SOE8D-INTERESC-CSUF
D0443949

The International Series in

ELEMENTARY EDUCATION

Consulting Editor

JOHN M. KEAN
University of Wisconsin

Building Mathematics Concepts in Grades Kindergarten Through Eight

Building Mathematics Concepts

INTERNATIONAL

An Intext Publisher

in Grades Kindergarten Through Eight

L. EDWIN HIRSCHI

Professor of Education
University of Arizona

TEXTBOOK COMPANY

Scranton, Pennsylvania 18515

Printed in the United States of America by The Haddon Craftsmen, Inc., Scranton, Pennsylvania. Library of Congress Catalog Card Number: 71–105079.

Standard Book Number 7002 2196 4

This text is dedicated to the hundreds of junior high and elementary school mathematics teachers scattered over the United States, Puerto Rico, and Guam who over the past decade have studied with me in the exciting area of contemporary mathematics. Their enthusiasm and encouragement have contributed greatly to both the production of the material and the personal satisfaction which I have received from the project.

Preface

Depending upon prerequisites, this course is designed for one or two semesters of college-level work for students planning to teach or presently teaching in the elementary school or junior high school. It is flexible in that it may be used for mathematics content, method, or combination courses.

The first two chapters cover current trends in mathematics education, goals of instruction, issues, and philosophy espoused by the author along with strategies of teaching. The remaining chapters summarize the basic mathematics concepts and ideas essential for teaching mathematics in grades K–8. Interwoven with the presentation of the ideas and concepts are methods and strategies designed for use with elementary school and junior high school students. No effort is made to separate method from mathematics content, since it is the contention of the author that for teaching to be practical and effective the two must be intermingled.

It is proposed that both college instructors and students use the text flexibly, altering the sequence of chapters and concepts as need and purpose might dictate.

The unique organization of the book emphasizes the vertical strands of mathematics as they unfold in grades K–8. In practice many of these strands move forward simultaneously, and the strength of the organization results from the assistance it gives to teachers and prospective teachers in seeing and understanding mathematics in large blocks which combine into a total interrelated whole.

Most of the material contained in the text has evolved in the form of instructional units and notes developed by the author over a period of thirty-five years of teaching and supervising at levels ranging from kindergarten to the graduate school. This extended experience as well as the preparation of the manuscript for this text have been exciting and challenging experiences which I invite you to share with me.

L. EDWIN HIRSCHI

Tucson, Arizona
January, 1970

Contents

Chapter 1

Objectives of Mathematics Education

THE LEARNER AND THE LEARNING PROCESS

Effective teaching requires that the teacher understand both the learner and the learning process. Learning is complex, involving the total organism and its complete environment. At no time can a teacher disassociate the mind of the learner from the reactions and interactions continually going on by virtue of a multiplicity of influences originating both within and outside the organism.

Every person, in his endless struggle to make his role status consistent with his self-image, faces certain basic needs and developmental hurdles with which he must cope. Robert J. Havighurst has identified three of these needs as security, growth, and faith in the future. The degree to which an individual achieves the first two of these will regulate the confidence and faith he can muster to face the certainties and uncertainties that lie ahead. This basic faith is as essential to learning and to personality adjustment as it is to the recovery of the pathologically ill or injured.

In the complex process of maturation, certain common hurdles confront the learner. The degree to which he can successfully take these hurdles largely determines the adjustment which the individual makes to his environment. Failure to make satisfactory adjustment in one or more areas results in a chain reaction which may have repercussions in every phase of the individual's life. While the meeting of these so-called "developmental tasks" may be accelerated at certain maturity levels, all of them have implications during the entire life cycle. Much research has been done on these "tasks" from birth to maturity, and several have been identified and generally accepted. Just how the schools can best expedite progress toward successful attainment of these objectives has long since been recognized as a basic problem of those concerned with both curriculum and methods of instruction.

Factors of human growth and development also play a tremendous role in the teaching-learning situation. These also require our most careful attention. It is not likely that as teachers we can guide the learner intelligently without knowing the basic principles of growth.

CONTENT AND METHOD

Subject matter is also tremendously important in the teaching-learning process. In fact, much of what a person learns takes place within the framework of some subject-matter field. It is the contention of this writer that it is unrealistic to speak of method and content in contrast to one another, since they are so basically interwoven that neither can function properly in practice without the other. Instead of the continued sniping which goes on between the experts in the two areas, there needs to be a coordination of effort to promote a maximum utilization of both of these facets of the teaching-learning problem.

One of the objectives of this methods text is to emphasize a balance between method and content and to provide for the vertical articulation of both these facets as they extend from kindergarten through grade 8. Admittedly this is an ambitious task and a frightening one. In fact, if one were to include with substantial completeness the psychological and sociological background and the historical development of mathematics teaching, a one volume work would be impractical. However, detailed treatments of these areas are available from several reputable sources, whereas the actual vertical development of basic concepts in grades kindergarten through eight seems not to have been given the attention it rightfully deserves. Dr. James R. Killian, then scientific advisor to President Dwight Eisenhower, speaking in October 1958, indicated that the way to produce an atomic scientist was to begin with a second-grader. Rightfully, perhaps we should start at the kindergarten. Furthermore, it is entirely plausible that the basic mathematical understandings desirable for an atomic scientist are not unlike those required by the intelligent citizen consumer who may not be highly specialized, or whose specialization may lie outside the field of mathematics and physical science. At least it would seem that there are certain quantitative concepts and skills that are essential for intelligent living and are the right of every citizen. The mathematics specialist will of course extend his competency beyond these basics.

COOPERATION BETWEEN ELEMENTARY AND SECONDARY

It is contended as a basic hypothesis to this treatment that two unsound notions have evolved in the American school system and among its patrons regarding the teaching of mathematics. The first is that the teachers of arithmetic in the elementary grades and the teachers of secondary mathematics have little in common. This has resulted in a failure to set long-term common objectives with cooperative plans for their achievement, which in turn has often placed the two groups at cross-purposes and left the student searching for articulation. The second notion implies that the specialist should have a rigorous treatment in mathematics, while the nonspecialist suffers from haphazard treatment in low-status courses such as general mathematics. Although this dual offering has usually been optional and concentrated at the secondary level, there is increasing pressure to impose this segregation and even move it into the elementary school.

The situations described above deserve our most thoughtful attention. It is hoped that a text such as this will aid in breaking the barrier between elementary arithmetic and secondary mathematics, and that as a result the treatment of concepts at all levels will become substantial and meaningful.

ABILITY GROUPING

It is also contended here that in keeping with American tradition, imposed ability grouping will be resisted in the United States, but that through improved techniques for dealing with individual differences within the classroom, through adequate guidance, testing, elective courses, equalizing the status of courses, better-trained teachers, creative teaching, more flexible class scheduling, programmed instruction, computer-centered practice and tutorical programs, team teaching, and many other democratic but perhaps undiscovered means we will be able to meet the needs of both specialists and nonspecialists without being panicked into the adoption of archaic continental systems which are even now under criticism in their own countries.

SPECIALIST AND NONSPECIALIST

The role of mathematics as part of our basic communication needs no longer be defended. With the emergence of rockets and satellites and our breakthrough into outer space has come a demand for an understanding of mathematics on the part of laymen unequaled in the history of civilization. The intelligent reading of a newspaper is becoming more and more dependent upon an understanding of the basic concepts of mathematics. Furthermore, our possibilities for intelligent living in our rapidly changing environment will continue to demand more and deeper mathematics background. As we look back now upon some of our shallow thinking of the past thirty-five years, we may wonder why some educators and the public considered a decrease of emphasis in mathematics at the more common levels of our everyday life experiences. We may question now whether we should have trusted the so-called expert to figure our carpeting, our income tax, our installment purchases, and our bank statement. First, we should have questioned from whence these experts were being drawn and, second, we should have thought more carefully of the freedom which our lack of mathematical knowledge was forcing us to surrender. Ignorance in any essential area of living can only result in dependence and subjection. We might just as well have decided that we could forgo learning to spell, write, and read, since the experts in grammar, stenography, and audiocommunication could take care of our needs in these areas.

A more intelligent interpretation of our mathematical needs might well recognize a spiraling demand at both the level of the laymen and of the technician. Also, it is likely that this increased emphasis must reflect a meaningful and adaptable mathematical philosophy rather than one steeped in mechanical manipulation and rote formalism.

BASIC OBJECTIVES AND CONCEPTS

If it is desired to state the basic objective of mathematics teaching, it might be stated as *To familiarize the student with the concept of quantity and space relationships and the associated patterns of thought as they relate to and affect his total life experience.* An objective as broad as this hardly requires psychological or sociological justification. One trembles to think of what would happen to either our society or the human mind were our culture suddenly void of quantification and space relations. As mentioned earlier, it is not the purpose of this text to be philosophical but rather to identify and develop the concepts of mathematics in a very concrete and functional manner.

Let us move then to the specific concepts which we wish to develop in mathematics and attempt to indicate where and how they should be introduced and maintained.

We may arbitrarily break the concept of quantity into the following subconcepts:

1. The concept of pairs of objects or elements.
2. The concept of a set or collection of objects or elements.
3. The concept of order in pairs and sets of objects or elements.
4. The concept of numbers.
5. The concept of one-to-one correspondence and counting.
6. The concept of combining and decomposing sets.
7. The concept of the relationship among elements, subsets, and sets.
8. The concept of measuring.
9. The concept of space relationships.
10. The concept of proof.
11. The concept of what constitutes the solution to a problem.

Before presenting a brief introduction to each of these concepts, let it be understood that the sequential numbering of the concepts does not imply mutual exclusiveness. Rather the teaching and learning should go forward simultaneously on many fronts, each concept reinforcing the others, with the total effort directed toward sound concepts of quantity, space relations, logic, and their interrelationships. Upon close examination the subconcepts have a tendency to merge into an integrated whole which seems to defy segmentation. The separation is retained here, however, as a means of attack upon what might otherwise become a prohibitive task.

The Concept of Pairs of Objects or Elements

Pairs and sets are the foundation stones for quantitative thinking. Children early become acquainted with pairs of persons, and objects. Father and mother, pairs of twins, pairs of shoes, pairs of stockings, pairs of bookends, and pairs of earrings are examples of concrete objects experienced as pairs. Each member of a pair may be thought of as an element and any grouping of two elements constitutes a pair. The fractions 2/3 or 3/5 are other examples of number pairs. The basic multiplication, addition, subtraction, and division facts illustrate effectively the role of number pairs in the teaching of arithmetic.

The Concept of a Set or Collection of Objects or Elements

Sets of objects are common experiences for children. The child's first contacts are with his mother, who is really a set containing one element. Pairs as referred to above constitute sets of two elements. Members of a family comprise a set. The child's life involves many sets: sets of dishes, sets of blocks, sets of dominoes, sets of tools, sets of books. A collection of elements consisting of less than the total elements in a set is said to be a *proper subset* of the original set. The concept of set is an integrating and unifying idea which ties in beautifully with elements and pairs and one which is much more basic than numbers and counting. Its use becomes even more apparent as the student extends the universal set of numbers with which he operates.

The Concept of Order in Pairs and Sets of Objects or Elements

The ordering of pairs and sets enters early into the child's experience. A pair is said to be *ordered* if order makes a difference. For example, in terms of the order of placing them on a foot, a shoe, and sock are ordered, while a pair of shoes is not. The numbers in the subtraction problem (3 - 2) are ordered in terms of difference obtained while the addends in (2 + 3) are not ordered as far as the sum is concerned. Sets are ordered or unordered, depending upon the property being considered. A child may order the members of his family by size, or he might consider without regard to order the individual marbles in his marble collection. The set of positive integers when arranged from smallest to largest is said to be an *ordered set.* The set of numbers from which the drawing is done in a bingo game is an *unordered set.*

Mathematicians are especially concerned about sets which can be ordered by placing their elements in one-to-one correspondence with the counting numbers. All finite sets may be theoretically ordered in this way. Infinite sets, however, cannot always be ordered although some ingenious techniques have been devised for ordering some of them.

The Concept of Number

Number as a concept is both abstract and difficult. It requires the use of symbols either verbal or written or both. Both order and quantity are involved through the ordinal and cardinal members and the previously discussed notion of ordered sets is extremely helpful as the quantitative aspect of number enters into the picture. For example, the idea of what constitutes 5 elements or fiveness requires careful nurturing if the student is to see its multiple ramifications. The concept of number has its roots deeply anchored in the relationships among collections or sets and the work here must move forward on many fronts if the student is to achieve a rational and meaningful picture of quantity.

The Concept of Counting

The process of counting was formerly thought to be basic in the teaching of arithmetic. In reality it is a rather difficult process and requires the placing of the elements of a set or subset into one-to-one correspondence with the set of counting members. Counting the elements of a set gives order to it even though the order may be related only to sequence. The complexity of counting becomes evident when we consider that it involves verbalization, symbolization, and one-to-one correspondence, in addition to whatever other factors may be involved in the sequential ordering. For example, we may be counting the girls in a schoolroom of children comprised of both boys and girls.

The Concept of Combining and Decomposing Sets

As mentioned earlier, a set may be comprised of zero or one or more elements. The operations of addition, subtraction, multiplication, and division involving these elements are major objectives of arithmetic. Later with the expansion of the universal set of numbers and the inclusion of the processes of extracting roots raising to powers and taking unions and intersections the job becomes even more formidable.

Combining and decomposing begins early with the student and his simple addition and subtraction facts need to be learned through concrete experiences and with full understanding. All algorisms[1] should be carefully developed through exploration and discovery on the part of the learner and should be used only after basic understanding has been achieved. The logic and sequences leading to meaningful use of algorisms constitutes a substantial part of this text.

The Concept of Relationships of Sets

Sets and subsets are related in many ways. A set of three blocks and a set of five blocks may be brought together to form a new set of eight blocks. In this case we write $3 + 5 = 8$. Equality is one of these basic relationships. However,

[1] An algorism is an arrangement of numbers and processes leading to solutions involving basic operation but which are not necessarily meaningful or logical to the person using them.

students learn early that a set of 6 objects contains twice as many objects as a set of 3 objects. Other relationships such as "greater than," (written $>$) and "less than," (written $<$) and "not equal to," (written $\neq$) also enter early into the mathematical experience of the child and should not be neglected. More mature relationships, such as ratio and function, should, of course, follow in proper sequence and with due consideration for the maturity and experience of the learner.

The Concept of Measuring

The concept of measuring is closely tied with relationships of sets. Also one aspect of division is basically a process of measurement, the divisor being the actual unit of measure. When children say that one boy is taller than another, they are not only observing a relationship of the heights of the two boys but they may actually be measuring the height of each boy in terms of some standard. Roughly, this standard may be the height of the shorter boy. Measuring could actually be classified under relationships since comparisons are always involved. The various kinds of measurement must receive consideration somewhere in the child's mathematical experience. Time, money, distance, liquid measure, and the like are all aspects of this concept.

The Concept of Space Relationships

Space relationship plays an important role in the mathematical experiences of children. Not only are measurement and relationships involved here but the recognition of shape, location, symmetry, projection and perspective. Children early have experiences with straight and curved lines, angles, squares, rectangles, triangles, spheres, and many other figures. The development of the concept of spaces having dimensions other than the three-dimensional space of our daily experience is an important and exciting experience for learners at all maturity levels.

The Concept of Proof

The concept of proof is both a complex and important aspect of mathematics. It involves a beautiful way of thinking which carries man's reasoning from probability to inductive uncertainty and on into the realm of deductive certainty. But the so-called facts of mathematics are no longer regarded as self-evident or absolute truths. Proven propositions are merely relative or contingent truths based upon a few undefined terms, definitions, and axioms. A mathematical proof merely employs the conventional laws of logic to show that, if certain assumptions are true, then a particular proposition must be accepted as true in the same sense. The elements of consistency and noncontradiction thus become the key to mathematical thought and, so long as they are respected, man has complete freedom to leave undefined, define, axiomatize, and postulate to his heart's content, and having done so he can, with Lobachevsky and Bolyai, unhesitatingly announce the proofs of propositions based upon the stipulations of the human mind. With such emancipation of thought, who can deny that many of the unconquered peaks lie in the realm of the intellect?

The Concept of What Constitutes the Solution to a Problem

The student needs to know early what constitutes the solution to a problem, what a mathematical problem really is, when it contains sufficient information to lead to a solution, when it can be solved axiomatically, when it is indeterminate, what elements can be drawn from in seeking a solution, how it can be stated through the use of mathematical symbolization, how it thus becomes an open sentence and finally what its solution set and complement set are.

These ideas, along with the ability and skill to arrange the solutions to problems in meaningful and logical order and to communicate mathematically with others, are all-important aspects of this concept.

CONCEPTS AT VARIOUS LEVELS

We will now look at the knowledge and understanding which should characterize the mathematical experiences of the learner at the various levels of development. Rather than segment this knowledge and understanding by grades we will divide it into

1. Primary level (kindergarten through 3)
2. Intermediate level (grades 4, 5, and 6)
3. Upper-grade level (grades 7 and 8)

Knowledge and Understanding—Primary Level (Kindergarten through 3)

The child should understand pairs ordered and unordered, concrete and abstract, finite and infinite. In the concrete he should see that a pair of stockings is unordered but that a stocking and a shoe is ordered in terms of sequence of use. In the abstract he should see that addition and multiplication are unordered as far as a sum or product is concerned; that is, $2 + 3 = 5$ as also does $3 + 2 = 5$ even though the concept of the arrangement of the addend groups may suggest some difference to the child. Also, $3 \times 2 = 6$, as does $2 \times 3 = 6$, even though here two groups of three each may seem quite different to the child than three groups of two each. The child should see that the 3 and 2 in $3 - 2 = 1$ is an ordered pair which does not allow for reversal of minuend and subtrahend. Also, he should recognize that $6 \div 3 = 2$ involves order and does not allow for interchange of dividend and divisor. Further, he should understand the meaning and symbol of the simple common fractions, with unit numerators up to 1/10, recognize them as ordered pairs, demonstrate them with concrete materials, and be able to add and subtract them when they have like denominators even though the sum may produce improper fractions and mixed numbers.

The child should be able to attach the proper cardinal number to any set containing from zero to one hundred elements, to read the counting numbers on a number line up to 100, know the names and symbols for each number in this set, be able to order them in proper sequence, and know certain subsets, as evidenced by his ability to count by 2's, 3's, 4's, 5's, and 10's up to 100. He should understand the four basic axioms of counting numbers. He should be able to use the number line as an attack upon his addition, subtraction, multiplication, and division facts.

The child should be able to write the digits from 0 to 9, operate them in one-to-one correspondence with objects, read and write three-place numbers, be able to give them base and place-value interpretation with objects in place-value pockets, and be able to compare modern modes of counting and calculating with those used by primitive cultures. He should be able within the limits of his own experience to apply numbers to the days of the week, months of the year, eggs in a dozen, pennies in a dime, quarter, half-dollar or dollar, minutes in an hour, hours in a day, inches in a foot, feet in a yard, ounces in a pound, and pints in a quart.

The child should understand the concepts and symbols of addition, subtraction, division, multiplication, equality, greater than, less than, and the cent and dollar symbols. He should know the abbreviations for hours, minutes, cents, inches, feet, yards, pounds, ounces, quarts, and pints. He should understand general quantitative words such as much, little, many, seldom, often. He should be able to read the roman numerals up to ten.

When the child has reached the second semester of the third grade, he should have a fair degree of mastery of and be able to demonstrate in the place value pockets the various counting numbers and the addition of facts involving a two-digit addend and a single-digit addend up to the sum 99. In a similar manner he should be able to handle minuends up to 99 with single-digit subtrahends. In these operations he should be able to borrow and carry with understanding. He should know with meaning the basic multiplication facts to a product of 30 and be able to multiply with a single-digit multiplier and a multiplicand of two digits where no part of the algorism leads to a product of more than 28. He should operate this algorism with full understanding. He should know and understand the basic division facts with single-digit divisors and dividends not greater than 30.

The child should begin to see each number within his present number set in its total role within the set. For example, he should see a number such as 6 as it relates to all the addition, subtraction, multiplication, and division facts which involve 6 and are within his experience. With children of this level this development might involve what is often referred to as *number families*. The child should be able to subject the quantitative problems arising within his experience to a sequential and logical analysis, arriving at solutions on the basis of the sum total of his mathematical knowledge, understanding, skill and competence. He should be able to translate from the symbolic to the written word and vice versa.

Very simple experiences with logic are in order at this level. The idea of tying ideas together to give them logical structure should be introduced. For example:

1. All children are either boys or not boys.
2. A number is either = 6 or ≠ 6.
   A number is either > 6 or ≯ 6.
3. Any number you can think of is equal to five, greater than five, or less than five.
4. If a number is greater than four it is also greater than three.

Geometric forms and shapes and their relationships to points and lines should be explored. Students should be able to locate three points in a plane and join them with line segments and recognize that they will get either a triangle or a straight line.

Knowledge and Understanding—Intermediate Level (Grades 4, 5, and 6)

The concept of ordered and unordered pairs should be extended and deepened. Reversals of unordered pairs in addition and multiplication should become less disturbing and more meaningful. The concept of finite and infinite sets should be developed, leading the child to recognize that the set of positive integers extends infinitely, and that the proper fractions which lie between 0 and 1 on the number line constitute an infinite set as do the improper fractions between 1 and 2, etc. The number line now includes many more elements whose position and relationship should be understood. Further facility with the subsets of nonnegative integers developed at the primary level should be achieved. In fact, at this stage the child should be able to count by 2's, 3's, 4's, and 5's, starting at any point in the whole number set. The basic addition and multiplication facts should be extended to include all single-digit combinations and subtraction and division should be extended to situations involving not more than two digits and resulting in a single-digit difference or quotient. All of the above should become automatic through meaningful habituation during this level. Fractions as ordered pairs and the notion of equivalent fractions should be developed and extended. The Golden Rule of Fractions, or law of the unit element, should be discovered. This, of course, takes fractions beyond the unit numerators introduced at the primary level. The concept of prime and composite numbers should be introduced with special treatment of 0 to 1. A lush experience with the numbers of our system should be interspersed throughout this level, drawing freely upon number theory for such exciting ideas as perfect, abundant, deficient, and amicable numbers, Goldbach's Conjectures, and the historical incidents from mathematics which are meaningful at this time.

The concept of number base and place should evolve from the concrete place-value pockets to the semiconcrete place value chart. Place value should be extended without limit, thus allowing for writing and reading of any whole number. With the introduction of decimal fractions, the place-value chart should be interrelated with proper understanding. The concept of a number system should be generalized to give at least a preview of systems with bases other than 10. Addition, subtractions, multiplication, and division of whole numbers should be extended without limit with full understanding of the algorisms involved. Raising to powers and extracting roots should be introduced. Union and intersection of sets should be developed and related to addition, subtraction, least common multiple, and greatest common divisor. The addition, subtraction, and multiplication of decimals should be introduced with meaningful development of the algorisms involved. Prime factors should be introduced and used in the renaming, multiplication, and division of fractions. The concept of equivalence class should be tied in with the renaming of fractions. The concept of canceling in division should evolve from the above as a shortcut operation and justified by the law of the unit element. The multiplication and division of fractions should be made completely understandable through a multistage development. Division of fractions should begin with like fractions and proceed through four-story fractions, with a complete understanding of the "inversion" of the divisor and multiplication technique. The conversion of unlike fractions to fractions having the same denominator should be taught and related to an equivalence class of fractions. Addition and subtraction of fractions should be developed by use of the prime-factor technique for finding a least common denominator and explained as an application of the law of the unit element.

The basic geometric notions begun in the earlier grades should be extended and two- or three-dimensional space recognized. The common geometrical figures should be understood and explained. Included here are triangle, square, rectangle, circle, cube, and sphere. The concepts of linear measure, area, and volume should be introduced, and measurement involving these three should be taught along with an extension of the measurement introduced at the primary level. Perimeter and circumference should be given meaningful interpretation. The notion of denominate and nondenominate numbers will enter here, and in the teaching of area and volume care should be taken to avoid contradiction of the basic meaning of multiplication.

The ability to choose appropriate mathematical processes in simple problems should be extended and increased, with emphasis given to appropriate and logical organizations of the problems leading to correct solutions. Experience in writing as well as solving problems should be provided.

Logic should be extended to include negation. For example:

Statement	*Negative of the Statement*
John is taller than Joe.	John is not taller than Joe.
The figure is a triangle.	The figure is not a triangle.
Jane is older than Mary.	Jane is not older than Mary.

The fundamental principles of logic should be discussed with regard to a proposition and logical implication introduced with the if-then notion. For example: If Joe goes to school, then he has a teacher.

Knowledge and Understanding—Upper Grade Level (Grades 7 and 8)

The concepts of the previous levels should be extended and deepened with the following specific developments.

The concept of number base should be so established that the student can set up a system in any base 2 through 9 and make conversions to and from any one of these and the decimal system. At least limited experiences should be had with the basic operations within these new systems. Unlimited operation (addition, subtraction, multiplication, and division) within the set of nonnegative rational numbers of our own system should now be achieved. The number line should again be revised to accommodate the new elements, and their order, position, and relationships should be thoroughly understood. This should include whole numbers, common fractions, and decimal fractions. Complete understanding of all the algorisms involved should support the above operations. The concept and use of prime and composite numbers should now be thoroughly established and utilized both as a final check on the basic number combinations and as a basic approach to operations with common fractions. The concept of percentage and its relationship to common and decimal fractions should be introduced, and the three basic types of percentage problems explored with meaningful and logical interpretation devoid of rote formulas at this stage. Number pairs and sets should be further developed, and the idea of equivalence class of ordered pairs used to introduce ratio and proportion. Simple equations involving nonspecified elements of the universal set should be explored and the notion of solution sets introduced. These simple equations should lead to standardized equations which we call formulas because of their general application. Special consideration should be given to the positive rational numbers which comprise the universal set at this level of development. The basic laws of numbers should now be given definite attention. The commutative and associative laws for both addition and multiplication as well as the distributive law of addition over multiplication should be explored with positive rational numbers. The uniqueness principles and closure should be discussed, and the cancellation laws for both finite and infinite sets are here in order. The definition of a positive rational number should be established, and terminating, repeating, and periodic decimals should be demonstrated. The positive irrational π should be recognized as not being in the universal set mentioned above. The number line should again be revised to accommodate these.

The discussion of π in this connection should be preceded by its introduction in connection with the area and circumference of a circle. At this level, measurement generally should be extended with increased emphasis upon the basic principles of linear, plane surface, and cubic measure. Linear measure should now be extended to include circumference of a circle, perimeter of the parallelogram, rhombus and trapezoid, and altitude of geometrical figures. Area should be extended to the rhombus and trapezoid and volume to cylinder, right prism, cone, and pyramid. Geometric forms and space relationships should be extended with brief introductions to such undefined concepts as line, point, plane surface, and terms such as angle, arc, radius, and diameter. Location of points on the earth's surface through the use of latitude and longitude or meridians should be introduced through the concept of great and small circles of a sphere. Longitude should be related to the time zones. The details of the geographical survey of the United States should be correlated with plane-surface measure introduced above, and extension made to include township, section, and quarter section. Care should be taken here to clarify that while the surface of the earth is spherical, the size of sphere allows us sufficient accuracy when it is considered as a plane surface. The understanding of measures should be thoroughly reviewed and extended to include rods, miles, square rods, square miles, acres, and cubic yards. The metric system should be introduced and comparisons made with the English system. The idea of relativism in mathematics should begin to restrain the tendency toward absolutism which often becomes dominant at this level. The student should be led to understand that hypotheses are tested and conclusions are reached in mathematics on the basis of previously accepted agreements or axioms; that arithmetic is a noncontradictory logical sequence of conclusions built upon certain basic definitions and assumptions.

The laws of logic should be extended from earlier treatments and deductive reasoning and related propositions introduced. The student should know that all measurements in applied mathematics are approximate except the placing of the counting numbers into a one-to-one correspondence with specific objects. The rounding of approximate numbers and the matter of the degree of accuracy resulting from operational involvement for approximate numbers should be given consideration here. The relationship between mathematics and science should become increasingly apparent, and the student should recognize that mathematics is the language of science.

The basic concepts involved in consumer mathematics should receive attention at this level. Quantitative terms and concepts contained in accounts available through the basic mass-communication media should become increasingly meaningful to the student. Fewer topics with a less superficial treatment are in order here. Topics at this level might well include:

1. Budgeting
2. Wise buying and consumer credit
3. Money and banking
4. Taxation (including income tax)
5. Statistics (including statistical graphs)
6. Stocks and bonds (investments generally)
7. Insurance (life, health and accident, fire, automobile, etc.)

The exciting and interesting events from the history of mathematics as well as developments in the contemporary scene should receive increased attention at this level. These should serve to broaden the horizons and extend the vision of the student of mathematics. An effort should also be made at this level to help the learner move from the concrete to the semiconcrete to the abstract. The solving of open sentences and word problems should be extended and refined with careful attention to student experiences in writing such problems, analyzing and attacking these logically, arranging solutions systematically, and seeing the problem and its solution in proper and meaningful perspective.

In concluding this section, we remind the reader that the grade placement of topics and concepts is presently in flux and that movement up or down will continue as research and the experimental programs dictate. Also new topics are continually being introduced at the elementary school level, some of which will undoubtedly find permanency in the program.

PROBLEMS

1. Explain how a lack of understanding of a mathematics concept may lead a teacher to an ineffective method of teaching it. Illustrate with a specific example.

2. Point up the dangers of teaching children limited application of mathematics concepts rather than broad general understandings. Center your discussion around the concept of addition of common fractions and the contention by some educators that we should concern ourselves only with the commonly used fractions such as halves, fourths, and fifths.

3. How might ignorance in a mathematics area such as percentage contribute to dependence and subjection in the life of an individual person?

4. Trace a single mathematics concept, such as primes, vertically through the curriculum, indicating where it should first be introduced, what extensions and uses should be made of it at each grade level, and what you would finally expect an eighth-grade student to know about it.

5. Use whatever information you can gather along with a bit of imagination to describe how a new mathematics concept might gain entrance into the elementary school curriculum.

Chapter 2

Strategies and Procedures for Teaching Mathematics

PURPOSE OF THE CHAPTER

This chapter is devoted to a series of topics centered around procedures and strategies, many of which are currently in vogue and about which mathematics teachers need to be informed. The discussions deliberately reflect the biases of the author and are presented as a stimulus for further thought and action on the part of prospective teachers as well as those presently in the field.

ENHANCING THE CLASSROOM ATMOSPHERE

Contemporary mathematics with its emphasis upon meanings, insights, and understandings requires a supporting classroom climate characterized by openness on the part of both students and teachers. The tightly structured classroom where the teacher dominates and imposes, where the next moves are predetermined, and where the students respond to the overt clues and habitual control patterns of an unimaginative teacher is hardly conducive to the achievement of the objectives of the so-called "new mathematics."

It is not likely that the conceptual advances currently available in mathematics will get through to the student unless he feels a challenge to become involved, a comfortable sort of freedom which invites his every idea, a security in which he dares to be wrong, and a commitment to mathematics which goes beyond his receiving a passing mark in the course.

Basic to the achievement of the classroom climate described above are certain considerations, among which the following appear to be essential.

1. A competent teacher trained in the content of the subject matter as well as in the principles of learning and the strategies of teaching.
2. A teacher aware of and responsive to the factors of human growth and development and who identifies well with students.
3. A teacher with a commitment to his profession generally and to the teaching of mathematics specifically.

4. A teacher who assumes responsibility for counseling students and who can open the frontiers and push back the horizons of mathematics for them.
5. An administration which is supportive of a well-conceived and clearly identifiable mathematics program.
6. An administration which involves its teachers in curriculum development and which provides adequate teaching stations, textbooks, and equipment.
7. An administration which provides for retraining and updating of teachers through:
   (a) Making current research and literature available for teachers.
   (b) Encouraging in-service and out-of-service study.
   (c) Promoting experimentation and innovation.
   (d) Providing sabbatical leaves and other subsidized extensions of training and experience.
8. Classes sufficiently small to allow a one-to-one relationship between every student and the teacher.
9. Helping-teachers and adequate secretarial service to free the teacher for the professional and technical facets of the teaching process.

METHODS OF TEACHING

An eclectic method of teaching seems to have evolved in many mathematics classrooms of the United States which can perhaps best be described as a mixture of lecture, demonstration, and interaction. The demonstration and interaction often draws heavily upon the students, with the teacher serving as consultant and resource person. To the degree that this method encourages involvement and guards against domination by the teacher, it appears to be sound and productive. If it is accompanied by the open type of classroom structure previously referred to, and if it produces a situation in which the students might be thought of as being junior engineers, with the teacher serving as the consulting engineer, then we might well be proud of this development.

This method of teaching is in clear contrast to a straight lecture method in which the classroom climate is often characterized by an "inmates and warden" atmosphere. The latter often degenerates to a point where the teacher finds himself devoting a large percentage of his time to classroom control rather than productive teaching. Studies have been done in this area in which the teaching act has been coded on a time basis, the results of which indicate that some teachers use as much as 50 percent of their teaching time for class-control functions. This is regrettable in this day in which the explosion of knowledge has provided us with so much to teach and learn and so little time in which to do it.

Another method of teaching which has drawn considerable attention is called the *discovery method*. The basic premise here is that students should be allowed or encouraged to discover the basic principles of mathematics, the implication being that such discovery will force involvement and thus lead to meanings, understandings, and insights of long or permanent duration.

The effectiveness of this method has probably been overrated and its application oversimplified. As a result students have developed a mathematical immunity to it, and instead of looking for basic principles and concepts students have reacted to teacher clues and found patterns without relating these patterns to the big ideas which supposedly were to have been included in the discovery.

Let us illustrate. Suppose we place the following on the chalkboard for a group of fourth-grade students, and ask them what they discover.

$$2 + (3 + 1) = (2 + 3) + 1$$
$$5 + (2 + 3) = (5 + 2) + 3$$
$$7 + (4 + 2) = (7 + 4) + 2$$
$$6 + (3 + 2) = (6 + 3) + 2$$

Most students may quickly discover the pattern, and the teacher might reward them by announcing that they have just discovered the *associative principle of addition.* Surely such observance of a pattern is important and may promote inquiry, but unless such inquiry training leads to discovery at a higher level of involvement there is real reason to question whether we might not have done as much for the students if we had explained in detail how the associative principle of addition operates and perhaps challenged them to find a counterexample. At least at present there is no evidence to indicate that either of the two methods is superior.

Perhaps we could have increased the depth of the involvement by presenting a more challenging situation. For example:

$$2 + (3 + 1) = (2 + 3) + 1$$
$$2 + (3 + \square\ = (2 + 3) + \square$$
$$2 + (\Delta + \square) = (2 + \Delta) + \square$$

$$\odot + (3 + \square) = (\odot + 3) + \square$$
$$\odot + (\Delta + \square) = (\odot + \Delta) + \square$$
$$95 + (5 + 9) = (\underline{?} + \underline{?}) + \underline{?}$$

With this example we do provide more opportunity for reaction and interaction leading to generalization and application.

The next example, which might justify the discovery technique, is designed for fifth-grade students in an effort to assist them in discovering a shortcut or algorism for multiplying a common fraction by a common fraction. By developing a pattern from the problems shown below can you find the product for $2/3 \times 3/4$?

$$2/3 \times 24 =$$
$$2/3 \times 12 =$$
$$2/3 \times 6 =$$
$$2/3 \times 3 =$$
$$2/3 \times 3/2 =$$
$$2/3 \times \Delta =$$

Note here that not only is the student confronted with finding the pattern of products but he must continue his pattern of factors in order to replace Δ. This forces his consideration of how to take half of a fraction.

A third example follows. Find the sum of the first 100 even whole numbers. Use a pattern developed in the following table if necessary.

Number of Consecutive Even Whole Numbers Added	Sum
First 2	
First 3	
First 4	
First 5	
First 6	
First 7	
.	
.	
.	
.	
.	
.	
n	

Hopefully students would discover $99 \cdot 100 = 9900$ = sum of first 100 even whole numbers. Or more generally, $(n - 1)n$ = sum of first n even whole numbers.

In summary, certain observations concerning the discovery method are presented:

1. Discovery, to be effective, should involve depth thinking and generalization. The generalizations, however, need not be verbalized.
2. Discovery, not unlike other methods of teaching, has its weaknesses and strengths.
3. Teachers using the discovery method should recognize that it requires uninterrupted time with minimum teacher direction.
4. Allowing the first volunteer student to respond deprives the remaining class members of discovery.
5. The teacher will do well to check quietly the early discoverers and encourage them to further check their discoveries, discover more, generalize, or pursue extensions or related problems.
6. When the discoveries are finally shared, they should be exploited for their full value.

PROGRAMMED INSTRUCTION

The field of mathematics has been an ideal medium for programmed instruction since it so readily lends itself to segmentation and sequential development. As a consequence many of the early programs appeared in mathematics, and considerable time has since been given to improvement and innovation in programmed mathematics at many levels. While programming has encouraged a rigorous investigation of mathematics concepts and how they are learned, at the same time it has in a sense been detrimental to the teaching of mathematics because it encouraged segmentation into small bits, called *frames*, and often left the student with little insight into the larger ideas and interrelationships so essential to a sound understanding of mathematics. Furthermore, the programming has been in process at a time when, under the influence of the so-called "new math," the trend was away from segmentation and toward the pervasive ideas and concepts which characterize the subject matter of mathematics. Although many commercial publishers and subsidized experimental programs sought to establish programmed instruction as *the* way in mathematics, most of the schools which tried individualized instruction through programming, experienced disappointing results and have long since returned to the conventional or directed their efforts toward other innovations.

Surely we must admit that as a complete method of teaching mathematics, programmed instruction has failed. Some useful information has, however, been salvaged from the experience and much progress has been made in the programming itself. More flexible formats are being developed, more challenging questions are being asked in the frames, and provisions for multiple responses are being built into both the programmed texts and the teaching machines. Some of the most promising developments related to programming in mathematics are coming out of the multimillion dollar project of Patrick Suppes at Stanford University, where expensive information centers and monitoring stations are providing networks designed to supplement and enrich regular classroom instruction by making programlike information available on a voluntary basis for specific remedial and enrichment purposes. This complex program with its expensive hardware could well lead to a valuable resource in the teaching of mathematics which may some day be generally available at a moderate cost.

The "systems" or "think tank" approach to the development of educational technology is spreading rapidly, and it was estimated that in 1967 the expenditure on hardware alone exceeded the $1 billion mark. The variety of technological aids is growing rapidly to include, television, videotape, computerized instruction, teaching machines, monitoring stations, talking typewriters, language laboratories, and microfilm. Where these innovations will finally take us in programmed instruction of mathematics is difficult to predict. It is, however very doubtful that even the ultimate in hardware or software will ever replace a good teacher.

In the meantime, the better-programmed texts and machines will continue to be useful as another teaching resource in the field of mathematics.

We conclude this discussion with a listing of the pitfalls which seem to be inherent in the use of programmed instruction as an exclusive means of teaching mathematics. Whatever benefits may occur from this method are not likely to overbalance these weaknesses in the foreseeable future.

1. The segmentation and isolation of concepts are factors which have as yet, not been completely overcome.
2. In many cases the extreme individualization leads to a loss of the benefits which can accrue from small and total group interaction.
3. Many students are not motivated or challenged by inching forward through endless frames of minutia and detail.
4. Students report actual loneliness and seek sharing of ideas and discussion of their mathematical experiences.
5. The lack of flexibility in responses is deadening and thwarts creativity.
6. Little provision is made for learning through flashes of insight and great leaps forward.
7. Voids in background information and deficiencies in learning are often ignored in the program.
8. Individual discoveries and generalizations are seldom shared with the group.

USE OF HIGHER MENTAL PROCESSES

One might consider the mental processes employed by students in responding to mathematical stimuli as being arranged in a hierarchial schema characterized by four levels, as follows.

Level I

Retrieving Remembering
Reflecting Recalling

Level II

Identifying Analyzing
Discriminating Comparing
Imagining Contrasting
Exploring Inferring
Organizing

Level III

Discovering Defining
Hypothesizing Judging
Abstracting Evaluating
Integrating

Level IV

Generalizing Synthesizing
Inventing Creating

No attempt is made here to defend the position of any process in the heirarchy and it is recognized that multiple processes often operate simultaneously;

however, there seems little doubt that creating requires a level of mental involvement above that of simple recall.

The point to be made here is that in our teaching of mathematics there is real danger of not encouraging the use of the higher levels of mental process. If the teaching emphasis leans heavily upon rote learning and simple recall, it is possible that the real message of contemporary mathematics, i.e., meanings, understandings, and insights, will never get through to the students.

We need then to gear our teaching and evaluation to involve the entire heirarchy of mental process. In our presentations, our class discussions, and our questions we should constantly provide students with adequate challenge and encourage them to respond at the appropriate mental level. Furthermore, we will need to be consistent and prove our concern for this involvement of the entire range of mental process by incorporating it into our tests and other evaluative experiences.

We now move to a series of examples of problems and questions which are posed in two different forms, one intended to promote the involvement of the higher mental processes, the other providing an escape through rote memorization and recall. The "A" items are geared to higher mental process, while the "B" items are not necessarily so geared. A suggested grade range is included for each pair of questions.

Primary Grades

A. Using two whole numbers at a time write all the addition problems you can such that sum for each shall be 12.

B. Add $7 + 5 =$ $8 + 4 =$ $6 + 6 =$ $10 + 2 =$

Intermediate Grades

A. Using axioms or other names for 7 and 9 show in as many ways as you can how you might find the answer for $7 \times 9 =$

B. Multiply $7 \times 9 =$

Intermediate Grades

A. How would you test a whole number to determine whether it is odd or even. Illustrate by testing several.

B. State which of the following whole numbers are even: 7, 4, 5, 12, 6, 4, 3

Upper Grades

A. Explain by pattern why it is logical that $n^0 = 1$, where $n \neq 0$. Begin with

$$2^4 = 16$$

B. Give the value of 6^0

Upper Grades

A. Is the $\sqrt{2}$ rational or irrational? Defend your answer. Does $\sqrt{2}$ exist on the number line?

B. What is an irrational number?

Intermediate or Upper Grades

A. Represent each of the whole numbers 1, 2, 3, etc., as far as you can go by using exactly four fours and no other numbers. You may use whatever operational signs you wish.

B. State the value of $\frac{4 \times 4}{4 + 4}$.

Intermediate Grades

A. Arrange the following fractions in order from least to greatest: 13/32, 23/64, 5/16, 1/3, 3/8, 11/32

B. Is 3/4 smaller or larger than 2/3?

Upper Grades

A. If we reverse the tens and units digits in any two digit number, why is their difference always divisible by nine?

B. If we reverse the digits in the number 67, is the difference between the original and the reversed number divisible by nine?

Intermediate Grades

A. If a retailer features blankets at $4 each and pillows at $3 each, in how many ways can you spend exactly $18 and have at least one of each item?

B. If a retailer features blankets at $4 each and pillows at $3 each, how much will three blankets and two pillows cost?

Intermediate Grades

A. Develop a shortcut for finding the sum of the first 100 positive integers.

B. Find the sum of the first 100 positive integers.

Upper Grades

A. Using what you know about binomials and factoring, determine whether 999991 is a prime number.

B. Is 999991 a prime number?

Intermediate Grades

A. Break the set of whole numbers < 50 into three subsets under the headings of specials, primes, and composites. Now choose one number from each subset and show why it belongs in that particular subset.

B. Define a prime, a composite, and a special.

Upper Grades

A. Are there more counting numbers than there are even counting numbers? Defend your answer.

B. Is it possible to set up a one-to-one correspondence between the counting numbers and the even counting numbers?

The preceding examples may encourage teachers to create in students an adventuresome attitude which welcomes difficult questions. Students' answers are seldom better than the questions and students who can answer difficult questions can usually ask difficult questions. Furthermore, this whole matter of difficulty is relative, since there is no more difficult question than a pure memory question for which one has forgotten the answer.

We conclude this section with a few suggestions which might increase the range of test items and encourage the use of higher mental processes.

1. More careful selection of test items by constantly asking "Can this item be answered by simple recall?"
2. Encouragement of a variety of attacks upon a problem, thus increasing the probability of success and the range of involvement.
3. Encouragement of several methods of solution for the same problem and the inclusion of all acceptable answers to the problem. Perhaps we should occasionally give only one problem and ask for many solutions.
4. The occasional abolition of time limits on tests, thus giving time for higher mental process to function. (Some students will need to be taught to utilize this time profitably.)
5. A consciousness on the part of the teacher as to what level of mental process is likely to be trigered by each test item.

MAKING ASSIGNMENTS IN MATHEMATICS

The matter of making appropriate assignments in elementary school mathematics has become more crucial with the advent of contemporary mathematics. The emphasis upon meanings, insights, and understandings, the trend toward the learning of big ideas and encompassing concepts, and the increased involvement of higher mental process on the part of the student have led many teachers to take a second look at their assignment practices. In like manner the trend away from workbooks, rote memory, drill for drill's sake, segmentation of concepts, and facts learned in isolation have also had their effect on the nature, amount, and content of assignments.

Reference is made here to certain innovative assignment practices which teachers may wish to consider as they establish or reappraise their own assignment patterns.

Self-Assignments

Self assignments—that is, assignments made by the students themselves, provide many worthwhile experiences for elementary school students which they otherwise may never get. It is likely that student's answers will be no better than their questions and unless they are encouraged to frame appropriate and challenging questions they may never rise to the level of responding well to questions framed by teachers, textbook authors, or testing experts.

Many experienced teachers will attest that writing a good test or framing a sequence of stimulating questions has often forced them into important insights of which they were not previously aware. That a similar experience is available for students who make their own assignments is not at all impossible.

The major problem confronting teachers, who have a desire to utilize this important strategy, is just how does one go about doing it in actual practice. A few suggestions are presented below, followed by some sample assignments geared to students at an indicated level of instruction.

1. Students will need to be assisted and motivated to try their hand at writing or stating their own questions and activities since tradition has generally assigned this task to the expert.
2. Student production of questions and other assignment activities for a particular content area often requires as much or more time than answering the questions or doing the activities. This should be taken into consideration by the teacher when utilizing this strategy.
3. Questions and assignment activities developed by students should be discussed and evaluated in class in order to lend prestige and importance to them.
4. Student produced questions and assignment activities should often be utilized by the teacher when designing tests and other evaluative materials for assessing pupil progress.
5. When scoring assignments the teacher should attach as much weight to the phrasing of the questions and assignment activities as to their solution and execution. The solutions and execution of the activities may be left for later work.
6. The teacher should not expect sophistication in mathematical preciseness and language usage beyond the maturity and experience level of the students.

As we now look at sample assignments let us be reminded of the work we do on open sentences, where we suggest that students write the word problems around open sentences. This is actually one application of students writing their own assignments, except that we provide the open sentence for the student. This assignment could now be altered to require the student to provide his own open sentence and then write the word problem. Such an assignment is appropriate at the intermediate and upper-grade level, with perhaps some limited use in the primary grades.

Another example is now in order. Assume that the class had just completed a development of the concept of prime numbers. We might then ask the student to frame two good questions concerning primes and answer them. Undoubtedly in such a situation with an average class we would get some very superficial questions and answers, such as "Is three a prime?," accompanied by the answer "Yes." But hopefully we would also get some questions of real import, such as "Is two the only even prime? Why?" Such a question accompanied by a good discussion could contribute much toward raising the level of questions submitted by class members, and is applicable in grades 4–8.

Another example might be centered around basic axioms and operations.

We might ask students to write and solve problems illustrating the axioms and at the same time leading to shortcuts in computation. Some results may be trivial, such as $3 + (7 + 4) = (3 + 7) + 4 = 10 + 4 = 14$, while others may come up with $497 + (17 + 3) = 497 + (3 + 17) = (497 + 3) + 17 = 500 + 17 = 517$, and relate the appropriate axiom to each step. An experience of this type is perhaps geared to the upper grades.

Once students have developed the skill and habit of writing their own assignments, the teacher can often use the general approach of merely asking students to write and solve as many problems as they can which relate to the concept at hand. This allows for flexibility and accommodates individual differences.

It is not to be assumed that the strategy of having students make their own assignments should be exclusive of teacher or textbook assignments. It is intended as an innovation that might well lead to more meaningful mathematics and productive involvement of students.

Open-Ended Assignments

The open-ended assignment is recommended as a means of meeting individual differences and allowing students to involve themselves to any depth and for any length of time that they may choose. In order to further clarify what is involved here, let us give a few examples:

1. Break the set of whole numbers into three subsets; specials, primes and composites, beginning with zero and going in sequence as far as you can.
2. Factor the successive composites beginning with four into primes. Go as far up the scale as you can.
3. Write as many abstract, unordered infinite sets as you can.
4. Find the sum of the first n odd whole numbers. Make a table as you go showing n in each case and the corresponding sums. Do you discover a pattern?
5. Write as many numerals as you can which represent the number 12.
6. Using exactly four 4's and any operational signs you wish but no other numerals, write the equivalent of each of the successive whole numbers, beginning with zero and going as far up the sequence as you can.
7. Write the set of perfect-square whole numbers as far as you can go, beginning with zero.
8. Write the sets of perfect squares, perfect cubes etc., as far as you can go for each.
9. Use the prime-factor technique to extract the square roots of the perfect-square whole numbers as far as you can go, beginning with four.
10. By geometric construction locate the square roots of 2, 3, 4, . . . on the number line.

In using the open-ended assignment teachers should guard against monotonous repetitions which do not open new vistas or increase in difficulty.

Furthermore, some students will need to be encouraged to devote a reasonable amount of time to the assignment yet not get carried away to the neglect of assignments in other subjects. It should also be recognized that it is just another kind of assignment and its use should not be overdone.

Some teachers may be at a loss as to the scoring of such assignments. This should create no problem, since the number of points possible also becomes open-ended. Suppose student A does 25 problems and receives 25 points, while student B does 500 problems and receives 500 points. This is all well and good, since the upper limit on test or assignment is merely a convention and perhaps one that should have disappeared long ago. If the teacher wishes to combine scores for final report-card marks, this can easily be done by converting the respective point scores to rank A, B, C, D, and F before combining for a final mark. Obviously to add raw scores before converting could seriously distort the child's progress since he may have scored a 1,000 points on some assignments which fascinated him and done almost nothing on all other assignments.

ACCELERATION OF THE RAPID LEARNER

Within the usual ability range of any group of students will be found those who require challenge beyond the basic content of the conventional text. Attention is here drawn to two commonly used types of acceleration which may be used with such students.

Vertical Acceleration

Modern teachers often individualize instruction to the point of allowing each child to move at his own rate through the text, often providing higher-grade level texts for those who can complete the text generally utilized in the current grade. While this type of acceleration has its advantages some problems arise in practice which deserve our attention.

Often the teacher is critized by her colleagues who teach the grades above for allowing students to move into their subject-matter topics, the contention being that such a procedure destroys for the student the adventure and excitement of the following year or years of mathematics instruction. This hardly seems a defensible criticism, since every teacher has the professional responsibility of taking the child as far as he can go without regard to grade level. As a matter of courtesy, however, a teacher might use a higher-grade level text of a publisher not used in the school, and while this text may cover approximately the same material it will at least use a different treatment.

Another more defensible criticism of vertical acceleration is the possibility that it will so separate the class members as to make total group development and discussion of mathematics topics almost impossible. Research indicates that the exchange of ideas resulting from group interaction contributes substantially to the learning and understanding of concepts, and therefore it is probably not desirable to forgo this valuable experience. One means of preserving this total group experience is to use it when all members of the class have completed a unit of learning, although some class members may have personally completed their experience in the unit many days earlier.

Generally the students will not object to returning to the unit, since they get satisfaction from contributing their ideas to the discussion and taking from it any new ideas of teacher or classmates. The results of a lively total group summary often are among the most valued experiences of the students. Furthermore, since small-group instruction lends itself to any kind of acceleration, the teacher has now incorporated individual, small-group, and total-group instruction, which seems entirely defensible.

Horizontal Acceleration

Some teachers prefer to keep their students together as far as topics are concerned, but to provide for acceleration by encouraging "in depth" extensions for the rapid learner. If the total class is studying primes at the fourth-grade level, as soon as the gifted students have mastered the fourth-grade treatment of primes they are led to extensions such as Goldbach's conjectures, Fermat's and Euler's factorization method, Mersenne and Fermat primes, proof that two is the only even prime, the distribution of primes, factor tables, and use of primes in extracting roots.

For the well-trained teacher little difficulty will develop in the use of horizontal acceleration. Those with lesser background will need to have resource materials available in the room. With the great number of supplemental and enrichment materials now available this approach is not impossible. A notable contribution to available resources is the *Twenty-Seventh Yearbook of the National Council of Teachers of Mathematics*, subtitled *Enrichment Mathematics for the Grades.*

The use of horizontal acceleration seems then to be a very practical procedure and one that perhaps avoids some of the disadvantages encountered in vertical acceleration. However, the teacher may wish to use a combination of the two, together with any other productive techniques that might provide a challenge for the gifted student.

PROBLEMS

1. Discuss briefly how you as a mathematics teacher would encourage your administrators to assist you in enhancing your classroom atmosphere. Be specific.

2. In parallel columns list the teacher behaviors that you believe will enhance open structure and those that will result in closed structure in a classroom.

3. Would you consider the lecture method of instruction to be more effective when teaching definitions or when teaching axioms? Why?

4. Describe in detail how you would teach that $N^0 = 1; N \neq 0$ by the discovery method. Emphasize depth thinking.

5. If you were a school superintendent and had valid evidence that completely programmed instruction was producing better results in a fourth-grade section than was produced when the same students were taught by the same teacher in a conventional program, would you continue the programmed instruction or reevaluate the teacher and the conventional text? Discuss.

6. Devise a half-dozen mathematics questions not mentioned in the text which you believe would trigger the use of higher mental process by an elementary school student. Identify for each question the processes which would be brought into play.

7. State what you consider to be the chief advantages and disadvantages of each of the following kinds of assignments:

(a) Questions and activities designed by the teacher.
(b) Questions and activities taken from the text.
(c) Self-assignments by students.
(d) Open ended assignments from many sources.
(e) Assignments having strict time limits.

8. Assume that you are converted to the use of horizontal acceleration as a means of caring for the individual differences in your classroom. Make a list of books, pamphlets, magazines, and other resources which you would accumulate within your classroom to be used for such acceleration. Be specific for a particular grade level.

Chapter 3

Sets, Pairs, Numbers, and Counting

As children enter the kindergarten they bring to the classroom a variety of experience involving sets and pairs. It is recommended that the teacher capitalize upon these basic understandings rather than begin with numbers and counting as has often been done in the past. The concept of number, an abstraction that is extremely difficult, is often introduced to children in rote fashion, with little meaning or understanding. Furthermore, counting is a difficult process requiring the notion of one-to-one correspondence between objects and an ordered set of numbers. It is much more logical to begin with students on common ground and talk of sets and pairs. Mathematicians speak of a pair of objects or elements as a set of two well-defined elements. Children are well aware of many such pairs, such as pairs of twins, pairs of shoes, pairs of skates, pairs of stockings; in fact their own bodies are characterized by the idea of twoness–two eyes, two ears, two hands, and two feet. The idea of set ties in nicely here, since it is a collection of well-defined objects or elements and the student talks freely of sets of dishes, sets of books, or sets of blocks. The teacher can help develop this concept by substituting the word "set" where she ordinarily may use the word "group." She might talk of the set of children in the classroom, the set of chairs or tables. Children should recognize that a pair is a set; in fact, a set can have any number of elements–zero, one, two, three, and so on. The teacher may draw to the attention of very young children the concept of the empty set by using the set of children left in the room when all of the children are out for recess. The idea of subsets should also be explored early. A subset of a larger set contains only elements from the larger set. For example, the set of all blue-eyed children in the room is a subset of all children in the room.

Students should be encouraged to identify many sets and pairs and to talk about their composition. They will begin to identify sets by the cardinal number which describes them. From this point it is a short step to number pairs and sets where the abstract begins to enter the picture. Students will now be able to recognize the numerals zero through nine as a set of numerals, and any two of them as being a pair of numerals.

The idea of order in pairs and sets will naturally evolve from the concepts above. Children will readily recognize that for certain pairs of objects order makes a difference, while for others it does not. They will see a washer and a nut in their relation to a bolt as being ordered, and a pair of earrings as being unordered. They will see that the set of whole numbers zero through nine takes on additional meaning when we speak of them as indicating quantity and arrange them in order from smallest to largest. If, when considering any two distinct elements of a set, one is less than the other in the same order, we say the set is *ordered*. From this point on the students will extend the set of whole numbers past nine by introducing combinations of basic symbols and moving upward decade by decade, up to one hundred, one thousand, and so on. With these successive extensions the counting numbers including zero finally become an infinite set and provide the student with his first excursion into the infinite. Prior to this, large nonnumber or concrete sets, such as the leaves on all the trees in the world or the grains of sand on all the seashores, will likely have been discussed and their finite nature recognized.

A few words are in order here concerning the distinction between a number and a numeral. While it is important that the concept involved here be established with students, the matter should not be labored. Under the proper tutelage, students will understand that number is an abstract notion which relates to a variety of mathematical situations. "Fiveness" as a characteristic of a set containing five elements is easily understood by the young students, and the numeral five is a symbol representing this situation which the student early learns to write and utilize in his communication.

A reasonable distinction between number and numeral should be expected of students. Undoubtedly there are situations in which the term to be used is debatable. To make an issue in such situations is senseless. Note the following examples of usage:

1. Write the numeral two.
2. The numeral two represents the number two.
3. Please write a large number. (The reaction here might be that one does not write numbers)
4. Please write a large numeral. (Now a student may write 12 in contrast to 12.)
5. Please write a numeral representing a large number. (This says what is intended but we may not wish to be so precise.)
6. Students should be able to use the numbers zero through nine with understanding. (Or should we say numerals?)

The important thing is not that students always use the correct word but that they can explain the difference between the two terms when pressed to do so and when the distinction is completely discernible.

NUMBERS

Many devices are available for helping the young student to master the concept of numbers. The use of sets, either concrete or semiconcrete, will assist students to tag the respective sets with the proper cardinal number. The closed line or cloud can be used in place of the set braces on the chalkboard, flannel board (with yarn) or on the table top (with yarn) and toy animals or letters representing animals can be used as elements of the sets, as shown in the illustrations.

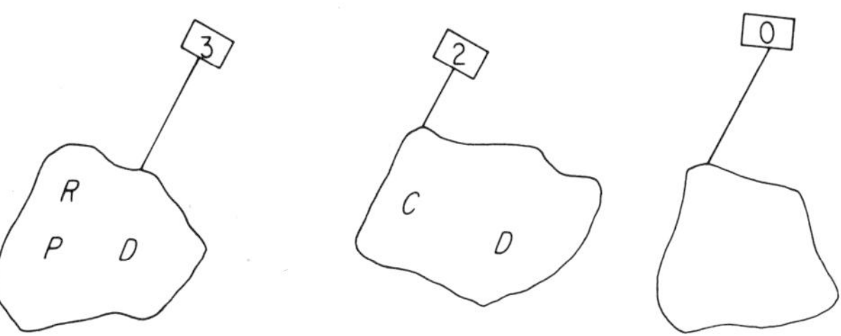

The number line is a useful semiconcrete device for teaching the four basic axioms of the counting numbers.[1] Namely:

1. There is a first counting number zero.
2. Every counting number has a successor.
3. Every counting number except zero has a predecessor.
4. Of any two distinct counting numbers, one is greater than the other.

These axioms give order and sequence to the counting numbers and the distances and points. The student soon learns to count by making loops with his pencil or finger from one point on the line to the next. He may also get experience with subsets by counting by 2's, 3's, etc., in each case making his loops at the same time. The arrow at the right end of the line helps the student to see the infinite nature of the counting numbers.

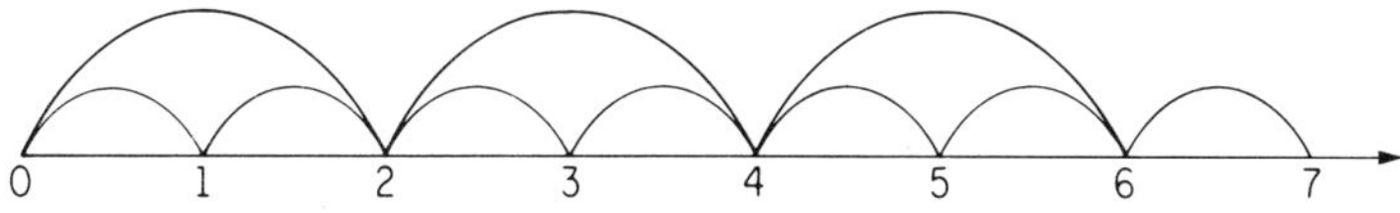

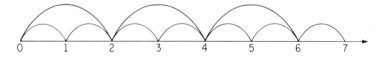

EXPANDING THE MASTER SET

Simultaneously with the counting numbers the students will develop the set of positive proper fractions. Beginning with simple fractions such as 1/2, 1/4, 1/3, they will gradually extend this set to include all of the so-called rational proper fractions between zero and one on the number line. The infinite

[1] In this treatment the counting numbers are considered to be the set $\{0, 1, 2, 3, \ldots\}$. This is consistent with using zero as the cardinal number describing the empty set.

nature of this set should now become apparent as students continue to divide the unit segment into more and more parts. This set poses a problem of distribution of these proper fractions and their corresponding points on the number line. Here for the first time we have numbers such that between any two of them there is always a third, and this holds regardless of how close together the two points are. In fact, we can exhibit a point or number between $\frac{1}{1{,}000{,}000}$ and $\frac{2}{1{,}000{,}000}$ simply by averaging these two. We get $\frac{3}{1{,}000{,}000} \div 2 = \frac{3}{2{,}000{,}000}$, which is greater than $\frac{1}{1{,}000{,}000}$ or $\frac{2}{2{,}000{,}000}$ and smaller than $\frac{2}{1{,}000{,}000}$ or $\frac{4}{2{,}000{,}000}$. Such a set is said to be a *dense set*. Note that our set of whole numbers was *not* such a set. This does not imply that all points on the number line are now represented.

From here it is a short step to the positive improper fractions or mixed numbers existing between 1 and 2, 2 and 3, etc. Each of these is again an infinite set. The student now has the concept of positive rational numbers which includes all of the positive numbers that can be expressed in the form a/b, where a and b are nonnegative integers, but b cannot equal zero. This set will meet his needs until he deals with negative numbers and numbers such as π, $\sqrt{2}$, etc., which require two further extensions of the set. It can now be seen that one of the major objectives of the student is to extend his number set to include more and more elements. These numbers become necessary to make his experiences meaningful and consistent.

ORDERING SETS AND PAIRS

The ordering of pairs and sets generally enters early into the child's experience. Young students often recognize a sort of built in order in certain sets. Some such sets and others which may appear to students to have no built in order are listed below:

Sets having built-in order	*Sets having no built-in order*
1. A set of socket wrenches.	1. A set of chairs.
2. A set of nested mixing bowls.	2. A set of dishes.
3. A washer and a nut in terms of the order in which one puts them on a bolt.	3. A set of random numbers.
4. The minuend and subtrahend in the binary operation of subtraction when considered in terms of the difference obtained.	4. A pair of shoes.

Sets having built-in order

5. The dividend and divisor in a division problem when considered in terms of the quotient obtained.
6. The terms of a fraction: $\frac{3}{4}$.
7. The terms of a ratio: 2:3.
8. A pair of coordinates used in graphing: (2,3).

Sets having no built-in order

5. A pair of water skiis.
6. The addends in an addition problem.
7. The factors in a multiplication problem.

Note that in this type of order or absence of order we consider properties of the elements such as weight, size, sum, difference, product quotient, value, and sequence of use.

Actually mathematicians are much more interested in determining whether the elements of a set can be put in one-to-one correspondence with the counting numbers. When this has been accomplished they say the set has been *ordered*. They are, however, also concerned about determining in what situations the order of the elements of a pair make a difference in the result of the property under consideration.

Returning to our list of sets having or not having built-in order, let us examine some number pairs. As children begin to operate with the elements of the nonnegative rational number set they will discover that order is important in some operations and notations while it is not important in others. For example, the number pairs in fractions are definitely ordered, since to interchange the numbers would alter the value of the fraction. Students will discover further that when adding or multiplying a pair of numbers the sum or product is not affected by the order. That is $3 + 4 = 7$, as does $4 + 3 = 7$ and $3 \times 4 = 12$ as does $4 \times 3 = 12$. The elements in the operations subtraction and division are ordered, however, $6 \div 3$ gives a different quotient than $3 \div 6$ and $5 - 3 = 2$ is not only different from $3 - 5 = -2$ but produces a difference completely outside the number set with which we are at present working.

Let us now summarize by diagram what we have been saying about sets and pairs. It is not intended that this diagram be used with younger students but it may be helpful for teachers and more mature students, as they attempt to articulate their understanding of these relatively new but basic ideas. For the sake of brevity we will refer to sets and pairs where objects are involved as being *concrete*, and those whose elements are not concrete as being *abstract* pairs and sets. Since set and pair are both undefined concepts, the descriptions of them are of course arbitrary. When we refer to a class of elements we mean elements possessing the same general characteristics and obeying the same laws. In many cases the use to be made of the set or pair will determine whether the elements are in the same class. We would correctly think of complex numbers as being in a different class than the positive integers. Also generally we would consider cows to be in a different class that planets even though in the nursery rhyme the cow and the moon may have been in the same class.

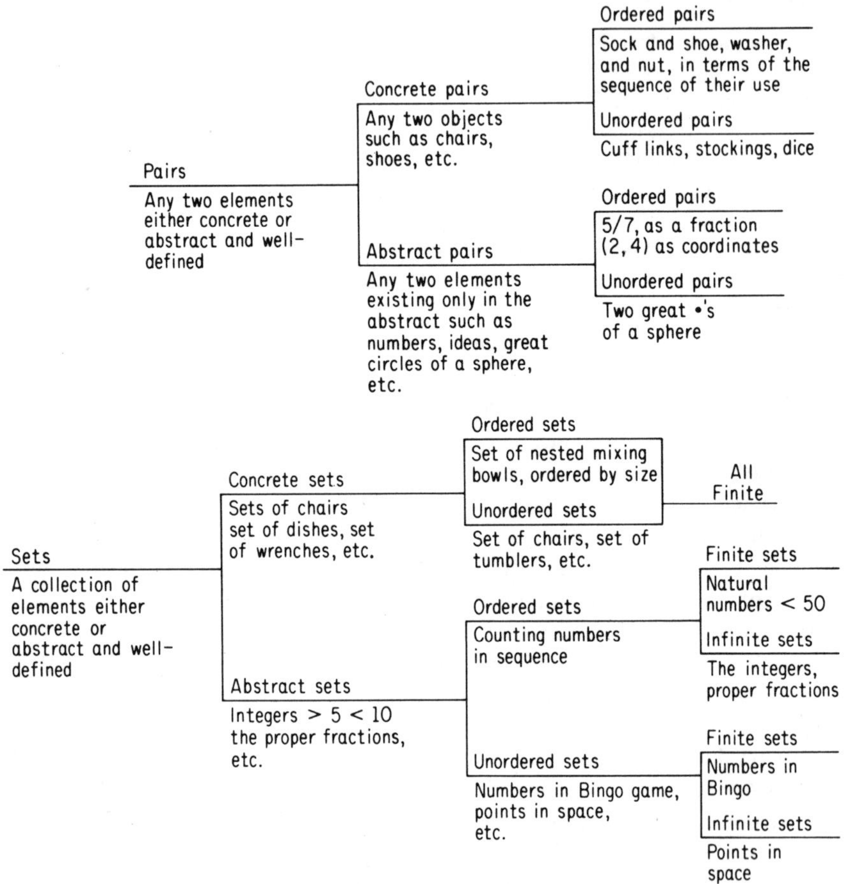

SUBSETS OF WHOLE NUMBERS

Another important aspect of number sets enters into elementary arithmetic in the study of subsets of the whole numbers. Children learn early to identify the subsets of the whole numbers, i.e., the even integers, odd integers, counting by 3's, by 5's, and by 10's. These are all basic subsets important in the child's number experiences. Primes and composites are other basic subsets of the whole numbers, which are extremely important tools for the mathematics student and which can be explored as early as fourth grade.

A whole number which has exactly two distinct factors with respect to the set of positive integers is a prime number. More generally in the set of integers an integer P is called a *prime number* when its only exact divisors are the trivial ones ± 1 and $\pm P$. An integer C which has exact divisors other than ± 1 and $\pm C$ is called a *composite*. In the set of nonnegative integers any integer other than zero and one and the primes is a composite. It is well for the young student to think of the nonnegative integer set as being comprised of a subset of primes, a subset of composites, and a special set containing zero and one. The definition of a composite leads us to observe that when a number is a composite it can be factored into two factors neither of which is trivial and the smallest possible one of these nontrivial divisors is a prime. For example, the composite 24 factors into nontrivial factor pairs 4 and 6, and 3 and 8, and 2 and 12, but the smallest possible of these not-trivial divisors is 2 which is a prime. We are now ready to state what is often called the *basic theorem of arithmetic*: "Every composite number can be factored uniquely into primes."[2] Let us illustrate: 12 factors into $2 \cdot 2 \cdot 3$, all of which are prime and there is no other set of factors consisting of strictly primes which will produce 12. We may change the order to read $2 \cdot 3 \cdot 2$ or $3 \cdot 2 \cdot 2$, but this is merely a change in order employing the same primes and therefore does not destroy the uniqueness provision of the theorem. This basic theorem of arithmetic is generally neglected in the elementary school when in reality it is the basis for the multiplication and division facts and for work with fractions. Its use in these areas will be discussed in a later chapter.

Students at all levels should have many experiences with the prime number set and composite number set and at an early age be able to identify the primes and composites up to 100 on a number board and with increasing maturity be able to break these composites into their prime factors. They should recognize that 2 is the only even prime, since all other even numbers are divisible by 2 and could, therefore, not be prime. More mature students will be interested in the prime factorization of large composites which will lead them from trial and error and factor-table methods to Fermat's and Euler's methods. These methods open up an entire area in number theory centered around such interesting items as the sieve of Eratosthenes, Mersenne and Fermat primes, the proof of the infinitude of primes, the distribution of primes, aliquot parts, the set of perfect numbers, the set of deficient numbers, the set of abundant numbers, amicable number pairs, relatively prime numbers, Euler's ϵ function, Goldback's conjectures, etc.[3]

Many of the topics mentioned above will be referred to in other chapters of this text. However, a few of them are so closely related to the concept of sets and pairs that they are given further consideration here.

The idea of numbers being relatively prime is of special significance when dealing with ordered pairs in fractions and ratios. Two or more numbers are

[2] Proof for this theorem may be found in Oystein Ore, *Number Theory and Its History* (New York: McGraw-Hill, 1948), pp. 51–52.

[3] A substantial treatment of these topics can be found on Ore, *op. cit.*, Chaps. 4 and 5.

said to be relatively prime if their greatest common integral divisor is one. For example, 9 and 25 are relatively prime even though neither is a prime number, the reason being that 9 and 25 are not both exactly divisible by any integer > 1. This concept helps us to understand when fractions or ratios have simplier names, and to recognize that the terms of a fraction must contain a common prime if the fraction has a simpler name. To illustrate: the fraction $9/25 = 3 \cdot 3/5 \cdot 5$ which contains no common prime, and 9 and 25 are therefore relatively prime and the fraction has no simplier name. On the other hand, $12/20 = 2 \cdot 2 \cdot 3/2 \cdot 2 \cdot 7$ contains two common primes and has a simpler name, 3/7.

Another topic relating to sets and of interest to a wide range of students is that of perfect, deficient, and abundant numbers. A number is said to be *perfect* if the sum of its exact divisors (excluding the number itself) is equal to the number. For example, under this agreement the number six is divisible by 1, 2, and 3, and $1 + 2 + 3 = 6$. Twenty-eight is the next greater perfect number. There is considerable numerological speculation in these two perfect numbers. God created the earth in six days and the moon goes through a complete cycle in 28 days. The succeeding perfect numbers have as yet not been associated with any such symbolic perfection. Only one general type of perfect number is known. It is $P = (2^{P-1})\,(2^P - 1)$, p being any prime. This formula always produces a perfect number P when $(2p - 1)$ is prime. First impressions from the preceding formula may lead one to believe that there are many perfect numbers, any number of which could be obtained by substituting larger and larger primes for p. This is not true, however, since $(2p - 1)$ is not always a prime. For example, the formula works beautifully for $p = 2$, 3, 5, and 7 but fails for $p = 11$. In fact, primes of the form $(2^p - 1)$ where p is itself prime are called *Mersenne primes* and are themselves very scarce—only sixteen of them having been discovered as of 1959. The primes 5 and 7 when substituted into the formula for perfect numbers give us the next two perfect numbers, 496 and 8,128. There was, in 1959, 16 known perfect numbers, one to correspond to each of the known Mersenne primes. Digital computers have made possible the finding of a few more perfect numbers, a task which mathematicians would likely not have pursued without the help of these machines. To date no odd perfect numbers have been found, but conclusive evidence of their nonexistence has not been established.

Another interesting number set consists of those numbers the sum of whose divisors are less than the number. These are called *deficient numbers.* Any prime or power of a prime is deficient, any divisor of a perfect or deficient number is deficient, but these are not the only deficient numbers. For example, 14 is deficient since its divisors are 1, 2, and 7 and $1 + 2 + 7 = 10$. Deficient numbers are plentiful in our natural number set. A third set of unusual numbers consists of those whose divisors add to produce a sum greater than the numbers themselves. These are called *abundant numbers.* The first few of these are 12, 18, 20, 24 . . . . There are only 20 abundant numbers below 100 and these are all even. The first odd abundant number is 945. Any multiple of an abundant or perfect number is abundant.

In connection with the number sets discussed above it is interesting to note that certain pairs of numbers are *amicable*. That is the sum of the divisors of one number produces the other, and conversely. The numbers themselves are excluded in these sums. An example of such a pair is 220 and 284. The divisors and their sum for 220 are

$$\begin{array}{r} 1 \\ 2 \\ 142 \\ 4 \\ \underline{71} \\ 220 \end{array}$$

and for 284 are

$$\begin{array}{r} 1 \\ 110 \\ 2 \\ 4 \\ 55 \\ 5 \\ 44 \\ 10 \\ 22 \\ 11 \\ \underline{20} \\ 284 \end{array}$$

According to some mystical philosophy, amicable numbers symbolize mutual harmony, perfect friendship, and love. These numbers have attracted the attention of mathematical writers for hundreds of years. Fermat formulated a rule for their determination, as did Descartes and Euler. In spite of the systematic investigation of these mathematicians, a sixteen-year-old Italian boy published the very small amicable pair 1,184 and 1,210, which had eluded all previous investigators. E. B. Escott in a 1946 article in *Scripta Mathematica* gives a complete survey of amicable numbers, listing 390 known pairs and their discoverers.

CLOSURE UNDER THE OPERATIONS

As students move on into the upper grades, the concept of closure within a given number set should be introduced. This can be done by assuming that each of the nonnegative rational numbers as previously defined is written on a square of cardboard and dropped into a basket. If the sum of any two elements drawn from the basket was originally contained in the basket, the set is said to be *closed under addition*. It is understood that since this set is infinite all of its elements could be contained in theory only. In a similar manner, students can test for closure under multiplication, division, and subtraction. Under subtraction it becomes evident that if we should agree to subtract the first number drawn from the second number drawn, we will not have closure.

FURTHER EXPANSION OF THE MASTER SET

This impasse leads to the need of extending the number set to include the negative rationals. This set is known as the *set of all rational numbers*, and is defined as the set of all ordered pairs of the form a/b, where a and b are integers and b does not equal zero. In practice the nonnegative rational number set should now be expanded by use of the number line and the concept of additive inverses. The additive inverse of a number a is defined as a number b such that $a + b = 0$. On the rational number line shown, the negatives are defined as the additive inverse of their positive counterparts, or in symbolic form $a + (-a) = 0$. Zero is its own additive inverse.

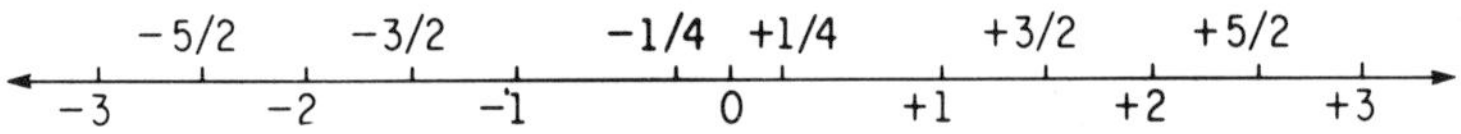

−5/2 −3/2 −1/4 +1/4 +3/2 +5/2

−3 −2 −1 0 +1 +2 +3

From what we have said above, the following are now true:

$$(+1) + (-1) = 0 \qquad (+1/4) + (-1/4) = 0$$
$$(+2) + (-2) = 0 \qquad (+3/2) + (-3/2) = 0$$

As the student studies open sentences such as $x + 2 = 10$ or $x^2 + y = 17$ the idea of *placeholders* comes into the picture, and students should be led to see that these placeholders may be replaced by elements of the rational number set some of which will make these expressions true, and some of which will make them false. In the first expression, 8 is the only element which makes the expression a true sentence while in the second expression we have an infinite set of elements which can replace x, but for each value replacing x only one value of y will pair up with this x to make the expression a true sentence. For example, if $x = 4$, then $y = 1$. Other pairs are (−4, 1), (1/2, 16 3/4), (−5, −8), etc. Thus we have an infinite set of ordered pairs, each pair of the set having the unique distinction of making the original expression a true sentence.

IRRATIONAL NUMBERS

As we move on in the solution of these open sentences we soon contact those of the form $x^2 - 2 = 0$. The solution to this equation gives us $(\sqrt{2})$ and $(-\sqrt{2})$, neither of which is in our present set of numbers.

This situation again invites us to extend our number set to include the irrationals, which now gives us the set known as the *real numbers*, which in reality is the set of all decimals where integers are considered decimals. For example, the integer 5 may be written in decimal form as 5.000. . . . That the number π is also one of the elements of this set was proven as early as 1761. Actually π has likely entered into the students' experience prior to irrationals such as $\sqrt{2}$, while its relationship to the circle and the fact that it is an unusual number should have been brought to the attention of the student earlier; its irrational nature might well be postponed until this stage.

The number line should now be modified to accommodate these new elements and their existence as specific points on the number line established. We use the number line and some geometry to identify the points representing $+\sqrt{2}$ and $-\sqrt{2}$, as shown in the drawing. We draw a unit square on the segment

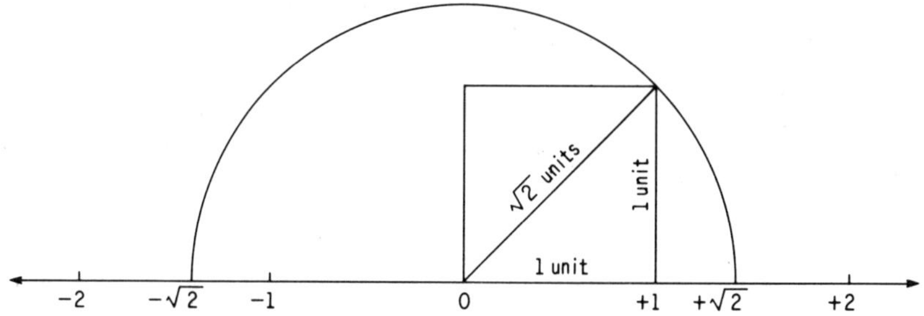

between (0) and (+1). The diagonal *OP* now represents the $\sqrt{2}$ by the Pythagorean theorem. If we pivot *OP* down on to the number line we then have the point *Q* which is $(+\sqrt{2})$. By rotating it on to the negative side of the line we

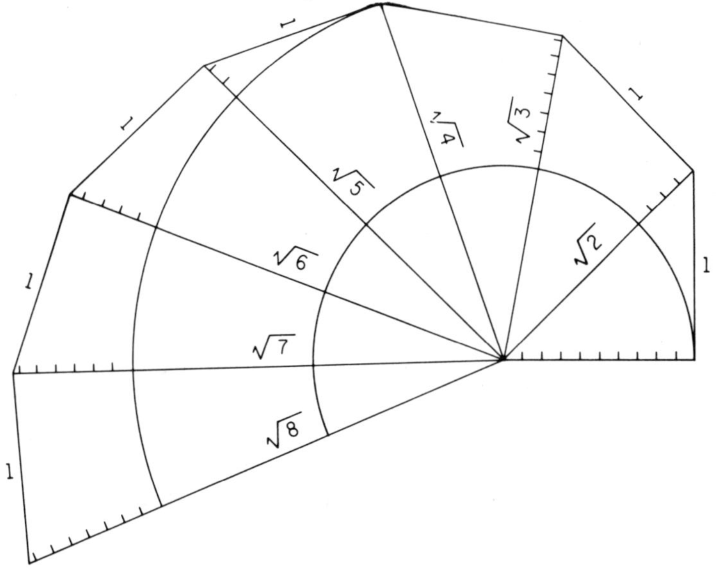

get $(-\sqrt{2})$. This not only illustrates the existence of $(+\sqrt{2})$ and $(-\sqrt{2})$ but from previous agreements we know that $(+\sqrt{2}) + (-\sqrt{2}) = 0$.

In a similar manner, we can show that all of the square roots of integers which are not perfect squares can be identified on the number line. We have gone only as far as $\sqrt{8}$, but we could go on indefinitely (see page 39).

We pause here to give formal proof that the $\sqrt{2}$ is irrational.

1. An integer m is divisible by an integer n provided there is an integer q such that $m = nq$.
2. An even integer, being an integer divisible by 2, is of the form $2q$, and an odd integer is of the form $2q + 1$ (q is an integer).
3. The square root of an even perfect square integer is an even integer since $(2q)^2 = 4q^2 = 2(2q^2)$. Similarly the square root of any odd perfect square integer is odd, since $(2q + 1)^2 = 4q^2 + 4q + 1 - 2(2q^2 + 2q) + 1$

We now do the proof by assuming $\sqrt{2}$ is rational and proving our assumption to be false.

Assume $\sqrt{2} = a/b$, where a and b are nonzero integers and not both even (this can be achieved by dividing a and b by two until a or b is odd.) Now $2b^2 = a^2$ (squaring and multiplying by b^2). Hence a^2 is even since it equals $2b^2$ and a is even by (3) of the previous paragraph. Now a being even may be written as $2q$, where q is an integer. Replacing a by $2q$ in the relation $2b^2 = a^2$, we get $2b^2 = 4q^2$ or $b^2 = 2q^2$. This shows that b^2 is even and hence b itself is even. We thus have a and b both even which is contrary to our earlier specifications. This contradiction establishes that $\sqrt{2}$ is irrational.

Rational and Irrational Decimals

As students encounter and begin to use the real number set they should be led to observe the difference between rational and irrational decimals. Let us classify decimals into four categories as follows:

1. Terminating decimals such as .25.
2. Repeating decimals such as .333 · · ·
3. Periodic decimals such as .272727 · · ·
4. Decimals in which none of the above patterns appear such as .1375493687 ⟶.

Now each of the first three types can easily be shown to be of the form a/b, where a and b are integers, $b \neq 0$. In other words, they can be shown to be rational numbers.

In the first example, $.25 = 25/100 = 1/4$, which is rational.

In the second example, let $n = .333 \cdots$, then $10n = 3.333 \cdots$ and subtracting, $9n = 3$; $n = 3/9$ or $1/3$, which is also rational.

In the third example, let $n = .272727 \cdots$, then $100n = 27.272727 \cdots$ and subtracting, $99n = 27$; $n = 27/99 = 3/11$, which is rational.

However, in the fourth type of decimal no such attack will work. Furthermore, from the fundamental theorem of arithmetic, it can readily be established that the $\sqrt{n}$ is irrational if n is not a perfect square.[4]

The above development should lead the student to the generalization that any of the first three types of decimals mentioned above can be converted to rational form by application of the process shown in the above examples. Two such decimals are especially interesting:

Let $$N = .999 \cdots$$
then $$10N = 9.999 \cdots$$

Subtracting the first equation from the second we get $9N = 9$ from which $N = 9/9 = 1$. We thus discover that .999... is another name for one.
For the second example:

Let $$N = .4999 \cdots$$
then $$10N = 4.999 \cdots$$

Subtracting the first equation from the second, we get $9N = 4.5$, and multiplying both sides of the equation by 10, we get $90n = 45$. Then $N = 45/90 = 1/2$. A second generalization to which students should be led states that any rational number of the form a/b, $b \neq 0$ will convert to one of the three kinds of decimals mentioned earlier. Most of these can be obtained by the usual division process:

$$3/4 = .75$$
$$1/3 = .333 \cdots$$
$$3/11 = .272727 \cdots$$

Of special interest are the two rationals 1 and 1/2 which resulted from .999... and .4999... respectively in our previous work. These can be returned to their decimal equivalents by using the modified algorism for our division. This is done as follows.

Rewriting 1 as in a/b form we have 1/1. Applying the algorism we get

1) 1.000	
.9	.9
.10	
.09	.09
.010	
.009	.009
.001	

If this process is continued the result will be $.999 \cdots$ when we sum the partial quotients.

[4] This is developed on page 15 of the *Twenty-third Yearbook of the National Council of Teachers of Mathematics.*

In the case of 1/2 we proceed in similar fashion.

2) 1.0000	
.8	.4
.20	
.18	.09
.020	
.018	.009
.0020	.0009

Summing the partial quotients, we get .4999 · · ·

A further observation is now in order. It is that we can now write any integer or any integer increased or decreased by 1/2 as a repeating decimal. To illustrate:

$$2 = 1.999... \qquad -5 = -4.999 \cdots$$
$$2\tfrac{1}{2} = 2.4999... \qquad -5\tfrac{1}{2} = -5.4999 \cdots$$

It may be helpful at this point to explore a number line and identify on this line the various sets to which we have referred.

$-\sqrt{3}$ $-\sqrt{2}$ $+\sqrt{2}$ $+\sqrt{3}$

$-\frac{5}{2}$ -2 $-\frac{3}{2}$ -1 $-\frac{1}{2}$ 0 $+\frac{1}{2}$ $+1$ $+\frac{3}{2}$ $+2$ $+\frac{5}{2}$ $+3$ $+\frac{7}{2}$ $+4$

Set	*Name of Set*		*Sample Elements*
Set *A*	The nonnegative integers	=	0, +1, +2, +3, ...
Set *B*	The positive fractions	=	+1/4, +1/2, +3/4, +3/2, ...
Set *C*	The nonnegative rational numbers	=	Set *A* and Set *B* above
Set *D*	The negative rational numbers	=	−1/2, −3/4, −1, − 3/2, −2, ...
Set *E*	The rational numbers	=	Sets *A*, *B*, *C*, and *D* above
Set *F*	The irrational numbers	=	$+\sqrt{2}, +\sqrt{3}, -\sqrt{3}, -\sqrt{2}$, ...
Set *G*	The real numbers	=	Sets *A*, *B*, *C*, *D*, *E*, *F*, and *G*

IMAGINARY AND COMPLEX NUMBERS

As the student moves into the solution of equations of the type $x^2 + 2 = 0$ it becomes apparent that our present U, that is the real numbers, again becomes inadequate, since the $\sqrt{-2}$ is not an element of the set and it thus becomes necessary to expand the set to include the imaginary numbers.

The symbol i is now introduced to represent the imaginary unit, its basic property being that $i^2 = -1$. $\{x|x^2 + 2 = 0\}$ thus becomes $\{+\sqrt{2}i, -\sqrt{2}i\}$ which can be verified by replacing x in the original set by either member of the solution set, as follows:

$$(+\sqrt{2}i)^2 + 2 = 0; \quad 2i^2 + 2 = 0; \quad 2(-1) + 2 = 0; \quad -2 + 2 = 0$$

also for:

$$(-\sqrt{2}i)^2 + 2 = 0; \quad 2i^2 + 2 = 0; \quad 2(-1) + 2 = 0; \quad -2 + 2 = 0$$

Now in solving equations of the type $x^2 - 4x + 13 = 0$, the quadratic formula gives $(2 - 3i)$, $(2 + 3i)$. Since these numbers contain the imaginary unit, they are not in the real-number set but are called *complex numbers.* More generally, all members of the form $a + bi$, where a and b are real numbers (a being called the *real part* and bi the *imaginary part*) are classified as complex numbers. The set of complex numbers encompasses the set of real numbers, since we need only let $b = 0$ in order to get the subset called the *real numbers.*

We have now arrived at a universal set sufficiently inclusive to provide the elements of solution sets for the general algebraic equation $ax^n + bx^{n-1} + \cdots + cx + d = 0$, where $a \neq 0$ and $a, b, \ldots, c, d$ are complex numbers. There are, how-

Logical Expansion of Number Set as it Evolves in Kindergarten through Grade Eight

Set	Description	Set Notation
Natural numbers	The set of elements 1, 2, 3...	$\{x \mid x \text{ is an integer} > 0\}$
+ Zero =	When referring to the absence of things or elements zero may be thought of as the cardinal number describing the empty set. As a point on the number line it is a set containing one element, namely zero.	$\{x \mid x \text{ is an integer} > -1 \text{ and} < +1\}$
Nonnegative integers	The set of elements ..0, +1, +2,..	$\{x \mid x \text{ is an integer} \geqslant 0\}$
+ Positive fractions =	The set of ordered pairs of the form a/b with a and b positive integers, $b \neq 0$, and a and b relatively prime.	$\{a/b \mid a$ and b positive integers b $\neq 0$ and a and b are relatively prime$\}$
Nonnegative rational numbers +	The set of ordered pairs of the form a/b with a and b nonnegative integers and $b \neq 0$.	$\{a/b \mid a$ and b nonnegative integers and $b \neq 0\}$
Negative rational numbers =	The set or ordered pairs of the from a/b with either a or b negative integers and $b \neq 0$.	$\{a/b \mid a$ or b is a negative integer and $b \neq 0\}$
Rational numbers +	The set of ordered pairs of the form a/b with a and b integers and $b \neq 0$.	$\{a/b \mid a$ and b integers and $b \neq 0\}$
Irrational numbers =	The set of decimals which cannot be expressed as rational numbers.	$\{x \mid x$ is a decimal which cannot be expressed as a rational number$\}$
Real numbers +	The set of all decimals.	$\{x \mid x \lesseqgtr 0\}$
Imaginary numbers =	The set of all numbers of the form bi, where b is real and $i = \sqrt{-1}$.	$\{bi \mid a$ is real and $i = \sqrt{-1}\}$
Complex numbers	The set of all numbers of the form $(a + bi)$, where a and b are real and $i = \sqrt{-1}$.	$\{a + bi/a$ and b are real and $i = \sqrt{-1}\}$

ever, other sets of supercomplex numbers such as "quaternions" and "Cayley numbers," both of which are beyond the scope of this treatment.

As we leave the classification of numbers which we have developed, let us set up a diagram which may be helpful in remembering the complex-number set and its subsets. Before doing so, however, it should be clear that the real number set is generally considered adequate for grades K–8, but since the universal set is such a basic idea in all of mathematics it seems desirable that teachers should at least be alerted to what lies ahead. It is with this in mind that the development in this area has proceeded to this rather advanced stage (see chart on page 43).

NUMERATION SYSTEMS

We now move from our summary of the various number sets to explore the Hindu-Arabic numeration system which is basic to all these sets and which serves as a pattern for developments of numeration systems in bases other than ten.

Five basic characteristics of the base ten system are:

1. Symbols 0, 1, 2, 3, 4, 5, 6, 7, 8, 9
2. Base . . . . the base 10 which repeats in decades and integral powers of 10
3. Place value . . . . the multiple of a power of 10 specified by a symbol is indicated by its position in the number
4. Zero . . . . a symbol specifying the empty or null set of objects and the set of integers > -1 and $< +1$
5. Decimal point . . . . a device for extending the place value idea to include fractions

The task of operating this numeration system within the various universal sets consists of a sequential development requiring extreme care. The child at the primary level may need numerous experiences with the number line, place-value pockets, and concrete objects such as cardboard tabs or tongue depressors placed in the pockets. Here the actual manipulation associated with counting and the basic processes of addition, subtraction, multiplication, and division helps substantially in teaching the concepts.

For some students this play upon the concrete will need to continue for many years, and teachers should feel free at any level to call upon the concrete manipulation technique. The use of the semiconcrete number line and place-value chart may be introduced as soon as students can understand it. To begin with, it should be used in conjunction with the concrete materials and the dependence upon the concrete gradually eliminated. The abstract is of course the ultimate objective and is gradually developed to a point where the impediments of sensory aids can be completely dispensed with.

In understanding the Hindu-Arabic system it is desirable at the upper-grade or junior high level to give students some experience with bases other than ten. This is not difficult and can lead to a general understanding of the operation of numeration systems similar to ours, but having a different base.

Let us look at what use can be made of the various bases in our regular mathematics program and where we can best fit the treatment into it. Systems with bases other than 10 may be desirable in certain situations. In fact, this actually is true today as electronic digital computers play an ever-increasing role in our culture. Because electronic calculators adapt themselves best to a number system having only two symbols (a circuit being either closed or open) the base 2 using the symbols 0 and 1 is practically a must for these machines. This leads us, as mathematics teachers, to a responsibility for familiarizing our students with this system on the basis of scientific and technical reasons as well as the traditional reason that understanding a system with another base gives students greater understanding of the decimal system. It may be desirable that we teach this system at several places in our curriculum, perhaps introducing it in a very simple way at grade 5 or 6 and reinforcing the ideas at one or two places further on in the curriculum.

Let us look at what use can be made of the various bases in our regular ings in a place-value chart for our own base 10. A sample number has been written into the chart.

Base 10 or Decimal System

10000	1000	100	10	1	1/10	1/100	1/1000
		3	7	4	5	2	

We observe certain characteristics of our base which parallel the bases which we will consider later and which go beyond the characteristics listed on page 44.

1. There is a column heading "1" which allows us to make single unit differences in the numbers we write.
2. We get the successive column headings to the left of "1" by multiplying one by successive powers of ten and we get the successive column headings on the right of "1" by dividing one by successive powers of ten. When students understand the zero exponent and negative exponents they will see that all column headings may be expressed as powers of 10 without using fractions.
3. Because of (2) above, any column heading multiplied by the base will produce the next column heading to the left.
4. The decimal in a base ten number locates the boundary line between the "ones" digit and the "one-tenth" digit. The number 374.52 has been inserted in the chart above.
5. The 3 in the hundreds column means 3 groups of 100 or $3 \cdot 100$. The five in the one-tenths column means $5 \cdot \frac{1}{10}$ etc. If we list each column

interpretation and then add we get:

$$\begin{aligned} 3 \cdot 100 &= 300 \\ 7 \cdot 10 &= 70 \\ 4 \cdot 1 &= 4 \\ 5 \cdot \frac{1}{10} &= .5 \\ 2 \cdot \frac{1}{100} &= .02 \\ \hline & 374.52 \text{ sum} \end{aligned}$$

6. Only single digits may be used in any column when writing numbers into the chart. This preserves the place value of each digit. Furthermore, the largest single digit is one less than the base.
7. A number can only be written correctly into the chart in one way. Using these observations let us build a place-value chart for base eight. Note that we write the column headings in base ten for convenience.

Base Eight Chart

512	64	8	1	1/8	1/64
	5	7	4		

The number 574_{eight} which has been written into the chart above may be converted to base ten by taking our clue from item 5 of our characteristics for base ten.

The 5 means $5 \cdot 64$ or 320_{ten}

The 7 means $7 \cdot 8$ or 56_{ten}

The 4 means $4 \cdot 1$ or 4_{ten}

Adding these base ten numbers we obtain a sum of 380_{ten}, and therefore

$$574_{\text{eight}} = 380_{\text{ten}}$$

Let us now convert in the opposite direction, i.e., convert a base ten number to a base eight number. To do this we reason as follows:

If we wish to convert 824_{ten} to base eight we refer to the base eight chart and note we can use one group of 512, so we place a "1" in that column. Now $824 - 512 = 312$. We can now use four groups of 64, so we place a "4" in that column. Now $312 - (4 \cdot 64) = 312 - 256 = 56$. We can now use seven groups of eight, so we place a seven in that column. Now $56 - (7 \cdot 8) = 56 - 56 = 0$, and we have used up all of our base ten number and can complete our work by placing a zero in the ones column. Our work now appears as follows:

Base Eight Chart

512	64	8	1	1/8	1/64
1	4	7	0		

We conclude then that

$$824_{ten} = 1470_{eight}$$

When students have learned to convert in both direction they can proceed to write the counting numbers in base eight. This is done by converting the base ten counting numbers to base eight through use of the chart. The conversions of the first twenty-one counting numbers are shown in the table.

$0_{ten} = 0_{eight}$
$1_{ten} = 1_{eight}$
$2_{ten} = 2_{eight}$
$3_{ten} = 3_{eight}$
$4_{ten} = 4_{eight}$
$5_{ten} = 5_{eight}$
$6_{ten} = 6_{eight}$
$7_{ten} = 7_{eight}$
$8_{ten} = 10_{eight}$
$9_{ten} = 11_{eight}$
$10_{ten} = 12_{eight}$
$11_{ten} = 13_{eight}$
$12_{ten} = 14_{eight}$
$13_{ten} = 15_{eight}$
$14_{ten} = 16_{eight}$
$15_{ten} = 17_{eight}$
$16_{ten} = 20_{eight}$
$17_{ten} = 21_{eight}$
$18_{ten} = 22_{eight}$
$19_{ten} = 23_{eight}$
$20_{ten} = 24_{eight}$

The next stage of the development involves the basic operations in the new base. In practice these should be demonstrated at the beginning stage with simple examples. For our purposes here, however, examples of medium difficulty seem more appropriate. The examples follow.

Addition, Base Eight

512	64	8	1	1/8	1/64
	3	7	4		
		5	6		
	4	5	2		

The process here is completely logical. We add 6 + 4 = 10_{ten} and convert to base eight to obtain 12_{eight}. The "2" is placed in the ones column and one group of eight carried to the eights column. The process then continues.

Subtraction, Base Eight

512	64	8	1	1/8	1/64
	5	6	3		
		7	5		
	4	6	6		

Note that we regroup by taking one group of eight to the ones column making 13_{eight} ones which is 11_{ten} and $11_{ten} - 5_{ten \& eight} = 6_{ten \& eight}$. We now have 5_{eight} groups of eight remaining from which we must subtract 7_{eight} groups of eight which again requires regrouping. The process continues.

Multiplication, Base Eight

4096	512	64	8	1	1/8	1/64
		4	3	7		
			5	3		
	1	5	3	5		
2	6	3	3			
3	0	0	6	5		

We multiply $3_{eight} \times 7_{eight} = 3_{ten} \times 7_{ten} = 21_{ten} = 25_{eight}$. We now place the "5" in the ones column and move the two groups of eight to the eights column, where we now multiply $(3_{eight} \times 3_{eight})$ and add $2_{eight} = (3_{ten} \times 3_{ten}) + 2_{ten} = 11_{ten} = 13_{eight}$. We place the "3" in the eights column and move one to the sixty-fours column. The process continues and finally the addition of the partial products must be done in base eight.

Division, Base Eight

		512	64	8	1
			4	3	7
53_{eight}	3	0	0	6	5
	2	5	4		
		2	4	6	
		2	0	1	
			4	5	5
			4	5	5

It is helpful to superimpose a place-value chart on the division bracket as above. We now proceed to divide as follows.

We are dividing 30065_{eight} by 53_{eight}. We try 4 in the sixty-fours column and multiply, getting 254_{eight}. (Note that 5 would have produced too large a product). Subtracting and bringing down another digit we get 246_{eight}.

The process continues. It must be understood that the explanations given for the multiplication and division algorisms above were not logically correct, since we were following the algorism and did not go into detail. The algorism can, however, be explained logically just as is done with the corresponding base ten algorisms elsewhere in this text. The processes in the preceding algorisms have been accomplished by converting back and fourth between base ten and base eight. We could have done the same work by constructing basic addition and multiplication charts for base eight and referring to them for our basic facts in base eight. These charts are shown adjacent, and as in base ten they may also be used to obtain the basic facts for the inverse operations of subtraction and division.

Addition and Subtraction Chart, Base Eight

±	0	1	2	3	4	5	6	7
0	0	1	2	3	4	5	6	7
1	1	2	3	4	5	6	7	10
2	2	3	4	5	6	7	10	11
3	3	4	5	6	7	10	11	12
4	4	5	6	7	10	11	12	13
5	5	6	7	10	11	12	13	14
6	6	7	10	11	12	13	14	15
7	7	10	11	12	13	14	15	16

Multiplication and Division Chart, Base Eight

× ÷	0	1	2	3	4	5	6	7
0	0	0	0	0	0	0	0	0
1	0	1	2	3	4	5	6	7
2	0	2	4	6	10	12	14	16
3	0	3	6	11	14	17	22	25
4	0	4	10	14	20	24	30	34
5	0	5	12	17	24	31	36	43
6	0	6	14	22	30	36	44	52
7	0	7	16	25	34	43	52	61

It is not intended that elementary students become familiar enough with these facts to give them from memory; rather, they should be able to do operations in bases other then ten by conversion between bases or by having access to the charts. Both are desirable.

Once the students have had considerable experience with bases they may wish to explore the following:

Division method for converting base ten numbers to base eight numbers.

Converting 974_{ten} to base eight:

8	9	7	4		
8	1	2	1	+	6
8		1	5	+	1
			1	+	7

Divide successively by 8, indicating the remainder in each case. Pick up the final quotient and the successive remainders from the bottom up. Thus in the example:

$$974_{ten} = 1716_{eight}$$

When students have achieved a reasonable mastery of base eight they may be led into a similar experience with another base such as two. (Base two is suggested because it is used in the computers). The sequence of development of another base might well follow that used here for base eight namely:

1. Build the proper place value chart.
2. Have some experience in writing the counting numerals for the new base.
3. Convert numbers from base ten into the new base using the chart.
4. Convert number from the chart to base ten.
5. Build basic fact charts for the operations (this is very simple in base two).
6. Perform the basic operations in the new base using both the conversion method and the chart method.
7. Have students check their own work by converting back to base ten.

Having had experience in at least two new bases the students can now likely find their way through any other of the bases less than ten.

The following is an interesting short cut method for converting from base eight to base two, and vice versa.

To change 725_{eight} to base two:

$$\begin{matrix} 7 & 2 & 5 \\ 111 & 010 & 101 \end{matrix}$$

By converting each digit of the base eight number to a three-digit base two number we find $725_{eight} = 111010101_{two}$. Note that each digit of the base eight number must produce a three-digit base two number, even if it requires placing an otherwise unnecessary zero on the left. The reason for this can be recognized when one parallels the place-value charts for the two numeration systems. This relationship is being utilized in some computers by programming in base eight, which involves fewer digits, and translating mechanically to base two before feeding the program into the computer. The process is then reversed when the computer has made its calculations.

In order to convey a more complete understanding of the place value chart and its headings the more mature students and surely the teachers will want to examine the following two tables showing column headings for base ten and base eight place-value charts.

Possible Column Headings for a Base Ten Place-Value Chart

10000_{ten}	1000_{ten}	100_{ten}	10_{ten}	1_{ten}	$\frac{1}{10_{ten}}$	$\frac{1}{100_{ten}}$	$\frac{1}{1000_{ten}}$	$\frac{1}{10000_{ten}}$
$(10)^4$	$(10)^3$	$(10)^2$	$(10)^1$	10^0	$(10)^{-1}$	$(10)^{-2}$	$(10)^{-3}$	$(10)^{-4}$
$(10)^4$	$(10)^3$	$(10)^2$	$(10)^1$	1	$\left(\frac{1}{10}\right)^1$	$\left(\frac{1}{10}\right)^2$	$\left(\frac{1}{10}\right)^3$	$\left(\frac{1}{10}\right)^4$
$10 \times 10 \times 10 \times 10$	$10 \times 10 \times 10$	10×10	10	1	$\frac{1}{10}$	$\frac{1}{10 \times 10}$	$\frac{1}{10 \times 10 \times 10}$	$\frac{1}{10 \times 10 \times 10 \times 10}$
10000	1000	100	10	1	$\frac{1}{10}$	$\frac{1}{100}$	$\frac{1}{1000}$	$\frac{1}{10000}$

Possible Column Headings for a Base Eight Place-Value Chart

10000_{eight}	1000_{eight}	100_{eight}	10_{eight}	1_{eight}	$\frac{1}{10_{eight}}$	$\frac{1}{100_{eight}}$	$\frac{1}{100_{eight}}$	$\frac{1}{1000_{eight}}$
8	8^3	8^2	8^1	8^0	8^{-1}	8^{-2}	8^{-3}	8^{-4}
8^5	8^3	8^2	8^1	1	$\left(\frac{1}{8}\right)^1$	$\left(\frac{1}{8}\right)^2$	$\left(\frac{1}{8}\right)^3$	$\left(\frac{1}{8}\right)^4$
$8 \times 8 \times 8 \times 8$	$8 \times 8 \times 8$	8×8	8	1	$\frac{1}{8}$	$\frac{1}{8 \times 8}$	$\frac{1}{8 \times 8 \times 8}$	$\frac{1}{8 \times 8 \times 8 \times 8}$
512	128	64	8	1	$\frac{1}{8}$	$\frac{1}{64}$	$\frac{1}{128}$	$\frac{1}{512}$

It will be noted here that as far as appearance of the numerals is concerned the column headings for all bases < 10 will appear the same when written in their respective bases. Note the first row of each of the charts above.

As we conclude this section on bases a few observations are in order:

1. Any work on bases other than ten in grades 4 and 5 should perhaps be limited to bases less than ten and emphasize the place value charts, translation from one base to another, counting in the new base and perhaps a few very simple operations.
2. In grades 6–8 more operations, more bases including those greater than ten, and depth involvement in numeration systems generally are in order (See chapter 10 for treatment of base twelve).
3. A reasonable understanding of bases by elementary students grades 6–8 will be evidenced when students generally can do an operational problem expressed in base ten by converting it to any base, less than ten, assigned by the teacher and doing the problem in the assigned base.
4. There are adequate extensions of the work on number bases to care for individual differences in the classroom. A few of these which are not elaborated in this text are:
   (a) Bases other than ten including the sexagesimal system of the Babylonians. (Base twelve is developed in Chapter 10 of this text).
   (b) Fractions in other bases.
   (c) Negative number bases.
   (d) Factorial number bases.
5. Teacher should use judgment in the amount of time devoted to the teaching of bases. To extend the treatment at the expense of more basic concepts can result in a weak mathematics program.
6. Teachers will do well to avoid the time-consuming tasks of checking a great number of student papers involving bases other than ten. This can better be handled by having students convert their calculations to base ten and thus do their own checking.

PROBLEMS

1. Give several examples of ordered pairs, both concrete and abstract, and identify the characteristic with regard to which they are ordered. Is the characteristic natural to the pair or is it a convention?

2. Explain with cloud sets and their associated cardinal numbers how you would show that $10 - 7 = 3$.

3. In language understandable to a fourth-grade student, explain the difference between "number" and "numeral."

4. Give an example of the following sets:

(a) A concrete, finite, ordered set.
(b) An abstract, infinite, ordered set.
(c) An abstract, finite, unordered set.

5. Find a common fraction which lies between $\frac{7}{1{,}000{,}000}$ and $\frac{8}{1{,}000{,}000}$ and show how you obtained it.

6. Devise an open-ended home assignment involving composite numbers which considers the individual differences of your students. (fourth-grade level)

7. Are the numbers 164 and 195 relatively prime? Show your work in detail.

8. Use the formula $P = 2^{p-1}\ (2^P - 1)$ to generate a perfect number when $p = 7$. Show by means of the sum of its divisors that P is perfect.

9. Is the set of odd whole numbers closed under addition? Subtraction? Multiplication? Division? Raising to a power? Show counterexamples in cases where the set is not closed.

10. By means of geometric construction and the number line show that the $\sqrt{3}$ exists on the line.

11. Convert the following to rational number form (i.e., the form a/b where a and b are whole numbers and $b \neq 0$):

(a) .4999 · · ·
(b) 1.274274274 · · ·
(c) .999 · · ·

12. Show that each of the following is a rational number by placing them in the a/b form:

(a) 7
(b) 0
(c) 2/3
(d) $1\frac{1}{2}$
(e) .75
(f) .4999 · · ·
(g) .102710271027 · · ·
(h) .4272727 · · ·
(i) .034888 · · ·

13. Convert the following numbers to base seven, then multiply them in base seven and check the product by converting back to base ten.

234, 86

14. If $2634_{\text{ten}} = 10452_N$, find N.

Chapter 4

Combining and Decomposing Sets

OPERATIONS

Having established in Chapter 3 the concepts of pairs, sets, numbers, counting and numeration systems, and having briefly explored some operations, we are now prepared to combine and decompose these sets further. At this point a diagram may be useful in identifying the job that lies ahead. We are concerned with what has been traditionally called the *fundamental operations.* These are tools that are necessary in order to carry the basic concepts of mathematics toward productive uses and broad concepts that may perpetuate and enrich our culture.

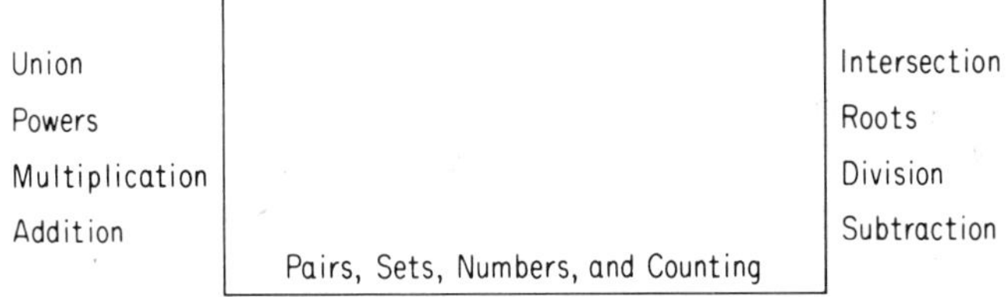

The base of the diagram represents the concepts discussed in Chapter 3, while the operations are identified along the vertical lines. Not only is there interrelationship among the operations as they are arranged vertically on the separate lines, but there also exist interrelationships among the operations from one vertical line to the other. For example, multiplication is not only a more powerful way of adding any number of equal addends but it is also closely related to all of the operations appearing on the other vertical line. Really the interrelationship among operations is the most challenging aspect of them, since the operations themselves are only necessary but routine tasks. The interrelationships are, however, not likely to be understood unless each operation has meaning and is logical. The uninitiated will need to learn the operations with full understanding and insight. Let us look at how we might build insight regarding these operations as the learner progresses from kindergarten through grade 8.

ADDING NONNEGATIVE INTEGERS

The primary grade child will need an abundance of experience in combining sets. One of his earliest experiences involves the bringing together of two single elements to make a pair. Symbolically this is written 1 + 1 = 2, but the initial experiences must, of course, occur in the concrete; i.e., "one block and one block" will be brought together to make a set of "two blocks." Let us deviate for a moment here to point out that learning generally will proceed from the concrete to the picture stage to the semiconcrete to the abstract. This sequence is especially necessary for most younger learners, but teachers should help the learner to free himself from the impediments of visual aids as his ability to deal with the abstract develops. However, reverting to the concrete at any stage or age in the learning process should not be frowned upon. While working in the abstract is an objective of the learning process, it is something that should evolve with comfort and ease under encouragement from the teacher and should never be forced or imposed.

Getting back now to our addition, the child will extend his experiences through discovery with concrete and semiconcrete objects, in sets. Once the student is able to identify the number of elements in a set by use of the proper cardinal number and understands the idea involved in the union of two disjoint sets it is a short step to the ideas represented in the sketch (the letters represent

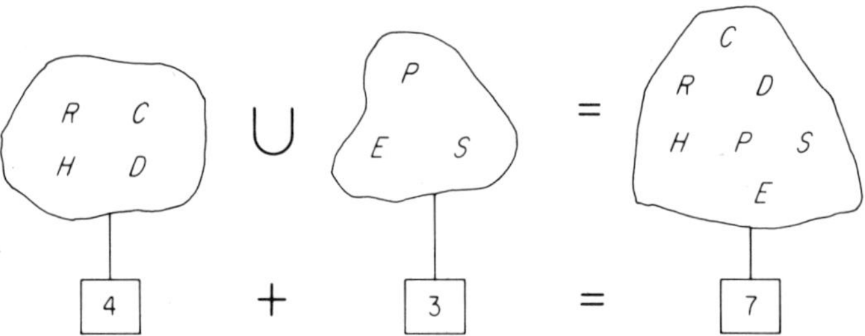

animals). The extension of abstract symbolism to where he recognizes the union of sets in some sequence as shown below is also helpful:

1 + 1 = 2	3 + 2 = 5
1 + 1 + 1 = 3	4 + 1 = 5
2 + 1 = 3	1 + 4 = 5
1 + 2 = 3	1 + 1 + 1 + 1 + 1 + 1 = 6
1 + 1 + 1 + 1 = 4	5 + 1 = 6
3 + 1 = 4	1 + 5 = 6
2 + 2 = 4	3 + 3 = 6
2 + 3 = 5	4 + 2 = 6
1 + 1 + 1 + 1 + 1 = 5	2 + 4 = 6
2 + 2 + 1 = 5	

There is no intent here to specify the exact sequences; the important thing is to provide many experiences with the addition facts without resorting to memorization of systematic patterns. There is value, however, in looking at patterns such as

$$\begin{aligned} 2 + 1 &= 3 \\ 2 + 2 &= 4 \\ 2 + 3 &= 5 \\ 2 + 4 &= 6, \text{ etc.,} \end{aligned}$$

but these are to be considered one of many experiences.

The student can get real help in learning his initial addition facts by utilizing the number line. For example, 2 plus 3 may be looped on the line in this manner:

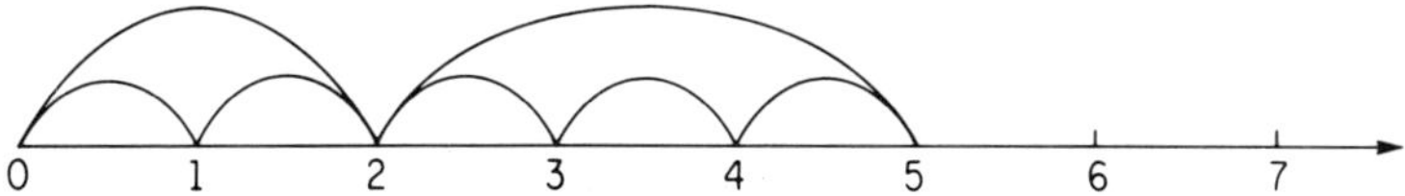

These experiences should continue until the student can handle with ease the sum of single-digit addends up to 81. For example,

$$9 + 9 + 9 + 9 + 9 + 9 + 9 + 9 + 9 = 81$$

or

$$8 + 8 + 8 + 8 + 8 + 8 + 8 + 8 + 8 = 72$$

These experiences evolve naturally from the easier ones, such as

$$\begin{aligned} 1 + 1 + 1 + 1 + 1 + 1 + 1 + 1 + 1 &= 9 \\ 2 + 2 + 2 + 2 + 2 + 2 + 2 + 2 + 2 &= 18 \end{aligned}$$

Students should not only use concrete objects in discovering and verifying these sums but they should also employ the number line and hundreds board to discuss and identify these subsets of integers. They thus learn to count by 2's, 3's, . . . , 9's and soon learn to handle with ease such problems as

$$\begin{array}{cc} 9 + 9 = 18 & 4 + 4 = 8 \\ 9 + 8 = 17 & 4 + 3 = 7 \end{array}$$

These are followed by parallel experiences such as:

$$\begin{array}{cc} 18 + 9 = 27 & 8 + 4 = 12 \\ \{18 + 8 = 26\} & \{8 + 3 = 11\} \\ 45 + 9 = 54 & 32 + 4 = 36 \\ \{45 + 8 = 53\} & \{32 + 3 = 35\} \end{array}$$

The subsets of integers identified by counting by tens and 5's are extremely important in understanding addition and will have received special attention when studying the nature of our numeration system.

It is important in teaching the basic facts for any of the four operations, to help the learner develop at least one logical attack upon each fact so that he will not be constantly harassed by fear of forgetting the answer. The particular attack used is not important so long as it is logical and ties in with his previous learnings. Tricks and rules should be avoided unless the student has insight into why they work. Several attacks upon each of two problems are illustrated below.

PROBLEM	ATTACK
$9 + 8 = ?$	$9 + 8 = 8 + 9 = 8 + (8 + 1) = (8 + 8) + 1 = 16 + 1 = 17$
	$9 + 8 = 9 + (1 + 7) = (9 + 1) + 7 = 10 + 7 = 17$
	$9 + 8 = 9 + (9 - 1) = (9 + 9) - 1 = 18 - 1 = 17$
	$9 + 8 = 8 + 9 = 8 + (10 - 1) = (8 + 10) - 1 = 18 - 1 = 17$
$7 + 4 = ?$	$7 + 4 = 7 + (3 + 1) = (7 + 3) + 1 = 10 + 1 = 11$
	$7 + 4 = 4 + 7 = 4 + (4 + 3) = (4 + 4) + 3 = 8 + 3 = 11$
	$7 + 4 = 4 + 7 = 4 + (6 + 1) = (4 + 6) + 1 = 10 + 1 = 11$
	$7 + 4 = 7 + (7 - 3) = (7 + 7) - 3 = 14 - 3 = 11$

Another productive means of visualizing the addition and subtraction facts results from the use of the following chart:

+ –	0	1	2	3	4	5	6	7	8	9
0	0	1	2	3	4	5	6	7	8	9
1	1	2	3	4	5	6	7	8	9	10
2	2	3	4	5	6	7	8	9	10	11
3	3	4	5	6	7	8	9	10	11	12
4	4	5	6	7	8	9	10	11	12	13
5	5	6	7	8	9	10	11	12	13	14
6	6	7	8	9	10	11	12	13	14	15
7	7	8	9	10	11	12	13	14	15	16
8	8	9	10	11	12	13	14	15	16	17
9	9	10	11	12	13	14	15	16	17	18

It will be noted that the facts in the shaded portion of the chart may be eliminated from the total task, since their counterparts from the commutative law of addition appear in the remainder of the chart. Also, the first row results from the additive law of zero. Another valuable use of this chart at the upper-grade level results from its use in a modified form as a test of a knowledge of the basic facts. This is done by using dittoed or photocopied charts in which the numerals at the top and side have been scrambled and the squares in the body of the chart left for the student to fill in. The time allowed should be adequate for automatic responses only. With this test individual difficulties can be quickly determined and special help given along the lines recommended on the previous pages.

The treatment of addition on the preceding pages, if handled adequately, leads to an easy development of the multiplication facts; however, one can easily restrict the addition facts to sums not greater than 18 and lighten the burden here with the expectation of later devoting more time to multiplication. It can be readily seen that all addition facts beyond those involving two single-digit addends may be done by means of the addition algorism. Before we develop this algorism, certain observations regarding the above development should be made.

1. The use of concrete and semiconcrete objects as members of sets should be encouraged with young children whenever the need arises.
2. The use of the commutative and associative laws of addition and the law of zero should be recognized as they occur in the experiences involved. The commutative law states where a and b are any elements of the set, that $(a + b) = (b + a)$. This is illustrated in $2 + 3 = 5$ and $3 + 2 = 5$. Even young students soon recognize that the order of addition does not affect the sum, even though there may be a slight difference in their thinking with regard to concrete objects in the two cases. This observation leads students to recognize that 2 and 3 is an unordered pair in the addition operation. The associative law states that $a + (b + c) = (a + b) + c$, where a, b, c, are any elements of the set. This principle was used in addition when we regrouped in problems such as $9 + 8 = ?$ $(1 + 8) + 8 = ?$ and $1 + (8 + 8) = 1 + 16 = 17$. The law of zero states: $a + 0 = a$, where a is any element of the set. While this is not a difficult concept, the student must always be conscious of it. In these situations the teacher should have full understanding and the students should be involved as far as their maturity will allow.
3. It should be recognized that all of the experiences described here are not to be had at any one time, but are to be distributed through the primary grades and on into the intermediate grades.
4. Addition is not to be taught in isolation from the other fundamental operations. Progress must go forward on all fronts simultaneously as the needs and interests of the students dictate. The treatment is here isolated only as a means of keeping our objective clear.
5. Time and meaningful experience are the bases for mastery of the basic facts. Students should not be given flash cards or other rote-memory devices nor asked to memorize these facts. Rather the emphasis should be on exploration, discovery, mulling over, and experiencing with an aim toward establishing a logical attack upon each fact. This builds confidence and removes the fear of forgetting.

6. The drill effort should be in the direction of meaningful habituation, should follow the initial establishment of the concept, and should not be expected to do more than develop facility, speed, and confidence.

UNDERSTANDING THE ADDITION ALGORISMS

The place-value pockets were referred to earlier and their use with children cannot be overemphasized. The pockets and counters are available from many sources along with directions for their use. No effort will be made here to picture the pockets, and the place-value chart will be used instead. These charts may be quickly drawn on a chalkboard and are a semiconcrete second-stage device to be used with older students after they have had access to the concrete place-value pockets. The basic principles involved were discussed in Chapter 3 and are not repeated here. Let us now use these charts to explain the addition algorism.

The sequence of problems confronting the learner should be about as follows:

1. Adding two single-digit numbers—no algorism necessary and should be treated as previously indicated.
2. Adding a two-digit number and a single-digit number, no regrouping required.

10	1
2	4 5
2	9

Add 4 units and 5 units to obtain 9 units. Add 2 tens and no tens to get 2 tens. If the addition facts to sums of 18 have been taught, this just becomes a verfication of what the student may have reasoned from a number line, hundred board, or experience with sets.

3. Adding a two-digit number and a single-digit number where regrouping is required:

10	1
2	4 7
1 2	1 0
3	1

4 units and 7 units = 11 units = 10 units + 1 unit, which may be written 1 group of ten and 1 unit. 2 tens and 0 tens = 2 tens, and no ones, which is written 2 in the tens column and 0 in the ones column. Now adding

these partial sums we get 3 tens and 1 unit. The algorism should now be shown and interpreted from the chart.

4. Adding a two-digit number and another two-digit number, no regrouping is required:

10	1
2 3	4 2
5	6

4 units + 2 units = 6 units; 3 tens + 2 tens = 5 tens. Show algorism without chart and verify by number line, hundred board, and sets.

5. Adding two two-digit numbers where regrouping is required from the units column:

10	1
2 3	9 4
1 5	3 0
6	3

9 units + 4 units = 13 units = 10 units + 3 units or 1 group of ten and 3 units. 2 tens + 3 tens = 5 tens and no units. Add partial sums, getting 3 units and 6 tens. Verify by number line, hundred board, and sets and show algorism as shortcut to work done in chart.

6. Adding two-digit numbers where regrouping is necessary in both columns:

100	10	1
	7 2	9 8
	1 9	7 0
1	0	7

9 units + 8 units = 17 units = 10 units + 7 units, or 1 group of ten and 7 units. 7 tens + 2 tens = 9 tens. Add partial sums, getting 7 units and 10 tens, but 10 tens make a group of 100, so we place a 1 in the hundreds column and a zero in the tens column. Now show the algorism as shortcut to work done in chart.

7. By similar reasoning, students may explore algorisms with many digits in both addends. The above development may require many grade levels, but every teacher should visualize the total job to be done and the care

and detail required if the algorisms are to be clearly understood. The teacher should not hesitate at any time to ask a student to explain any algorism he uses by means of this place-value chart or even the place-value pockets.

Another valuable experience which assists the learner to understand the addition algorism is centered around expanded notation. Expanded notation merely means that the multiples of the various powers of ten have been handled separately and their sum indicated with plus signs. For example, 3784 in expanded notation becomes 3000 + 700 + 80 + 4. The addition algorism can now be explained as follows:

284 + 96 becomes

$$\begin{array}{r} 200 + 80 + 4 \\ 90 + 6 \\ \hline 200 + 170 + 10 \end{array}$$

which in turn equals 300 + 80 + 0 when we put the sum back into true expanded notation, and this then becomes 380.

ADDING NONNEGATIVE RATIONAL NUMBERS

Having traced the adding of subsets of the universal set of integers, let us consider this operation as we expand the universal set. Our next universal set will be the nonnegative rational numbers. This set in addition to the whole numbers includes the positive rational fractions, both common and decimal. Actually in the learning experience of the child these fractions will not come into the picture after a thorough treatment of the nonnegative integers, but to a large extent evolve simultaneously with them. The addition of these fractions will not be treated at this point, however, since they can be more economically included under the more complete treatment of fractions generally which follows. When the treatment is given later, it will be observed that the commutative and associative laws of addition and the law of zero hold throughout the entire set of rational numbers.

ADDING THE INTEGERS

While it is true that learners in the grade school are constantly expanding their set of nonnegative integers to include larger elements, this expansion requires no extended concepts other than the inclusion of more columns in the place value chart. The next significant expansion of the set usually occurs beyond the fifth grade when negative numbers are brought into use. The set of all integers now becomes our universal set. We are now faced with the task of analyzing the operation called addition as it relates to subsets of our new universal set. Five possibilities seem to face us.

1. We must learn to add two elements of this set when the upper addend is positive and the lower negative (vertical arrangement).
2. We must learn to add two elements when the upper addend is negative and the lower positive.
3. We must learn to add two elements when both are negative.
4. We must recognize that adding two elements, both nonnegative, is identical to the addition of whole numbers in arithmetic which we have already covered.
5. We must recognize the addition involving zero may be handled by the additive law of zero; i.e., $N + 0 = N$.

Again consistent with our policy of discovering our own generalizations or rules, let us set up a pattern that will illustrate (1) above. Instead of placing the addends under each other, let us for convenience use the optional horizontal notation:

(+4) + (+3) = +7
(+4) + (+2) = +6
(+4) + (+1) = +5
(+4) + (0) = +4
(+4) + (-1) = +3
*(+4) + (-2) = +2
(+4) + (-3) = +1
**(+4) + (-4) = 0
(+4) + (-5) = -1

Since the first four problems come within our previous experience we accept them as true statements and, knowing what we do about the relative size of the negative integers as developed in Chapter 3, we are led to accept the remaining sums as being the only possible logical results. The problem marked with the double asterisk (**) illustrates what is known as the *law of the additive inverse.* In general terms it states: $a + (-a) = 0$ where a is any element of the set. Students should become conscious of this law and see its relation to $a - a = 0$.

Now let us in a similar fashion consider possibility 2 above. This time by reference to item 2, we will continue to make each successive first addend exactly two units smaller than the previous one and keep the second addend constant:

(+8) + (+4) = +12
(+6) + (+4) = +10
(+4) + (+4) = + 8
(+2) + (+4) = + 6
(0) + (+4) = + 4
*(-2) + (+4) = + 2
(-4) + (+4) = 0
(-6) + (+4) = - 2
(-8) + (+4) = - 4

The first five sums are again within our previous experience. The remaining sums are the only logical results as evidenced by the pattern and our knowledge of the relative size of the elements. Furthermore, the two starred examples in this and the previous sequence of problems leads us to suspect that, as with the positive integers, the order of the addends is immaterial.

This last conjecture can be further verified by setting up other sequences of problems. At this point students should be encouraged to draw some generalized observation on how to add in the set of integers when the addends have opposite signs. This should lead to the conventional rule: *When adding elements having unlike signs, subtract the smaller absolute value from the larger absolute value and give the sum the sign originally carried by what is now the larger absolute value.*

We define the absolute value of an element as follows:

1. The absolute value of a positive element or zero element is the element itself.
2. The absolute value of a negative element is its additive inverse.
3. The absolute value of N is written $|N|$.

Let us now look at possibility 3. We can capitalize upon our previous discovery to set up a suitable pattern:

$$
\begin{aligned}
(-3) + (+5) &= +2\\
(-3) + (+4) &= +1\\
(-3) + (+3) &= 0\\
(-3) + (+2) &= -1\\
(-3) + (+1) &= -2\\
(-3) + (0) &= -3\\
(-3) + (-1) &= -4\\
(-3) + (-2) &= -5\\
(-3) + (-3) &= -6
\end{aligned}
$$

The first six sums are again within our previous experience. The remaining sums are expected by logic and pattern. We can, therefore, generalize and come up with the rule. *When adding elements from this set having like signs, add their absolute values and attach the common sign.* It is noted that this rule also covers the case of two positive addends from arithmetic.

We look now at the addition of rational numbers, including placeholders. To begin with we will restrict ourselves to whole numbers used as factors with placeholders and we will use frames instead of the usual letters. The theory here can, of course, be extended to cover the rationals. Let us first add some monomials. We recognize that $2 \cdot 3 + 5 \cdot 3 = 7 \cdot 3$ because we can check it as $6 + 15 = 21$. We would expect then that $2 \cdot \square + 5 \cdot \square = 7 \cdot \square$ regardless of the value of $\square$. It appears then that we could have used the $\square$ as a multiplier in front of the sum of the whole numbers in this fashion $\square \cdot (2 + 5)$. We have thus discovered an example of the distributive law of multiplication over addition and can now generalize this axiom to read $\Delta \cdot (\square + \odot) = (\Delta \cdot \square) + (\Delta \cdot \odot)$. With this axiom as a tool we are now ready to add monomials: and can extend the theory to cover polynomials:

$$\begin{array}{r} 3\,\square + 2\,\Delta + 5\,\odot \\ \underline{2\,\square + 5\,\Delta + 3\,\odot} \\ 5\,\square + 7\,\Delta + 8\,\odot \end{array}$$

Later when powers have been mastered we can add the following:

Add

$$\begin{array}{r} 2\,\square^3 - 5\,\Delta^2 + 2\,\odot \\ \underline{3\,\square^3 + 3\,\Delta^2 + 3\,\odot} \\ 5\,\square^3 - 2\,\Delta^2 + 5\,\odot \end{array}$$

As we move on into the addition of fractions, these same basic rules apply and no further attention will be devoted to their verification, since both the irrational and rational fractions are points on the same number line which contains the integers. We should, however, recognize that the so-called *law of the additive inverse* has now been established. This law states that for any element of the universal set, $(+a) + (-a) = 0$. We demonstrated this law in our development of possibility 1, when we found that $(+4) + (-4) = 0$.

A word of caution is here in order. Students should be allowed and encouraged to discover as much of the preceding development as possible. Insight will not generally come from teachers' lectures.

ADDING THE RATIONAL FRACTIONS

We shall now extend our universal set to include the rational fractions. Our set is now comprised of all numbers of the form a/b, when a and b are integers and $b \neq 0$. This set has been introduced in Chapter 3 and our attention is here directed toward the addition of those members of the set which we ordinarily call the common fractions.

In beginning the development of fractions with primary-grade children, it is necessary that they begin to develop a sound definition of a fraction. Basically a fraction is part of a whole. The whole may be a single unit or a group of units. For example, we may speak of half an apple, or of half the apples in a bushel. Students should recognize early that the denominator of a fraction tells into how many equal parts the whole has been divided, while the numerator tells how many of these equal parts we are working with. The student will need many concrete experiences with fractions and the fraction kit, fraction line, and other demonstrative material to help him establish the concept. Statements such as "Your half of the apple is larger than mine" indicate either a lack of understanding of half or carelessness, either of which is dangerous. Once the student clearly understands what fractions are he can begin to combine them through the process of addition. He may see very early that $\frac{1}{2} + \frac{1}{2} = 1$; that $\frac{1}{3} + \frac{1}{3} + \frac{1}{3} = 1$; that $\frac{1}{3} + \frac{1}{3} = \frac{2}{3}$; that $\frac{1}{2} + \frac{1}{2} + \frac{1}{2} = 1\frac{1}{2}$, etc. This experience is known as adding like fractions and poses little difficulty. As the student attempts to add unlike fractions he will recognize the need for converting from one fraction to an equivalent fraction. From his fraction kit he will have observed that 1/2 = 2/4 = 3/6 = 4/8 = 5/10. This series of equal fractions is known as an equivalence class of numbers and the student should be led to see that this series is infinite. In other words, there are an infinite number of ways of writing 1/2. Having explored many of these sets of equivalent fractions, the student will be led to the discovery of the basic law of fractions. This is often called the *golden rule of fractions*, and states that the numerator and denominator of any fraction may be multiplied or divided by the same nonzero number without altering the value of the fraction. The student should recognize that this process is equivalent to multiplying the fraction by one which does not alter the value of the fraction and is in reality the law of the identity element discussed under multiplication. By applying this rule the student can now develop sets of equivalent fractions which are not so obvious as that referred to above. For example: 3/7 = 6/14 = 9/21 = 12/28 = 15/35 = 18/42 = 21/49, etc. The young student should verify these equivalent fractions by means of diagrams like the ones shown.

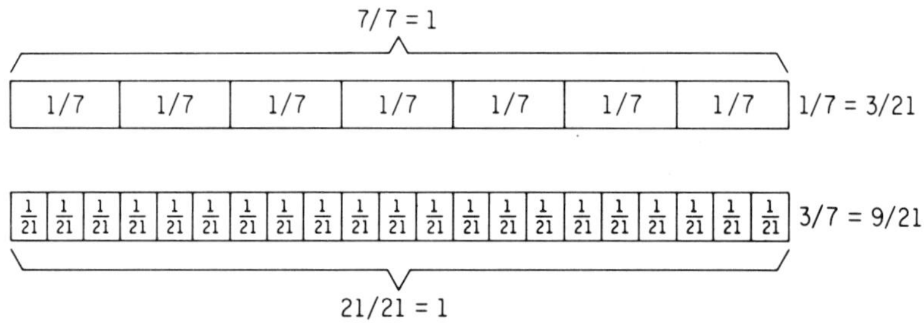

Having gained facility in equivalence classes of fractions, we can now add unlike fractions by choosing members of their equivalence classes which are like fractions as follows:

2/3 = 4/6 = 6/9 = 8/12 = 10/15= 12/18, etc.
3/4 = 6/8 = 9/12 = 12/16 = 15/20 = 18/24, etc.

Now we choose 8/12 from the first group of equal fractions and 9/12 from the second group. We now have like fractions: 8/12 + 9/12 = 17/12 = 1 5/12. We now need a shorter way of converting to like fractions. Using the same example, we note that if we apply the golden rule of fractions to each fraction and select the proper multipliers for each, we can get like denominators. That is, we multiply numerator and denominator of 3/4 by 3 to get 9/12. We now observe that if we choose the smallest whole number exactly divisible by both 3 and 4 we get 12. Twelve is known as the lowest common denominator of the two original denominators. We further observe that having chosen 12 as the L.C.D. we can quickly make the conversion by dividing the L.C.D. by the denominator of the fraction and multiplying the quotient by the numerator. For example, to convert 2/3 to twelfths we divided 12 by 3 to get 4 and multiply 4 X 2 thus getting 8/12.

This attack works satisfactorily for cases where the L.C.D. can be easily determined by observation, but eventually we will need a more powerful technique. Let us resort then to what we will call the *prime-factor technique.* Using the same example, we first factor the denominators into their primes, observing that in this case the first denominator is already prime: 2/3 + 3/2 X 2. Next we build our L.D.C. by using each prime factor the greatest number of times that it occurs in any one denominator. The L.C.D. thus becomes a 3 X 2 X 2 or 12. Proceeding in our conversion to an equivalent fraction as we did previously, we can divide the denominators in factor form into the L.C.D. in factor form andshorten our work. Thus:

For 2/3,

$$\frac{\text{L.C.D.}}{3} = \frac{3 \times 2 \times 2}{3} = 2 \times 2 = 4$$

and we now multiply 2/3 · 4/4 to get 8/12.

For 3/2 · 2,

$$\frac{\text{L.C.D.}}{2 \times 2} = \frac{3 \times 2 \times 2}{2 \times 2} = 3$$

and we now multiply 3/2·2 · 3/3 to get 9/12:

$$\frac{8}{12} + \frac{9}{12} = \frac{17}{12} = 1^5/_{12}$$

Let us illustrate with a more difficult problem:

$$\frac{9}{17} + \frac{5}{51} + \frac{9}{68} = \frac{9}{17} + \frac{5}{3 \times 17} + \frac{9}{2 \times 2 \times 17}$$

$$\text{L.C.D.} = 2 \times 2 \times 3 \times 17; \quad \frac{2 \times 2 \times 3 \times 17}{17} = 12$$

$$\frac{2 \times 2 \times 3 \times 17}{3 \times 17} = 4; \quad \frac{2 \times 2 \times 3 \times 17}{2 \times 2 \times 17} = 3$$

Multiplying,

$$\frac{9}{17} \cdot \frac{12}{12} = \frac{108}{\text{L.C.D.}}; \quad \frac{5}{51} \cdot \frac{4}{4} = \frac{20}{\text{L.C.D.}}$$

and

$$\frac{9}{68} \cdot \frac{3}{3} = \frac{27}{\text{L.C.D.}}$$

$$\frac{108}{\text{L.C.D.}} + \frac{20}{\text{L.C.D.}} + \frac{27}{\text{L.C.D.}} = \frac{155}{\text{L.C.D.}} = \frac{155}{2 \times 2 \times 3 \times 17} = \frac{5 \times 31}{2 \times 2 \times 3 \times 17} = \frac{155}{204}$$

Note that the L.C.D. was left in factor form until the final step and that we factored the numerator in order to determine whether the fraction had a simpler name. In this case it did not.

Teachers and students using this technique should exploit it thoroughly not only for its strength in adding fractions but for its splendid review of prime factors, division and multiplication in factor form, finding the simplest name for fractions by the prime-factor method, etc. Students exploring it with time and personal involvment will discover why this attack always produces the L.C.D., and why any C.D. as well as the lowest one will produce the correct results.

Teachers will note that this is the same method used in adding algebraic fractions and with this development at the elementary arithmetic level, algebra students are better able to understand its operation in algebra. One algebraic example is given here as a means of continuing the concept of addition vertically from grade to grade. Further examples may be obtained from a good algebra text.

$$\frac{2X+3}{X^2-7X+12} + \frac{X-6}{X^2-6X+9} = \frac{2X+3}{(X-4)(X-3)} + \frac{X-6}{(X-3)(X-3)}$$

$$\text{L.C.D.} = (X-3)^2\,(X-4)$$

$$\frac{(2X+3)(X-3)}{\text{L.C.D.}} + \frac{(X-6)(X-4)}{\text{L.C.D.}} = \frac{2X^2-3X-9+X^2-10X+24}{\text{L.C.D.}}$$

$$= \frac{3X^2-13X+15}{(X-3)^2(X-4)}$$

Let us look now at the rational decimals. As explained in Chapter 3, the rational decimals are only those which terminate, repeat, or become periodic. The addition of such decimals is handled with full meaning through the use of a place-value chart, but before doing this let us look briefly at the process of changing from common to decimal fractions and vice versa. The first approach might well be that of applying the golden rule of fractions to make the denominator a multiple of 10. For example, 3/4 may be converted to decimal by multiplying numerator and denominator by 25, thus getting $3/4 \times 25/25 = 75/100$ which interpreted into the place value chart becomes .75. Many fractions may be easily converted in this manner, but it is not recommended that students be asked to memorize these equivalents. Better that they should understand the concept involved and the attack rather than be plagued by forgotten equivalents or fractions with which they have had no experience.

Some rational fractions resist the approach described above; for example, 3/7 is one of these. Now 3/7 may be accurately interpreted as 3 ÷ 7. Performing this by long division will, of course, convert it to a decimal—in this case a periodic one. This method may be used as soon as the student has studied long division involving decimals in the quotient. This is treated in the Division section of this chapter.

To get back to our primary objective, that of adding rational decimals, it should be clear that the algorisms must be built from the very simple, such as .5 + .3, to decimals involving any number of places. This process so closely parallels that of adding integers that only one example of medium difficulty is given here:

1	1/10	1/100	1/1000	1/10000
	7	8	9	
	4	3	5	
		1	4	
	1	1	0	
1	1	0	0	
1	2	2	4	

.789 + .435

$$\frac{9}{1000} + \frac{5}{1000} = \frac{14}{1000} = \frac{10}{1000} + \frac{4}{1000} = \frac{1}{100} + \frac{4}{1000}$$

$$\frac{8}{100} + \frac{3}{100} = \frac{11}{100} = \frac{10}{100} + \frac{1}{100} = \frac{1}{10} + \frac{1}{100}$$

$$\frac{7}{10} + \frac{4}{10} = \frac{11}{10} = \frac{10}{10} + \frac{1}{10} = 1 + \frac{1}{10}$$

The sums are worked out in common fractions by the above process and then placed in the chart. From this logical analysis the algorism quickly emerges to appear as follows:

$$\begin{array}{r} .789 \\ .435 \\ \hline 1.224 \end{array}$$

Since the process works exactly as in adding integers, the student need only discover the rule for placing the decimal.

This, then, completes our discussion of the addition of rational fractions. Obviously this development needs to be interwoven with the other operations and each inched forward with full consideration for the cumulative nature of the content and the maturity of the learner.

ADDING IRRATIONAL NUMBERS

As we proceed in our study of addition we find it necessary to extend the universal set to include the irrational numbers. Our new set is now known as the real-number set. We find a need for irrationals in solving as simple an equation as $X^2 - 2 = 0$. Here $x = \sqrt{2}$ but, as explained in Chapter 3 this number is not in the rational number set. It is a non-periodic, nonrepeating infinite decimal and as such is classified as an *irrational number*. In practical use we may choose to operate with the so-called radical form (for example $\sqrt{2}$) which is theoretically accurate or we may use the decimal form which is only approximate (for example $\sqrt{2} \approx 1.414$). The wavy equals sign signifies "is approximately equal to."

If we use the approximate decimal form, these decimals will be added as are the rational decimals except, of course, the sums will always be approximate, while in the rational decimals some (the terminating decimals) will be exact. The degree of accuracy to be sought in using these nonterminating decimals is an arbitrary matter.

If we use the radical form we discover that certain laws hold. These laws are similar to those governing the addition of like terms in algebra. For example: $(3 \cdot \sqrt{2}) + (2 \cdot \sqrt{2}) = (5 \cdot \sqrt{2})$. But $3 \cdot \sqrt{2} + 2 \cdot \sqrt{3}$ cannot be further simplified in its radical form. This is to be expected, since these examples parallel the following examples involving nonspecified elements of the set: $3X + 2X = 5X$, but $3X + 2Y$ cannot be further simplified unless X and Y are either equal or their values are known. In the example of our irrational numbers $\sqrt{2}$ and $\sqrt{3}$, neither is the case.

The addition of irrational fractions requires some attention at this point. Here again, like rational fractions, those having the same denominators are easily handled by merely adding numerators and retaining the denominators. Examples are:

1. $$\frac{2}{\sqrt{2}} + \frac{3}{\sqrt{2}} = \frac{5}{\sqrt{2}} = \frac{5\sqrt{2}}{2}$$

2. $$\frac{2+\sqrt{2}}{3} + \frac{3+\sqrt{2}}{3} = \frac{5+2\sqrt{2}}{3}$$

3. $$\frac{5}{\sqrt{3}+\sqrt{2}} + \frac{2}{\sqrt{3}+\sqrt{2}} = \frac{7}{\sqrt{3}+\sqrt{2}} = \frac{7(\sqrt{3}-\sqrt{2})}{(\sqrt{3}+\sqrt{2})(\sqrt{3}-\sqrt{2})}$$
$$= \frac{7(\sqrt{3}-\sqrt{2})}{3-2} = \frac{7(\sqrt{3}-\sqrt{2})}{1} = 7(\sqrt{3}-\sqrt{2})$$

4. $$\frac{2}{\sqrt{3}} + \frac{3}{\sqrt{2}} = \frac{2\sqrt{2}}{\sqrt{3}\sqrt{2}} + \frac{3\sqrt{3}}{\sqrt{3}\sqrt{2}} = \frac{2\sqrt{2}+3\sqrt{3}}{\sqrt{2}\cdot\sqrt{3}} = \frac{\sqrt{2}\sqrt{3}(2\sqrt{2}+3\sqrt{3})}{\sqrt{2}\sqrt{3}\sqrt{2}\sqrt{3}}$$
$$= \frac{4\sqrt{3}+9\sqrt{2}}{6}$$

Note that the sums in their original forms have radicals in the denominators. Since it is customary to rationalize the denominators in mathematics, we do this by applying the golden rule of fractions. In the first two examples we apply the law by multiplying numerator and denominator by the radical found in the denominator, thus getting the final results. In the third example we multiply both numerator and denominator by the conjugate of the denominator (that is, the binomial whose last term has the opposite sign). This rationalizes the denominator in cases where the irrational radical contained in the denominator is a square root. Students working at this level have had polynomials and sufficient experience with the real-number set to understand and interpret the solutions shown in the examples above.

Before we leave the addition of irrational numbers, let it be recognized that the inclusion of these numbers in our set has in no way nullified the operation of the basic laws of addition. To illustrate:

$$\sqrt{2} + \sqrt{3} = \sqrt{3} + \sqrt{2} \text{ or } \sqrt{5} + \sqrt{7} = \sqrt{7} + \sqrt{5} \qquad \text{Commutative law}$$

$$\sqrt{2} + (\sqrt{3} + \sqrt{5}) = (\sqrt{2} + \sqrt{3}) + \sqrt{5}$$

or

$$\sqrt{7} + (\sqrt{3} + \sqrt{2}) = (\sqrt{7} + \sqrt{3}) + \sqrt{2} \qquad \text{Associative law}$$

$$\sqrt{2} + (-\sqrt{2}) = 0 \qquad \text{Law of additive inverse}$$

$$\sqrt{2} + 0 = \sqrt{2} \qquad \text{Additive law of zero}$$

We conclude, therefore, that these basic laws hold for all elements of the real number set.

SUBTRACTING THE NONNEGATIVE INTEGERS

Having previously dealt with the combining of sets under addition, we find the decomposition of sets under the operation called subtraction is now a much less formidable task. We can use the number line to illustrate subtraction in a manner somewhat opposite to our looping process used for addition. We shall not pause here to show this procedure since the reader can easily supply it. The so-called basic subtraction facts should be taught simultaneously with those of addition and the sequence of development is identical. As a child discovers that $4 + 5 = 9$ he should also recognize the corresponding subtraction facts, i.e., $9 - 5 = 4$ and $9 - 4 = 5$. The basic approaches through sets, the number line, hundred board, and place-value pockets apply here as with addition. Always the method should be one of logical attack and exploration of patterns rather than rote memorization. Experiences in addition and subtraction centered around a certain number are valuable. These may be explored in a situation where the learner is asked to avoid involvement of any number larger than the specified one; that is, using the number 12 we get

9 + 3 = 12	8 + 4 = 12	5 + 7 = 12	12 + 0 = 12
12 - 3 = 9	12 - 8 = 4	12 - 7 = 5	12 - 0 = 12
12 - 9 = 3	12 - 4 = 8	12 - 5 = 7	
6 + 6 = 12	10 + 2 = 12	11 + 1 = 12	
12 - 6 = 6	12 - 2 = 10	12 - 1 = 11	
	12 - 10 = 2	12 - 11 = 1	

Another possibility for older students is that of having a single-digit number, say 9, involved as a sum or difference in every experience but allowing the use of any other positive integers elsewhere in the problems. This opens the situation to infinite possibilities in subtraction

9 + 0 = 9	9 - 0 = 9	30 - 21 = 9
8 + 1 = 9	10 - 1 = 9	29 - 20 = 9
7 + 2 = 9	11 - 2 = 9	28 - 19 = 9
6 + 3 = 9	12 - 3 = 9	27 - 18 = 9
5 + 4 = 9	13 - 4 = 9	26 - 17 = 9
	14 - 5 = 9	25 - 16 = 9
	15 - 6 = 9	24 - 15 = 9
	16 - 7 = 9	69 - 60 = 9
	17 - 8 = 9	89 - 80 = 9
	18 - 9 = 9	86 - 77 = 9

Let us stress again that while these examples exhibit a pattern, it is not intended that this always be so. The learner should have both random and patterned experiences. Experiences such as those in the last column are not essential, since these differences may be obtained through use of the subtraction algorism; however, many students will handle these with complete insight, given time and encouragement. This is especially true of problems such as the three in the last column which have both minuend and subtrahend within the same decade. Bridging the decade as is required in the remaining problems of the column is more difficult.

Another observation appropriate at this time is that of closure referred to in Chapter 3. The learner should recognize here that we cannot always subtract any element of the present universal set from another element and obtain a difference which is an element of the set. For example, we cannot subtract 9 from 5 in our present set. Our subtracting here is limited to situations where the subtrahend is smaller than or equal to the minuend. Note that we faced no comparable limitation under addition. In mathematical language, we say that the set of nonnegative integers is closed under addition but is not closed under subtraction.

Having studied with logic and understanding the subtraction facts at least up to 18 - 9 = 9, the learner is now ready to explore the algorisms for subtraction.

Here the sequence parallels that used in addition; i.e., working up from a single-digit subtrahend and a two-digit minuend requiring no regrouping. Here again the approach is through the place-value pockets and place-value charts. Only one example taken well along in the sequence will be illustrated here, since the detailed treatment necessary when working with children can easily be adapted from the previous development of addition. Let us consider the case of a three-digit minuend and a two-digit subtrahend requiring regrouping. Specifically we will illustrate the problem:

$$243 - 78 =$$

100	10	1
2	4	3
	7	8
1	6	5

Since we cannot subtract 8 units from 3 units, we regroup by taking one group of ten from the tens column and combine it with the 3 units there to make 13 units. Now 13 - 8 = 5. We are now confronted with subtracting 7 tens from the 3 tens remaining in the minuend. Again we must regroup. One group of 100 taken from the hundreds column gives us 10 groups of ten to combine with the 3 groups of ten remaining in the tens column to give us 13 groups of 10 from which we subtract 7 groups of ten to give 6 groups of ten. One group of 100 now remains in the hundreds column. The algorism is now established and the shortcuts are in order. Expanded notation also adds to the explanation of the subtraction algorism. For example, the problem

$$846 - 98 =$$

becomes

$$\begin{array}{r} 800 + 40 + 6 \\ \underline{90 + 8} \end{array}$$

Modifying the notation and regrouping the problem becomes

$$\begin{array}{r} 700 + 130 + 16 \\ \underline{90 + 8} \\ 700 + 40 + 8 \end{array}$$

or 748 which agrees with the algorism

$$\begin{array}{r} 846 \\ \underline{98} \\ 748 \end{array}$$

As in addition, the fractions enter into subtraction almost as early as do the integers but the subtraction of fractions both common and decimal so closely parallels addition that the reader is left to establish the detailed treatment.

SUBTRACTION IN THE SET OF ALL INTEGERS

We will now extend our universal set to include the negative integers and consider subtraction in the larger set. Again as in addition, our job consists of exploring subtraction under five headings:

1. Subtracting a negative integer from a positive integer.
2. Subtracting a positive integer from a negative integer.
3. Subtracting a negative integer from a negative integer.
4. Subtraction involving zero.
5. Subtracting a positive integer from a larger positive integer. (This, of course, is the subtraction we have been doing up to this point.)

Considering situation 1, we set up a pattern as follows:

$$
\begin{aligned}
(+4) - (+3) &= +1\\
(+4) - (+2) &= +2\\
(+4) - (+1) &= +3\\
(+4) - (\ 0) &= +4\\
(+4) - (-1) &= +5\\
(+4) - (-2) &= +6\\
(+4) - (-3) &= +7
\end{aligned}
$$

The first four problems are easily verified by previous experience. That the remainders in the last three problems are correct follows from the logic of the pattern; i.e., since the subtrahend is getting one unit smaller in each successive problem and the minuends remain the same, we expect the remainders to get one unit larger. Students should now be encouraged to generalize and discover a rule which might simplify the process. Such a rule could eventually take the form: When subtracting a negative integer from a positive integer, change the sign of the subtrahend and proceed as in algebraic addition.

Students should be led to observe that this same rule also takes care of the first four problems of the sequence if we change the introductory statement to fit the situation. This fact later assists us to make an overall rule for subtraction.

We next consider situation 2 and again construct a sequence of problems exhibiting a pattern:

$$
\begin{aligned}
(+5) - (+2) &= +3\\
(+4) - (+2) &= +2\\
(+3) - (+2) &= +1\\
(+2) - (+2) &= +0\\
(+1) - (+2) &= -1\\
(\ 0) - (+2) &= -2\\
(-1) - (+2) &= -3\\
(-2) - (+2) &= -4
\end{aligned}
$$

Here again the first four problems are merely examples of our work with positive integers and are true statements. Now since our minuend decreases by one unit in each successive problem and our subtrahend remains constant, we logically expect the remainders to get one unit smaller in each successive example. Again we are led to generalize as follows: When subtracting a positive integer from a negative integer, change the sign of the subtrahend and proceed as in algebraic addition.

Note again that this rule holds in the first four problems where we, of course, were not at all dependent upon it.

Let us now consider situation 3. In doing so we shall capitalize upon the discovery made in situation 2.

$$(+4) - (-2) = +6$$
$$(+3) - (-2) = +5$$
$$(+2) - (-2) = +4$$
$$(+1) - (-2) = +3$$
$$(\ 0) - (-2) = +2$$
$$(-1) - (-2) = +1$$
$$(-2) - (-2) = \ 0$$
$$(-3) - (-2) = -1$$
$$(-4) - (-2) = -2$$
$$(-5) - (-2) = -3$$

The first five problems of the sequence are true statements on the basis of our discoveries under situation 2 above. That the remainders in the remaining problems are correct follows from the fact that the minuends are decreasing by one unit while the subtrahend remains constant. This should then cause the remainders to become sucessively one unit smaller. Once more we generalize our discovery: When subtracting a negative integer from a negative integer, change the sign of the subtrahend and proceed as in algebraic addition. Situation 4 has already been verified from our arithmetic experience, but since zero is neither positive nor negative we do not apply the sign-change rule when it occurs as a subtrahend but rather depend upon the axiom $N - 0 = N$. Combining our observations, excluding zero, into one statement, takes care of all other situations: *When subtracting elements of the set of integers, change the sign of the subtrahend and proceed as in algebraic addition.*

SUBTRACTION OF FRACTIONS AND POLYNOMIALS

The above rule becomes a convenient and easily remembered guide for not only subtracting all possible combinations of the negative and positive integers but it can be extended logically to all points on the number line and therefore works equally well for the positive and negative fractions both rational and irrational. (Again, zero as a subtrahend is handled by $N - 0 = N$.)

The subtraction of monomials, polynomials, and fractions with placeholders presents little problem. Having established the rules of signs above and already having handled these situations for addition when placeholders are involved, we have only to change the sign of the subtrahend and proceed as in algebraic addition. We illustrate:

1. Subtract

$$\begin{array}{r} 5\square + 3\Delta - 5\odot \\ 2\square - 2\Delta - \odot \\ \hline 3\square + 5\Delta - 4\odot \end{array}$$

2. Subtract

$$\begin{array}{r} 3\square^2 - 4\Delta + \odot \\ 5\square^2 + 3\Delta - 6\odot \\ \hline -2\square^2 - 7\Delta + 7\odot \end{array}$$

3. $\dfrac{3}{\square + 2} - \dfrac{5}{3\square + 6} = \dfrac{9}{3\square + 6} - \dfrac{5}{3\square + 6} = \dfrac{4}{3\square + 6}$; $\dfrac{3}{\square + 2}$ was multiplied by $\dfrac{3}{3}$

4. $\dfrac{3}{\square - \Delta} - \dfrac{4}{\Delta - \square} = \dfrac{3}{\square - \Delta} + \dfrac{4}{\square - \Delta} = \dfrac{7}{\square - \Delta}$

   Since it was necessary to multiply the second fraction by $\dfrac{(-1)}{(-1)}$ in order to obtain an L.C.D., the latter problem actually turned out to be an addition problem.

5. The subtraction of fractions having no placeholders parallels the work on addition.

SUBTRACTION OF IRRATIONAL NUMBERS

We shall pause only briefly here to discuss the irrationals in radical form. Since the logic here parallels that of addition, we shall consider only a few examples.

1. $5\sqrt{2} - 2\sqrt{2} = 3\sqrt{3}$
2. $3\sqrt{2} - 2\sqrt{3} =$ cannot be further simplified for reasons as discussed under addition
3. $(+2\sqrt{2}) - (+5\sqrt{2}) = -3\sqrt{2}$
   Extension of our universal set to include the negative numbers and the irrationals now makes it possible to perform this operation. Previously $-3\sqrt{2}$ was not in the universal set and the problem had no solution or, in other words, the solution set was empty. Note that $-3\sqrt{2}$ is excluded from the set of numbers used in primary arithmetic for two reasons. First, the set contained no negative numbers, and second, $-3\sqrt{2}$ is irrational and this set did not include the irrationals.

MULTIPLICATION OF WHOLE NUMBERS

Let us now devote our attention to the combining of sets under the operation known as multiplication. Here again experiences begin early in the life of the child and there should be no effort to postpone the development of the concept. As previously mentioned, multiplication is merely a short means of adding two or more equal addends. The learner should observe that $2 \times 2 = 2 + 2$, $3 \times 2 = 2 + 2 + 2$, $4 \times 2 = 2 + 2 + 2 + 2$, $5 \times 2 = 2 + 2 + 2 + 2 + 2$, etc. His earliest experiences will likely occur with concrete objects. Two groups of blocks each composed of 2 blocks makes 4 blocks. Three groups of blocks each composed of 2 blocks makes 6 blocks, etc. Actual multiplication in the abstract may not occur for some students until third grade or later, while for others the concept may develop simultaneously with addition and subtraction. The basic multiplication facts should always be taught in conjunction with the corresponding division facts and should give due consideration to the maturation of the learner. Some of the earliest experiences with multiplication will take place within the set of positive integers less than 10.

The young student will want to experience multiplication on the number line which he may think of as three groups of two or two groups of three. As soon as the student understands the basic concept of multiplication we will observe that any integer multiplied by one will produce the integer, since in reality this means just one group of size indicated by the integer. This is known as the *multiplicative law of one*, or one is said to be the *identity element of multiplication.*

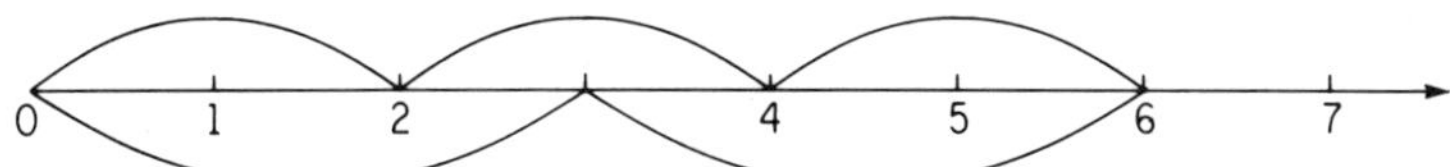

The logic here is that, for example, in $1 \times 6 = 6$, we are taking one group of six elements. The student should include among his experiences $1 \times 0 = 0$. This is known as the *multiplicative law of zero.* While it is not here implied that we should begin the multiplication experience with the facts involving zero and one, it is imperative that they receive early and thoughtful consideration. Later these same concepts must be verified in the realm of fractions. Too often teachers have considered these facts trivial or have imposed them through memorization and without meaning. Such treatment will often redound to the disadvantage of the learner throughout his later experiences.

In teaching the basic multiplication facts through $9 \times 9 = 81$, it is here suggested that there be no emphasis upon rote memorization in table form. Rather, as was suggested under addition and subtraction, the approach should be one of developing an attack based upon previous experiences. Among these basic experiences leading to mastery of the multiplication facts should be an abundance of experiences with subsets of the integers, counting by 2's, 3's, 5's, and 10's. The number line, sets, and hundred board will assist here. From these experiences should evolve a good understanding and mastery of what was traditionally called the 2, 3, 5, and 10 times tables. Actually there is no harm in looking at these facts in pattern or table form; in fact this should definitely be one of many experiences leading to the mastery.

Each of the successive integers up to 81 should be explored in terms of two integers which will multiply together to produce it. This is illustrated in detail in the table on pages 76-78.

While the total analysis here illustrated appears a formidable task, in actual practice it evolves gradually, first perhaps only to 9, then to 18, and so on. Regardless of how much of the total is used at any one time, the part used should be thoroughly exploited. We will exploit the entire development here.

1. The prime numbers—that is, those exactly divisible by themselves and one only—are readily identified. These can be products for only trivial multiplication facts . They have been starred.
2. Some composites factor into two primes; since this factorization is unique, by the basic theorem of arithmetic, no other two factors will produce them—except, of course, the trivial factors one and the number itself. All such examples have been identified by two asterisks. This set also includes all other multiplication facts which we call basic.
3. The experience involves many more multiplication facts than those ordinarily considered basic. These we can exclude for our present purposes, since they can be had by means of algorisms. Before leaving them, however, we should observe that at least one factor is always a single digit, which makes the factors possible to find just by exploration and is a good experience for the learner at this stage—even though we do not utilize the discovery in working toward mastery of the basic multiplication facts. These we have identified with three asterisks. Note that we have, of necessity, used both two and three asterisks on some facts, since they meet both criteria. Also we should point out that many of the facts marked with three asterisks are very simple and the student will likely remember many of these as easily as the basic facts. This should be encouraged but is, of course, not basically necessary. It should be noted that while our table did not lend itself to inclusion of all the zero facts, the axiom $N \cdot 0 = 0$ takes care of these facts for all values of N and generally they pose little difficulty.

1 X 1 = 1	7 X 1 = 7*	12 X 1 = 12
2 X 1 = 2*	8 X 1 = 8	3 X 4 = 12**
3 X 1 = 3	4 X 2 = 8**	2 X 6 = 12**
4 X 1 = 4	9 X 1 = 9**	13 X 1 = 13*
2 X 2 = 4**	3 X 3 = 9**	14 X 1 = 14
5 X 1 = 5*	10 X 1 = 10	2 X 7 = 14**
6 X 1 = 6	2 X 5 = 10**	15 X 1 = 15
2 X 3 = 6**	11 X 1 = 11*	3 X 5 = 15**

16 × 1 = 16
4 × 4 = 16**
2 × 8 = 16**
17 × 1 = 17*
18 × 1 = 18
3 × 6 = 18**
2 × 9 = 18**
19 × 1 = 19
20 × 1 = 20
4 × 5 = 20**
2 × 10 - 20***
21 × 1 = 21
3 × 7 = 21**
22 × 1 = 22
2 × 11 = 22*****
23 × 1 = 23*
24 × 1 = 24
3 × 8 = 24**
4 × 6 = 24**
2 × 12 = 24***
25 × 1 = 25
5 × 5 = 25**
26 × 1 = 26
2 × 13 = 26*****
27 × 1 = 27
3 × 9 = 27**
28 × 1 = 28
2 × 14 = 28***
4 × 7 = 28**
29 × 1 = 29*
30 × 1 = 30
3 × 10 = 30***
5 × 6 = 30**
2 × 5 = 30***
31 × 1 = 31*
32 × 1 = 32
2 × 16 = 32***
4 × 8 = 32**
33 × 1 = 33
3 × 11 = 33*****
34 × 1 = 34
2 × 17 = 34*****
35 × 1 = 35
5 × 7 = 35**
36 × 1 = 36
3 × 12= 36***
2 × 18 = 36***
6 × 6 = 36**
4 × 9 = 36**
37 × 1 = 37*
38 × 1 = 38
2 × 19 = 38*****
39 × 1 = 39
3 × 13 = 39*****
40 × 1 = 40
4 × 10 = 40***
5 × 8 = 40**
2 × 20 = 40***
41 × 1 = 41*
42 × 1 = 42
2 × 21 = 42***
6 × 7 = 42**
3 × 14 = 42***
43 × 1 = 43*
44 × 1 = 44
22 × 2 = 44***
4 × 11 = 44***
45 × 1 = 45
15 × 3 = 45***
5 × 9 = 45**
46 × 1 = 46
23 × 2 = 46*****
47 × 1 = 47
48 × 1 = 48
24 × 2 = 48***
16 × 3 = 48***
12 × 4 = 48***
6 × 8 = 48**
49 × 1 = 49
7 × 7 = 49**
50 × 1 = 50
25 × 2 = 50***
5 × 10 = 50***
51 × 1 = 51
3 × 17 = 51*****
52 × 1 = 52
26 × 2 = 52***
13 × 4 = 52***
53 × 1 = 53*
54 × 1 = 54
27 × 2 = 54***
3 × 18 = 54***
6 × 9 = 54**
55 × 1 = 55
5 × 11 = 55*****
56 × 1 = 56
28 × 2 = 56***
14 × 4 = 56***
7 × 8 = 56**
57 × 1 = 57
19 × 3 = 57*****
58 × 1 = 58
29 × 2 = 58*****
59 × 1 = 59*
60 × 1 = 60
30 × 2 = 60***
15 × 4 = 60***
6 × 10 = 60***
5 × 12 = 60***
20 × 3 = 60***
61 × 1 = 61*
62 × 1 = 62
31 × 2 = 62*****
63 × 1 = 63
21 × 3 = 63***
7 × 9 = 63**
64 × 1 = 64
32 × 3 = 64***
16 × 4 = 64***
8 × 8 = 64**
65 × 1 = 65
5 × 13 = 65*****
66 × 1 = 66
33 × 2 = 66**
22 × 3 = 66***
6 × 11 = 66***
67 × 1 = 67*
68 × 1 = 68
34 × 2 = 68***

4 X 17 = 68***	73 X 1 = 73*	39 X 2 = 78***
69 X 1 = 69	74 X 1 = 74	13 X 6 = 78***
23 X 3 = 69*****	37 X 2 = 74*****	26 X 3 = 78***
70 X 1 = 70	75 X 1 = 75	79 X 1 = 79*
35 X 2 = 70***	25 X 3 = 75***	80 X 1 = 80
7 X 10 = 70***	15 X 5 = 75***	40 X 2 = 80***
14 X 5 = 70***	76 X 1 = 76	20 X 4 = 80***
71 X 1 = 71*	38 X 2 = 76***	16 X 5 = 80***
72 X 1 = 72	19 X 4 = 76***	8 X 10 = 80***
36 X 2 = 72***	77 X 1 = 77	81 X 1 = 81
18 X 4 = 72***	7 X 11 = 77*****	9 X 9 = 81**
24 X 3 = 72***	78 X 1 = 78	27 X 3 = 81***
8 X 9 = 72**		

4. Omitting the primes and all other trivial facts where one of the factors is unity, also those marked with three stars, we now have remaining:

2 X 2 = 4	4 X 4 = 16	3 X 9 = 27	5 X 9 = 45
2 X 3 = 6	2 X 8 = 16	4 X 7 = 28	6 X 8 = 48
2 X 4 = 8	3 X 6 = 18	5 X 6 = 30	7 X 7 = 49
3 X 3 = 9	2 X 9 = 18	4 X 8 = 32	6 X 9 = 54
2 X 5 = 10	4 X 5 = 20	5 X 7 = 35	7 X 8 = 56
3 X 4 = 12	3 X 7 = 21	6 X 6 = 36	7 X 9 = 63
2 X 6 = 12	3 X 8 = 24	4 X 9 = 36	8 X 8 = 64
2 X 7 = 14	4 X 6 = 24	5 X 8 = 40	8 X 9 = 72
3 X 5 = 15	5 X 5 = 25	6 X 7 = 42	9 X 9 = 81

By means of the distributive law we can now handle all facts above since they break into trivial facts or facts already included in the list. For example:

$2 \times 2 = 4 = 2 \times (1 + 1) = 2 + 2 = 4$
$3 \times 3 = 9 = 3 \times (2 + 1) = 6 + 3 = 9$
$3 \times 4 = 12 = 3 \times (2 + 2) = 6 + 6 = 12$
$9 \times 9 = 81 = 9 \times (4 + 5) = 36 + 45 = 81$, etc.

Now at this point students will have had considerable experience with the multiplication and division facts. In fact, they will be able to respond to many of these, having made no effort at all toward memorization.

For those facts still causing trouble, the student should be encouraged to organize his own attack. The attack upon a particular problem will vary from learner to learner, and no effort should be made in the direction of uniformity. Most students will now know the multiplications by 2 and 3 because of their experience with the number line. Many will know those involving 4 as well as those involving a number multiplied by itself. These then become means of attack upon other facts. A teacher should not depend entirely upon any one organizational scheme but allow and encourage a variety of attacks. For example, 9×8 may be attacked by using $(10 \times 8) - 8 = 80 - 8 = 72$, or 6×7 is attacked by using $(5 \times 7) + 7 = 42$; 8×7 is attacked by using $(8 \times 8) - 8 = 56$.

Another attack upon these facts might be made through the use of prime factors. Students at this level should be able to factor composites to 81 into their prime factors. They might then attack 8×9 as $2 \times 2 \times 2 \times 3 \times 3 = 6 \times 6 \times 2 = 72$. Still another attack is through the distributive law, i.e., $a(b + c) = ab + ac$. For example, we may multiply 8×9 by using $8(4 + 5) = (8 \times 4) + (8 \times 5) = 32 + 40 = 72$. The associative law of multiplication also is helpful here. $8 \times 9 = (4 \times 2) \times 9 = 4 \times (2 \times 9) = 4 \times 18 = 72$. Instantaneous responses to the basic multiplication facts are just as desirable as they ever were. It is just that a student removed from the pressure of memorizing and the fear of forgetting seems to get and retain the facts more satisfactorily.

During the learning experience surrounding the multiplication facts the learner should be led to discover the commutative law of multiplication. In generalized form it is that $a \times b = b \times a$. The very young child will interpret 2×3 as being different than 3×2, since he thinks in the first instance of 2 groups of 3 and in the second instance of 3 groups of 2. He quickly discovers, however, that the product is the same in either case and that the order of multiplication does not alter the product. He thus recognizes 2 and 3 in the multiplication operation as being unordered and extends this notion to triplets or any number of factors. This concept makes possible the prime-factor attack referred to above. As one of the many experiences of the learner in establishing the basic multiplication facts, he may wish to set up the summary given in the adjoining table and observe the patterns that are created.

×	0	1	2	3	4	5	6	7	8	9
0	0	0	0	0	0	0	0	0	0	0
1	0	1	2	3	4	5	6	7	8	9
2	0	2	4	6	8	10	12	14	16	18
3	0	3	6	9	12	15	18	21	24	27
4	0	4	8	12	16	20	24	28	32	36
5	0	5	10	15	20	25	30	35	40	45
6	0	6	12	18	24	30	36	42	48	54
7	0	7	14	21	28	35	42	49	56	63
8	0	8	16	24	32	40	48	56	64	72
9	0	9	18	27	36	45	54	63	72	81

An additional observation is here in order. Multiplication by zero and by one are clearly discernible in the chart. Students must recognize early and remember always that multiplying any number by zero produces zero and that multiplying any number by 1 produces the number. These two facts are extremely basic and have important implications in later mathematics. They are known as the *multiplicative law of zero* and the *multiplicative law of one*. Also, the cummutative law eliminates the facts shaded on the chart.

UNDERSTANDING THE MULTIPLICATION ALGORISMS

Having established the basic multiplication facts, we are now prepared to extend multiplication through a sequential development of the algorisms. The sequence, like those of addition and subtraction, proceeds from a two-digit multiplicand and a single-digit multiplier involving no regrouping to many-digit multipliers and multiplicands involving regrouping. Let us illustrate one very simple and one more complex example:

$$3 \times 42 = ?$$

100	10	1
	4	2
		3
		6
1	2	0
1	2	6

Using the place-value chart, we proceed as follows: 3 units × 2 units = 6 units, 3 units × 40 units or 4 tens = 120 units which may be written 100 + 20 placed in the chart as one group of 100, two groups of ten and no units. Adding the partial products we get 126. Now simplifying the process we get the algorism:

$$\begin{array}{r} 42 \\ \underline{3} \\ 126 \end{array}$$

which without logic becomes a process of multiplying 3 × 2 to get 6 and 3 × 4 to get 12.

Now let us move to a more difficult example, such as 278 × 4346 = ?

1000000	100000	10000	1000	100	10	1	
			4	3	4	6	
				2	7	8	
					4	8	
				3	2	0	*
			2	4	0	0	
		3	2	0	0	0	
				4	2	0	
			2	8	0	0	△
		2	1	0	0	0	
	2	8	0	0	0	0	
			1	2	0	0	
			8	0	0	0	⊡
		6	0	0	0	0	
	8	0	0	0	0	0	
1	2	0	8	1	8	8	

Without elaboration the basic logic is as follows: 8 X 6 = 48 = 4 tens and 8 units. 8 X 40 = 320 = 3 hundreds + 2 tens + no units. 8 X 300 = 2400 = 2 thousands = 4 hundreds + no tens + no units. 8 X 4000 = 32000 = 3 ten thousands + 2 thousands. 70 X 6 = 4 hundreds + 2 tens. 70 X 40 = 2800 = 2 thousands + 8 hundreds. 70 X 300 = 21000 = 2 tens thousands + 1 thousand. 70 X 4000 = 280000 = 2 hundred thousands + 8 ten thousands. 200 X 6 = 1200 = 1 thousand + 2 hundreds. 200 X 40 = 8000 = 8 thousands. 200 X 300 = 60000 = 6 ten thousands. 200 X 4000 = 800000 = 8 hundred thousands. Adding we get 1208188. Now let us simplify this reasoning to produce the algorism. The sum of the partial products marked * is 34768 which is the first partial product in the algorism. The sum of the partial products marked Δ is 304220, which is the second partial product in the algorism. The sum of the partial products marked ⊡ is 869200, which is the third partial product in the algorism. Note that in the algorism zeros which do not effect the final result are not generally shown. These have been marked through with a cross in the example. In the algorism they are accounted for by moving one place to the left with each successive multiplication.

```
   4346
    278
-------
  34768
 304220
 869200
-------
1208188
```

Having now established the algorism at this level of difficulty, students should be able to apply it with multipliers and multiplicands having any number of digits. Teachers should feel free to ask students to verify the logic of any algorism used by them. In other words, their use of a short cut should be contingent upon their ability to explain why it works.

Another approach to the multiplication algorism centers around expanded notation. In our previous explanation one weak spot is quite apparant. Students may inquire why it is necessary to multiply each digit in the multiplicand by each digit in the multiplier. This deserves an explanation. Let us examine a multiplication problem using expanded notation. The problem 25 X 12 is a good example. In expanded notation a student will recognize that to obtain the correct product we must use the cross-products; i.e.,

```
      20 +  5              20 +  5
      10 +  2      NOT     10 +  2
-------------          ---------
      40 + 10            200 + 10
200 + 50
-------------
200 + 90 + 10
```

Having established this requirement, we can now do a more difficult problem which will better illustrate the algorism.

$$297 \times 46 = 297$$

$$\begin{array}{r} 200 + 90 + 7 \\ 40 + 6 \\ \hline 1200 + 540 + 42 \\ 8000 + 3600 + 280 \\ \hline 8000 + 4800 + 820 + 42 \end{array} = 10000 + 3000 + 600 + 60 + 2 = 13662$$

$$\begin{array}{r} 297 \\ 46 \\ \hline 1782 \\ 1188 \\ \hline 13662 \end{array}$$

In this result we can detect the carrying process which takes:

1. 40 or $4 \cdot 10$ to the tens column, giving 860
2. 800 or $8 \cdot 100$ to the hundreds column, giving 5600
3. 5000 or $5 \cdot 1000$ to the thousands column, giving 13000
4. 10000 or $1 \cdot 10000$ to the ten-thousands column, giving 100000

MULTIPLICATION OF THE NONNEGATIVE RATIONALS

Let us first consider proper and improper fractions. Under addition of fractions we have already developed the golden rule of fractions and the concept of prime factors. From the primary grades students should be led to understand that $^1/_2$ of $^3/_4$ is interpreted mathematically to mean $^1/_2 \times {}^3/_4$. If we now set up a pattern beginning with the multiplication of a fraction and a whole number and leading into the multiplication of two fractions, we can quickly establish our process:

$$\begin{array}{l} ^1/_2 \times 8 = 4 \\ ^1/_2 \times 4 = 2 \\ ^1/_2 \times 2 = 1 \\ ^1/_2 \times 1 = {}^1/_2 \\ \hline ^1/_2 \times {}^1/_2 = {}^1/_4 \\ ^1/_2 \times {}^1/_4 = {}^1/_8 \\ ^1/_2 \times {}^1/_8 = {}^1/_{16} \end{array}$$

The first four problems should be verified by a variety of techniques. (a) The student may feel perfectly comfortable in just saying $^1/_2$ of 8 is 4.
(b) He may remember that multiplication is unordered and therefore $({}^1/_2 \times 8)$ equals $(8 \times {}^1/_2)$ which means we can add $^1/_2 + {}^1/_2 + {}^1/_2 + {}^1/_2 + {}^1/_2 + {}^1/_2 + {}^1/_2 + {}^1/_2 = 4$. (c) He can also see that $^1/_2$ of 8 can be represented by a diagram.

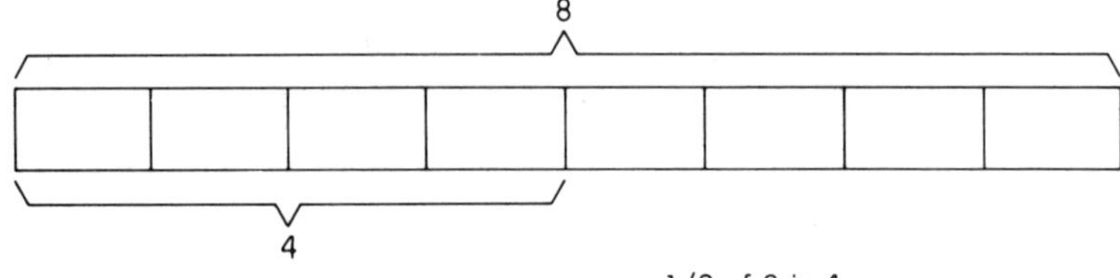

1/2 of 8 is 4

This diagram system can be extended through all the problems in this pattern. $1/2 \times 1/4$ is illustrated as follows:

1 rectangle

1/8	1/8	1/4	1/4	1/4

We want 1/2 of 1/4 which is 1/8

Students should now study the pattern recognizable in the series of problems. Note that the multiplier remains the same. The multiplicand is successively cut in half.

At this point the question arises as to how we determined that half of 3 is 3/2 and half of 3/2 is 3/4, etc., as we set up our pattern of problems. This can easily be handled by developing two ways of taking half of a fraction. If the numerator is even, half of the fraction can be obtained by taking half of the numerator and leaving the denominator as it is. This amounts to taking half as many of the equal parts. If the numerator is odd, we can easily take half of the fraction by keeping the same number of equal parts (leaving the numerator as is) but making the size of the equal parts half as large (doubling the denominator).

A further question may arise with older students as to the use of the word "of" meaning multiplication. It should be made clear that "of" does not necessarily always mean multiplication in mathematics, but in this particular situation it does. The next step should involve a more difficult series. For example:

$$2/3 \times 12 = 8$$
$$2/3 \times 6 = 4$$
$$2/3 \times 3 = 2$$
$$2/3 \times 3/2 = 1$$
$$2/3 \times 3/4 = 1/2$$
$$2/3 \times 3/8 = 1/4$$
$$2/3 \times 3/16 = 1/8$$

Again, use whatever verification is necessary but capitalize upon the pattern. Usually at this stage we are ready to establish the algorism. This is done by illustrating to the student that these same answers can be obtained by factoring numerators and denominators into prime factors and eliminating factors which are equal to unity. Example:

$$2/3 \times 3/4 = 2/3 \cdot 3/2 \cdot 2 = 2 \cdot 3/3 \cdot 2 \cdot 2 = \frac{3 \cdot 2 \cdot 1}{3 \cdot 2 \cdot 2} = 1 \cdot 1 \cdot \frac{1}{2} = \frac{1}{2}$$

All of the answers in the two series of problems used in the patterns can be obtained in this way, and the student should do as many as necessary to convince himself that this method produces the correct answer.

It should be pointed out that eliminating factors which result in 1 or technically 1/1 is known as the *law of the unit element* and may be done in shortcut ways after the principle is thoroughly understood. The student should now be in a position to multiply accurately in any problem involving proper and/or improper fractions and should see that mixed numbers need only be converted to improper fractions to fit the same process.

MULTIPLICATION OF RATIONAL DECIMALS

We consider now the multiplication of positive rational decimals. Since this work parallels the multiplication of integers, we give only an example but point out that the development must be carefully done with a final transition step to the algorism. Examples: 2.34 X .245 = ? Since multiplication is unordered we may rearrange the problem to be .245 X 2.34 = ?

	1	$\frac{1}{10}$	$\frac{1}{100}$	$\frac{1}{1000}$	$\frac{1}{1000000}$
	2	3	4		
		2	4	5	
		0	0	0	2
.0117 ←		0	0	1	5
		0	1	0	0
		0	0	1	6
.0936 ←		0	1	2	0
		0	8	0	0
		0	0	8	0
.4680 ←		0	6	0	0
		4	0	0	0
		5	7	3	3

$$\frac{5}{1000} \times \frac{4}{100} = \frac{20}{100000} = \frac{2}{10000}$$

$$\frac{5}{1000} \times \frac{3}{10} = \frac{15}{10000} = \frac{10}{10000} + \frac{5}{10000} = \frac{1}{1000} + \frac{5}{10000}$$

$$\frac{5}{1000} \times 2 = \frac{10}{1000} = \frac{1}{100}$$

$$\frac{4}{100} \times \frac{4}{100} = \frac{16}{10000} = \frac{10}{10000} + \frac{6}{10000} = \frac{1}{1000} + \frac{6}{10000}$$

$$\frac{4}{100} \times \frac{3}{10} = \frac{12}{1000} = \frac{10}{1000} + \frac{2}{1000} = \frac{1}{100} + \frac{2}{1000}$$

$$\frac{4}{100} \times 2 = \frac{8}{100}$$

$$\frac{2}{10} \times \frac{4}{100} = \frac{8}{1000}$$

$$\frac{2}{10} \times \frac{3}{10} = \frac{6}{100}$$

$$\frac{2}{10} \times 2 = \frac{4}{10}$$

and

$$\frac{234}{100} \cdot \frac{245}{1000} = \frac{57330}{100000} = \frac{5733}{10000}$$

These results check with the partial products of the algorism shown below:

```
   2.34
   .245
  -----
   1170
   936
  468
  -----
 .57330
```

The mechanics of the algorism, such as staggering the partial products and placing the decimal, now become apparent.

MULTIPLYING RATIONAL NUMBERS

As we now extend our universal set to include both positive and negative rationals, we are confronted again with five possible situations. In brief, they are:

1. Multiplying a negative rational by a positive rational.
2. Multiplying a positive rational by a negative rational.
3. Multiplying a negative rational by a negative rational.
4. Multiplying a positive rational by a positive rational.
5. Multiplying involving zero.

Again let us build our logic from a sequential pattern involving integers:

$$(+3) \times (+3) = +9$$
$$(+3) \times (+2) = +6$$
$$(+3) \times (+1) = +3$$
$$(+3) \times (0) = 0$$
$$(+3) \times (-1) = -3$$
$$(+3) \times (-2) = -6$$
$$(+3) \times (-3) = -9$$
$$(+3) \times (-3) = -9$$

The first four examples are true statements verified by our experience in elementary arithmetic. Since the pattern reveals that the multiplicands are decreasing by one and the multipliers are remaining the same the products should decrease by three. Students will quickly recognize that the products in the last three problems can be obtained by multiplying absolute values and attaching the negative sign.

Illustrating the second situation in a similar way:

$$\begin{aligned}
(+3) \times (+3) &= +9 \\
(+2) \times (+3) &= +6 \\
(+1) \times (+3) &= +3 \\
(0) \times (+3) &= \ \ 0 \\
(-1) \times (+3) &= -3 \\
(-2) \times (+3) &= -6 \\
(-3) \times (+3) &= -9 \\
(-4) \times (+3) &= -12
\end{aligned}$$

Again, the first four statements are true from arithmetic. Since the multipliers are decreasing by one while the multiplicands remain constant, the products should decrease by three; again the rule stated above can be observed to apply to the last four problems.

Let us look now at the multiplication of a negative by a negative.

$$\begin{aligned}
(+4) \times (-3) &= -12 \\
(+3) \times (-3) &= -9 \\
(+2) \times (-3) &= -6 \\
(+1) \times (-3) &= -3 \\
(0) \times (-3) &= \ \ 0 \\
(-1) \times (-3) &= +3 \\
(-2) \times (-3) &= +6 \\
(-3) \times (-3) &= +9 \\
(-4) \times (-3) &= +12
\end{aligned}$$

The first five statements are true on the basis of our experience in situation one. Since the multipliers are decreasing by one and the multiplicands are remaining constant, we would expect the pattern of products for the last four problems to follow that of the first five, i.e., they will increase successively by three units. We conclude therefore that the product of two negative numbers can be obtained by multiplying their absolute values and attaching the positive sign. Because this rule has been traditionally difficult to establish with any semblance of logic understandable to the average learner, time is taken here to offer an alternate development which ties back with previous learning in a more direct way. Let us set up three series similar to that utilized in situation one, applying the same reasoning to establish the logic of each pattern.

$(+3) \times (+3) = +9$	$(+2) \times (+3) = +6$	$(+1) \times (+3) = +3$
$(+3) \times (+2) = +6$	$(+2) \times (+2) = +4$	$(+1) \times (+2) = +2$
$(+3) \times (+1) = +3$	$(+2) \times (+1) = +2$	$(+1) \times (+1) = +1$
$(+3) \times (0) = 0$	$(+2) \times (0) = 0$	$(+1) \times (0) = 0$
$(+2) \times (-1) = -3$	$(+2) \times (-1) = -2$	$(+1) \times (-1) = -1$
$(+3) \times (-2) = -6$	$(+2) \times (-2) = -4$	$(+1) \times (-2) = -2$
$(+3) \times (-3) = -9$*	$(+2) \times (-3) = -6$*	$(+1) \times (-3) = -3$*

Now let us select the three starred problems to begin a fourth pattern, the last four problems of which lead up to the situation we were seeking. Again the rule emerges as in the previous approach.

$$
\begin{aligned}
(+3) \times (-3) &= -9 \\
(+2) \times (-3) &= -6 \\
(+1) \times (-3) &= -3 \\
(0) \times (-3) &= 0 \\
(-1) \times (-3) &= +3 \\
(-2) \times (-3) &= +6 \\
(-3) \times (-3) &= +9
\end{aligned}
$$

Some teachers may feel that the establishment of this rule is unduly labored in the above treatment. It should be recognized, however, that this generalization does not lend itself to interpretation on the directed number line, and for this reason has been a trouble spot in the teaching of negative numbers. A teacher need only seek for another practical and/or logical illustration of this rule short of the propositional calculus to find how frustrating this problem can be. Students given plenty of time for personal involvement in the above development seem to accept it readily and with good understanding.

The fourth situation is again readily recognized to be the experience of elementary arithmetic, and we need only point out that these same arithmetic answers can be obtained by applying the rule of multiplying the absolute values and attaching the positive sign.

We are now ready to further summarize our discoveries:

1. When multiplying elements one of which is negative and the other positive, multiply their absolute values and change the result to its opposite (or make it negative).
2. When multiplying elements both of which are negative or both of which are positive, multiply their absolute values.
3. Multiplication involving zero as a multiplier always results in zero. Rational fractions without nonspecified elements follow the same multiplication laws previously developed with positive rational fractions. Of course the two laws developed above must now come into play, since we have both positive and negative elements in the set.

MULTIPLICATION OF RATIONAL EXPRESSIONS INVOLVING PLACE HOLDERS

Let us look first at monomials and polynomials which are not fractional. We begin by defining $\square \cdot \square = \square^2$; $\Delta \cdot \Delta \cdot \Delta = \Delta^3$; etc. Multiplying monomials thus becomes merely a matter of multiplying specified elements according to previous development and following the definition above. Thus $(-2\square^2\Delta)(3\square\Delta^3) = -6\square^3\Delta^4$. We generalize with the law $\square^m \cdot \square^n = \square^{m+n}$ for handling nonspecified elements.

We now exhibit through arithmetic the means for multiplying polynomials:

$$\begin{array}{r} 20 + 4 \\ \underline{12 + 6} \\ 240 + 48 \\ \underline{+ 120 + 24} \\ 240 + 168 + 24 = 432 \end{array}$$

$24 \times 18 = 432$ by the usual algorism

Using the technique developed for monomials it is apparent that we have only to multiply each monomial of the multiplicand by each monomial of the multiplier. To illustrate:

$$\begin{array}{l} 2\Delta + 3\square \\ \underline{3\square - \Delta} \\ 6\Delta\square + 9\square^2 \\ \underline{\qquad\qquad -2\Delta^2 - 3\Delta\square} \\ 6\Delta\square + 9\square^2 - 2\Delta^2 - 3\Delta\square \\ \qquad \text{or} \\ 3\Delta\square + 9\square^2 - 2\Delta^2 \end{array}$$

Since there were two like terms in the partial products, combining of terms was possible.

In the multiplication of fractions involving nonspecified elements and monomials and polynomials, we merely draw upon previously developed fraction theory and factoring to handle the situation. To illustrate:

$$\left(\frac{4\square^2\Delta}{\square^2 - \Delta^2}\right) \cdot \left(\frac{\square^2 + 2\square\Delta + \Delta^2}{2\square^2 + 2\square\Delta}\right) = \frac{(2 \cdot 2 \cdot \square \cdot \square \cdot \Delta)}{(\square - \Delta) \cdot (\square + \Delta)} \cdot \frac{(\square + \Delta)(\square + \Delta)}{2 \cdot \square(\square + \Delta)}$$

$$= \frac{2 \cdot 2 \cdot \square \cdot \square \cdot \Delta \cdot (\square + \Delta) \cdot (\square + \Delta)}{2 \cdot \square \cdot (\square - \Delta)(\square + \Delta) \cdot (\square + \Delta)} = \frac{2\square\Delta}{(\square - \Delta)}$$

which is obtained by factoring and using the multiplicative law of one.

MULTIPLYING IRRATIONAL NUMBERS

Here again let us consider only the irrationals in radical form since the decimal forms of irrationals are infinite and cannot be converted to common fractions.

Basically the definitions of the irrational radicals govern their multiplication since $\sqrt{2} \times \sqrt{2} = 2$ by definition; $\sqrt[3]{3} \times \sqrt[3]{3} \times \sqrt[3]{3} = 3$ by definition. Further, we know from previous experiences that the order of multiplication does not alter the product. If we wish then to multiply $2\sqrt{2} \times 3\sqrt{2}$ we can multiply the 2 and 3 to get 6 and the $\sqrt{2}$ and $\sqrt{2}$ to get 2 and then multiply the 6 and 2 to get 12. Students having this experience for the first time may wish to verify it with rational radicals. For example, $2\sqrt{9} \times 3\sqrt{9}$ by the above attack will be $6 \times 9 = 54$. By extracting the roots first we get $2 \times 3 \times 3 \times 3 = 54$.

In examples where the radicals are not alike we can only multiply numbers under the radicals as follows:

$$3\sqrt{2} \times 4\sqrt{3} = 12\sqrt{6}$$

Again this process may be verified by rational radicals:

$$3\sqrt{4} \times 4\sqrt{9} = 12\sqrt{36} = 12 \times 6 = 72$$

or extracting roots first, $3 \times 2 \times 4 \times 3 = 72$.

The above is merely a brief treatment of the multiplication of irrationals and is dependent upon an understanding of powers and roots which is handled in a separate section of this text.

BASIC LAWS OF MULTIPLICATION

Before leaving multiplication we should correlate our discoveries with the basic law of multiplication.

1. We have already mentioned the commutative law of multiplication. It states that for any elements a,b in the universal set $(a \times b) = (b \times a)$. This may be extended to include any number of elements. A specific example is: $2 \times 3 \times 11 = 11 \times 2 \times 3$.
2. The associative law of multiplication states that for any elements a, b, and c of the set, $a \times (b \times c) = (a \times b) \times c$. This is illustrated as follows: $3 \times (4 \times 5) = (3 \times 4) \times 5$. In words, it states that 3 times the product (4×5) is equal to the product of 3 and 4 multiplied by 5. Algebraically it may of course appear much more complex, for example: $(2 - 3)[(-2)(+3)] \doteq [(2 - 3)(-2)]\ (+3)$.
3. Our experience has led us to the law of the identity element which states that for any element a in the set, $a \times 1 = a$. Examples are.

   $9 \times 1 = 9$ or $0 \times 1 = 0$ or algebraically $(2 - 4)\,1 = 2 - 4$

4. The law of the multiplicative inverse has also come within our experience as we worked with fractions. It states that for any element a in the universal set, except $a = 0$, $a \times \frac{1}{a} = 1$. For example, $12 \times \frac{1}{12} = 1$.
5. Having developed both addition and multiplication we are now ready for the law which ties the two relationships together. It is called the *distributive law* and states that for any elements a, b, and c of the set, $a(b + c) = ab + ac$. This law or axiom was previously referred to under addition. Example:

$$3 \times (4 + 5) = (3 \times 4) + (3 \times 5)$$
$$3 \times 9 = 12 + 15$$
$$27 = 27$$

Algebraically, $2x(x + 9) = 2x^2 + 18x$, which may be verified by letting $x = 3$ or any other element of the set.

$$2 \cdot 3\,(3 + 9) = 2\,(3)^2 + 18 \cdot 3$$
$$6\,(12) = 2 \cdot 9 + 54$$
$$72 = 18 + 54$$
$$72 = 72$$

DIVISION

Two aspects of the division operation should be recognized in mathematics. The first is that of finding how many sets of a particular size are contained in the set to be divided. This is called *separation*. The other aspect considers what size each equal set will be if an original set is divided into a certain number of equal parts. This is called partitioning. For example; if we wish to know how many sets of 3 elements each are contained in a set of 12 elements we find there are 4. If we want to divide a set of 12 elements into 4 equal sets, we find there are 3 elements in each of the 4 equal sets. For those who have completely integrated these two aspects, little attention need be given to the distinction between the two.

DIVISION OF NONNEGATIVE INTEGERS

The decomposition of sets of nonnegative integers should parallel the combining process called multiplication. As in multiplication, the young learner will need an abundance of experiences in the concrete and semiconcrete. Here again the number line and sets will be useful for younger students. The process is not unlike that illustrated for multiplication except that the reasoning is reversed. For example, $12 \div 3 = 4$ may look like this on the number line:

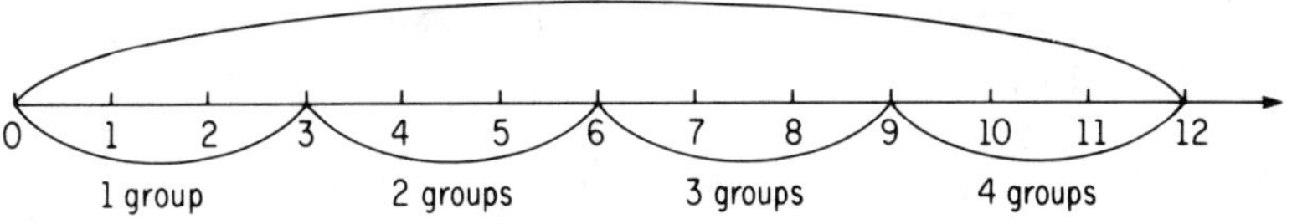

With the use of sets it might appear as shown on the accompanying illustration.

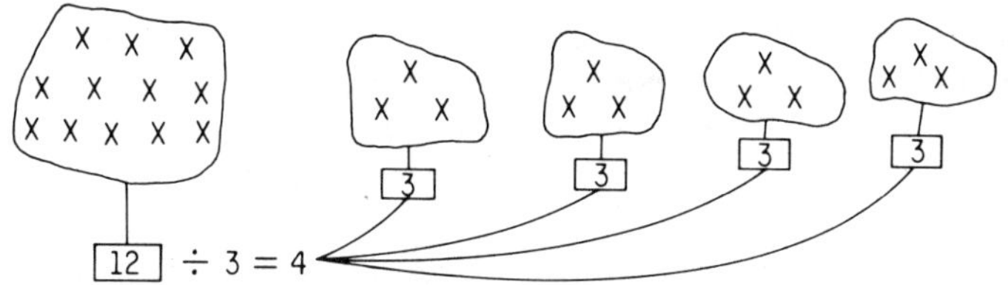

In words, we are asking how many sets of 3 elements each are contained in a set of 12 elements.

Both aspects (separation and partitioning) can and should be experienced in the concrete. The basic division facts up to $81 \div 9$ should be taught jointly with the multiplication facts and should be an important part of the experience recommended elsewhere in this text. The whole concept of primes and prime factors depends upon an understanding of division. Students should become progressively more efficient at breaking larger and larger composites into primes and combining these primes in various combinations to illustrate both the division and multiplication facts. Here again, counting by 2's, 3's, 5's, and 10's is the starting point. For example: 18 contains 9 sets of 2 or $18 = 9 \cdot 2$; 2 sets of 9 or $18 = 2 \cdot 9$; 3 sets of 6 or $18 = 3 \cdot 6$; now 18 contains 3 sets each of which is composed of 2 sets of 3 elements each written, $18 = 3\,(2 \cdot 3)$; finally, 18 contains 2 sets each of which is composed of 3 sets of 3 elements each written, $18 = 2\,(3 \cdot 3)$. This ultimately leads to the prime factorization of 18; i.e., $18 = 2 \cdot 3 \cdot 3 = 3 \cdot 3 \cdot 2 = 3 \cdot 2 \cdot 3$. Note that we have here illustrated the associative law of multiplication, and below have related the multiplication facts to the corresponding division facts:

$18 = 9 \cdot 2$	$18 \div 9 = 2$	and $18 \div 2 = 9$
$18 = 3 \cdot 6$	$18 \div 3 = 6$	and $18 \div 6 = 3$
$18 = 3(2 \cdot 3)$	$18 \div 3 = (2 \cdot 3)$	and $18 \div (2 \cdot 3) = 3$
$18 = 2(3 \cdot 3)$	$18 \div 2 = (3 \cdot 3)$	and $18 \div (3 \cdot 3) = 2$

Furthermore, it may be desirable at this point to relate multiplication and division to addition and subtraction.
$18 = 2 + 2 + 2 + 2 + 2 + 2 + 2 + 2 + 2$ or the sum of nine 2's. $18 - 2 = 16$; $16 - 2 = 14$; $14 - 2 = 12$; $12 - 2 = 10$; $10 - 2 = 8$; $8 - 2 = 6$; $6 - 2 = 4$; $4 - 2 = 2$; $2 - 2 = 0$; or we have subtracted 2 nine times. Similarly, $18 = 6 + 6 + 6$ and $18 - 6 = 12$; $12 - 6 = 6$; $6 - 6 = 0$. $18 = 3 + 3 + 3 + 3 + 3 + 3$, and $18 - 3 = 15$;

$15 - 3 = 12$; $12 - 3 = 9$: $9 - 3 = 6$; $6 - 3 = 3$; $3 - 3 = 0$. $18 = (2 \cdot 3) + (2 \cdot 3) + (2 \cdot 3)$ and $18 - (2 \cdot 3) = 12$; $12 - (2 \cdot 3) = 6$; $6 - (2 \cdot 3) = 0$. $18 = (3 \cdot 3) + (3 \cdot 3)$ and $18 - (3 \cdot 3) = 9; 9 - (3 \cdot 3) = 0$.

The process of breaking composites into prime factors thus becomes extremely important for both the multiplication and division facts. However, a student who can count by 2's, 3's, and 5's with real understanding will encounter little difficulty factoring up to the composite 81, except that $7 \times 7 = 49$ and its companion division fact $49 \div 7 = 7$ poses a special problem. While it may be expected that any composite having 7 as a factor would give like trouble, this is not so, since 2, 3, and 5 help to break the others down. For example, 56 can be successively divided by 2 until the prime factors $2 \cdot 2 \cdot 2 \cdot 7$ are obtained and the twos then multiplied back to get $56 = 8 \cdot 7$ and $56 \div 7 = 8$.

The thing to be noted here is that it takes considerable planning to provide all the essential experiences with the composites involved in the basic division facts, and that these things should be explored and discovered by the learner whenever possible, rather than told by the teacher. Further, no effort should be made to teach a single process in isolation but rather to move all processes forward as rapidly as the maturity and interest of the student will allow.

DIVISION ALGORISMS

Once we have mastered the fundamental division facts, the next job is that of dividing nonnegative integers beyond those involved above. Before introducing the division algorism some experience should be had at this point with the prime factor techniques of division. For example:

$$68 \div 17 = \frac{68}{17} = \frac{2 \cdot 2 \cdot 17}{17} = 4$$

where the 17/17 is equivalent to 1. After pursuing this attack as far as the maturity of the learner will allow, we then help students discover the algorisms. Only one example is given here since this seems adequate to set the pattern for both the simpler and more difficult divisions. Example:

		100	10	1
12)	1728	1	0	0
	1200			
	528		4	0
	480			
	48			4
	48	1	4	4

A modification of this form places the partial quotients and final quotient above the bracket as illustrated.

	1000	100	10	1
	0	1	0	0
	0	0	4	0
	0	0	0	4
	0	1	4	4
12)	1	7	2	8
	1	2	0	0
		5	2	8
		4	8	0
			4	8
			4	8

We first decide whether 12 is contained in 1728 one thousand times. The answer is no, since 12 X 1000 = 12000. We then ask is it contained 100 times or 200 times, etc. Since 200 X 12 = 2400 it must be contained only 100 times. We then place the one in the 100's column, multiply 100 X 12 = 1200, place it under 1728 and subtract. We next ask how many groups of 10 times 12 is contained in 528. Five groups of 10 multiplied by 12 is 600, which is too large, therefore we try 4 groups of 10 and get 40 X 12 = 480, placing this under 528 and of course placing 40 in the quotient. Again we subtract and get 48. We now ask how many unit times 12 is contained in 48. The answer being 4, we place 4 in the unit column and multiply 4 X 12 = 48, which leaves no remainder when we subtract. We now add the partial quotients to obtain 144. When students understand the algorism the place-value columns may be eliminated and the quotient placed above the division bracket.

Before leaving this algorism, let it be observed that actually the process breaks the dividend into parts which are exactly divisible by (in this case) 100, 10 and one. If there is a remainder, it will show up in the units operation. Note that in this example 1728 was broken into 1200 + 480 + 48 and 1200 ÷ 12 = 100; 480 ÷ 12 = 40 and 48 ÷ 12 = 4.

DIVISION OF FRACTIONS

We move first to the division of common fractions. Commonly students are taught that this is done by inverting the divisor and proceeding as in multiplication. Such a procedure should perhaps not be used until students can understand why the algorism works. In fact the four-story algorism is perhaps more useful and may be taught instead. If this method is used it too will require explanation of why it works.

Before either method is employed, the students should be led to some logically correct solutions of problems through pattern and diagram. Let us set up two patterns, the first leading to 3/4 ÷ 1/2 and the second to 3/4 ÷ 2/3.

$$12 \div 1/2 = 24$$
$$6 \div 1/2 = 12$$
$$3 \div 1/2 = 6$$
$$3/2 \div 1/2 = 3$$
$$3/4 \div 1/2 = 3/2$$

Note that we can easily verify the first three problems by asking how many times 1/2 is contained in 12 whole numbers, etc. Also we can easily diagram any of the first four problems, for example, $3 \div 1/2 = 6$.

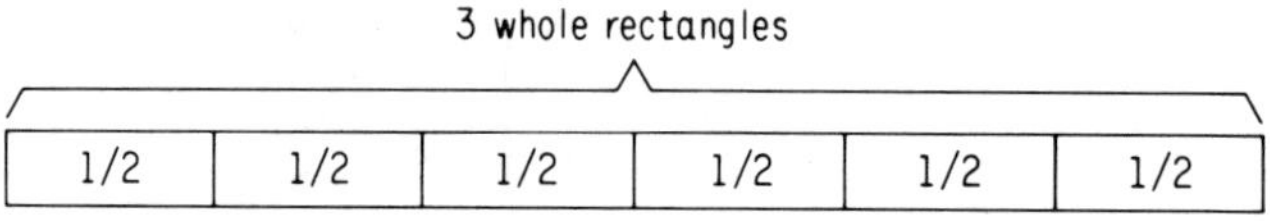

3 whole rectangles

1/2	1/2	1/2	1/2	1/2	1/2

Three whole rectangles contain 6 half rectangles. Having once verified the first four quotients; we find the pattern is easily discernible. That is, our divisor remains 1/2 while our dividend is successively cut in half and the quotients are likewise successively cut in half. Logically, then, $3/4 \div 1/2$ must equal 3/2. Illustrating $3/4 \div 2/3$ without detailed analysis:

$$12 \div 2/3 = 18$$
$$6 \div 2/3 = 9$$
$$3 \div 2/3 = 9/2$$
$$3/2 \div 2/3 = 9/4$$
$$3/4 \div 2/3 = 9/8$$

Again the quotients can be verified by diagram and pattern as was done with multiplication.

We are now ready to establish the two algorisms. Since we are accustomed to writing $12 \div 4$ as 12/4, in a like manner we can write $\frac{3}{4} \div \frac{1}{2} = \frac{3/4}{1/2}$; now apply the golden rule of fractions or multiplicative law of one. We can multiply both numerator and denominator of this four-story fraction by $\frac{2}{1}$, thus $\frac{3/4}{1/2} = \frac{3/4 \times 2/1}{1/2 \times 2/1} = 3/4 \times 2/1$, which agrees with our previously obtained quotient and verifies the rule of inverting the divisor and multiplying. It also verifies that we could have multiplied the extremes for a new numerator and the means for a new denominator and obtained the same quotient. To illustrate:

$$\frac{3}{4} \div \frac{1}{2} = \frac{\frac{3}{4}}{\frac{1}{2}} = \frac{6}{4} = \frac{3}{2}$$

The 3 and 2 in the four story fraction are called the extremes while the 4 and 1 are called the means. Either algorism may now be used. Applying the second one to 3/4 ÷ 2/3, we get $\frac{3}{4} \div \frac{2}{3} = \frac{3/4}{2/3} = \frac{9}{8}$. At this point students should be helped to see that in using this last algorism for a whole number divided by a fraction or a fraction divided by a whole number, we establish the main division line and complete the four-story fraction before applying the mean and extreme algorism. Examples:

$$4 \div \frac{2}{3} = \frac{4}{2/3} = \frac{4/1}{2/3} = \frac{12}{2} = 6, \text{ and } \frac{3}{4} \div 3 = \frac{3/4}{3/1} = \frac{3}{12} = \frac{1}{4}$$

In developing the division of common fractions it should be observed that multiplication serves as a check for division, and this check should be used often throughout the development. We utilize this idea to establish one of the most important laws governing numbers. This is that division by zero is not defined in our number set.

Let us consider the two cases of division by zero. The first is $\frac{0}{0}$. Note that this division checks equally well for any quotient. If $\frac{0}{0} = N$, then $0 \times N = 0$ is true, regardless of whether $N = 5$, 2/3, or 1000000. This leaves us with no unique quotient and of course, would bring inconsistency into our mathematics, which is plainly contrary to its nature. The second case is $\frac{N}{0}$ where $N \neq 0$. Here we note that no element of our number set will serve as a quotient because in checking, 0 times any other element is zero, and we have already said that $N \neq 0$. The existence principle thus fails, and we say then that $\frac{N}{0}$ where $N \neq 0$ is undefined in our set. It therefore has no meaning and cannot be allowed. This important concept often receives too little attention. It should be taught in the primary grades and reemphasized as often as necessary to insure against falling into this trap even when zero may be disguised in complex expressions involving nonspecified elements.

A notable example of the disguised zero division is shown below:

1. Let $\square = \Delta$
2. Then $\square^2 = (\square \cdot \Delta)$
3. Now $\square^2 - \Delta^2 = (\square \cdot \Delta) - \Delta^2$
4. and $(\square - \Delta) \cdot (\square + \Delta) = \Delta \cdot (\square - \Delta)$
5. Also, $\frac{(\square - \Delta) \cdot (\square + \Delta)}{(\square - \Delta)} = \frac{\Delta \cdot (\square - \Delta)}{(\square - \Delta)}$
6. and $\square + \Delta = \Delta$
7. But since $\square = \Delta$

8. then $\Delta + \Delta = \Delta$
9. and $2\Delta = \Delta$
10. Therefore $2 = 1$

The error was introduced in step 5 because $\square = \Delta$ in step 1 and therefore $(\square - \Delta) = 0$.

DIVISION OF DECIMALS

The algorism used in the division of positive rational decimals requires careful verification. Such verification is not unlike that utilized for the division of positive integers. Naturally this must be established with the young learner by working from the very simple to the more difficult situations. An example of medium difficulty is:

$$.03979 \div .17 = \frac{.03979}{.17} = \frac{3979}{17000}$$

when we multiply numerator and denominator by 100000. Now, proceeding:

		$\frac{1}{10}$	$\frac{1}{100}$	$\frac{1}{1000}$	$\frac{1}{10000}$	$\frac{1}{100000}$
17000)	3979.00	2				
	3400					
	579		3			
	510					
	69			4		
	68					
	1.00				0	5
	.85					
	.15	2	3	4	0	5

We ask how many $\frac{1}{10}$ times is 17000 contained in 3978? $\frac{2}{10} \times 17000 = 3400$, but $\frac{3}{10} \times 17000 = 5100$, which is too large. We, therefore, place 2 in the $\frac{1}{10}$ column and multiply and subtract. We ask how many $\frac{1}{100}$ times is 17000 contained in 578? $\frac{3}{100} \times 1700 = 510$ but $\frac{4}{100} \times 17000 = 680$, which is too large. We therefore, place 3 in the $\frac{1}{100}$ column and multiply and subtract. We, ask how many $\frac{1}{1000}$ times is 17000 contained in 68? $\frac{4}{1000} \times 17000 = 68$. We, therefore, place 4 in the $\frac{1}{1000}$ column and multiply and subtract. We ask how many $\frac{1}{10000}$ times is 17000 contained in 1.0? $\frac{1}{10000} \times 17000 = 1.7$, which is too large. We place 0 in the $\frac{1}{10000}$ column and then ask: how many $\frac{1}{100000}$ times is 17000 contained in 1.0? $\frac{5}{100000} \times 17000 = .85$. We therefore place 5 in the $\frac{1}{100000}$ column and multiply and subtract. The quotient is now correct to the fifth decimal place. We could continue indefinitely or until there was no remainder in case this happens. From here the transition to the standard algorism is a short step.

DIVISION OF RATIONAL NUMBERS

As we expand our number set to include the negative members, it becomes necessary to explore division in four separate situations:

1. Dividing a negative element by a positive element.
2. Dividing a positive element by a negative element.
3. Dividing a negative element by a negative element.
4. Dividing a positive element by a positive element.

Again we illustrate by means of patterns:

$$
\begin{aligned}
(+6) \div (+2) &= +3\\
(+4) \div (+2) &= +2\\
(+2) \div (+2) &= +1\\
0 \div (+2) &= 0\\
(-2) \div (+2) &= -1\\
(-4) \div (+2) &= -2\\
(-6) \div (+2) &= -3
\end{aligned}
$$

The four problems being arithmetic, they suffice to establish the pattern and give us the answers for the last three. Note the dividends are decreasing by 2, the divisors are constant, and the quotients decrease by one. This illustrates situation 1. Division being ordered, it becomes necessary to illustrate situation 2.

$$
\begin{aligned}
(+12) \div (-3) &= -4\\
(+\ 9) \div (-3) &= -3\\
(+\ 6) \div (-3) &= -2\\
(+\ 3) \div (-3) &= -1\\
(\ \ 0) \div (-3) &= 0
\end{aligned}
$$

This series may be verified by multiplying each quotient by the divisor to obtain the dividend.

We are now in a position to write a rule covering situation 1 and 2. It is: When dividing elements having unlike signs, divide the absolute values and attach the negative sign.

Situation 3 may be handled by extending the pattern of 2. We get:

$$\begin{array}{ll} (+12) \div (-3) = -4 & (\ \ 0) \div (-3) = \ \ 0 \\ (+\ 9) \div (-3) = -3 & (-\ 3) \div (-3) = +1 \\ (+\ 6) \div (-3) = -2 & (-\ 6) \div (-3) = +2 \\ (+\ 3) \div (-3) = -1 & (-\ 9) \div (-3) = +3 \\ & (-12) \div (-3) = +4 \end{array}$$

We note that here again we have our pattern and of course we can verify each problem by multiplication. We now write a rule covering situation 3: When dividing elements having like signs, divide the absolute values and attach the positive sign. This rule also handles situation 4 but is not essential here, since 4 is purely arithmetic.

Having established the basic rules for division of integers, we can extend the same rules to all real numbers, since in this respect the integers are not unique.

The division of rational fractions is now readily handled by applying the sign rules stated above and proceeding as with positive rational fractions.

DIVIDING RATIONAL NUMBERS INVOLVING PLACEHOLDERS

At this point we consider the rational numbers involving placeholders in the form of frames. We use only the definition of powers developed under multiplication and the axioms $\forall_{\square \neq 0};\ \frac{\square}{\square} = 1$, and $\forall_{\square};\ \square \cdot 1 = \square$. A more sophisticated treatment of exponents and the power laws is given later in the chapter. We proceed now to illustrate the division of monomials:

Example 4-1

$$\frac{\square^3}{\square^2} = \frac{\square \cdot \square \cdot \square}{\square \cdot \square} = \square \qquad \text{using the axioms above}$$

Example 4-2

$$\frac{-4\square^2}{+2\square} = -2\square \qquad \text{because} \qquad \frac{(-2)\,(+2)\,(\square)\,(\square)}{(+2)\,(\square)} = (-2)\,(\square)$$

Example 4-3

$$\frac{-10\square^2\,\Delta^3}{-5\,\square\Delta} = 2\square\,\Delta^2 \text{ because } \frac{(-5)\,(+2)\,(\square)\,(\square)\,(\Delta)\,(\Delta)\,(\Delta)}{(-5)\,(\square)\,(\Delta)} = 2\square\,\Delta^2$$

The division of polynomials by monomials is now considered. Here as in arithmetic we must divide each term of the numerator by the monomial denominator.

We illustrate with an arithmetic example:

$$\frac{12 + 20}{2} = \frac{12}{2} + \frac{20}{2} = 6 + 10 = 16$$

In a similar manner,

$$\frac{6\square^2\,\Delta^3 + 12\square^4\,\Delta^2 - 18\square^3\,\Delta^2}{6\square^2\,\Delta^2} = \frac{6\square^2\,\Delta^3}{6\square^2\,\Delta^2} + \frac{12\square^4\,\Delta^2}{6\square^2\,\Delta^2} - \frac{18\square^3\,\Delta^2}{6\square^2\,\Delta^2}$$

$$= \Delta + 2\square^2 - 3\square$$

The division of a polynomial by a polynomial is now illustrated by arithmetic numbers. $675 \div 25$ may be divided by first converting the numbers to polynomials.

$$\begin{aligned} 675 &= 400 + 240 + 35 \\ 25 &= 20 + 5 \end{aligned}$$

We now divide as follows:

$$\begin{array}{r|l} & 20 + 7 \\ \hline 20 + 5 & 400 + 240 + 35 \\ & 400 + 100 \\ \hline & \quad\;\; + 140 + 35 \\ & \quad\;\; + 140 + 35 \\ \hline\hline \end{array}$$

Note that in the process the individual parts of the quotient are chosen to make the first term of the dividend disappear in each case. In multiplying, each term of the divisor must be multiplied by the partial quotient.

We now illustrate algebraically:

$$\begin{array}{r|l} & x - 4 \\ \hline x - 3 & x^2 - 7x + 12 \\ & x^3 - 3x \\ \hline & \quad\; - 4x + 12 \\ & \quad\; - 4x + 12 \\ \hline\hline \end{array}$$

We make the shift from frames to letters at this point, realizing that the student will make the change at about this time.

Having taught the algorism, teachers will often find it helpful to suggest arranging dividend and divisor in descending or ascending powers, and perhaps supplying for the beginner missing powers of the nonspecified element through the use of zero coefficients.

Multiplication and division both play a major role in algebraic factoring, and this rule should be capitalized on when teaching the factoring process. Since factoring in algebra is not treated elsewhere in this text, we comment briefly here that factoring is merely the application of division and should be taught by the insight method rather than by cases. The initial progress is slow by this method, but the retention is better and the process much more meaningful. This is not to say that students should not be encouraged to discover the short-cuts, but these should follow the concept and are valuable chiefly for speed and facility. The student should not be dependent upon the remembering of the cases in order to be able to factor.

It should be observed at this point that all of the traditional cases of factoring may be handled by means of the distributive law. We illustrate:

$$xy + x^2 = x(y + x) \qquad \text{(direct application)}$$
$$x^2 - y^2 - xy + xy - y^2 = x(x - y) + y(x - y) = (x - y)(x + y)$$
$$x^2 + 2xy + y^2 = x^2 + xy + xy + y^2 = x(x + y) + y(x + y) = (x + y)(x + y)$$
$$x^2 - 2x - 15 = x^2 + 3x - 5x - 15 = x(x + 3) - 5(x + 3) = (x + 3)(x - 5)$$
$$2x^2 - x - 6 = 2x^2 + 3x - 4x - 6 = x(2x + 3) - 2(2x + 3) = (x - 2)(2x + 3)$$

Factoring beyond these elementary cases involves special cases, the remainder theorem, the factor theorem, synthetic division, and so on. These can be had from any good algebra series and are generally not difficult for students who have the foundations of factoring.

DIVISION OF IRRATIONAL NUMBERS

Using the sign rules and the techniques employed above along with our limited knowledge of roots, we illustrate as follows:

Example 4-4

$$\frac{2\sqrt{2}}{2} = \sqrt{2}$$

Example 4-5

$$\frac{4\sqrt{2} - 6\sqrt{2}}{\sqrt{2}} = \frac{4\sqrt{2}}{\sqrt{2}} - \frac{6\sqrt{2}}{\sqrt{2}} = 4 - 6 = -2$$

Example 4-6

$$\frac{3(2 - \sqrt{3})}{(2 - \sqrt{3})} = 3$$

The division of irrational decimals presents no new problems, since the process is like that for dividing rational decimals except that the quotients will be approximate values of the irrationals.

Example 4-7 Irrational divided by a rational

$$.272172117 \rightarrow \div 5 \approx .27217 \div 5 \approx .5444$$

The $\rightarrow$ is used to indicate the infinite nature of the irrational decimal.

Example 4–8

$$.656056005 \rightarrow \div .232132113 \rightarrow \approx .65605 \div 23213 \approx 2.8$$

POWERS

Roots and powers are merely methods of dividing and multiplying in situations where the factors are identical. They are also related to addition and subtraction just as are division and multiplication. Since extracting roots and raising to powers are rather unique operations, they are handled here in a separate treatment, although there is no implication that this material must or should be taught apart from the other operations. While traditionally these operations have been reserved for the secondary school, there is no sound basis for excluding them from elementary school, and many modern programs do include them there. Surely a sequential unfolding of the concepts involved is not only in order in the elementary school, but where such is given the shock of sudden exposure at the secondary level is averted.

The concept of powers and roots may enter the childs experience as soon as he knows that $1 \times 1 = 1$ or $2 \times 2 = 4$. This means then that the student in the intermediate grades is surely mature enough to handle powers and roots in a rather sophisticated manner. The basic notion with regard to powers begins with an integral base and integral exponent. The following sequence illustrates the concept.

$$2^1 = 2$$
$$2^2 = 2 \cdot 2 = 4$$
$$2^3 = 2 \cdot 2 \cdot 2 = 8$$
$$2^4 = 2 \cdot 2 \cdot 2 \cdot 2 = 16, \text{etc.}$$

In this illustration it is evident that the exponent tells how many times the base shall be used as a factor to produce the desired product. The student should recognize that in the example $2^5 = 32$, 2 is called the *base*, 5 is the exponent and 32 the product resulting from raising two to the 5th power. Another way of stating this equality is to say that 2 with the exponent 5 is equal to 32.

Younger children will usually be motivated by the subset of the whole numbers known as the perfect squares. These are the numbers which result from raising each successive whole number (beginning with zero) to the second power or to the square. The sequence to 10 follows:

$$0, 1, 4, 9, 16, 25, 36, 49, 64, 81, 100$$

These are not difficult since all but the last are products learned with the basic multiplication facts; i.e.,

$0 \times 0 = 0^2 = 0$	$3 \times 3 = 3^2 = 9$
$1 \times 1 = 1^2 = 1$	$4 \times 4 = 4^2 = 16$
$2 \times 2 = 2^2 = 4$	$5 \times 5 = 5^2 = 25$

$$6 \times 6 = 6^2 = 36 \qquad 8 \times 8 = 8^2 = 64$$
$$7 \times 7 = 7^2 = 49 \qquad 9 \times 9 = (9^2) = 81$$

From here the student will quickly move to the perfect cubes, perfect 4th powers, perfect 5th powers, etc. These are illustrated below for products less than 100:

Perfect cubes	Perfect 4th powers	Perfect 5th powers
$0 = 0 \cdot 0 \cdot 0 = 0^3$	$0 = 0 \cdot 0 \cdot 0 \cdot 0 = 0^4$	$0 = 0 \cdot 0 \cdot 0 \cdot 0 \cdot 0 = 0^5$
$1 = 1 \cdot 1 \cdot 1 = 1^3$	$1 = 1 \cdot 1 \cdot 1 \cdot 1 = 1^4$	$1 = 1 \cdot 1 \cdot 1 \cdot 1 \cdot 1 = 1^5$
$8 = 2 \cdot 2 \cdot 2 = 2^3$	$16 = 2 \cdot 2 \cdot 2 \cdot 2 = 2^4$	$32 = 2 \cdot 2 \cdot 2 \cdot 2 \cdot 2 = 2^5$
$27 = 3 \cdot 3 \cdot 3 = 3^3$	$81 = 3 \cdot 3 \cdot 3 \cdot 3 = 3^4$	
$64 = 4 \cdot 4 \cdot 4 = 4^3$		

This experience can be extended to products greater than 100 and powers greater than the 5th. Such flexibility allows for individual differences in the class.

We are now ready to generalize the power laws for integral bases and exponents. Specific examples accompany the laws. For every positive integer,

1. $A^n \cdot A^m = A^{n+m}$

   $2^3 \cdot 2^2 = 2 \cdot 2 \cdot 2 \cdot 2 \cdot 2 = 2^{3+2} = 2^5$

2. $\dfrac{A^n}{A^m} = A^{n-m}$

   $\dfrac{2^3}{2^2} = \dfrac{2 \cdot 2 \cdot 2}{2 \cdot 2} = 2^{3-2} = 2^1 = 2$

3. $(A^n)^m = A^{n \cdot m}$

   $(2^2)^3 = 2^2 \cdot 2^2 \cdot 2^2 = 2 \cdot 2 \cdot 2 \cdot 2 \cdot 2 \cdot 2 = 2^6$

These laws can now be extended to include nonintegral bases. For example.

1. $(2/3)^2 \cdot (2/3)^1 = 2/3 \cdot 2/3 \cdot 2/3 = (2/3)^{2+1} = (2/3)^3 = 8/27$

which is an application of $A^n \cdot A^m = A^{n+m}$

2. $\dfrac{(3/4)^3}{(3/4)^2} = \dfrac{3/4 \cdot 3/4 \cdot 3/4}{3/4 \cdot 3/4} = (3/4)^{3-2} = 3/4$

Which is an application of $A^n/A^m = A^{n-m}$

3. $[(2/5)^2]^3 = (2/5)^2 \cdot (2/5)^2 \cdot (2/5)^2 =$

   $2/5 \cdot 2/5 \cdot 2/5 \cdot 2/5 \cdot 2/5 \cdot 2/5 = (2/5)^6 = \dfrac{64}{15625}$

Which is an example of $(A^n)^m = A^{n \cdot m}$.

We are now prepared to extend our exponents to include zero and the negative integers. Let us set up a sequence of problems leading to these exponents:

$$
\begin{aligned}
2^4 &= 2 \cdot 2 \cdot 2 \cdot 2 = 16\\
2^3 &= 2 \cdot 2 \cdot 2 = 8\\
2^2 &= 2 \cdot 2 = 4\\
2^1 &= 2 = 2
\end{aligned}
$$

\- - - - - - - - - - - - - - - - - - - -

$$
\begin{aligned}
2^0 &= \text{no interpretation} = 1\\
2^{-1} &= \text{"} \quad \text{"} \quad \text{"} = 1/2 \text{ or } 1/2^1\\
2^{-2} &= \text{"} \quad \text{"} \quad \text{"} = 1/4 \text{ or } 1/2^2\\
2^{-3} &= \text{"} \quad \text{"} \quad \text{"} = 1/8 \text{ or } 1/2^3
\end{aligned}
$$

Note that the products above the dotted line come from previous experience and are varified. The results below the dotted line while having no interpretation in terms of factors do have products consistant with the sequence of problems. The exponent is decreasing by one and the products are decreasing by half of the preceding product.

From the above we can conclude (perhaps with further illustration) that for any $N > 0$; $N^0 = 1$ and for any $N > 0$ and any integral $n > 0; N^{-n} = 1/N^n$. At this point we should pause to illustrate that the basic power laws also hold for integral exponents $\leqslant 0$ and for any positive base.

Example 4-9

$$A^n \cdot A^m = A^{n+m}$$

$$2^2 \cdot 2^{-1} \cdot 2^0 = 2^{2+(-1)} \cdot 2^0 = 2^1 \cdot 2^0 = 2^{1+0} = 2^1 = 2$$

which is consistent with our interpretation of $2^{-1} = 1/2$ and $2^0 = 1$. Substituting these values in the original we get $2^2 \cdot 1/2 \cdot 1 = 4 \cdot 1/2 \cdot 1 = 2$ as obtained by using the power law.

Example 4-10

$$\frac{A^n}{A^m} = A^{n-m}$$

$$\frac{2^3 \cdot 2^0}{2^{-1}} = \frac{2^{3+0}}{2^{-1}} = \frac{2^3}{2^{-1}} = 2^{3-(-1)} = 2^{3+1} = 2^4 = 16$$

which is consistent with our interpretation of $2^0 = 1$ and $2^{-1} = 1/2^1$.

Substituting these values into the original, again we get

$$\frac{2^3 \cdot 1}{1/2^1} = \frac{8 \cdot 1}{1/2} = \frac{8/1}{1/2} = 16/1 = 16$$

consistent with the result obtained by means of the power law.

Example 4-11

$$(A^n)^m = A^{n \cdot m}$$
$$(2^0)^{-3} = 2^{0 \cdot (-3)} = 2^0 = 1$$

which is consistent with our interpretation of $2^0 = 1$ and $(2^0)^{-3} = \frac{1}{(2^0)^3}$. Substituting these values in the original we get:

$$(2^0)^{-3} = 1^{-3} = 1/1^3 = 1/1 = 1$$

again consistent with our previous result.

ROOTS

Let us look at the unique notation used by mathematicians to express roots:

The symbol for square root is $\sqrt{\ }$ or $\sqrt[2]{\ }$.
The symbol for cube root is $\sqrt[3]{\ }$.
The symbol for fourth root is $\sqrt[4]{\ }$.

From this point on the pattern is clear. The "overbar" — , called a *vinculum*, is used in conjunction with the root sign to indicate what we are taking the root of. For example, $\sqrt{16}$ or $\sqrt{16} + 25$. In the latter case we are taking the square root of the 16 only, not the 25, we therefore do not allow the vinculum to cover the 25.

We shall now explain what is meant by the root of a number, but first let it be clear that in this treatment we deal only with positive numbers for N.

$\sqrt{N}$ = one of two equal factors whose product is N
$\sqrt[3]{N}$ = one of three equal factors whose product is N
$\sqrt[4]{N}$ = one of four equal factors whose product is N

From here on the pattern is clear. We now illustrate with specific examples.

$$\sqrt{4} = \sqrt{2 \cdot 2} = 2; \quad \sqrt{9} = \sqrt{3 \cdot 3} = 3$$
$$\sqrt[3]{8} = \sqrt[3]{2 \cdot 2 \cdot 2} = 2; \quad \sqrt[3]{27} = \sqrt[3]{3 \cdot 3 \cdot 3} = 3$$
$$\sqrt[4]{16} = \sqrt[4]{2 \cdot 2 \cdot 2 \cdot 2} = 2; \quad \sqrt[4]{81} = \sqrt[4]{3 \cdot 3 \cdot 3 \cdot 3} = 3$$

The relationship of root and the corresponding power is

$$\sqrt{4} = 2 \quad \text{and} \quad 2^2 = 4$$

also

$$\sqrt[3]{8} = 2 \quad \text{and} \quad 2^3 = 8.$$

This leads to another law or axiom, which states that $\forall_{\substack{N \geq 0 \\ n > 1}}; (\sqrt[n]{N})^n = N$ which in words says that for any $N \geqslant 0$ and $n > 1$ the nth root of any number N

when raised to the nth power is N. Since we will deal only with positive N and positive n we will also concern ourselves only with positive roots, i.e. $\sqrt{4} = +2$ and $-\sqrt{4} = -2$. Even though positive 4 can be obtained by squaring (-2), we shall exclude this value because of the confusion which the dual interpretation may create.

It is interesting to note when examining the square roots of the successive integers that many of them are not integers nor even rational. That is, only the square roots of the perfect-square integers are rational, and all others are irrational:

$$\begin{array}{ll} \sqrt{0} = 0 & \sqrt{3} \approx 1.732 \\ \sqrt{1} = 1 & \sqrt{4} = 2 \\ \sqrt{2} \approx 1.414 & \sqrt{5} = 2.230 \end{array}$$

The approximate roots are actually infinite decimals and are irrational. Experiences similar to the above can be had with the successive cube roots, fourth roots, and so on.

We move now to three methods of extracting the square root of numbers, all of which have relevance in grades K–8. The algorism method which is treated in Chapter 10 is not nearly as popular as it was traditionally and is therefore treated as supplemental and enrichment in this text.

Prime Factor Method

From our previous discussion of roots, it can be seen that the factors (prime or otherwise) of perfect square numbers can occur in pairs of identical factors and, from our definition of square root, one of the pair is the square root of the product of the pair. Furthermore, since it can be shown that the square root of the product of two or more numbers is the same as the product of their square roots taken separately, we have then in the prime factor method a very understandable and practical means of extracting square root.

1. $\sqrt{36} = \sqrt{2 \cdot 2 \cdot 3 \cdot 3} = 2 \cdot 3 = 6$
2. $\sqrt{144} = \sqrt{2 \cdot 2 \cdot 2 \cdot 2 \cdot 3 \cdot 3} = 2 \cdot 2 \cdot 3 = 12$
3. $\sqrt{176400} = \sqrt{2 \cdot 2 \cdot 2 \cdot 2 \cdot 3 \cdot 3 \cdot 5 \cdot 5 \cdot 7 \cdot 7} = 2 \cdot 2 \cdot 3 \cdot 5 \cdot 7 = 420$

Note that in the perfect square numbers the factors always occur in pairs of identical factors and we need only take one of each pair into our final set of factors to produce the square root. It can be observed that if the original number is not a perfect square an approximation can often be obtained if the student has available the square roots of some of the smaller nonperfect square whole numbers. For example:

$$\sqrt{288} = \sqrt{2 \cdot 2 \cdot 2 \cdot 2 \cdot 2 \cdot 3 \cdot 3} = 2 \cdot 2 \cdot 3 \cdot \sqrt{2} \approx 16.968$$

providing the child knows that $\sqrt{2} \approx 1.414$. This method is also applicable to cube root, fourth root, etc., if we remember that for perfect cubes the prime factors will occur in groups of three identical factors and that for perfect fourth powers in groups of four identical factors and so on.

$$\sqrt[3]{216} = \sqrt{2 \cdot 2 \cdot 2 \cdot 3 \cdot 3 \cdot 3} = 2 \cdot 3 = 6$$

The Successive Mean Method

This method is based on the fact that if we estimate the square root of a number and then divide by this estimate we will get a quotient equal to our divisor, and thus have the square root, or we will get some number different than our estimate and the square root will lie between the two. By averaging those two numbers and using this mean as our new divisor we can then by successive applications close in on the square root. To illustrate, let us find the square root of 144. Suppose we estimate the square root to be 10.

$$\begin{array}{r} 14 \\ 10\,\overline{)\,144} \\ \underline{10} \\ 44 \\ \underline{40} \\ 4 \end{array}$$

Obviously we did not estimate correctly so let us average 10 and 14 which gives us $\frac{10 + 14}{2} = \frac{24}{2} = 12$. We now divide 144 by 12 and find we have the square root.

Note that we obtained our correct root with only averaging once. In many cases this will not occur and we will perhaps need to repeat the process many times. Note also that in our first division we ignored the remainder. This can be done whenever the original number is a perfect square. In other cases it is desirable to carry one, two, or even more decimals into the averaging and continue the averaging process until we have the desired accuracy. For example, in finding the $\sqrt{288}$, suppose we estimate 15.

$$\frac{288}{15} = 19.2; \quad \frac{15 + 19.2}{2} = 17.1$$

$$\frac{288}{17.1} \approx 16.84; \quad \frac{17.1 + 16.84}{2} = 16.97$$

$$\frac{288}{16.97} \approx 16.97$$

Our result is now accurate to two decimal places.

It should be pointed out to students that the initial estimate is not critical to the success of the method. A poor guess may or may not increase the number of steps. It is helpful to the student if he is told initially whether or not the number is a perfect square since this will guide him in deciding whether to ignore remainders.

Algorism Method

The logic of this method is not readily discernable by elementary students. The process and explanation of why it works can be found in Chapter 10.

Fractional Exponents

In order to correlate our roots and powers more closely we now introduce a unit fraction notation for roots; i.e.,

$\sqrt{N}$ may be written $N^{1/2}$
$\sqrt[3]{N}$ may be written $N^{1/3}$
$\sqrt[4]{N}$ may be written $N^{1/4}$

The pattern is now clear. We can combine our powers and roots in the form of fractional exponents. $8^{2/3}$ is interpreted to mean $(\sqrt[3]{8})^2$ or $(8^{1/3})^2$. Note that this is all consistent as far as basic meanings and the power laws are concerned; i.e., $(8^{1/3})^2 = 8^{1/3 \cdot 2} = 8^{2/3}$, and since $8^{1/3} = 2$ then $(2)^2 = 4$ and when using the notation $(\sqrt[3]{8})^2$ we get $\sqrt[3]{8} = 2$ and $(2)^2$ is 4.

We are now in a position to involve negative powers and test the validity of our new notation.

Example 4–12

$$(16)^{-3/4} = \frac{1}{(16)^{3/4}} = \frac{1}{2^3} = \frac{1}{8}$$

Let us also evaluate $(16)^{-1/4}$, which means

$$\frac{1}{(16)^{1/4}} = \frac{1}{\sqrt[4]{16}} = \frac{1}{2}$$

We will now multiply $(16)^{-3/4} \cdot (16)^{-1/4}$. By means of the power law this becomes $(16)^{(-3/4)+(-1/4)} = (16)^{-1} = 1/16$. This checks with our previous results where $(16)^{(-3/4)} = 1/8$ and $(16)^{-1/4} = 1/2$ and $1/8 \cdot 1/2 = 1/16$.

We now have the combined strength of positive, negative, zero, and integral exponents as well as positive and negative fractional exponents at our disposal, and have developed several consistent and convenient relationships between roots and powers, all of which obey the basic power laws.

UNION AND INTERSECTION OF SETS

In the early stages of our addition section we mentioned that sets could be used to teach the foundations for addition. This actually involved the union of two disjoint sets. Let us develop set theory more thoroughly at this stage and discuss in particular the two operations known as *union* and *intersection of sets*. Two sets are said to be *disjoint* when they have no elements in common. Little difficulty is encountered here when using concrete elements, since the student can observe that the elements are discrete. For example, if we have two sets one of which contains a toy rabbit, a toy dog, and toy cat and the other contains a toy rabbit, a toy horse, and a toy pig, the children will recognize that the two rabbits are two distinct toys. However, should we shift to letters representing the animals, it is no longer entirely clear to the children that the two *R*'s are distinct, as shown in the sketch.

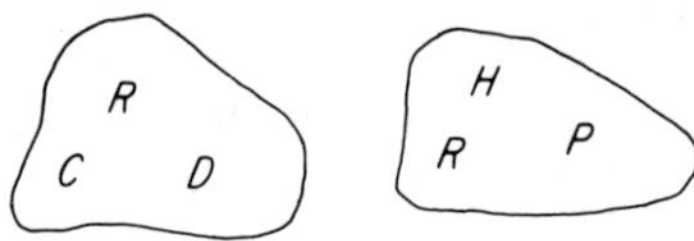

Children at the primary-grade level should be exposed only to disjoint sets in order to avoid confusion. Later children should be helped to see that we must clarify whether or not like element occurring in two different sets are the same or different elements. It should also be made clear that two cats or two "2's" occurring in the same set are always discrete elements. We often indicate this discreteness by using different subscripts on the like elements. For example, if we have two sets containing abstract elements such as numbers we use the subscripts as shown in the sketch.

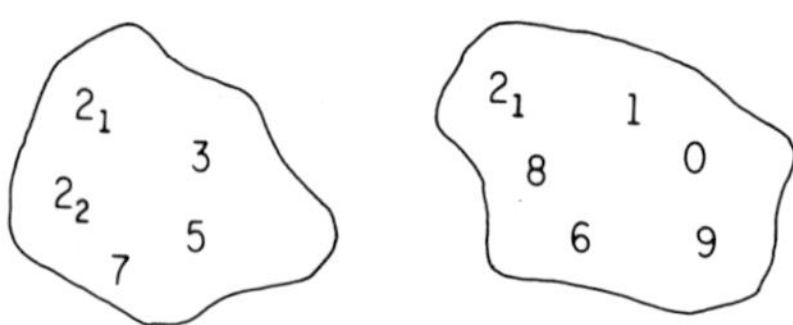

Since the 2's here are nondenominate, the 2_1's in the two sets refer to the same 2 while the 2_2 occurring in the first set is discrete from the 2_1.

UNION OF SETS

We now examine the operation called *the union of sets*. The union of two sets consists of all the discrete elements belonging to either set.

Example 4–13 (disjoint sets)

Set *A* Set *B* Union of set *A* and set *B*

R, P, C, D ∪ H, E, M = R, P, C, D, H, M, E

The union of sets A and B is written $A \cup B$

Example 4–14

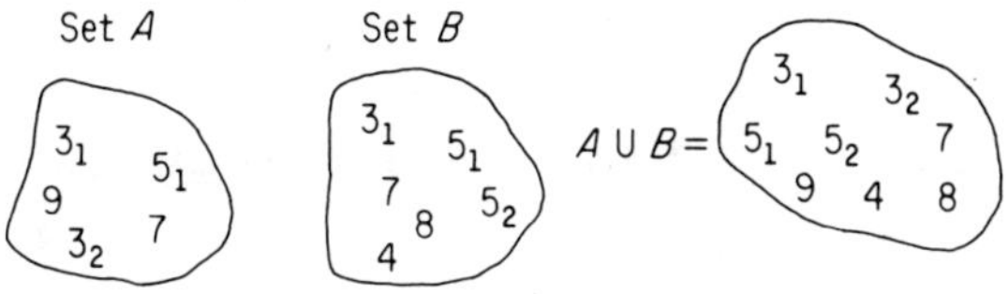

Set A: 3_1 5_1 9 3_2 7

Set B: 3_1 5_1 7 8 5_2 4

$A \cup B =$ 3_1 3_2 5_1 5_2 7 9 4 8

Example 4–15

In this example we will use the braces to represent the sets instead of the clouds. This transition should probably be made in the 4th grade.

$$\text{Set } A = \{A_1, A_2, B, F, M\}$$
$$\text{Set } B = \{B, F, R, W_1, W_2\}$$
$$A \cup B = \{A_1\ A_2\ B, F, M, R, W_1, W_2\}$$

Note that indentical elements occur only once in the union.

Nonmathematical situations may also be used to illustrate union. Suppose set A represents all students in Miss Jones room who take private music lessons and set B represents all students in the room who are scouts:

A = {Joe, Mary, Jane, Sue, John}

B = {John, Pete, Joe, Mary, Bill, Edward}

$A \cup B$ = {Joe, John, Mary, Jane, Sue, Bill, Edward, Pete}

The idea of subscripts may be illustrated here in case there were two John's in the room and the John appearing in set A is different than the John appearing in set B. We could then call them John_1 and John_2 and both would appear in the union.

INTERSECTION OF SETS

With the background we have developed above we can now handle the operation called *intersection of sets*. The intersection of two sets consists of all elements common to both sets. The intersection of set A and set B is written $A \cap B$. Illustrations follow:

Example 4–16

Using the same sets used in example #1 of union,

$A \cap B = \{\ \}$ the empty set since there are no elements which are common to sets A and B

Example 4–17

Using the same sets used in Example 4–14,

$$A \cap B = \{3_1, 5_1, 7\}$$

Example 4–18

Using the same sets used in Example 4–15,

$$A \cap B = \{B, F\}$$

Example 4–19

Using the same sets of children from Miss Jones' room as used in union,

$$A \cap B = \{\text{Joe, Mary, John}\}$$

VENN DIAGRAMS

Venn diagrams may be used to represent sets, master set[1], and union and intersection of sets. This diagram was named after the logician John Venn (1834–1923), who also utilized Euler's circles as part of his diagram. Euler was also a noted mathematician.

The Venn diagram consists of circles inside a rectangle. The rectangle represents the master set while the circles represents subsets of the master set. Illustrations follow:

Example 4–20

Using sets *A* and *B* from example #1 for union and intersection

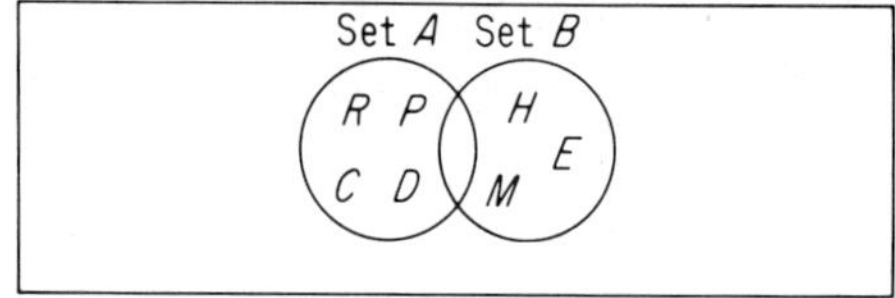

$$A \cup B = \{R, P, C, D, H, M, E\}$$
$$A \cap B = \{\ \}$$

If these letters represent animals (rabbit, dog, pig, cow, horse, elephant, mouse) then the master set could be all animals and all other animals such as bear, wolf, etc. would be in the rectangle but not in the circles.

Example 4–21

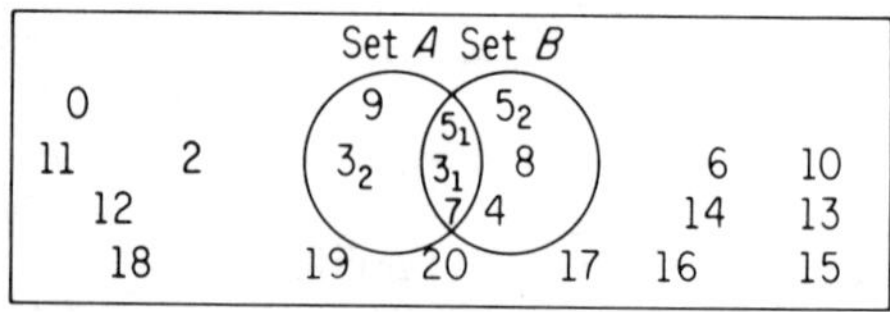

The master set here might consist of the whole numbers less than or equal to 20. Those not in the circles would then show in the rectangle. It would also be necessary in this particular case to recognize that the master set contains as many of

[1] *Master set* is often used instead of *universal set*.

each number as we need. Note in this case we used two different 3's and two different 5's.

$$A \cup B = \{3_1, 3_2, 5_1, 5_2, 4, 7, 8, 9\} \qquad A \cap B = \{3_1, 5_1, 7\}$$

Example 4–22

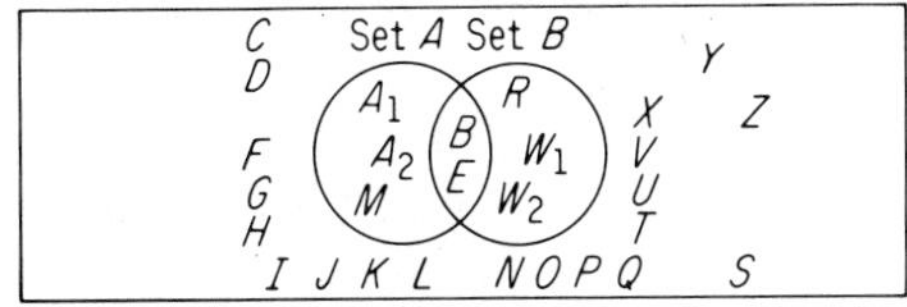

The master set here might contain all the letters of the alphabet with as many of each letter as we wish

$$A \cup B = \{A_1, A_2, B, M, E, R, W_1, W_2\}$$
$$A \cap B = \{B, E\}$$

Example 4–23

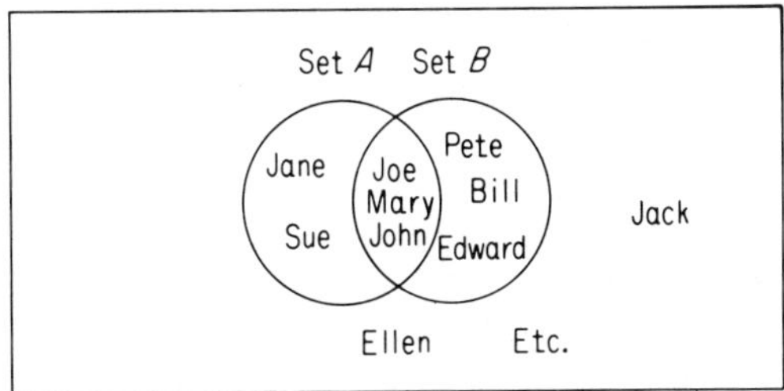

Master set consists of all children in Miss Jones' room.

$$A \cup B = \{\text{Jane, Sue, Joe, Mary, Bill, John, Pete, Edward}\}$$
$$A \cap B = \{\text{Joe, Mary, John}\}$$

The Venn diagram is not limited to two subsets or circles. Many challenging situations involving three or more subsets may be devised for the gifted students who need supplemental work.

USING UNION AND INTERSECTION TO FIND LCM AND G.C.D.

These operations may be used to find the least common multiple and greatest common divisor of two or more whole numbers. Let us first illustrate the least common multiple. We will use the two numbers 12 and 18. We first factor these into their prime factors:

$$12 = 2 \cdot 2 \cdot 3$$
$$18 = 2 \cdot 3 \cdot 3$$

We now form set A and set B using the first set of factors and second set of factors respectively:

$$A = \{2_1, 2_2, 3_1\}$$
$$B = \{2_1, 3_1, 3_2\}$$

Note these were different 2's, hence the subscripts, also different 3's in set B.

$$A \cup B = \{2_1, 2_2, 3_1, 3_2\}$$

Note that we use only the discrete elements. We now form a product using the elements of the union set. This becomes

$$\text{L.C.M.} = 2 \cdot 2 \cdot 3 \cdot 3 = 36$$

This method of finding an L.C.M. was adapted to finding the L.C.D. in our treatment of fractions.

We now find the intersection of A and B.

$$A \cap B = \{2_1, 3_1\}$$

Using the elements for a product we get the G.C.D.:

$$\text{G.C.D.} = 2 \cdot 3 = 6$$

The G.C.D. is used for finding the simplest name for fractions and in other mathematical situations.

Throughout this chapter we have discussed many facts concerning zero. These have been interspersed among the operations and since zero is such as important number and so often misunderstood we bring this chapter to a close by summarizing the basic facts concerning zero.

ESSENTIAL FACTS INVOLVING ZERO

1. $\{\ \}$; zero is the cardinal number which describes the empty set.
2. $\{0\}$; the set containing zero is described by the cardinal number one.
3. $N + 0 = N$; zero as the identity element of addition.
4. $N \cdot 0 = 0$; the multiplicative law of zero.
5. $\frac{0}{0}$ is undefined, since every element of the universe checks.
6. $\frac{N}{0}$ where $N \neq 0$ is undefined, since no element of the universe checks.
7. Zero is a point on the number line.
8. Zero is a digit.
9. Zero is an element of the set of integers.
10. Zero is the first element of the ordered set of whole numbers.
11. Zero is not an element of the set of positive integers.
12. Zero is not an element of the set of negative integers.

13. Zero is an element of the set of nonnegative integers.
14. Zero is generally considered as not being an element of the counting numbers.
15. The sum of any positive number and its opposite is zero; $N + (-N) = 0$
16. $N^0 = 1, N \neq 0$
17. Zero is an even integer.
18. The expression $\frac{9}{2x - 6}$ is undefined for $x = 3$ because of (6).
19. Zero is not essential to a useful numeration system, a blank would do as well. Its value is as a concept and not as a symbol.
20. Zero is a placeholder only in the sense that any other digit is a placeholder. This relates closely to (1).
21. The major impact of the invention of zero was not necessarily its use in numeration (it is of course convenient there) but its greatest contribution came in providing and clarifying the concepts contained in this list.
22. Zero is neither prime nor composite.
23. The set of nonnegative nonpositive integers contains only the number zero.
24. The reciprocal law $a \cdot \frac{1}{a} = 1$ does not hold when $a = 0$.
25. The axiom, if $a \cdot c = b \cdot c$, then $a = b$, does not hold when $c = 0$.
26. To say that zero means nothing in mathematics is dangerous, since it has this meaning only when naming the empty set.

PROBLEMS

1. Show how you would help a fifth-grader learn an addition fact with which he has had consistent difficulty. Emphasize a variety of experiences conventional and modern. Use 8 + 9 as the fact.

2. Use cloud sets and the number line to show how you would help a third-grader learn that 3 + 4 = 7.

3. State and illustrate the following addition axioms:

(a) Commutative axiom of addition
(b) Associative axiom of addition
(c) Additive axiom of zero

4. Explain in detail the algorism for adding 347 and 256.

5. Beginning with positive addends, develop a pattern of problems leading to $(-3) + (-2) = (-5)$.

6. State how you would help a child answer problems such as the following:

(a) What number is 6 units smaller than (+2)?
(b) Which number is the larger (−7) or (−2)?
(c) What number must be added to (−5) to produce zero?
(d) How can we describe in a meaningful way what is meant by $a\,(-3)$?

(e) What is the absolute of $(-a)$ if a itself is negative? This question could be written: Find $|-a|$ when a itself is negative.

7. Show by diagram how a fifth-grader might visualize the addition of 3/8 and 3/4. Now do this same problem using the prime factors for finding the L.C.D.

8. By means of the place-value chart, explain the algorism for adding .654 and .2798.

9. Add the following:

(a) 3□ + 5□ =

(b) 2□ + 3△ + 7□ + △ =

(c) 5△ + 4□ + 7△ =

(d) 2□ + 3△ + 5.
 4□ + 2△ + 3.

10. Illustrate with cloud sets and also by the number line how you would help a third-grader understand 7 − 3 = 4.

11. What relation exists between addition and subtraction? Does this lead to a mathematical definition of subtraction? State such a definition.

12. Set up a pattern of problems leading to (−3) − (−4) = +1.

13. Use every device, old and new, that you can think of to help a sixth-grader learn the multiplication fact 8 × 9 = 72. If he has not learned this fact it may indicate a psychological block. Direct your efforts at overcoming such a difficulty.

14. Set up a basic multiplication chart zero through nine and cross out the facts on the chart which the child should have learned from the following sources:

(a) The multiplicative axiom of zero

(b) The multiplicative axiom of one

(c) Duplications resulting from the commutative axiom of multiplication.

Now show how the remaining facts may be built from the trivial ones by applying the distributive axiom, the associative axiom, or primes.

15. Explain in detail the algorism for multiplying 128 by 64.

16. Present a logical development for showing a fifth-grade student two ways of taking one-half of a fraction. Verify this by means of a diagram.

17. Show by a pattern of problems the logic behind (−3) × (−2) = 6. (Assume a knowledge of how to multiply a positive element by a negative element.)

18. Explain in detail the algorism involved in multiplying .541 by .68.

19. Using expanded notation and polynomial theory, multiply 64 by 37. Now show how you would convince a sixth-grade child that the cross-products must be involved.

20. By means of cloud sets and the number line, illustrate the problem 15 ÷ 5 = 3.

21. Use the modified algorism and show in detail how to divide 1824 by 12.

22. Define division in terms of multiplication.

23. What basic ideas should a student have concerning:

(a) The relation between addition and subtraction
(b) The relation between multiplication and division
(c) The relation between addition and multiplication
(d) The relation between multiplication and subtraction
(e) The relation between division and subtraction

24. Set up a pattern of problems leading to $(-15) \div (-3) = (+5)$. (Assume a knowledge that a positive element divided by a negative element produces a negative quotient.)

25. Show how the multiplicative axiom of one enters into the division of a monomial by a monomial.

26. Indicate the dangers involved in teaching elementary students to cancel. (Use a polynomial divided by a monomial.)

27. Show how a thorough understanding of the distributive axiom might prevent abuse of the cancelation principle.

28. Illustrate the division of polynomials by using expanded notation to do the problem $952 \div 28 = 34$.

29. Explain power notation as an abbreviated form for writing the product of two or more equal factors.

30. Illustrate the basic power laws by using specific examples.

31. Set up a series of problems, beginning with 3^4, which will show the logic of interpreting $3^0 = 1$ and $3^{-1} = 1/3^1$, etc.

32. In the true statement $\frac{2^0 \cdot 2^2}{2^3} = \frac{1}{2}$ use the power laws to show the consistency of $2^0 = 1$ and $2^{-1} = 1/2^1$.

33. It is true that for all positive exponents greater than or equal to one the exponent tells how many times the base is to be used as a factor in the product? Consider only integral exponents.

34. Is it true that the cube root of a number is one of three equal factors which produces the number?

35. Write the perfect cube integers up to 1,000.

36. Is it true that for all positive N the $\sqrt{N}$ is a positive number whose square in N?

37. Find $\sqrt{592900}$ using each of the three methods taught in this chapter.

38. Is it true that $-\sqrt{36} = -6$?

39. Construct a segment equal to $\sqrt{3}$.

40. What interpretation should be given to $9^{3/2}$?

41. How might a teacher use the union of two disjoint sets to teach addition to a first-grade student?

42. Draw a Venn diagram to represent the following problem:

Let U = the set of all presidents of the United States to date.

Set A = all presidents who were past 50 years of age at the time of election.

Set B = all presidents who were single at the time of election.

Set C = all presidents who served more than one full term.

Show all presidents who were past age 50 at election, who were single, and who served more than one full term.

43. Find the least common multiple for 24 and 56, using the union of sets of the prime factors of the numbers.

44. State the essential facts which a sixth-grade student should know about zero.

45. Show in detail why division by zero is undefined. Consider both cases.

Chapter 5

Relations Within and Among Sets

THE SYMBOLISM OF RELATIONS

Much of mathematics is concerned with relations among sets. Children's early experience requires a basic understanding of this concept. John speaks of having more marbles than Joe, Mary says she is younger than Susan, Martha says she and Betty are the same height. From these early associations children should go on toward a more complete understanding of the basic relations of mathematics as well as their counterpart in nonmathematical situations. Let us now identify some of the common mathematical relations and introduce a simple symbolic system for writing them. We shall concern ourselves with the following relations:

1. Is equal to (=)
2. Is not equal to ($\neq$)
3. Is greater than ($>$)
4. Is not greater than ($\not>$)
5. Is less than ($<$)
6. Is not less than ($\not<$)
7. Is paralled to ($\|$)
8. Is perpendicular to ($\perp$)
9. Is congruent to ($\cong$)
10. Is approximately equal to ($\approx$)
11. Is a subset of ($\subset$)
12. Is a superset of ($\supset$)
13. Is greater than or equal to ($\geqslant$)
14. Is not greater than or equal to ($\not\geqslant$)
15. Is less than or equal to ($\leqslant$)
16. Is not less than or equal to ($\not\leqslant$)

DEVICES FOR TEACHING RELATIONS

Many of the modern elementary texts are utilizing what they call "number machines," "function machines," "what's my rule," etc., as devices and games designed to help students discover relationships among numbers. While these are usually motivating to students and encourage creativity, teachers should be careful to limit the time devoted to them, since they surely cannot teach all that is to be known in mathematics. We shall not attempt here to glamorize this area but merely to utilize the idea for what it can and should do.

Example 5-1

□	Δ
0	2
1	4
2	6
3	8
4	?
5	12

The relation here is $\Delta = 2\,\square + 2$

One way to invite discovery is to ask children to find "?". In this case this may not reveal the relation, however, since the student could get the 10 by observing the Δ values only.

Example 5-2

□	Δ
0	0
1	3
2	8
3	15
4	24

This one could be used after studying exponents. The relation is $\Delta = \square^2 + 2\square$.

Obviously the possibilities for using this device are unlimited. Note that the young student is generally dependent upon observation for finding the relation. There are systematic ways of finding these relations. Some of these are discussed later in this chapter.

PROPERTIES OF A RELATION

Let us proceed to a general discussion of relations. For convenience, we consider R as referring to any relation whatsoever, including any of those in the previous list. If we choose for the moment to let R stand for the relation "is equal to," we could write xRy, meaning "x is equal to y, or $x = y$." This use of R gives us a precise and brief way of expressing any relation. Now any relation may be tested for certain properties which reveal the nature of the relation. Let us examine these properties.

1. A relation is said to be *reflexive* in a set P if for every element x of P, xRx is true. For example, if R stands for $>$, then xRx is not true and R is not a reflexive relation.
2. A relation is said to be *symmetric* if, when xRy is true, reversing the

elements involved to read yRx does not, destroy its truthfulness. Equality is symmetric since if $x = y$, then $y = x$.

3. A relation is said to be *transitive* if when xRy and yRz are both true then xRz is true. The relation "is greater than" is transitive, since if $6 > 5$ and $5 > 3$ then $6 > 3$.
4. A relation is said to be *asymmetric* if reversing the order of the sets in the relation produces the opposite or inverse relation. For example, if $P > Q$ then $Q < P$.

Some of the most significant relations in the mathematics are those that are both symmetric and transitive and those which are assymmetric and transitive. If a relation R is reflexive, symmetric, and transitive it is called an *equivalence relation*. In the accompanying table many relations previously listed, as well as some nonmathematical relations, have been analyzed under the four properties just discussed. The reader should verify each analysis in terms of some concrete examples.

Relation	Reflexitivity	Symmetry	Transitivity	Assymetry
$\supset$	Yes	No	Yes	Yes
$\subset$	Yes	No	Yes	Yes
$=$	Yes	Yes	Yes	No
$\neq$	No	Yes	No	No
$>$	No	No	Yes	Yes
$\ngtr$	Yes	No	Yes	Yes
$<$	No	No	Yes	Yes
$\nless$	Yes	No	Yes	Yes
$\parallel$	No	Yes	Yes	No
$\perp$	No	Yes	No	No
$\cong$	Yes	Yes	Yes	No
$\approx$ "is approximately equal to"	No	Yes	No	No
"is a descendant of"	No	No	Yes	Yes
"is a brother of"	No	No	Yes	No
"is part of"	Yes	No	Yes	No
"is the complement of"*	No	Yes	Yes	No

*Refers to complementary angles.

The reader in verifying the above should recognize that the property must hold generally and not just for special cases. One exception is sufficient to exclude the property.

RELATIONS WITHIN SETS

Let us now look briefly at some sets which have a relation built in. Generally speaking, these relations describe or define the set. Among such relations are the following:

1. The successive positive integers
2. The successive even positive integers
3. The successive odd positive integers
4. The prime numbers
5. The exact multiples of an integer (multiples of five: 5, 10, 15, 20, 25, etc.)
6. The integral powers of an integer: $2^1, 2^2, 2^3, 2^4, 2^5$, etc.
7. A set of equivalent rational numbers:

$$\frac{1}{2} = \frac{2}{4} = \frac{3}{6} = \frac{4}{8} = \frac{5}{10} = \frac{6}{12} = \frac{7}{14} = \frac{8}{16} = \frac{9}{18}, \text{ etc.}$$

These simple sets exhibiting relations within themselves should be exploited for their value in understanding mathematical concepts. This was done to some extent in Chapter IV, but let us extend it here.

The first three of our list deserve attention at the primary-grade level and should be later generalized to recognize that the successor to any integer n is $(n + 1)$; that the even numbers may be represented by $(n + 2)$, where n is even and the odd numbers by $(n + 2)$, where n is odd. The primes are not easily generalized. It can be proven that 2 is the only even prime and all other primes are of the form $4n + 1$ or $4n + 3$, but no formula has as yet been found which will always produce a prime. Here then we find a very important number set in which the relation between successive elements has so far eluded mathematicians. There is, however, a tremendous body of mathematics related to prime numbers and developed by such great mathematicians as Fermat, Euler, Gauss, and Eratosthenes, phases of which are of interest of students at practically all grade levels. In fact, Eratosthenes' sieve might be utilized by primary children. The reader is referred to the *Twenty-fourth Yearbook of National Council of Teachers of Mathematics*, page 297, and Oystein Ore, *Number Theory and Its History* (New York: McGraw-Hill, 1948), Chapter 4.

In a like manner the integral powers of an integer can be exploited in many ways including their application in number bases for numeration systems as discussed in Chapter 4.

Let us now look at a set of equivalent rational numbers. This set technically contains only one element expressed in an infinite number of forms. It may also be thought of as a set of equivalent ordered pairs. This set enters into the work on fractions, ratios, proportions, etc.

Technically speaking, a relation R defined on a set of elements is an equivalence relation if, for any elements a, b, and c in the set, the reflexive, symmetric, and transitive principles hold. Furthermore, if for every a and b in the set, aRb, then the elements of the set constitute an equivalence class.

SPECIAL RELATIONS

We now move to special kinds of relations known as equations, inequalities, identities, ratios and proportions. In order to understand these concepts, let us develop carefully the ideas involved in their definition. The statement "Descartes was a great mathematician" is a true statement. If we should place a question mark or a blank in place of Descartes we would have an open sentence which is neither true or false. Now there are many great mathematicians whose names would make the sentence true, but we could also select names of persons who were not great mathematicians which would make the sentence false. The set of all names from which we can make a selection is known as the *universal set*, written **U**; and the subset of names which make the sentence true constitutes the domain for this particular relation. Let us now consider some mathematical sentences which are open (that is, have nonspecified element in them). The inequality $x + 3 > 5$ is such a sentence. For convenience, let us here limit our universal set to the natural numbers. The nonspecified elements may now be any natural number greater than 2. This set is known as the *range* of the nonspecified element, since each element in this set makes the sentence true. This set is also known as the *solution set.* The natural numbers 1 and 2 constitute all of the elements of the universal set which make the sentence false. This set is known as the *relative complement set* or *complement set.*

Let us discuss another example but one that is somewhat different in that the sentence contains two variables. The formula for the perimeter of a square, $P = 4S$, is such a sentence. We will take the rational numbers as our universal set for this example. If we entertain the limit case of a square having its sides equal to zero units, we can conclude that the range for S (the independent variable) will now be the nonnegative rational numbers. Likewise the domain for P (the dependent variable) is also the nonnegative rational numbers. The ordered pairs (S,P), i.e., $(1,4)$ $(^1/_2,2)$ $(^3/_4,2^2/_5)$ etc. which make the sentence true is the solution set of the sentence. It should be noted that this is an infinite set of ordered pairs. All other ordered pairs (those that make the sentence false) comprise the relative complement set. The original open sentences $x + 3 > 5$ and $P = 4S$ are known as the *set selectors*, since they select from **U** only those elements which make the sentence true.

Consider one further example to illustrate these ideas. Take the open sentence or set selector $x + 6 = 2$. If our universal set consists of the integers then (-4) comprises the solution set. This set consists of only one element, and may be written $\{-4\}$. The relative complement set consists of all the integers greater than or less than (-4). It may be written $\{x/x \gtrless -4\}$, read, "the set of all x such that x is greater than or less than a negative 4." Note now that if we had limited our universal set to the natural numbers there would be no element in the **U** set which would make the sentence true and the solution set would then be empty.

A unique relation involves what is called an *identity*. An identity is a relation in which any element of the universal set for which both the right- and left-hand members of the relation are defined makes the relation true. An example will serve to clarify the idea. Consider the equations

1. $3\square - 5 = 13$
2. $\square \cdot (2 + 5) = 2\square + 5\square$
3. $\dfrac{\square^2 - 5\square + 6}{(\square - 2)} = \dfrac{(\square - 7)(\square - 3)}{(\square - 7)}$

The first equation is satisfied only by $\square = 6$; that is, the only value of the non-specified element which makes the sentence true is 6.

The second equation is satisfied by any element of the universal set. The third equation is satisfied by any element of the universal set of which the right- and left-hand members are defined. Note that the left-hand member is not defined when $\square = 2$ and the right member is not defined for $\square = 7$, since in both cases the result is division by zero. Both equations 2 and 3 are called *identities.* In fact 2 above will be recognized as an example of the distributive axiom. All axioms are identities within their universe.

The idea of an identity is useful in solving certain equations where one member can be transformed to an equivalent form. For example, $\square^2 - 9 = 0$. may be transformed to $(\square - 3)(\square + 3) = 0$; which is now easily solved.

We will now consider a relation known as *ratio*. If we wish to do so, we can set up any relationship we desire between elements of number pairs. When we take the ordered pair (a,b) and designate R as division of the first element by the second (instead of identifying the notation as a division problem or a fraction), we often identify it as a ratio. We can define a ratio as a set of equivalent ordered pairs (a,b), $b \neq 0$. Now this concept of ratio, while not unlike a sophisticated concept of a fraction, has some uses which are not generally thought of as being associated with fractions. For example, if there are 60 students in one group and 20 students in another, the ratio of the number of students in the first group to the number in the second group is 60/20 or 3 to 1. In expressing the ratio of denominate numbers we must always be certain that each element of the ordered pair is expressed in the same unit. For example, the ratio of a foot to a yard is 1/3, or 1 to 3. It can be seen from the above that in finding the ratio of one number to another we merely choose the simplest member of the set of equivalent ordered pairs.

Any identity may be thought of as a proportion. We can therefore test an expression to determine if it is a proportion in the same way that we test an equation to determine if it is an identity. That is, we can convert both the right- and left-hand members of the equation or inequality to equivalent fractions having the same denominators. If the numerators thus obtained are alike, the original was a proportion. This process can often be expedited by finding the simplest name for both members of the original before converting to equivalent fractions having the same denominators.

Let us now generalize the above experience. If we write the generalized proportion $\frac{a}{b} = \frac{c}{d}$, a and d are called the *extremes*, and b and c are called the *means*. These terms likely come from the older notation in which the above proportion was written in one line using a (:) and would appear as

$$\overbrace{a : \underbrace{b = c}_{\text{means}} : d}^{\text{extremes}}.$$

Here the lines indicate the means and extremes. Going back to the more popular $\frac{a}{b} = \frac{c}{d}$, if we multiply both members of the proportion by $(b \cdot d)$ we get: $\not{b}\, d \frac{a}{\not{b}} = \frac{c}{\not{d}} b\, \not{d}$ or $(a \cdot d) = (b \cdot c)$. It can be observed now that $(a \cdot d)$ is the product of the extremes and $(b \cdot c)$ is the product of the means. We can conclude therefore that in any proportion the product of the means must equal the product of the extremes. Not only does this give us another method of checking to determine whether an expression is a proportion but it assists us in solving for nonspecified elements in conditional proportions as we shall see later.

As can be observed in previous examples, the numbers in ratios involved in conditional proportions may contain nonspecified elements. If all elements of the universal set verifies the proportion when substituted for the nonspecified element, then we have an identity and there is no question about the validity of the proportion. For example: $\frac{2x}{12} = \frac{x}{6}$. If, however, the expression contains one nonspecified element but cannot be verified generally, it is classified as a *conditional proportion*, and a solution set can be found which will contain all of the elements capable of making the original a proportion. For example, in $\frac{3x}{5} = \frac{9}{10}$, if $x = 1^1/_2$ then $\frac{(3 \cdot 1^1/_2)}{5} = \frac{9}{10}$; $\frac{4^1/_2}{5} = \frac{9}{10}$; $45 = 45$, and the conditional proportion becomes a proportion. Obviously we can solve these conditional proportions just as we did fractional equations, or we may apply our shortcut of equating the product of the means and extremes in the proportion.

Using this last technique on the equation used in our previous illustration, we proceed as follows:

$$3x \cdot 10 = 45, 30x = 45, x = 1^1/_2$$

The type of proportions which we have been discussing to this point may have resulted from direct relationships and thus produced direct proportions. For example, in a basketball game John scored two points for every three points scored by Jack. If Jack scored thirty points, how many points did John score? Note here that the ratio of John's points to Jack's points is 2 : 3. The proportion thus becomes $\frac{x}{30} = \frac{2}{3}$, where x represents John's points. Note here that as Jack's points increase, so also do John's.

There is a second type of proportion called *inverse*. Let us illustrate the second type. If we have 120 marbles to divide equally among ten boys, this would allow 12 marbles per boy, but if we increase the number of boys to 15 the number of marbles each will receive would now be only 8. That is, $\frac{10}{15} = \frac{8}{12}$, or the number of boys in the first instance is to the number of boys in the second instance, as the number of marbles each will receive in the second instance is to the number each will receive in the first. We say then that the number of marbles each boy will receive vaires inversely as the number of boys receiving the marbles. In table form the data appear like this.

Number of boys receiving an equal number of marbles	*Number of marbles received by each boy*
10	12
15	8

Problems involving inverse proportions are very common in our daily lives. The faster we walk the less time it takes us to reach our destination; the greater the distance of a satellite from the earth the less the pull of the earth's gravitation upon it; the higher the unit price of an item the fewer items we can purchase with a given sum of money.

DIRECT AND INVERSE VARIATION

When we study first-degree equations involving two nonspecified elements we find an infinite number of ordered pairs satisfying each such equation. For example, the formula for the perimeter of an equilateral triangle $P = 3S$ is such an equation and upon substituting ever-increasing values for S into this equation we note that each successive value of P increase. A few of the infinite number of ordered pairs which satisfy this formula are shown in the table.

When S	0	1	3	4	8
When P	0	3	9	12	24

This type of relation between P and S is called *direct variation*, or we say that P varies directly as S.

In the equation $x = \frac{10}{y}$ we have a different type of variation. Here we see that as y increases x decreases as shown by the table:

y	1	2	5	10	15
x	10	5	2	1	2/3

DETERMINING VARIATION

In the above discussion we analyzed variation in a general way but when we express a relationship in four ways—that is, verbally, in equation, in table, and in graph—in going from the table to the other three methods it is difficult in some cases to determine the exact relationship by observation. Let us now try an example and from it devise a systematic method of determining the relationship between two nonspecified elements. Using a relationship expressed in table form, let us attempt to find the corresponding equation. Suppose our table relationship is as follows:

M	1	2	3	4	5
C	20	25	30	35	40

We first determine the change in C as we uniformly change the value of n. We call this change in C (ΔC). Vertical columns better portray this analysis:

M	C	ΔC
1	20	
		5
2	25	
		5
3	30	
		5
4	35	
		5
5	40	

When the change (ΔC) is uniform as in this case, we can be sure the relationships are linear or of first degree.

The general type form of the equation will then be $C = AM + b$, where a and b are to be determined. Let us now substitute two ordered pairs from the table into the general equation. Using the first two we get

$$20 = 1a + b$$
$$20 = 2a + b$$

Solving these equations simultaneously, we get $a = 5$ and $b = 15$. The equation therefore becomes $C = 5M + 15$. This equation checks for the other ordered pairs in the table.

Relationships leading to higher degree equation can also be determined systematically. Suppose we consider the number of segments which can be drawn between various numbers of points in a plane. The table showing the relation is

P	L	ΔL	$\Delta^2 L$
2	1	2	
3	3	3	1
4	6	4	1
5	10	5	1
6	15		

If we set up the ΔL as we did in the previous example we find them unlike; however, if we take the $\Delta^2 L$ that is the differences in the ΔL's we find them alike, each being one. The relation is, therefore, of the second degree and of the general form of the quadratic $L = aP^2 + bP + c$. Substituting the value of three successive L's and their corresponding P's into this general formula we get

$$1 = 4a + 2b + c \tag{5-1}$$
$$3 = 9a + 3b + c \tag{5-2}$$
$$6 = 16a + 4b + c \tag{5-3}$$

Solving the first two equations simultaneously, we get

$$-2 = -5a - b \tag{5-4}$$

Solving the first and third, we get

$$-5 = 12a - 2b \tag{5-5}$$

Solving Eqs. 5-4 and 5-5 simultaneously, we get $a = 1/2$, then $b = 1/2$, and $c = 0$.[1] The equation thus becomes $2L = P^2 - P$ when we substitute the values for a, b, and c into the general equation. The formula may now be checked with the table values or used to determine additional values for the table.

THE SUBSET AND SUPERSET RELATIONS

We now consider the relations known as subset and superset. A set is a *subset of its superset* if it is comprised entirely of elements of the superset and contains the same or a lesser number of elements. If the superset is

[1] For assistance in solving simultaneous equations the reader is referred to "Systems of Open Sentences," Chapter 10.

$A = \{\Delta, \square, \odot\}$, then its subsets are

$$\begin{array}{ll} B = \{\Delta, \square, \odot\} & F = \{\Delta\} \\ C = \{\Delta, \square\} & G = \{\square\} \\ D = \{\Delta, \odot\} & H = \{\odot\} \\ E = \{\square, \odot\} & I = \{\ \} \end{array}$$

The number of subsets possible when the superset contains N element is 2^N. The symbol used for subset is $\subseteq$ and we write in reference to the above sets that set $D \subseteq$ set A. This symbol can be easily remembered, since the $\subset$ points in the same direction as the less than symbol ($<$) and $\subseteq$ may then be compared to less than or equal to, which is consistent with the number of elements in the subsets as compared to the superset.

The subsets which contain at least one less element than their superset are called proper subsets. The symbol is ($\subset$) and without the line under it, makes the situation consistent. From our previous example of sets we can then write set $C \subset$ set A, but set $B \not\subset$ set A (read "set B is not a proper subset of set A"). The number of proper subsets possible from a superset having N elements is $(2^N - 1)$ since from the definition a set cannot be a proper subset of itself.

The relations of subset and superset have many uses in grades K–8. For example: When we take the subset $\{\Delta, \square\}$ from the superset $\{\odot, \Delta, \square\}$ we have the subset $\{\odot\}$ remaining. When these sets are associated with the cardinal numbers which describe them we have an illustration of the subtraction problem $3 - 2 = 1$. This approach may be used with addition, multiplication and division.

The subset and superset terminology fits into a variety of related experiences and assignments such as:

1. Break the set of whole numbers < 100 into three subsets; specials, primes, and composites.
2. Classify the set of whole numbers into the subsets; perfect, abundant, and deficient as far up the scale as you can go.
3. Is the set of even whole numbers a proper subset of the set of all whole numbers?
4. Make a superset covering all of the subsets below:

$$\begin{array}{ll} A = \{5, 3, 1\} & C = \{0, 2, 4\} \\ B = \{7, 9, 11, \ldots\} & D = \{6, 8, 10 \ldots\} \end{array}$$

We shall not discuss in detail all of the relations listed on the first page of this chapter. Three of these, namely, ($\parallel, \perp, \cong$,), relate to geometric figures, and the combinations of relations such as $\geqslant$ and $\not\geqslant$ can be analyzed in terms of their components. Furthermore, the list is by no means intended to be exhaustive.

DEFINING A RELATION

A *relation* may be adequately defined as a set of ordered pairs with a domain consisting of the first components of the pairs and a range consisting of the second components of the pairs within the domain and range. If we let R represent the relation between the various pairs of components, say x and y, and if d represents the domain and r the range, within which the relation operates, then we can define the relation by $F = \{(x,y)/x \in d,\ y \in r \text{ and } R(x,y)\}$ If $\mathbf{U}$ = the natural numbers, then d = the natural numbers, r = the natural number > 0 and < 10. We now define the relation by $F = \{(x,y)/x \in d, y \in r, \text{ and } x + y = 10\}$. This definition is read "the set of all ordered pairs (x,y) such that x is an element of d, y is an element of r and $x + y = 10$." As an example let us take the relation R to be $x + y = 10$ and restrict ourselves to the natural number set. Then the d or domain for the first components of the ordered pairs (x,y) is $\{x|x$ is natural number$\}$ and r or the range is $\{y|y$ is a natural number $> 0 < 10\}$. As we study the number pairs constituting this relation we find them to be (1,9), (2,8), (3,7), (4,6), (5,5), (6,4), (7,3), (8,2), (9,1). While this is the precise definition of the relation, students should recognize that this same relation might be described by a table, or by the formula $x + y = 10$ [x and y

x	1	2	3	4	5	6	7	8	9
y	9	8	7	6	5	4	3	2	1

natural numbers], by the graph as shown, and by verbal description, "The sum of two natural numbers is 10."

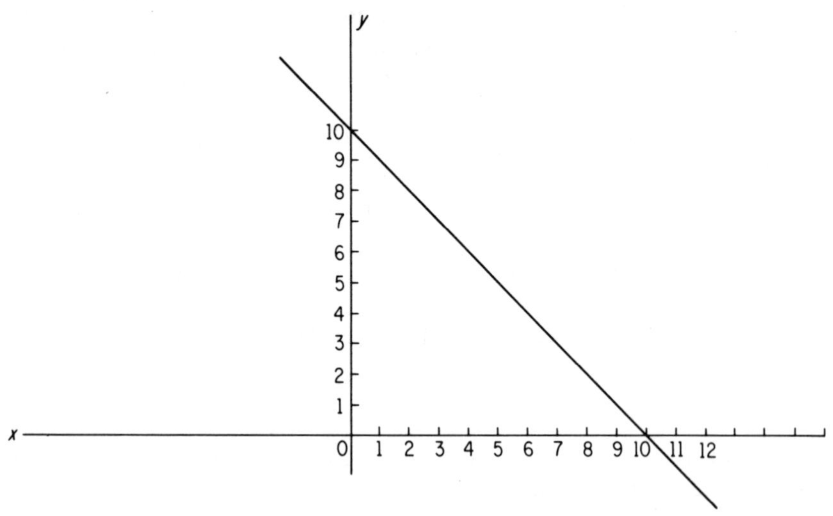

In the above example we have confined ourselves to a definite set of ordered pairs, and furthermore we have used an "equals" relationship. Students will need to extend their experience to other relationships and infinite sets.[2]

[2] *Twenty-fourth Yearbook of National Council of Teachers of Mathematics*, pp. 73–81.

FUNCTION AS A SPECIAL RELATION

Having defined a relation in our previous discussion, it is now relatively simply to define a special kind of relation known as a *function*. A function is a relation in which each element of the domain belongs to only one ordered pair. If we wish to bypass the term *relation* in our definition and get back to fundamentals, we can define a function as a set or ordered pairs no two of which have the same first element. Both of these definitions provide that for any value of x in the domain there is only one corresponding value of y in the range. Graphically, this requires that any line drawn parallel to the y-axis crosses the graph of the function only once. The graphs illustrate a functional and nonfunctional relation.

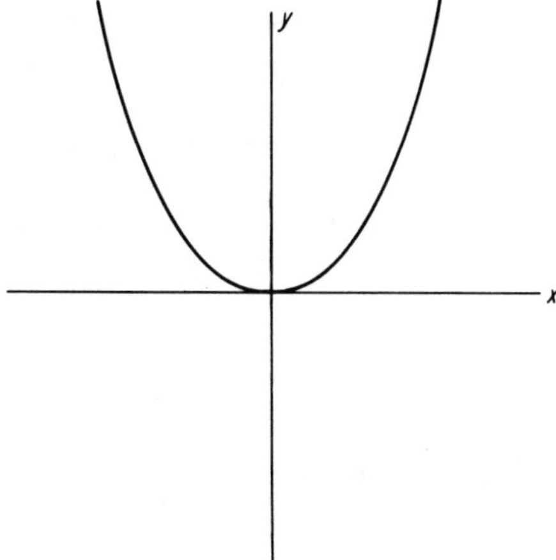

Graph of $y = x^2$ is a function of x

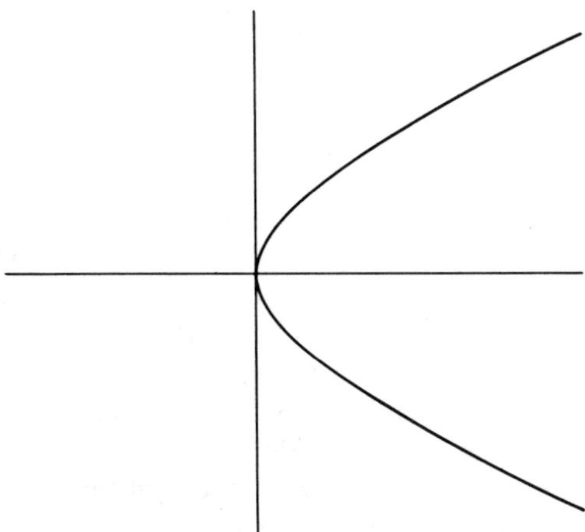

Graph of $y^2 = x$ is not a function of x

RELATIONS ANALYZED BY OPERATIONS

The development of the concepts of "relation" and "function" through the use of sets and ordered pairs insures an interpretation which was often overlooked in the traditional treatment. The solution of all types of equations can now comfortably be thought of in terms of sets of points in two-dimensional or multidimensional space. While most of mathematical experiences of the elementary and secondary student will be concerned with Cartesian or two-dimensional space, his thinking should in no wise be limited to it. He may often explore sets of ordered triples in three-dimensional space and can easily find solution sets of systems of equations containing three of more nonspecified elements. As we refer again to Cartesian coordinates in the plane and consider the concepts of "relation" and "function" within the universe of real numbers, we find that any linear equation is a function unless its graph is parallel to the y-axis. We may state that a linear function is a set of ordered pairs (x,y) obeying the relation $y = mx + b$ where m, x, and b are elements of the real number set and $m \neq 0$. When solving two such equations simultaneously the solution set is often referred to as *intersection* of the two sets defined by the original equations. For example, if we are seeking the solution set for the two simultaneous linear equations

$$\begin{aligned} 2x + y &= 10 \\ x - y &= 5 \end{aligned}$$

the solution or intersection set is the ordered pair (5,0). In set notation,

$$\left\{(x, y) \;\middle|\; \begin{aligned} 2x + y &= 10 \\ x - y &= 5 \end{aligned}\right\} \quad \text{is} \quad \{(5,0)\}$$

The first equation designates a set of ordered pairs among which are

$$(1,8), (2,6), (^1\!/_2,9), (5,0) \ldots$$

The second equation designated a set of ordered pairs among which are

$$(6,1), (5,0), (9,4) \ldots$$

Now the set of elements common to both sets is (5,0) and this constitutes the *solution set* or *intersection set.* If we consider the first set of number pairs to be the set A and the second set to be the set B, then the intersection set is written $A \cap B$ and read "A intersection B," or "A cap B." If we wished to speak of the set of number pairs obtained by combining sets A and B, we would write $A \cup B$, read "A union B," or "A cup B." These two notations are used generally when dealing with sets and are not necessarily restricted to the use made of them above. They are set operations and were discussed further in Chapter 4. The close tie between relation and operation can be demonstrated through the use of the so-called Venn diagram as illustrated.

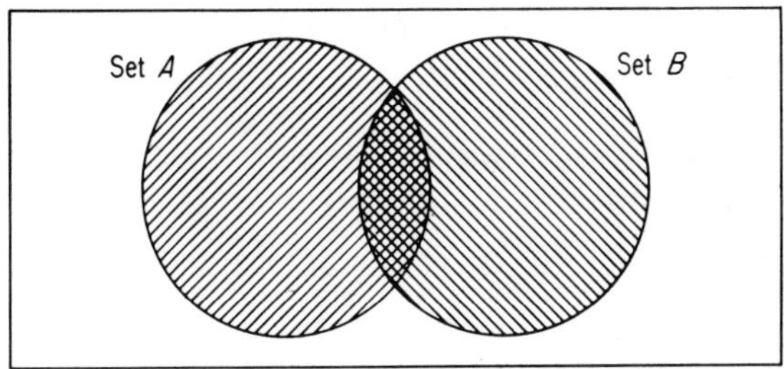

If A represents the set of elements or points enclosed by the left-hand circle and B represents the set of elements or points enclosed by the right-hand circle the double shaded part is designated as $A \cap B$ and all of A and B including the overlap is designated $A \cup B$. **U** represents the universal set. These diagrams are not used on the rectangular coordinate axis, since they do not illustrate location of points in the sets but merely portray the existence of points and elements in sets and subsets.[3]

From the foregoing discussion it can be seen that the concepts of relation and operation of sets and pairs gets so basically involved in the mathematical picture that one can foresee their use throughout the entire sequence. One also becomes intrigued by the language and symbolism to a point where traditional statements of problems may take on a new look. For example, instead of saying "solve the following equation for x," we might say, "find $\{x|x^2 + x - 2 = 0\}$."

The development in this chapter merely characterizes the sequential nature of relations within and among sets. It is in no way exhaustive but should serve as an important reminder to teachers that here is a basic concept of mathematics which must be developed and maintained at all grade levels.

PROBLEMS

1. Find the relation exhibited in the following pairs of numbers:

0	1	2	3	4
10	$10^2/_3$	$11^1/_3$	12	$12^2/_3$

2. Is the relation ">" an equivalence relation? Show the analysis which supports your answer.

3. Find by observation the solution set and complement set for the following open sentences. (Consider the master set to be the rational numbers.)

(a) $2\square + 3 = 13$ (c) $3\square + 4 > 13$

(b) $\dfrac{\square - 3}{2} + 5 = 9$ (d) $2\square + 6 < +12$

[3] *Twenty-Third Yearbook of National Council of Teacher of Mathematics*, pp. 39–41.

(e) $12 + \square \geqslant \square^2$

(f) $\dfrac{2\square + 5}{5} = \square - 2$

(g) $3 \cdot \square - 7 \leqslant -5$

(h) $\square^2 + 6 = 8$

4. Provide evidence which might support the conclusion that the following open sentence is an identity.

$$\square(\square + 3) + \square^2 = 3\square + 2\square^2$$

5. Express the ratio of

(a) one foot to one inch
(b) three to fifteen
(c) one-half to three-fourths
(d) one pound to eight ounces

6. Are the following proportions?

(a) $6 : 9 = 12 : 18$
(b) $7/12 = 35/60$
(c) $17 : 64 = 51 : 190$
(d) $1\frac{2}{3} : \frac{5}{7} = \frac{5}{3} : \frac{15}{21}$

7. Find the values for $\square$ which will make the following proportions true:

(a) $2\square : 6 = 2 : 12$
(b) $15 : \square = 3 : 2$
(c) $7 : 35 = \square : 70$
(d) $3/4 = 6/\square$
(e) $9 : \square = \square : 4$

8. In the relation $p = 4s$, does p vary directly or inversely as s? How did you reach your conclusion?

9. How would you assist a sixth-grade student to develop the concept of function?

10. Will the relation shown in the following table be linear or quadratic? (Complete the table to assist you in your decision.)

x	y	Δx	$\Delta^2 x$
0	3		
1	4		
2	9		
3	18		
4	31		
5	48		

11. Students in the elementary grades may in many cases be unable to use the systematic method of finding the relationship between two variables as described in this chapter. Can you suggest means of helping them discover the relationships by observations and experimentation? Be specific.

12. Explain the difference between a relation and an operation in mathematics.

13. Consider the nonmathematical relation "Is a brother of." Is this relation (1) reflexive (2) symmetric, (3) transitive, (4) asymmetric? Use examples to support your conclusion.

14. How many proper subsets can be made from a set containing seven elements?

15. Define a mathematical relation involving two variables and use a specific example to illustrate the four forms in which such a relation might appear.

Chapter 6

Solving Open Sentences and Word Problems

BASIC IDEAS

Students in the primary grades can get very excited about solving open sentences by observation and trial and error. The concept of what constitutes an open sentence may be introduced by using frames instead of letters to represent the nonspecified element. Such simple open sentences as $\square + 3 = 7$ and $\square + 4 < 12$ should be among their first experiences. The principal concepts involved can then be gradually developed each at successive stages of sophistication to fit the maturity of the students and thus carried to mastery in the secondary school.

Let us examine the basic notions involved in open sentences.

1. The open sentence itself is merely a relation involving one or more placeholders and each of these may occur in one or more positions in the open sentence and may be raised to the first power or a higher power. Examples follow:

   (a) $\square - 6 = 10$
   (b) $2\square + 10 = \square + 15$
   (c) $\square^2 + 6 = 15$
   (d) $\square^2 + 3\square = 28$
   (e) $\square + 2\Delta = 14$
   (f) $2\square - 6 = \Delta$
   (g) $\square + 8 = \Delta^2$
   (h) $\frac{\square}{2} + 4 = 8$

2. The solution set for an open sentence consists of all the elements taken from the master set which will make the sentence true. In the examples given under (1), some sentences have one element in the solution set, others have two. Those having two different placeholders require a pair of numbers to make them true, and the solution set in this case will consist of an infinite set of pairs.

3. The complement set for any open sentence consists of those elements of the master set which make the sentence false. The complement set plus the solution set must always equal the master set. Attention to the complement set avoids overlooking possible solutions.

4. The master set consists of the set of elements from which choices may be made when finding the solution set. It may be fixed by agreement in advance, or it may be left for the student to decide just how large a set is necessary to make solutions possible. When dealing with sets of numbers smaller than the complex numbers, it is generally better to call the set the *master set* rather than the *universal set*, since the universal set should be reserved for the ultimate set.
5. In the primary grades and to some extent in the intermediate grades the solution sets will be found by observation and trial and error. The ultimate power sought by the student should be solution of the open sentences by axioms. Once the student has mastered the axiomatic method, shortcuts and time saving procedures are perfectly in order.
6. Students should be encouraged at all levels to organize their problems orderly and logically and to communicate their process and procedures in a manner comprehensible to colleagues, teachers, and others concerned with the mathematics involved. We have in this text already developed the basic operations and have listed and examined several relations. Open sentences involve relations and often require the application of axioms and operations for their solution. We shall begin our solutions by first tracing the observation technique to approximately the eighth-grade level. Beginning with the fifth grade, students will want to develop the more powerful axiomatic approach, but they should feel free to use observation at any stage or level as long as the process is productive and does not interfere with other objectives.

SOLVING OPEN SENTENCES BY OBSERVATION

We begin with examples of increasing difficulty and in each case indicate the master set, solution set and complement set. M will represent the master set, S the solution set, and $\overline{S}$ the complement set.

Example 6-1

$$\square + 3 = 10$$

Note that with primary grade children no fuss is made about the symbolism or terminology. They just discuss the elements that make the sentence true and false and what choices they have.

M = whole numbers
$S = \{7\}$
$\overline{S}$ = {all whole numbers except 7}
This may be written

$$\overline{S} = \{\square | \square \neq 7\}$$

and is read "The set of all elements in the master set represented by □ such that □ does not equal seven."

Example 6-2

$\square - 4 = 12$ | M = whole numbers
$S = \{16\}$
$\overline{S} = \{\square | \square \neq 16\}$

Example 6-3

$2 \times \square = 10$ | M = whole numbers
$S = \{5\}$
$\overline{S} = \{\square | \square \neq 5\}$

Example 6-4

$\frac{\square}{2} = 6$ | M = whole numbers
$S = \{12\}$
$\overline{S} = \{\square | \square \neq 12\}$

Example 6-5

$2 \cdot \square + 6 = 16$ | M = whole numbers
$S = \{5\}$
$\overline{S} \neq \{\square | \square \neq 5\}$

Note that we have shifted from the old multiplication sign to the dot, which is a more flexible symbol.

Example 6-6

$\frac{3 \cdot \square}{2} - 4 = 5$ | M = whole numbers
$S = \{6\}$
$\overline{S} = \{\square | \square \neq 6\}$

The process on this last problem uses the reasoning that $\frac{3 \cdot \square}{2}$ must = 9. $3 \cdot \square$ must = 18, therefore $\square$ must be 6.

Example 6-7

$\frac{2 \cdot \square + 7}{3} - 4 = 5$ | M = whole numbers
$S = \{10\}$
$\overline{S} = \{\square | \square \neq 10\}$

The reasoning here is that $\frac{2 \cdot \square + 7}{3}$ must equal 9. $2 \cdot \square + 7$ must equal 27 and $2\square$ must be 20, therefore, $\square = 10$. Students having had this kind of experience in the observation method can solve many open sentences which appear to require the axiomatic approach.

Example 6-8

$\square + 6 > 10$ | M = whole numbers
$S = \{5,6,7,\cdots\}$
$\overline{S} = \{0,1,2,3,4,\}$

Note here that the solution set becomes infinite while the complement set is finite.

Example 6-9

$2\square - 4 < 16$

M = whole numbers
$S = \{9,8,7,6,5,4,3,2,1,0\}$
$\overline{S} = \{10,11,12,\cdots\}$

Example 6-10

$\dfrac{3\square + 6}{2} > 9$

M = nonnegative rationals
$S = \{\square | \square > 4\}$
$\overline{S} = \{\square | \square \leqslant 4\}$

Note that here it was necessary to change our master set since we ran into fractions as we substituted whole numbers for $\square$. Specifically when we try $\square = 5$ we get $10^1/_2 > 9$, which of course is true but the experience has forced us beyond the whole numbers.

GRAPHING SOLUTIONS

As a useful device for helping students visualize the solution and complement set we use what is called a *line graph.* The heavy line exclusive of the

circled point "4" represents the solution set, while the circled point and the remainder of the line represents the complement set. Actually not all numbers and points on the line are represented, since the irrationals were not in our master set for this problem. This is a technicality, however, which need not be labored with the students at this point unless they ask about it.

Example 6-11

$\dfrac{2\square}{3} + 9 \leqslant 11$

M = nonnegative reals
$S = \{\square | \square \leqslant 3\}$
$\overline{S} = \{\square | \square > 3\}$

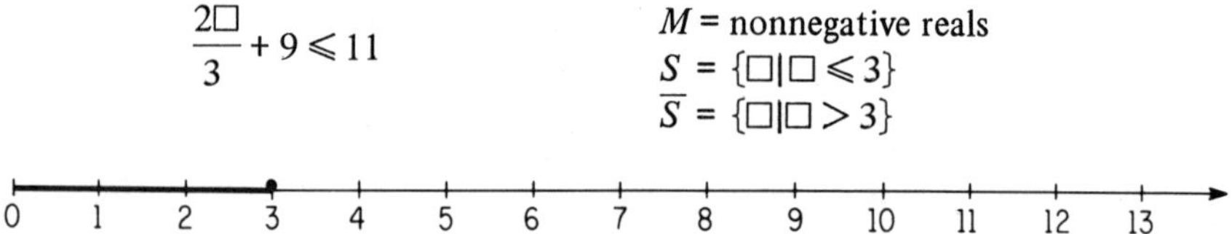

Note that in this instance the point 3 is in the solution set and is blacked in. Also we have used the nonnegative reals as M and, therefore, all points on the line are now represented.

SOLVING OPEN SENTENCES HAVING TWO PLACEHOLDERS

Let us now consider some open sentences containing two placeholders which do not necessarily represent the same number. Again we resort to examples and as explained earlier each solution will involve a pair of numbers.

Example 6-12

$\square + \Delta = 6$

M = whole numbers
S = {(2,4), (3,3), (5,1), (6,0), (4,2), (1,5), (0,6)}
$\overline{S}$ = {($\square$,Δ)|($\square$,Δ) $\neq$ any of the above pairs.}

If we extend the master set to the nonnegative rationals we would increase the solution set, because we could then use fractions such as the pair (9/2,3/2). If we let M = the reals we then admit negatives and irrationals and would have among our solutions such pairs as (+9, −3) but no irrational solutions, since the sum of an irrational and a rational or two irrationals is never rational. However, had the open sentence been $\square \cdot \Delta = 6$ we could have had the pair of irrationals $(\sqrt{6}, \sqrt{6})$ in the solution set, or if we had had the open sentence $\square \cdot \Delta = -7$, $\square$ could $= (\sqrt{2} - 3)$ and Δ could $= (\sqrt{2} + 3)$, and the pair $[(\sqrt{2} - 3), (\sqrt{2} + 3)]$ would be an element of the solution set.

Example 6-13

$\square + \Delta < 6$

M = the whole numbers
S = {(0,1), (0,2), (0,3), (0,4), (0,5), (1,1), (1,2), (1,3), (1,4), (2,0), (2,1), (2,2), (2,3), (3,0), (3,1), (3,2), (4,0), (4,1), (5,0)}
$\overline{S}$ = {($\square$,Δ)|($\square$,Δ) = none of the above}

GRAPHING SOLUTIONS ON A COORDINATE SYSTEM

In order to graph the solution and complement set for this type of open sentence we resort to our conventional rectangular coordinate system of graphing. This can be introduced to students by telling them that we are imposing a second number line on our regular one so that the zero points coincide and the lines are perpendicular to each other. Since our master set was the whole numbers in Example 6-12, the lattice points indicated there constitute the graph of the solution set. Note that the points fall in a straight line (see page 140).

The graph of the solution set for Example 6-13 consists of all the lattice points in the first quadrant which are below a line drawn through the lattice points representing the solution-set graph for Example 6-12. This experience has tremendous implications for the mathematics involved with the solution of simultaneous pairs of open sentences, a part of secondary mathematics. We shall not pursue this matter further at this point, but gifted students in the upper grades may wish to do so.

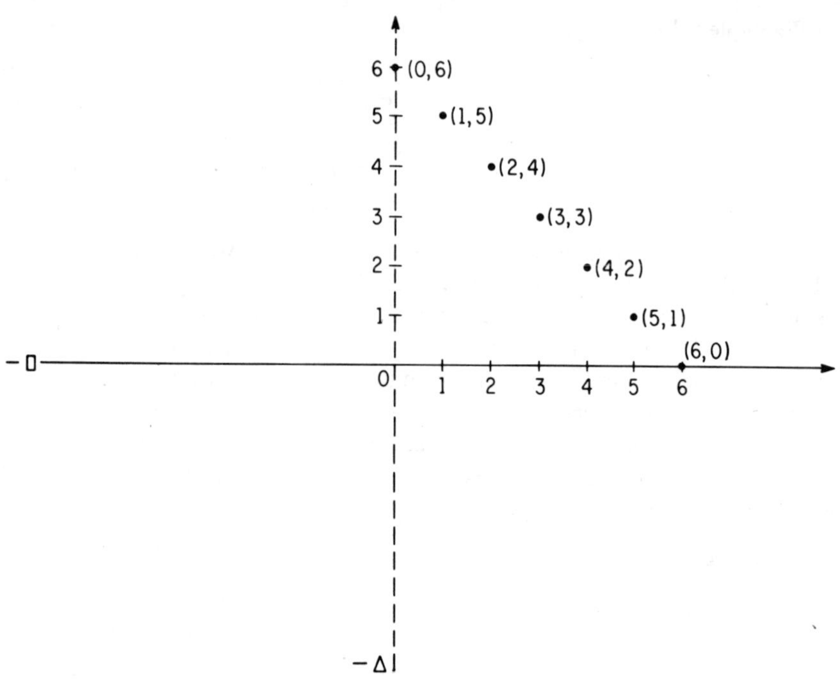

SOLUTION BY AXIOMS

We begin this section by discussing and later listing the axioms which are essential for our treatment of this area. Many of these have been developed earlier in the text, while others have not. It should be understood that these axioms should emerge gradually in grades K–8 and should be introduced by the discovery technique, each axiom being reinforced at successive grade levels after its introduction. All axioms included in this list should be understood by students in the eighth grade, and in many situations most or all of them can be handled by sixth-grade students. Teachers should avoid rote memorization of these axioms by students. Understanding meaning and insight are the keys here. If the teacher can instill in students a comprehensive understanding of these axioms along with skill and facility in their use, a large part of the mathematics teaching responsibility at the elementary school level will have been met.

Before listing the axioms let us be reminded that they are merely basic agreements by which we live in mathematics. Their place in a mathematical system is portrayed in the diagram on the last page of Chapter 9. Most axioms hold for all elements of the master set, including the ultimate or universal set. Occasionally, however, we find a useful relation which holds in all except perhaps one case. These we often retain in our list of axioms by limiting the universal quantifier. Let us remember that the notation for the universal quantifier is "$\forall$". We use it as follows: If we write the axiom $a + b = b + a$ and it holds for all elements a

and b in the master set we indicate this by writing $\forall_{a,b}; a + b = b + a$. It is read, "For every element a in the master set and for every element b in the master set $a + b = b + a$." There are other quantifiers in mathematics, one of which is the existential quantifier used in the following manner: $\exists_x | x + 6 = 12$. This is read, "There exists some element x in the master set such that $x + 6 = 12$." We have not used this symbol elsewhere in this text, but the concept pervades our work on open sentences, as well as referring directly to the existence and closure principles.

BASIC AXIOMS

We now list the axioms with the quantifiers and examples:

1. $\forall_{a,b}$; $a + b = b + a$ — Commultative axiom of addition
   $2 + 3 = 3 + 2$
2. $\forall_{a,b,c}$; $a + (b + c) = (a + b) + c$ — Associative axiom of addition
   $5 + (6 + 4) = (5 + 6) + 4$
3. $\forall_a$; $a + 0 = a$ — Additive axiom of zero
   $6 + 0 = 6$
4. $\forall_a$; $a + (-a) = 0$ — Axiom of the additive inverse
   $6 + (-6) = 0$
5. $\forall_{a,b,c}$; If $a = b$, then $a + c = b + c$
   If $6 = \frac{12}{2}$, then $6 + 4 = \frac{12}{2} + 4$
6. $\forall_{a,b}$; $a \cdot b = b \cdot a$ — Commutative axiom of multiplication
   $5 \cdot 6 = 6 \cdot 5$
7. $\forall_{a,b,c}$; $(a \cdot b) \cdot c = a \cdot (b \cdot c)$ — Associative axiom of multiplication
   $(3 \cdot 4) \cdot 5 = 3 \cdot (4 \cdot 5)$
8. $\forall_a$; $a \cdot 0 = 0$ — Multiplicative axiom of zero
   $7 \cdot 0 = 0$
9. $\forall_a$; $a \cdot 1 = a$ — Multiplicative axiom of one
   $8 \cdot 1 = 8$
10. $\forall_{a \neq 0}$; $a \cdot \frac{1}{a} = 1$ — Axiom of the multiplicative inverse
    $6 \cdot \frac{1}{6} = 1$
11. $\forall_{a,b,c}$; If $a = b$, then $a \cdot c = b \cdot c$
    If $6 = \frac{18}{3}$, then $6 \cdot 4 = \frac{18}{3} \cdot 4$
12. $\forall_{a,b,c}$; $a(b + c) = a \cdot b + a \cdot c$ — Distributive axiom of multiplication over addition
    $4(3 + 7) = 4 \cdot 3 + 4 \cdot 7$
13. $\forall_{a,b,c}$; If $a > b$, then $a + c > b + c$
    If $6 > 5$, then $6 + 4 > 5 + 4$

14. $\forall_{c>0,a,b}$; If $a > b$, then $a \cdot c > b \cdot c$
If $7 > 6$, then $7 \cdot 4 > 6 \cdot 4$
15. $c_{c<0,a,b}$; If $a > b$, then $a \cdot c < b \cdot c$
If $9 > 8$, then $9 \cdot (-2) < 8\,(-2)$

This list of axioms is adequate for our present purposes.

APPLYING THE AXIOMS

We now proceed to solve by axioms each of the examples used with the observation technique. It should be kept in mind that while the axiomatic method is not required on these easy examples, it is well to use them in teaching the new process. Our objective here is, of course, to teach the more powerful axiomatic approach so that students will have it available when solving more difficult problems that cannot readily be done by observation. Note also that we show each step in detail with special emphasis upon organization and logic. As has been stated previously, shortcuts should be allowed only after students have good understanding of the axioms and processes involved.

Example 6-14

$\square + 3 = 10$	*Problem*
$(\square + 3) + (-3) = (7 + 3) + (-3)$	If $a = b$, then $a + c = b + c$
$\square + [(+3) + (-3)] = 7 + [(+3) + (-3)]$	$(a + b) + c = a + (b + c)$
$\square + 0 = 7 + 0$	$a + (-a) = 0$
$\square = 7$	$a + 0 = a$

M = integers. $S = \{7\}$. $\overline{S} = \{\square | \square \neq 7\}$.

Note that after successive applications of the axioms the open sentence became so simple that the solution set was obvious. Note also that we often used a legitimate modification of the original axioms.

Example 6-15

$\square - 4 = 12$	We first rewrite this problem since we have no subtraction or division axioms. Actually none are necessary.
$\square + (-4) = 12$	*Equivalent problem*
$[\square + (4)] + (+4) = 12 + (+4)$	If $a = b$, then $a + c = b + c$
$\square + [(-4) + (+4)] = 16$	$(a + b) + c = a + (b + c)$ + addition
$\square + 0 = 16$	$(-a) + (+a) = 0$
$\square = 16$	$a + 0 = a$
M = integers. $S = \{16\}$	$\overline{S} = \{\square | \square \neq 16\}$

Example 6-16

$2 \cdot \square = 10$	*Problem*
$\frac{1}{2}(2 \cdot \square) = \frac{1}{2} \cdot 10$	If $a = b$, then $c \cdot a = c \cdot b$
$(\frac{1}{2} \cdot 2) \cdot \square = 5$	$a \cdot (b \cdot c) = (a \cdot b) \cdot c$ & multiplication
$1\square = 5$	$\forall_{a \neq 0};\ \frac{1}{a} \cdot a = 1$
$\square = 5$	$1 \cdot a = a$
M = nonnegative rationals; $S = \{5\}$.	$\overline{S} = \{\square \mid \square \neq 5\}$

Example 6-17

$\frac{\square}{2} = 6$	
$\frac{1}{2} \cdot \square = 6$	*Problem rewritten*
$2\,(\frac{1}{2} \cdot \square) = 2 \cdot 6$	If $a = b$, then $c \cdot a = c \cdot b$
$(2 \cdot \frac{1}{2}) \cdot \square = 12$	$a\,(b \cdot c) = (a \cdot b) \cdot c$ & multiplication
$1\square = 12$	$\forall_{a \neq 0}; a \cdot \frac{1}{a} = 1$
$\square = 12$	$1 \cdot a = a$
M = nonnegative rationals; $S = \{12\}$	$\overline{S} = \{\square \mid \square \neq 12\}$

Example 6-18

$2 \cdot \square + 6 = 16$	*Problem*
$(2\square + 6) + (-6) = (10 + 6) + (-6)$	If $a = b$, then $a + c = b + c$
$2\square + [(+6) + (-6)] = 10 + [(+6) + (-6)]$	$(a + b) + c = a + (b + c)$
$2\square + 0 = 10 + 0$	$a + (-a) = 0$
$2\square = 10$	$a + 0 = a$
$\frac{1}{2}\,(2\square) = \frac{1}{2} \cdot 10$	If $a = b$, then $c \cdot a = c \cdot b$
$(\frac{1}{2} \cdot 2 \cdot \square = 5$	$a \cdot (\,b \cdot c) = (a \cdot b) \cdot c$
$1\square = 5$	$\forall_{a \neq 0};\frac{1}{a} \cdot a = 1$
$\square = 5$	$1 \cdot a = a$
M = rationals. $S = \{5\}$	$\overline{S} = \{\square \mid \square \neq 5\}$

Example 6-19

$\frac{3\square}{2} - 4 = 5$	*Problem*
$\frac{3\square}{2} + (-4) = 5$	*Problem rewritten*

$\left[\frac{3\square}{2} + (-4)\right] + (+4) = 5 + (+4)$	If $a = b$, then $a + c = b \pm c$
$\frac{3\square}{2} + [(-4) + (+4)] = 9$	$(a + b) + c = a + (b + c)$ + addition
$\frac{3\square}{2} + 0 = 9$	$(-a) + (+a) = 0$
$\frac{3\square}{2} = 9$	$a + 0 = a$
$1/2 \cdot 3\square = 9$	*Problem rewritten*
$2\,(1/2 \cdot 3\square) = 2 \cdot 9$	If $a = b$, then $a \cdot c = b \cdot c$
$(2 \cdot 1/2) \cdot 3W = 18$	$a\,(b \cdot c) = (a \cdot b) \cdot c$
$1 \cdot 3\square = 18$	$\forall_{a \neq 0}\,; a \cdot \frac{1}{a} = 1$
$3\square = 18$	$1 \cdot a = a$
$1/3\,(3\square) = 1/3 \cdot (3 \cdot 6)$	If $a = b$, then $c \cdot a = c \cdot b$ and $18 = 3 \cdot 6$
$(1/3 \cdot 3)\,\square = (1/3 \cdot 3) \cdot 6$	$a\,(b \cdot c) = (a \cdot b) \cdot c$
$1\square = 1 \cdot 6$	$\forall_{a \neq 0}\,; 1/a \cdot a = 1$
$\square = 6$	$1 \cdot a = a$
M = rationals; $S = \{6\}$	$\overline{S} = \{\square \mid \square \neq 6\}$

Example 6-20

$$\frac{2\square + 7}{3} - 4 = 6$$

$1/3\,(2\square + 7) + (-4) = 5$	*Problem rewritten*
$[1/3\,(2\square + 7) + (-4)] + (+4) = 5 + (+4)$	If $a = b$, then $a + c = b + c$
$1/3\,(2\square + 7) + [(-4) + (+4)] = 9$	$(a + b) + c = a + (b + c)$
$1/3\,(2\square 7) + 0 = 9$	$(-a) + (+a) = 0$
$1/3\,(2\square + 7) = 9$	$a + 0 = a$
$3\,[1/3\,(2\square + 7) = 3 \cdot 9$	If $a = b$, then $c \cdot a = c \cdot b$
$(3 \cdot 1/3)\,(2\square + 7) = 27$	$a\,(b \cdot c) = (a \cdot b) \cdot c$
$1\,(2\square + 7) = 27$	$\forall\, a \neq 0; a \cdot 1/a = 1$
$2\square + 7 = 27$	$1 \cdot a = a$
$(2\square + 7) + (-7) = (20 + 7) + (-7)$	If $a = b$, then $a + c = b + c$
$2\square + [(+7) + (-7)] = 20 + [(+7) + (-7)]$	$(a + b) + c = a + (b + c)$
$2\square + 0 = 20 + 0$	$a + (-a) = 0$
$2\square = 20$	$a + 0 = a$
$1/2\,(2\square) = 1/2 \cdot (2 \cdot 10)$	If $a = b$, then $c \cdot a = c \cdot b$
$(1/2 \cdot 2)\,\square = (1/2 \cdot 2)\,10$	$a\,(b \cdot c) = (a \cdot b) \cdot c$

$1 \cdot \square = 1 \cdot 10$	$\forall a \neq 0; 1/a \cdot a = 1$
$\square = 10$	$1 \cdot a = a$
M = rationals; $S = \{10\}$	$\overline{S} = \{\square \mid \square \neq 10\}$

Example 6-21

$\square + 6 > 10$	*Problem*
$(\square + 6) + (-6) > (4 + 6) + (-6)$	If $a > b$, then $a + c > b + c$
$\square + [(+6) + (-6)] > 4 + [(+6) + (-6)]$	$(a + b) + c = a + (b + c)$
$\square + 0 > 4 + 0$	$a + (-a) = 0$
$\square > 4$	$a + 0 = a$
M = rationals; $S = \{5,6,7,\cdots\}$	$\overline{S} = \{0,1,2,3,4,\}$

Example 6-22

$2\square - 4 < 16$	*Problem*
$2\square + (-4) < 16$	*Problem rewritten*
$[2\square + (-4)] + (+4) < 16 + (+4)$	If $a < b$, then $a + c < b + c$
$2\square + [(-4) + (+4)] < 20$	$(a + b) + c = a + (b + c)$
$2\square + 0 < 20$	$(-a) + (+a) = 0$
$2\square < 20$	$a + 0 = a$
$1/2 \cdot (2\square) < 1/2 \cdot 20$	If $a < b$, then $c \cdot a < c \cdot b$
$(1/2 \cdot 2)\square < 10$	$a(b \cdot c) = (a \cdot b) \cdot c$
$1\square < 10$	$\forall a \neq 0; 1/a \cdot a = 1$
$\square < 10$	$1 \cdot a = a$
M = rationals. $S = 9,8,7,6,5,4,3,2,1,0$	$\overline{S} = 10,11,12,\cdots\cdots$

Example 6-23

$\dfrac{3\square + 6}{2} > 9$	*Problem*
$[1/2\,(3\square + 6)] > 9$	*Problem rewritten*
$2\,[1/2\,(3\square + 6)] > 2 \cdot 9$	$\forall a > 0$; If $a > b$, then $c \cdot a > c \cdot b$
$(2 \cdot 1/2)(3\square + 6) > 18$	$a(b \cdot c) = (a \cdot b) \cdot c$
$1\,(3\square + 6) > 18$	$\forall a \neq 0; a \cdot 1/a = 1$
$3\square + 6 > 18$	$1 \cdot a = a$
$1/3\,(3\square + 6) > 1/3 \cdot 18$	$\forall a > 0$; If $a > b$, then $c \cdot a = c \cdot b$
$(1/3 \cdot (3\square) + 1/3 \cdot 6 > 1/3 \cdot 18$	$a(b + c) = a \cdot b + a \cdot c$
$(1/3 \cdot 3)\square + 2 > 6$	$a(b \cdot c) = (a : b) \cdot c$
$1\square + 2 > 6$	$\forall a \neq 0; 1/a \cdot a = 1$
$\square + 2 > 6$	$1 \cdot a = a$
$(\square + 2) + (-2) > (4 + 2) + (-2)$	If $a > b$, then $a + c > b + c$
$\square + ((+2) + (-2)) > 4 + ((+2) + (-2))$	$(a + b) + c = a + (b + c)$
$\square + 0 > 4 + 0$	$a + (-a) = 0$
$\square > 4$	$a + 0 = a$
M = rationals $S = \{\square \mid \square \neq 4\}$	$\overline{S} = \{\square \mid \square \leqslant 4\}$

Example 6-24

$\frac{2\Box}{3} + 9 \leqslant 11$	*Problem*
$\left(\frac{2\Box}{3} + 9\right) + (-9) \leqslant (2 + 9) + (-9)$	If $a \leqslant b$, then $a + c \leqslant b + c$
$\frac{2\Box}{3} + [(+9) + (-9)] \leqslant 2 + [(+9) + (-9)]$	$(a + b) + c = a + (b + c)$
$\frac{2\Box}{3} + 0 \leqslant 2$	$a + (-a) = 0$
$^2/_3\ \Box \leqslant 2$	$a + 0 = a$ & rewriting $\frac{2\Box}{3}$
$^3/_2 \cdot (^2/_3 \cdot \Box) \leqslant {}^3/_2 \cdot 2$	$\forall\, c > 0$; If $a \leqslant b$, then $c \cdot a \leqslant c \cdot b$
$(^3/_2 \cdot {}^2/_3)\, \Box \leqslant 3$	$a \cdot (b \cdot c) = (a \cdot b) \cdot c$ & multiplication
$1\Box \leqslant 3$	$\forall\, a \neq 0 \quad a \cdot 1/a = 1$
$\Box \leqslant 3$	$1 \cdot a = a$
M = rationals $S = \{\Box \mid \Box \leqslant 3\}$	$\overline{S} = \{\Box \mid \Box > 3\}$

Example 6-25 (two placeholders)

$$\Box + \Delta = 6$$

No solution by axioms, since we must have two independent relations before we can solve for two placeholders by axioms.

Example 6-26

$$\Box + \Delta < 6$$

No solution by axioms (see above).

OBSERVATIONS ON WORD PROBLEMS

We make a series of important observations concerning word problems before giving some examples.

1. Word problems should begin in the kindergarten and develop simultaneously with open sentences.
2. All word problems can be expressed as open sentences and solved either by observation or by axioms, depending upon their difficulty.
3. Word problems should never be delayed because of reading difficulties. Appropriate problems can be given at any level and can become part of the learning to read experience.
4. Students should have the dual experience of going from the open sentence to the word problem as well as setting up open sentences from the word problems. This becomes a reading, writing, spelling, and arithmetic experience.

5. Preciseness of language is the primary consideration in writing word problems. The quality and sophistication of the narration are secondary. However, the latter should be encouraged and necessary mathematical vocabulary should be built through deliberate exercises and experiences.

WRITING WORD PROBLEMS FOR OPEN SENTENCES

Example 6–27

$$3¢ + 4¢ = \square ¢$$

A primary-grade child may build a word problem around this open sentence as follows:

John has 3 cents and Mary has 4 cents. How many cents do John and Mary have together? The children may then take a word problem similar to this one and write the open sentence. In either case the children should solve the problem before leaving it.

Example 6–28

$$7 + 3 = \square$$

This time we leave the numbers nondenominate to allow more flexibility in writing the word problem. One child may write: I am seven years old. My brother is three years older. How old is my brother?

Another child may write: If I have seven marbles and John gives me three more, how many marbles do I have?

Another: Seven days and three days makes how many days?

The possibilities here are unlimited, and each child should have the opportunity to create a problem of his own and solve it.

Example 6–29

$$\square - 5 = 12$$

I gave Joe five marbles out of my bag and have twelve left. How many marbles did I have to begin with?

Example 6–30

$$5 \cdot \square = 35$$

Pencils are 5 cents each. I spent 35 cents for pencils. How many did I buy?

Example 6–31

$$6\square + 3 = 15$$

One possibility: If we add three to six times a certain number it equals 15. Find the number.

A more sophisticated possibility: If six times a certain number is increased by three the result is fifteen. Find the number.

An effort lacking in precision: Six times a certain number increased by three is 15. Find the number. Note this could come from $6(\square + 3) = 15$ or $6\square + 3 = 15$, and the solution set to the two problems is different.

Example 6–32

$$\square - 3 < 7$$

If I give three of my marbles away I will have less than seven. How many do I have?

Note here that students are having experience with problems which have more than one element in the solution set.

$$S = \{9,8,7,6,5,4,3\}$$

$$\overline{S} = \{0,1,2,10,11,12,\ldots\}$$

when M = the whole numbers.

Some students may argue here that M should be $\{3,4,5,\ldots\}$ since the situation requires that the person have at least three to begin with. This is a good observation and should be praised. Note also that an M which contains negatives or fractions is not practical here since we cannot have a negative number of marbles or a fraction of a marble. (At least the latter is very unlikely.)

Example 6–33

$$3\square + 2 \geqslant 17$$

One possibility: When two is added to three times a certain number the result is at least 17. Find the number.

If M = the whole numbers,

$$S = \{5,6,7,\ldots\}$$

$$\overline{S} = \{0,1,2,3,4\}$$

Note that the solution set and complement set change if we make M = nonnegative rationals, or if M = the reals or any master set different from the whole numbers.

It is not likely that many students would devise a word problem which reads as smoothly as this example. Many lesser efforts should surely be acceptable.

Example 6–34

$$\frac{2\square + 5}{3} => 4$$

A possibility: One third the result obtained when twice a certain number is is increased by five is greater than four. Find the number.

If M = nonnegative rational,

$$S = \{\square \mid \square > 3^1/_2\}$$

$$\overline{S} = \{\square \mid \square \leqslant 3^1/_2\}$$

Example 6–35

$$3\square + \frac{\square}{2} \leqslant 14$$

A possibility: When three times a number is increased by one-half of itself, the result is at most 14. Find the number.

If M = the reals,

$$S = \{\Box \mid \Box \leqslant 4\}$$

$$\overline{S} = \{\Box \mid \Box > 4\}$$

Note that in this case the negatives, irrationals and in fact all numbers on the number line are included.

Example 6–36

$$\frac{\Box + 4}{3} + 6 = 2\Box - 16$$

A possibility: If twice a certain number is diminished by sixteen, the result will be six more than one-third of the sum obtained when the number is increased by four. Find the number.

If M = the reals,

$$S = \{14\}$$

$$\overline{S} = \{\Box \mid \Box \neq 14\}$$

Note how easily errors can enter into a word problem. If we leave out the phrase "the sum obtained when" and the last "is" the open sentence may be written

$$(\Box/3 + 4) + 6 = 2\Box - 16$$

which has an entirely different solution set.

In concluding this development of word problems it should be clear that the possibilities are infinite for every example. By merely letting □ represent something else such as the height of a flagpole, etc., we can get a different statement but the basic relations will remain the same. In some cases the solutions to the problems may make certain statements impractical. For example under certain conditions the flagpole may turn out to be −3 ft high, but this is incidental to the concepts and skills being taught.

WRITING OPEN SENTENCES FOR WORD PROBLEMS

Having had the experiences suggested above, students should now be able to proceed with word problems and translate them into open sentences. Care should be taken to establish clearly with the students the new vocabulary which has evolved. It is not out of place to utilize such exercises as the following.

Write the following symbolically:

1. 12 increased by 7
2. □ diminished by 3
3. Twice □ increased by 5

4. Twelve greater than $3\square$
5. The product of $\square$ and 4
6. The result when the quotient of $\square$ divided by 6 is diminished by 10
7. The sum of $\square$ and Δ divided by 2
8. 12 less than $\square$
9. The remainder when 12 is decreased by Δ
10. Twice the product of $\square$ and Δ
11. Half the product of 5 and $\square$
12. Five less than the square of Δ

The above examples may be too sophisticated for the lower grades, but teachers can devise simpler expressions to be used with younger students. Let it here be emphasized that in solving open sentences that have already been set up, or open sentences resulting from word problems, the students at all levels should be encouraged to arrange their solutions logically and systematically. A good test of the arrangement consists of considering whether another person with comparable background in mathematics could understand the written solution without supplemental explanation. It requires considerable effort to get students to accept this responsibility and refrain from submitting a hodge-podge of numbers and other symbols as a finished problem.

An example of an acceptable solution is shown below. It is not intended that a specific format be followed, merely that communication be enhanced through some kind of meaningful organization.

Problem

Twice a certain positive integer when increased by 12 is at most 24. Find the integer.

Solution: Let $\square$ represent the certain positive integer. Then $2\square + 12 \leqslant 24$ describes the situation. Solving,

$2\square + 12 = 24$	If $a = b$, then $a + c = b + c$
$(2\square + 12) + (-12) = 24 + (-22)$	$(a + b) + c = a + (b + c)$ and algebraic addition
$2\square + (12 + (-12)) = 12$	
$2\square + 0 = 12$	$a + (-a) = 0$
$2\square = 12$	$a + 0 = a$
$\frac{1}{2}(2\square) = \frac{1}{2} \cdot 12$	If $a = b$, then $a \cdot c = b \cdot c$
$(\frac{1}{2} \cdot 2)\square = 6$	$a(b \cdot c) = (a \cdot b) \cdot c$ + arithmetic
$1 \cdot \square = 6$	$\forall a \neq 0 \;\; 1/a \cdot a = 1$
$\square = 6$	$1 \cdot a = a$

Now since the open sentence involved $<$ as well as equals, and because we are only interested in positive integers the solution set becomes:

$$S = \{6,5,4,3,2,1,\}$$

each element of which makes the original sentence true. In this solution the axiomatic detail was employed. The problem can also be solved by observation or by shortcut application of the axioms. Both methods are in order, depending on the purpose of the experience. If, however, any other method is employed both logic and sequence should be retained in the solution.

The solution given is not intended to preclude other implications inherent in the problem and which may provide exciting points of departure for class discussion. Some other facets of the problem are listed below:

1. What is the complement set?
2. Does $S + \overline{S} = M$
3. What would happen if we eliminated "positive" from the original problem?
4. Suppose we changed "positive integer" to "number" in the original, what then?
5. In view of our use of $^1/_2$ in one of the steps can we correctly say that our universe was the positive integers?

An interesting observation from the above problem is that conventional mathematics often did not exploit problems for their true worth. Perhaps we were too anxious to move to other problems rather than treat fewer problems in depth.

PERCENT

The concept of percent leads to many open sentences and word problems which elementary students should be able to interpret and solve. Let us begin by clarifying the concept, then move to the solutions of problems involving percent. Elementary students may well think of percent as being a special name for hundredths. They should understand that 20 percent means 20/100, 115 percent means 115/100, $^1/_2$ percent means $^1/_2$/100, etc. Students should be taught to express any number as a percent, a decimal, or a common fraction. The early skills in percent should include conversion of any one of these forms to the other two. Illustrations follow.

1. Change $^3/_4$ to percent and decimal.

$$\frac{3}{4} = \frac{3 \cdot 25}{4 \cdot 25} = \frac{75}{100} = 75\% = .75$$

2. Change 80% to decimal and simplest common fraction.

$$80\% = 80/100 = .80 = .8 = 8/10$$

3. Change .45 to percent ana simplest common fraction.

$$.45 = 45/100 = 45\%; \quad 45/100 = \frac{5 \cdot 9}{5 \cdot 20} = \frac{9}{20}$$

More difficult problems should be attacked with rigor. For example the solution to "Convert .002 to per cent and common fraction" might well be arranged as follows:

Example 6–37

$$.002 = 2/1000 = 2/1000 \cdot \frac{1/10}{1/10} = \frac{2/10}{100} = 2/10\%$$

since hundredths means percent. Also, going back to 2/1000 we find its simplest name to be 1/500 which now gives us common fraction form:

$$\therefore .002 = 1/500 = 2/10\% = .2\%$$

Example 6–38

Change .05% to decimal and common fraction.

$$.05\% = .05/100 \text{ because percent is hundredths}$$

and

$$.05/100 = .05 \cdot 100/100 \cdot 100 = 5/10000 = 1/2000$$

which is in common-fraction form

and

$$.05/100 = \frac{.05 \cdot 1/100}{100 \cdot 1/100} = \frac{5/100 \cdot 1/100}{1} = 5/10000 = .0005$$

which is decimal form

Example 6–39

Change 7/45 to percent and decimal.

$$7/45 \cdot \frac{20/9}{20/9} = \frac{7 \cdot 20/9}{100} = \frac{140/9}{100} = 140/9\% = 15.5/9\% = 15.555\ldots\%$$

Any of these last three being the answer in percent. $7/45 = 7 \div 45 = .1555\ldots$, which is the decimal answer.

We are now prepared to solve such word problems as the following:

1. Find 12 percent of 60.
2. 7.2 is what percent of 60?
3. 7.2 is 12 percent of what number?

Students should understand that each of these word problems can be stated in many ways. For example, (1) could read "What is 12 percent of 60?" or "12 percent of 60 is what?" or "How much is 12 percent of 60?"

The solutions to the above can be found by solving the proper open sentences.

1. Let □ = the answer to the problem. Then

$$12\% \text{ of } 60 = \square$$
$$12/100 \cdot 60 = \square$$

$12/100 \cdot 60/1 = \square$
$\square = 720/100 = 7.2 \quad S = \{7.2\}$
$\bar{S} = \{\square | \square \neq 7.2\}$

2. Let $\square$ equal the percent, then

$\square \cdot 60 = 7.2$
$\square = 7.2/60 \quad S = \{12\%\}$
$\square = .12 = 12/100 = 12\% \quad \bar{S} = \{\square | \square \neq 12\%\}$

An alternate attack on this problem is as follows. We first ask what fraction 7.2 is of 60 and then convert the fraction to percent. 7.2/60 is the fraction and

$$7.2/60 = \frac{72/10}{60} = \frac{72/10 \cdot 5/3}{60 \cdot 5/3} = \frac{360/30}{100} = \frac{12}{100} = 12\% \qquad s = \{12\%\} \quad \bar{s} = \{\square | \square \neq 12\%\}$$

3. Let $\square$ = the number

$12\% \text{ of } \square = 7.2$
$12/100 \cdot \square = 7.2$
$12\square/100 = 7.2$
$12\square = 720 \quad S = \{60\}$
$\square = 60 \quad \bar{S} = \{\square | \square \neq 60\}$

In choosing other examples the teacher should make certain that percents of less than one and more than 100 get involved. For example:

1. 1/200 is what percent of 500?
2. 165 is what percent of 50?

Other word problems center around percent of decrease and percent of increase. Examples follow:

3. Joe's class had 30 members last year. This year it has 40 members. What is the percent of increase?

Solution:

40 − 30 = 10 is the increase

10/30 is the fraction of increase

$$10/30 = \frac{10 \cdot 10/3}{30 \cdot 10/3} = \frac{10/1 \cdot 10/3}{30/1 \cdot 10/3} = \frac{100/3}{300/3} = \frac{100/3}{100} = \frac{33\ 1/3}{100} = 33\ 1/3\%$$

4. Mary earned \$60 last year. This year she earned only \$40. What is the percent of decrease?

\$60 − \$40 = \$20 is amount of decrease

$$20/60 = \frac{20 \cdot 5/3}{60 \cdot 5/3} = \frac{20/1 \cdot 5/3}{60/1 \cdot 5/3} = \frac{100/3}{100} = 33^1/_3\%$$

Teachers will quickly recognize that percent is not a difficult concept when properly related to common and decimal fractions. It should not be isolated and handled as if it were new, strange, or unrelated.

PROBLEMS

1. Describe what is meant by an open sentence in mathematics and what role the master set, solution set, and complement set play when an open sentence is under consideration.

2. Can the solution set for an open sentence be empty? Give an example.

3. Can the complement set be empty? Illustrate.

4. Illustrate how the master set may limit or extend the solution set and complement set for a specific open sentence.

5. Find by observation the solution set and complement set for each of the following open sentences (the master set to be considered in each case is indicated):

(a) $2\square + 3 = 13$ $\quad M$ = whole numbers
(b) $3\square - 4 = 14$ $\quad M$ = nonnegative rationals
(c) $\dfrac{\square}{4} + 6 = 9$ $\quad M$ = nonnegative reals
(d) $\square + 15 = -2$ $\quad M$ = integers
(e) $\square + 6 = 4$ $\quad M$ = positive integers
(f) $\dfrac{2\square + 7}{3} + 5 = 14$ $\quad M$ = reals
(g) $\sqrt{2}\,\square + 10 = 12$ $\quad M$ = reals
(h) $5\square + 4 > 14$ $\quad M$ = whole numbers
(i) $3\square - 6 < 12$ $\quad M$ = nonnegative integers
(j) $\dfrac{\square + 4}{2} \geqslant 12$ $\quad M$ = nonnegative even integers
(k) $12 > \square + 8$ $\quad M$ = rationals
(l) $2(\square + 3) = 6 + 2$ $\quad M$ = reals
(m) $2\square > \square + \square$

6. Use the number line to graph the solution sets for parts (c) and (h) in Prob. 5.

7. Solve each of the parts in Prob. 5 by the axiomatic process. Choose your own master set in each case to be sufficiently large to cover all of the numbers involved in the solution. This change may, of course, alter your solution set and complement set from what they were when the observation technique was employed.

8. Set up open sentences for the following word problems then find their solution sets and complement sets. Choose your own master set to fit the problem. If you cannot do the problem by observation use the axiomatic method.

(a) If apples are 10 cents each, how much will six apples cost?
(b) John is 10 years old, his sister is three years older. How old is the sister?
(c) James has 60 cents. He is working today and will earn at most 40

cents, depending on how much work he does. How much money will he have at the end of the day?

(d) Mary is twelve years old. Her brother is five years less than twice her age. How old is her brother?

(e) If twice a number is diminished by 10, the result is at least six. Find the number.

(f) If a bottle and its stopper costs $1.10 and the bottle costs a dollar more than the stopper, how much does the stopper cost?

(g) How many oranges costing 9 cents each can be purchased for $1.17?

(h) If blankets are $3 each and pillows are $2 in how many ways can you spend $20 if in each case you use all of the money and buy at least one of each article?

(i) When twice the height of a certain flagpole is increased by 8 ft the result is 73 ft. How high is the pole?

(j) If a whole number greater than 5 is tripled and the result increased by 7, the result is less than 30. Find the number.

(k) When five times a certain number is divided by 2, the result is at most 15. Find the number.

(l) A warning buzzer sounds every 40 seconds. If it sounds at exactly 12:00 noon, when will it again sound exactly on the hour?

(m) Jane is now a certain number of years old. Her mother will be twice as old as Jane in five years from now. What are the present ages? of Jane and her mother?

9. Make as many true statements as you can about the solution set and complement set for an open sentence. These statements may concern the sets separately or taken together.

10. What is the meaning of percent?

11. Can we have percents smaller than one?

12. Can we have percents larger than 100?

13. Change 23 percent to decimal and common fraction, explaining your work in detail.

14. Change .0005 to common fraction and percent. Show the logic of your solution.

15. Convert 5/37 to decimal and percent. Explain in detail.

16. Solve the following percent problems showing each step in detail.

(a) What is 30 percent of 675?

(b) 16 is what percent of 80?

(c) 24 is 60 percent of what number?

(d) If a class had 36 children last year but has 42 this year, what is the percent of increase?

(e) If a company's income was $260,000 last year and $240,000 this year, what is the percent of decrease?

17. 128 is what percent of 64?

Chapter 7

Measurement

THE NATURE OF MEASUREMENT

Much of our daily living is concerned with measurement. Things generally do not have their measurements stamped upon them. Furthermore, these things whose properties or observable characteristics we measure are not always concrete material things. True, we measure the properties of boards, people, rooms, and automobiles, but we also measure the properties of light waves, electrical charges, sound, and heat. Note that we always measure their width, length, thickness, weight, density, and the like. Note also that while we may measure color or smoothness, these measurements are usually in terms of an arbitrary or relative scale and are not true mathematical measurements. Basically all measurement involves the assignment of numbers through the process of counting.

While technically the counting of the number of people in a room or the number of rungs in a ladder does concern itself with properties of things, these are trivial and hardly worthy of being classified as measurement. When we count we assign cardinal numbers to the elements of a set, but when we measure we assign a ratio to represent a property of a thing. The act of measuring involves the use of a standard of the property being considered and comparing this standard to the similar property of the thing to be measured. By repeated appropriate applications of this standard to the thing to be measured, we find the ratio of the measure of the things to the measure of the standard. This is known as the *measurement of the property* of the thing. Another important fact must be borne in mind. Really, the measurement is never sharply defined but lies between an upper and lower limit. In other words, excluding the trivial counting situation referred to earlier, all measurements are approximate. The approximate nature of any measurement stems from two sources: (1) certain measurements such as length of a diagonal of a square requires the use of irrational numbers which, of course, must be written in rational approximate form for practical use; (2) physical measurements are always subject to errors, which may be due to imperfections in instruments, personal errors in using the instrument, errors in method, accidental errors, or lack of accuracy due to the size of the standard unit. As you will see later, the relative error decreases as the size of the standard unit decreases.

One need hardly argue the approximate nature of measurement when we consider the never-ending struggle to establish a standard for a defined unit. Students will be interested in reading the history associated with the establishment of standard units of length and mass.[1]

We now move to a discussion of measurement and measuring as it evolves in the life of the individual person. Young children face the task of learning the standards of measurement peculiar to their culture and applying these to measuring the properties of various things. A primary-grade child not yet familiar with the units and standard of length may say "John is three times as tall as his baby brother." Here the child may actually, in his mind's eye, be using the height of the baby brother as a standard of length. Later, when he, through experimentation, finds that the yardstick is three times as long as a foot rule, he is actually engaged in measuring.

Children learn early to compare and measure time, distance, and size. Size, to the child, may be at first a combination of length, area, volume, mass, and weight. Later he learns to distinguish among these properties of things and utilize the units and standards applicable to each. The primary teacher will find herself devoting much of her effort toward the teaching of the measurement of time, linear measure, and the measure of monetary value as it is associated with coins and currency. The measurement of time will include both the clock and the calendar. Volume as it relates to common units of liquid measure also enters early into the experience of the child. Ideally, the concept of square measure of area should precede cubic measure or volume, but the demands of the culture usually reverse the sequence. Weight also enters early as a property of things and its measurement will generally parallel those mentioned above.

SEQUENCE FOR DEVELOPING MEASUREMENT

Let us now present in table form a sequential development of measurement and measuring, realizing, of course, that many of the concepts develop simultaneously. The first column indicates the property or concept, the second column shows sample applications, and the third column specifies the common standard units used to measure this property.

The teaching of measurement to younger students requires elaborate concrete illustrations and demonstration. The use of the cardboard clock face, calendar, coins, currency, and charts showing comparative size of units for time and money are musts for the primary teacher.

[1]William L. Schaaf, *Basic Concepts of Elementary Mathematics*, 2d ed. (New York: Wiley, 1965), Chapter 7.

Concept	Application	Units
Time	Meal time, school time, play time, rest time, day, night, seasons, moon phases, time for orbit, gestation period, life span, etc.	Seconds, minutes, hours, days, weeks, months, years, decades, centuries, milleniums, etc.
Linear Measure	Length, height, width, distance, length of curve, circumference, diameter, radius, round trip, perimeter, trajectories, wavelength, length of orbit, slant height, edge, altitude, apothem.	Inch, foot, yard, rod, mile, nautical mile, light years, radian. Metric system, millimeter, centimeter, decimeter, meter, kilometer.
Money	Buying treats, paying lunch money, buying for a party, going to the grocery store, collecting transportation costs for a field trip, etc.	Penny, nickel, dime, quarter, fifty-cent piece, dollar, currency.
Square Measure or Area	Areas enclosed by plane geometric figures and parts of some, such as sectors, etc. Surface area of solid geometric figures and parts of surface area such as lateral area, area of base, area of zones, etc., area within an irregular closed curved line.	Square inch, square feet, square yard, square rod, acre, square metric units.
Cubic Measure or Volume	Volume of space enclosed by three-dimensional geometric figures; volume as it relates to liquid measure. Volume as it relates to dry measure.	Cubic inch, cubic foot, cubic yard, cubic rod, cubic mile, acre foot, teaspoon, cup, pint, quart, gallon, barrel, bushel, peck, cubic centimeter and other metric units of cubic measure.
Weight	Results from product of volume and density where density of a substance is a ratio of any volume of substance to an equal volume of water	Ounce, pound, ton, gram, and other metric units of weight.
Angular and Circular Measure	Angular measure indicates the amount of rotation of the terminal ray of an angle from the initial ray. Circular measure indicates the length of an arc in terms of the total circle from which it is taken.	Angle seconds, minutes, and degrees. Arc seconds, minutes, degrees, and radians.
Pitch Velocity Work Horsepower Electric current Electrical Energy Explosive Power Radio-activity	Some of these concepts use compound units to measure specific properties of things.	vib/sec ft/sec ft/lb ft-lb/hr watts kw-hr vib/sec roentgens

LINEAR MEASURE

The concept of linear measure or length should be taught carefully and well. Length is purely a one-dimensional property. Even the primary child should recognize that length is void of width and thickness. Standard units such as the inch, foot, or yard are always simulated to the student by the abstract notion that the length is associated with the path designated by the edge of the ruler or other device used for linear measuring. A piece of very fine wire often helps a student to comprehend length disassociated from width and thickness. Furthermore, the student can see that the piece of wire has the same length regardless of the shape it is forced to assume. The changing of the shape merely alters the path along which the measurement is made.

The measuring of the property called length as well as all other measuring involves two basic concepts toward which teachers should keep their sights set: (1) Measuring involves the relative magnitude of the thing to be measured and a conventional standard or unit. For example, if we are measuring the length of a table in feet and find the relative magnitude to be approximately 12 to 1, we say the table is 12 feet long. (2) All quantities whose properties we measure are continuous. For example in measuring length, this means that if we select any two points along the path to be measured no matter how close together these points may be, there is an infinitude of points lying on the path and between these two points. Here we are saying two things: first, that points occupy no space, but merely specify a location, and second, that the length measured along the path from one point to another corresponds to some real number (rational or irrational) of the standard unit being used. This actually makes it reasonable to apply other mathematical processes to these numbers and use them in conjunction with exact abstract numbers, keeping in mind at all times the limits of accuracy imposed by the approximate nature of measurements. It is likely appropriate at this point to summarize by stating that the concept of linear measure or length is sufficiently complex to warrant continued review and extension throughout the entire learning span of the pupil.

Furthermore, students will need to relate length to the common geometrical figures and the special segments and arcs associated with them. Perimeter, circumference, altitude, median, apothem, diagonal, radius, diameter, semicircle, base, width, and length are among them. Student experiences are not limited to these, however, since they may speak of the length of a highway (measured along a path designated by its center stripe) or the distance around a lake, having irregular shape, etc.

SQUARE MEASURE

Let us now look at the property of things known as area or square measure. We now introduce a standard unit involving a specific portion of two-dimensional space and in many cases possessing straight-line dimensions known as width and length.

Area never has depth or thickness. Students should recognize that this standard unit is characterized by its size and not its shape, but that for convenience we most often think of it as being the amount of area enclosed by a square one inch on a side. Most early experiences in measuring area are associated with formulas. These may be found from a variety of sources.[2] Care should be taken when making the transition to formulas that students understand the development of the formula as well as its use. Another aspect of area which requires clarification for young students is the matter of justifying the units obtained. Let us illustrate a case in point. In measuring the area of a rectangle having, say, a width of 2 inches and a length of 3 inches, students are often taught to multiply 2 inches by 3 inches to get 6 square inches. Such operations become contradictory in the minds of students who understand the process called multiplication. These students consider multiplication a short way of adding, and the multiplier thus signifies how many of the multiplicands should be added. In such capacity, the multiplier cannot be inches, feet, or yards, but must be a nondenominate number—that is, an abstract number which does not refer to any kind of unit. If we were to remain precise in our basic understandings we would find the area of rectangles as follows:

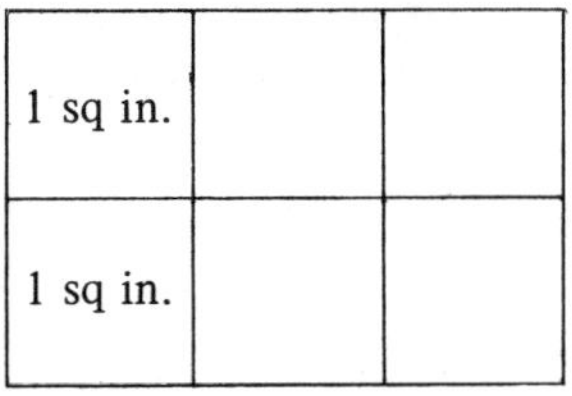

1 sq in.		
1 sq in.		

Our job is to find how many square inches are contained in the rectangle. This may be done by superimposing the standard unit on the rectangle and counting the number of units contained therein.

Applying the shortcut, we reason as follows: The first column contains 2 square inches and there are three such columns, so we multiply 2 square inches by 3 and obtain 6 square inches.

It is here recognized that this process is not likely to be retained, nor should it be, by the advanced student who understands and feels comfortable with the shortcuts and algorisms arising in physics and other fields where compound units are commonplace. While it is basically nonsensical to multiply 2 feet by 3 pounds and get 6 foot-pounds, yet for the student who understands why the algorism works it is not only legitimate for him to use this shortcut, it may actually help him keep his compound units straight and help him better understand the science concept involved.

In teaching area to beginning students, the teacher should utilize copious chalkboard demonstrations as well as a chart illustrating a square inch, square foot, and a square yard, superimposed upon each other.

[2] An excellent source is William H. Schaaf, *op. cit.*, pp. 238–241. See also Chapter 9 of present text.

CUBIC MEASURE

The concept of cubic measure or volume, while involving three dimensions, is usually easier to teach than is area, since it is further removed from linear measure. The notion of volume might best be demonstrated through the use of a cube made of plastic or plywood, with one side left open, the inside dimensions being one foot, and using one-inch cubes to illustrate its volume. While it may not be practical to have 1,728 cubes available, by using one layer of 144 cubes, and then stacking an additional eleven cubes up one corner to illustrate the number of such layers, the desired effect may be obtained.

As with area, the student should interpret the shortcut technique of multiplying units to get cubic units as really being an algorism. In reality we first find the number of cubic inches in a row, then in one layer, then multiply the number of cubic inches in a layer by the number of layers. The calculations for the cubic foot referred to above would thus become:

12 × 12 cu in. in a row = 144 cu in. in a layer
12 × 144 cu in. in a layer = 1,728 cu in. in a cube

Here again, once the learner understands the logical interpretation, he should be allowed to use the shortcut and the point should not be labored.

Volumes of common geometric space figures other than the cube should also be discussed and formulas developed, as maturation will allow. The cube, regular pyramid, right prism, right circular cylinder, right circular cone, sphere, and lune are basic solids from which the work on volumes may be extended. The technique of finding the volume of irregular solids by immersing them in a right circular glass, metal, or plastic cylinder partly filled with water and measuring the volume of water between the original and final level is a concept understandable to any student who understands and can calculate the volume of a right circular cylinder.

OTHER ASPECTS OF MEASUREMENT

As was stated earlier, measuring involves many properties of many things. The table set up earlier illustrated many areas of measurement which we have not discussed in this treatment. Even the common measures of weight and standard volume such as teaspoon, tablespoon, cup, pint, quart, and gallon are not treated here, but these generally give little trouble if the concepts back of them are understood. If weight is understood to result from volume and density, the units, both English and metric, are not particularly difficult.

Another aspect of measuring centers around proportional parts of similar geometric figures. This requires a knowledge of ratio and proportion as well as similarity of figures. While Boy Scouts and other young learners often use the principles involved here in estimating inaccessible distances, the ultimate objective should be a complete understanding of how and why these tricks work. Any good plane geometry hook may be used as a reference to develop this very important facet of measuring, but it is not recommended that time be devoted to it until the supporting concepts—namely ratio, proportion, and similarity—have been established. Extension into the use of scale drawings and problems involving navigation, travel on land, travel in space, angles of depression, angles of elevation, angles determined by direction from a fixed line, or points of the compass are all within the scope of an elementary development of this topic.

The use of trigonometric concepts and tables provides a powerful tool for measuring and opens up vast possibilities. Vectors which show both the direction and the magnitude of force or of velocity involve a very useful kind of measuring and one that is becoming increasingly important in modern mathematics and science. Although the basic notions of vectors are relatively simple, the measuring involved is intricately tied up with the whole area of vector analysis, aspects of which are fairly sophisticated. A good introduction to vectors may be found in the *Twenty-third Yearbook* of the National Council of Teachers of Mathematics.

ACCURACY IN MEASUREMENT

Let us move now to a discussion of the degree of accuracy of measurements and how this affects the results obtained when measurements are involved in computations. We have already established the approximate nature of all measurements, but just how approximate are they?

The precision of a measurement is defined by the unit used to make it. The smaller the unit the more precise the measurement. This means that if we measure a segment to the nearest inch as being 3 inches, the actual length of the segment is between $2^1/_2$ and $3^1/_2$ inches. If we measure the segment in half-inch units, the actual length lies between $2^3/_4$ inches and $3^1/_4$ inches, thus increasing the accuracy. We call this interval, within which the measurement must lie, the *tolerance interval*.

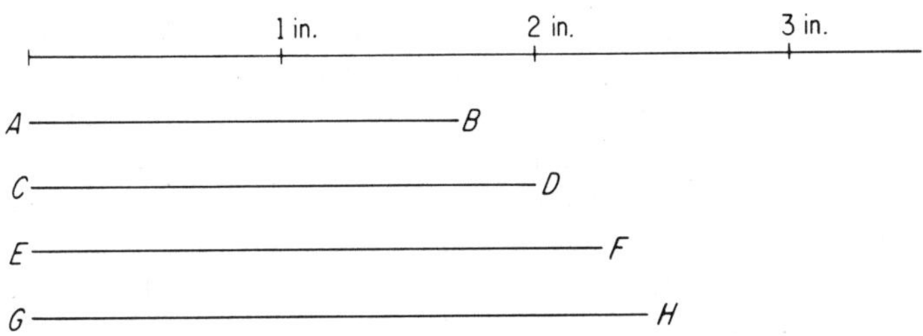

If in the accompanying figure the top line represents our measuring instrument, and it has only the markings 1 inch, 2 inches, 3 inches, etc., then anyone of the four segments *AB*, *CD*, *EF*, and *GH* would measure 2 inches to the nearest inch. In other words, any segment whose right-hand terminal point is closer to 2 inches long than it is to 1 inch or 3 inches would be classified as being 2 inches long. If we consider the imaginary midpoints (remember these are not really marked on the instrument) the tolerance interval lies between $1^1/_2$ inches and $2^1/_2$ inches. Now we observe also that for anyone of the four segments shown the greatest possible error is $^1/_2$ inch, since if the measurements of each of the four segments is given as 2 inches, it is not likely that any of these terminal points B, D, F, H, is more than $^1/_2$ inch from the 2-inch mark. This can be generalized to be true about any terminal point within the tolerance interval. We conclude, therefore, that the greatest possible error is one-half the unit of measure used.

Let us apply this analysis to another measurement, say $5^1/_8$ inches, measured to the nearest $^1/_8$ inch. The tolerance interval is now between $5^1/_{16}$ inches and $5^3/_{16}$ inches. Precision measurements often indicate the tolerance interval with the $\pm$ sign. This is read "plus or minus," and the notation for the tolerance interval above would read $5^1/_8$ inches $\pm$ $^1/_{16}$ inch. In notations of this kind $^1/_{16}$ inch is said to be the tolerance and corresponds with what we previously called the greatest possible error. This notation of tolerance is also used in industry in a little different sense. For example, a machinist may be required to produce a steel pin whose diameter is .025 inch $\pm$ .001 inch. This would mean that his finished product could have a diameter of not less than .024 inch and not more than .026 inch.

Another modification of tolerance comes from the dispensing of materials by merchants. Since the law requires full measure, only positive tolerances may be practical. For example, if one requests an 8-foot board at a lumber yard, he may be most unhappy to find he had received a board as short as 7.5 feet. Yet our previous discussion might justify such a measurement. However, some state and federal laws do allow slight negative tolerances for weight, volumes, areas, lengths, and the like. Scientific notation also has a method for indicating precision of measurement; for example, 5.71×10^4 cm means that the measurement was made to the nearest hundred centimeters, while 4.30×10^{-4} cm indicates precision to the nearest millionth centimeter. Note that in the first case we subtract the number of decimal places in the multiplier from the power of 10 to get an exponent of 2 indicating hundred centimeters, while in the case of the negative exponent we do the same thing, $(-4) - (+2) = -6$, getting an exponent -6 or millionths of a centimeter.

We now discuss briefly another measure of accuracy called the *relative error*, or the ratio of the greatest possible error to the measured value. If, for example, we measure the length of a room to be $15^1/_2$ feet to the nearest half-foot, then the greatest possible error is $^1/_4$ foot. Now dividing by $15^1/_2$ we get the relative error. Assuming that all measurements are made correct to the precision indicated for them, a measurement having a smaller relative error is more accurate than one having a larger relative error. Thus the distance from the earth to the sun, 93,000,000 miles measured to the nearest million miles, is about as accurate as the length of a table 9.7 feet measured to the nearest tenth of a foot. Note the calculation below:

Measure	*Greatest possible error*	*Relative error*
93,000,000 miles	500,000 miles	$\frac{500,000}{93,000,000} \approx .005$
9.7 feet	1/20 foot	$1/20/9.7 \approx .005$

When the relative error is expressed in percent, it is called *percent of error*.

Modern technology, with its mass-production and precision requirements, draws heavily upon measurement and tolerance. Students need an exposure to and understanding of these important aspects of modern living.

COMPUTATIONS INVOLVING APPROXIMATIONS

We shall begin this discussion by reviewing two elementary agreements which enter into these computations. The first is the matter of rounding numbers. This process is governed by the following ground rules.

1. If the number is an integer any digits dropped when rounding must be replaced by zeros, i.e., 537 feet rounded to the nearest 10 feet becomes 540 feet.
2. If the number involves a decimal fraction any digits dropped to the right of the decimal are never replaced with zeros, e.g., 9.724 miles becomes 9.7 when rounded to the nearest tenth of a mile.
3. If the last digit dropped (that is the one farthest to the left) is 5, 6, 7, 8, or 9, the first digit retained is increased by one. Only the last digit dropped figures in the rounding; digits to the right of it are completely ignored.
4. If the last digit dropped is 4, 3, 2, 1, or 0, the retained digits are unchanged.
5. If the only nonzero digit dropped is 5 and it occupies the highest place value of the dropped digits, it is customary to round to the nearest even digit, e.g., 907.50 becomes 908 but 906.50 remains 906.

With regard to significant figures the following agreements are generally accepted.

1. All nonzero figures are always significant.
2. Zeros occurring between nonzero digits are always significant. For example, in 3002, if we know the number of thousands to be 3 and the number of ones to be 2, we also know there are no hundreds and no tens.
3. Terminal zeros following a decimal are always significant: 4.0 miles means the distance has been measured to the nearest tenth of a mile.
4. If a decimal is less than one, zeros immediately following the decimal point are not significant; e.g., in the measurement 0.005 inch, the unit of measure is one-thousandth of an inch, and only the five is significant.

5. Terminal zeros in an integer are not significant unless so indicated, e.g., a measurement of 3,500 miles may be considered to have only two significant digits unless information to the contrary is given. If the units or tens have been measured we should be told so, or if the number has been rounded this should be stated. Scientific notation overcomes this ambiguity by placing all the significant figures in the multiplier. Furthermore, it is standard practice in scientific notation to place the decimal between the first and second significant figures.

We now discuss the adding and subtracting of measurements. Suppose we have the measurement 5.3 feet correct to the nearest tenth of a foot and 7.635 feet correct to the nearest thousandth of a foot. If we add these as they stand we get 5.3 feet + 7.635 feet = 12.935 feet. Here we have taken the idenfensible liberty of considering 5.3 to be equivalent to 5.300 or we are considering 5.3 to be correct to the nearest thousandth foot, which is contrary to the original information. This we would expect to lead us into difficulty. Let us analyze the situation.

The measurement 5.3 feet could be as small as 5.25 or as large as 5.35, whereas the measurement 7.635 could be as small as 7.6345 or as large as 7.6355. Let us consider the two extremes 5.25 + 7.6345 = 12.8845 as the smallest possible sum, while 5.35 + 7.6355 = 12.9855 is the largest possible sum. There is then only one chance in approximately 100 that our first sum 12.935 is the largest possible sum. There is then only one chance in approximately 100 that our first sum 12.935 is the correct one. We would have been just as accurate had we added 5.3 feet to 7.6 feet and gotten the sum of 12.9 feet which is well within the range and does not leave us with any false sense of accuracy, as did the first sum.

In multiplying or dividing numbers arising from approximations, we again find a false notion of accuracy. Basically we can be guided by the principle that we cannot make a measurement or other approximate value more precise by involving it in a computation. Let us consider the area of a circle whose radius is

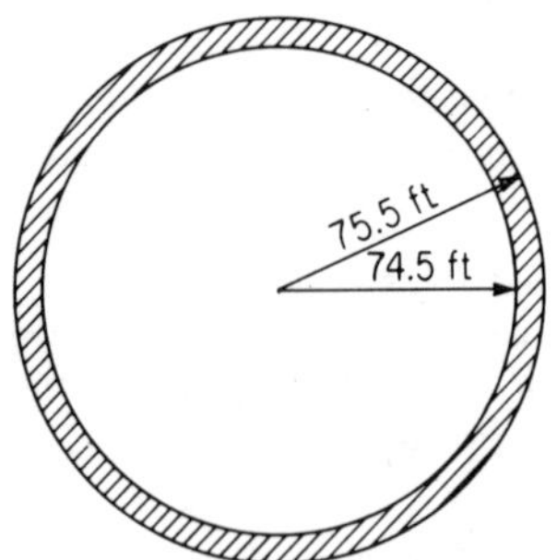

given as 75 feet, measured to the nearest foot. Actually, then, the tolerance interval of the radius is from 74.5 feet to 75.5 feet. Let us now diagram the above situation.

Now the desired area will include the area of the inner circle plus part of the shaded area between the two concentric circles. Using the minimum and maximum values of the radius, we find the smallest and largest areas to be:

$$(74.5)^2 \times 3.14159 = 17{,}436.6098984 \text{ sq ft}$$

$$(75.5)^2 \times 3.14159 = 17{,}907.8433975 \text{ sq ft}$$

We are justified here in using pi to 5 decimals or 6 significant figures, since the 74.5 and 75.5 are considered exact numbers and the squares have 7 significant figures. Now note that there is a difference between the two extremes of approximately 470 square feet. Any area within the two limits is then as good an approximation as any other, since the chances are 1 in approximately 470 for any value chosen within the limits. Let us take an easy and sensible computation rounding as seems logical and see whether our area falls within the limits.

$(75)^2 = 5{,}625 \approx 5{,}600$ rounded to two digits. Multiplying by a reasonably accurate value for pi, say, 3.14, we get $5600 \times 3.14 = 17{,}584.00$, and rounding to two significant digits we get 18,000 square feet to the nearest thousand square feet. This agrees with our limits, since of 471 possibilities only 64 could be closer to 17,000 than 18,000. We rounded our final product to 2 significant digits because the least accurate number involved in the multiplication had only two significant digits, and the number of significant digits does give a rough idea of accuracy.

Let us now state the guidelines for rounding and give some illustrations.

1. To add or subtract numbers arising from approximations, first round each number to the accuracy of the least precise number involved, then perform the addition or subtraction and round the result to same degree of accuracy.
2. When multiplying or dividing numbers arising from approximations, keep as many significant digits in the product or quotient as there are in the least accurate number entering into the particular computation.
3. When using a rounded value of π in either multiplication or division, retain one more significant figure in π than is contained in the least accurate measurement entering into the computation.
4. To find the square root of a number arising from approximation, retain as many significant digits in the root as the number contains.

It will be noted that no demonstration is given in support of guidelines 3 and 4. Experimentation on the part of the reader will, however, support this plausibility.

ILLUSTRATIONS

Multiplication: 2.34 inches $\times$ .0006 $\approx$ .001404 $\approx$ .001 inch

Division: 7.6432 $\div$ .015 inch $\approx$ 509.5 $\approx$ 510 inches

Multiplication with pi: Find the circumference of a circle whose radius = 7.6 inches.

$$C = 2 \times 3.14 \times 7.6 \approx 47.728 \approx 48 \text{ inches}$$

Note that 2 is not an approximate number but part of the formula. Since the radius which is approximate has two significant digits we use three significant digits for π.

Square Root: Find the square root of .0096 sq ft.

$$\sqrt{.0096} \approx .0979 \approx .10$$

In concluding this chapter on measurement the reader will recognize that while this may be a fairly good effort toward organizing this material, at the same time it leaves a great deal to be desired. This area of mathematics is receiving considerable current attention, and the answers lie not in so elementary a treatment as is presented here but in the sophisticated areas of statistics and the theory of errors. Accordingly we will do well not to labor the notions of accuracy and error below the college level.

PROBLEMS

1. What do we mean when we say that we measure the property of a thing rather than the thing itself?
2. How would you defend the proposition that all measurement is approximate before a group of fourth-grade students?
3. What do we mean by a standard unit of measure?
4. Differentiate among linear measure, square measure, and cubic measure.
5. Which kind of measure should one use to measure the following:
   (a) The perimeter of a rectangle
   (b) The area of the interior of a circle
   (c) The height of a tree
   (d) The amount of water in a bucket
   (e) The circumference of a circle
   (f) The hypotenuse of a right triangle
   (g) The amount of goods for a dress
   (h) The amount of water in a reservoir
   (i) The elevation of a city
   (j) The diagonal of a square
   (k) The amount of land in a lot
6. When you study Chapter 9, "Space and Relationships Within It," you will be reminded of the need for a volume kit in teaching cubic measure. Can you at this point predict what items such a kit should contain?
7. What do we mean by the greatest possible error for a particular measurement? Illustrate with an example.
8. Calculate the relative error for the following measurements and tell which has the greatest accuracy.
   (a) 86745000 lb
   (b) 2.3 oz
9. Round the following:
   (a) 874 ft. rounded to the nearest 10 ft
   (b) 98.323 rd rounded to the nearest tenth of a rod

(c) 876.5296 yd rounded to the nearest yd
(d) 93,486 ft rounded to the nearest ft
(e) 47.7500 lb rounded to the nearest tenth of a pound
(f) 47.8500 lb rounded to the nearest tenth of a pound

10. How many significant figures are there in the following measurements?
(a) 8765.497 in.
(b) 930007.6 ft
(c) 870.00 cm
(d) .0007 yd
(e) 93000000 miles

11. Perform the following operations rounding your results to a degree of accuracy consistant with the measurements given:
(a) Add 9.3 in. and 8.659 in.
(b) Subtract 857.62 ft from 900 ft.
(c) Multiply 4.2 yd by 87.294 yd.
(d) Divide 864 lb by 9.2 lb.
(e) Find the area of a circle whose radius is 3.2 ft.
(f) Find the square root of 9.86 sq ft.

12. Show by diagram and calculation the plausibility of the area of the following rectangle being approximately 20 sq in.

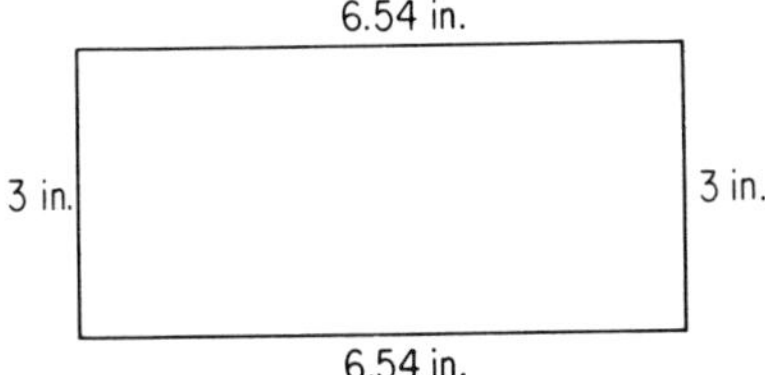

Chapter 8

Logic and Proof in the Teaching of Mathematics

THE TASK AND THE SEQUENCE

Students should be helped to become aware of the nature of logic and proof at all grade levels. These concepts should be treated as vertical strands in the learning experience from kindergarten through grade 8. The ideas should be expanded and reinforced as the maturity and understanding of the students will allow. A brief outline of the treatment of each level is shown below. The details should be interspersed as necessary and numerous examples and experiences provided.

LOGIC IN GRADES K-3

Some basic strategies of logic are here in order. The following examples illustrate them.

1. All children are either boys or girls. If a child is not a girl, he must be a boy. This is a matter of exhausting the possibilities.
2. Any real number is equal to five, smaller than five, or greater than five. If you can show that a number is not either of two of these, then it must be the third. Again, we have exhausted the possibilities.
3. If a real number is larger than four, then it is larger than any number smaller than four.
4. If two numbers are not equal, then one must be greater than the other.
5. The children may now be led to the law of the excluded middle. It states that a thing is either "A" or "non-A." For example, a number is either six or not six. (Emphasize the *logic*, not the name with students of this age.)
6. Now we move to the law of non-contradiction. It says a thing cannot be "A" and "non-A" at the same time. For example, a number cannot be six and not six at the same time.

LOGIC IN GRADES 4–6

1. The negation or denial of a proposition may now be stated by introducing the term "not."

   (a) John is a Republican. (a) John is not a Republican.
   (b) Jack is taller than Mary. (b) Jack is not taller than Mary.
   (c) Ten is greater than nine. (c) Ten is not greater than nine.

   Review from level one that either the statement is true or its negation is, but not both.
2. The implication or conditional structure using "if. . .then" is now introduced.
   (a) If John is elected, then he will be president
   (b) If a natural number is not odd, then it is even.
   (c) If a person lives in Utah, then he lives in the United States of America.
3. Review and extend all of the concepts from the previous level.

LOGIC IN GRADES 7 AND 8

At this level, the treatment of logic and proof may be more formal. The common connectives and modifiers, their symbols and names may now be introduced. We include here two expressions previously mentioned.

Connectives or Modifiers	Symbol	Name
"not"	$\sim$	Negation or denial
"and"	$\wedge$	Conjunction
"or"	$\vee$	Disjunction or alternation
"if. . . .then"	$\rightarrow$	Implication or conditional
"if and only if"	$\leftrightarrow$	Biconditional

At this level the names should be mentioned, but not over emphasized. Examples using each word or phrase follows:

1. Sixteen is a perfect square. Sixteen is not a perfect square.
2. A quadrilateral is a polygon and a hexagon is a polygon.
3. Angle x equals angle y, or angle z equals angle w. In the inclusive sense this means either or both. In the exclusive sense this means either, but not both. Mathematicians usually use the inclusive sense.
4. If two angles are equal to the same angle, then they are equal to each other. This is a most fruitful form of logic at this grade level. The beginner may wish to think of "if" as meaning "whenever."
5. A set of points in a plane is a circle if and only if all the points are equidistant from a given point.

At this level we look at deductive inference in contrast to simple implication. In simple implication we do not necessarily mean that the premise is true but that if it is true then the conclusion follows. For example, "If the figure is a square, it is a rectangle," does not insure that the figure is a square. But if we say: "The figure is a square and a square is a rectangle, then the figure is a rectangle," we have used deductive inference by insuring that both premises are true; and, therefore, the conclusion is necessarily true. Another example: If a man lives in Utah, he is a Utahan. Joe Blake lives in Utah, therefore, Joe Blake is a Utahan.

At this stage it is well to review the fact that every proposition is true or not true in the exclusive sense of "or" and we may now again identify this statement as the *law of the excluded middle.* Also, *the law of noncontradiction* should now be reviewed and called by its name. It states that a proposition cannot be both true and false at the same time.

Law of the Excluded Middle

1. Rational numbers are either whole or not whole.
2. A geometric figure is either a circle or not a circle.

Law of Noncontradiction

1. A number cannot be both an integer and not an integer.
2. A line cannot be both perpendicular and not perpendicular to the same line.

Logical implication employing the "if-then" form now leads us to the identification of "hypothesis" and conclusion. We state: If a person is 21 years old, then he is old enough to vote in the United States. The "if" clause sets up a condition or premise and is called the hypothesis of the proposition. The "then" clause specifies an inference and is called the conclusion.

In the examples which follow some propositions are arranged in the usual way while in others the clauses are reversed; the "then" is omitted, or the "if-then" arrangement is completely omitted. These changes in no way affect the logic.

1. If a person lives in Los Angeles, then he lives in California.
2. If a person lives in Los Angeles, he lives in California.
3. A person lives in California if he lives in Los Angeles.
4. A resident of Los Angeles is a Californian.
5. If two angles are vertical, then they are equal.
6. If two angles are vertical, they are equal.
7. Two angles are equal if they are vertical.
8. Vertical angles are equal.

Note that all of these propositions may be put into the standard "if-then" form without changing the meaning.

Now let us introduce some symbols. Actually the logic of a pattern is not affected by the contents of the proposition; so if we identify the "if" clause as

p and the "then" clause as q, we can accurately and tersely say $p \longrightarrow q$. Consider the proposition: "If I study, then I will learn." Here "I study" is p and "I will learn" is q. Now if we accept the implication, $p \longrightarrow q$ and also p then the conclusion q must follow. Diagrammatically:

$$\text{If}\begin{cases} 1.\ p \longrightarrow q \text{ is true} \\ 2.\ p \qquad\ \ \text{is true} \end{cases}$$
$$\overline{\text{Then } q \text{ follows}}$$

This kind of reasoning is called *deductive inference*, and our example exhibits the *fundamental rule of inference*. Note that the implication $p \longrightarrow q$ does not necessarily mean that either p or q is true; but the truth of both p and $p \longrightarrow q$ insures that q be true.

Example 8-1

Premise 1. If unemployment increases, the national income will decrease.
Premise 2. Unemployment has increased.
Conclusion. The national income will decrease.
Symbolically,

$$\begin{array}{ll} 1.\ p \longrightarrow q & (p \text{ implies } q) \\ 2.\ p & (p \text{ holds}) \\ \hline 3.\ \therefore q & (q \text{ holds}) \end{array}$$

This, as was previously stated, is called the *fundamental rule of inference.* An extension of this rule is known as the *chain rule of inference.* It states:

$$\begin{array}{l} 1.\ p \longrightarrow q \\ 2.\ q \longrightarrow r \\ \hline 3.\ \therefore p \longrightarrow r \end{array}$$

1. $p \longrightarrow q$	1. Every element of the set of positive integers is an element of the set of integers.
2. $q \longrightarrow r$	2. Every element of the set of integers is an element of the set of rational numbers.
3. $p \longrightarrow r$	3. Every element of the set of positive integers is an element of the set of rational numbers.

Euler's circles and Venn diagrams are useful means for illustrating the fundamental rule of inference and the chain rule. Using the notion of elements of sets and by confining the elements of a particular set to a circle, Euler has diagrammatically represented the logic involved.

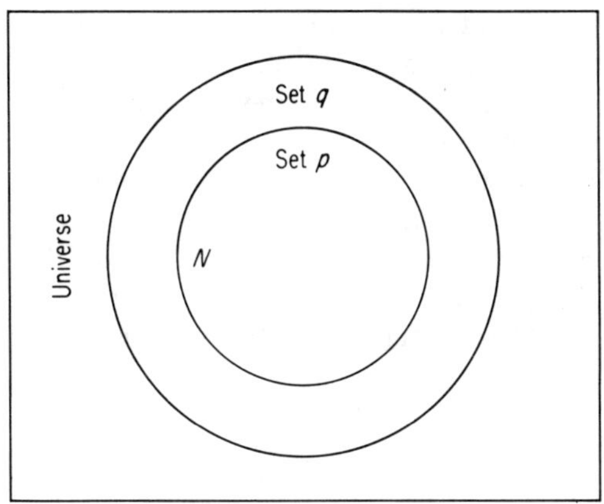

Symbolism

1. $p \longrightarrow q$	1. Every element of p is an element of q.
2. p	2. N is an element of p.
3. $\therefore q$	3. N is an element of q.

Extending the illustration to the chain rule we have:

1. $p \longrightarrow q$	1. Every element of p is an element of q.
2. $q \longrightarrow r$	2. Every element of q is an element of r.
3. $\therefore p \longrightarrow r$	3. $\therefore$ every element of p is an element of r.

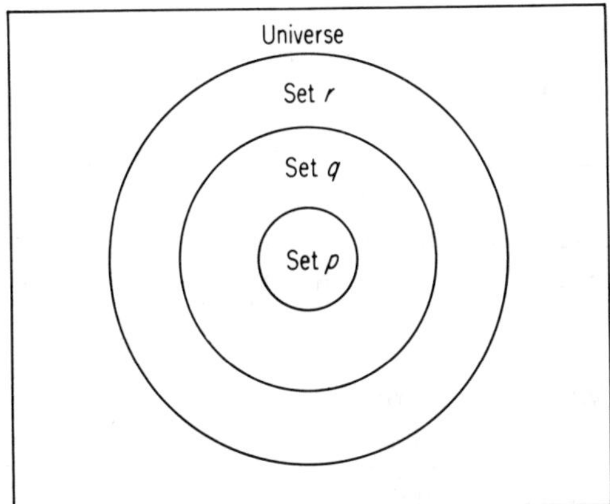

We now introduce three versions of a proposition known as the *converse*, *inverse*, and *contrapositive*. Let us consider the proposition: "If he is a man, he is a *Homo sapiens*." The converse is: "If he is a *Homo sapiens*, he is a man." Note that the original "if" clause becomes the conclusion (or "then" clause) and the original conclusion is changed to an "if" clause. We now write the inverse:

"If he is not a man, he is not a *Homo sapiens*." Note that here we do not reverse the clauses, but merely negate both of them.

It should be noted from the two previous examples that converses and inverses may or may not be true[1] even though the original proposition is true. The teacher should assist students in examining many of both kinds.

The contrapositive of the original proposition is:

"If he is not a *Homo sapiens*, he is not a man." Note that this statement is true, as are all contrapositives of true propositions. Further, it should be observed that contrapositives are formed by interchanging the clauses and negating each of them.

Symbolically,

$$(p \longrightarrow q) \longleftrightarrow (\sim q \longrightarrow \sim p)$$

Diagrammatically,

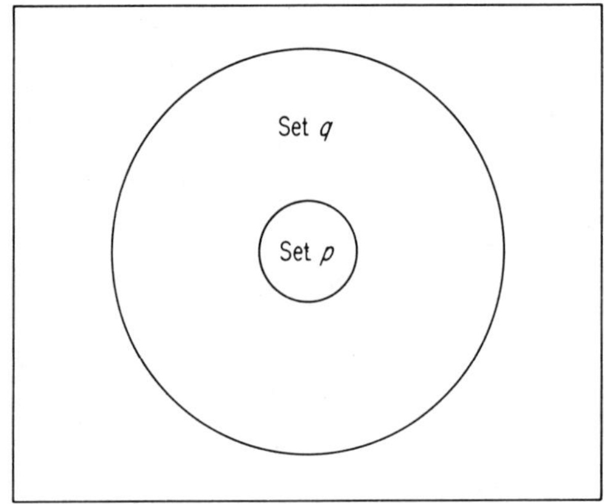

If an element is not in q, then it is not in p.

Some forms of invalid reasoning are exhibited below in both symbolic and sentence notation.

Case 1

1. $p \longrightarrow q$ 1. All apples are fruit.
2. q 2. This is a fruit.

3. $\therefore p$ 3. $\therefore$ this is an apple.

Case 2

1. $p \longrightarrow q$ 1. All apples are fruit.
2. p 2. This is not an apple.

3. $\therefore \sim p$ 3. $\therefore$ this is not a fruit.

[1] If we limit man not to include women, then the converse and inverse are not true.

Diagrammatically, Case 1 and Case 2 appear as follows:
Case 1

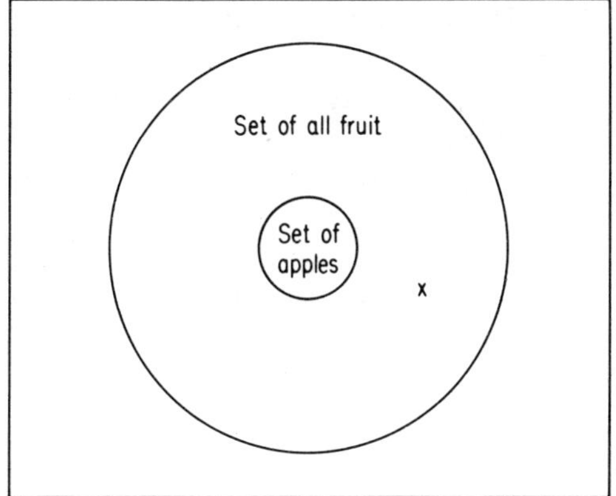

Obviously, an element x could be fruit without being an apple.
Case 2

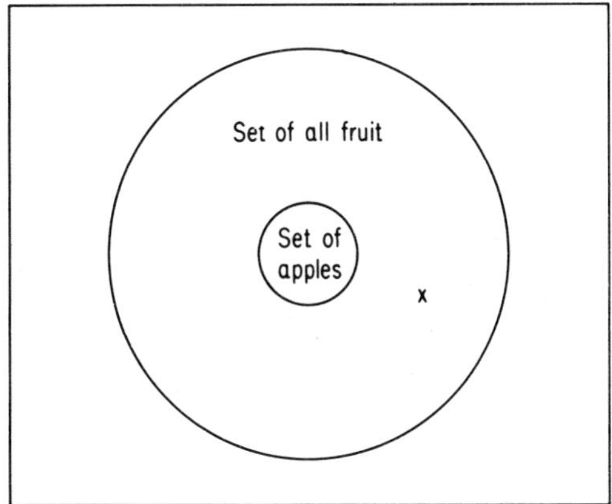

Just because an element x is not an apple does not assure that it is not a fruit.

Note here that considering p, q, $\sim q$, etc., as sets of elements helps to diagram the situation and thus arrive at the truth or falsity of the reasoning. Note further that one counterexample is sufficient to disprove a conclusion. Teachers should encourage their students to analyze each case separately rather than memorize generalizations.

In mathematics we often refer to relationships as being necessary or sufficient or both. For example, it is a necessary condition that water be a chemical compound. However, it is not a sufficient condition since a substance could be a compound without being water. For a substance to be a compound it is sufficient that it be water, but it is not necessary that it be water, since it could be a compound without being water; e.g., it could be salt or sugar or any of many compounds.

A second example: It is necessary that a prime number be integral, but it is not sufficient that it be integral since there are many integral numbers which are not prime. For a number to be prime, it is sufficient that it be 2, 3, or 5, but is not necessary that it be one of these, since there are many other prime numbers. It is both necessary and sufficient that a prime number have exactly four integral divisors if we are considering the rational number set. We illustrate this second example by means of Euler's circles:

1. It is necessary that a prime number be integral.

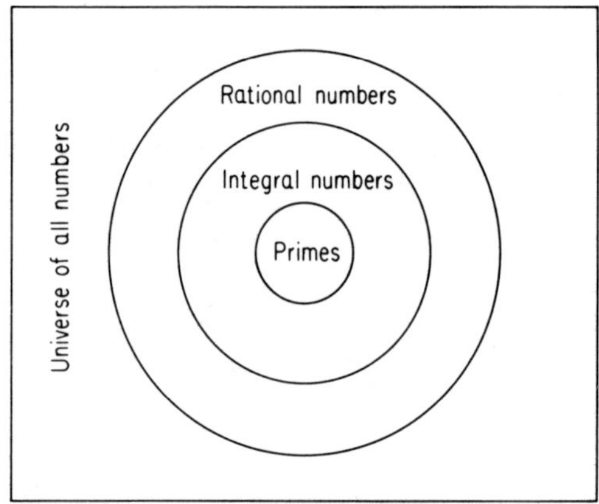

2. It is sufficient that a prime number be 2, 3, or 5.

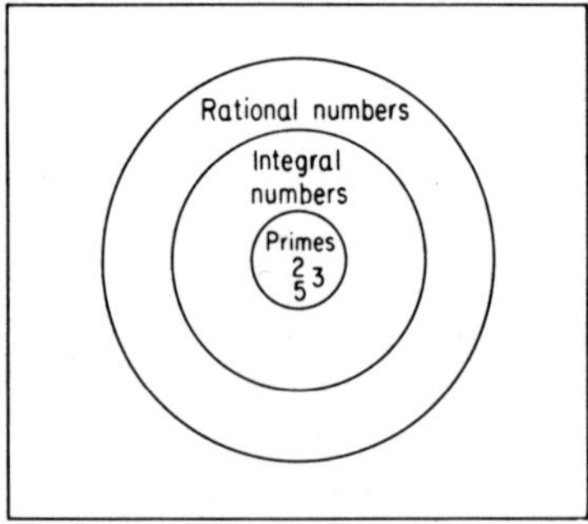

It is a necessary and sufficient condition that a prime rational have exactly four integral divisors. Note that the prime rationals and the rational numbers having exactly four integral divisors are the same set. Note further that these last two sets illustrate the biconditional relationship; that is $p \longleftrightarrow q$.

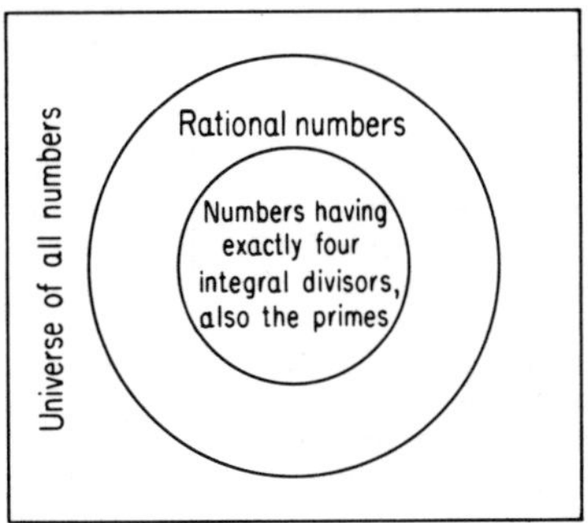

We see then that "necessary and sufficient" conditions parallel "if and only if" conditions. Now since $p \longleftrightarrow q$ implies that both the proposition and its converse is true, theorems of this type will require separate proofs for the "if" part and the "only if" part, or the "necessary" part and the "sufficient" part. The reason for having to prove both parts is that the converse of a proposition is not necessarily true.

From the above discussion it can be seen that all logically correct definitions are biconditional, or the conditions stated are both necessary and sufficient. Technically we are generally careless in our statement of definitions since often the biconditional situation is understood, but not stated.

Common definitions:

1. An isosceles triangle has two equal sides.
2. If a triangle has two equal sides, it is isosceles.
3. If a triangle is isosceles, it has two equal sides.

Note 2 and 3 are converse, both do hold.

Definition stated in biconditional form: A triangle is isosceles if and only if it has at least two equal sides.

Definition stated by use of "necessary and sufficient": It is a necessary and sufficient condition that an isosceles triangle have at least two equal sides. The true meaning of a definition becomes quite apparent when we consider that it is merely a name or symbol for a set of properties. The definition thus becomes an equivalence relation and as such must be reversible. "If and only if" or "necessary and sufficient" thus become essential to logical equivalence. We now summarize our definitions of the symbolic statements which are used in argument forms and give examples of each.

Symbol	Possible Meanings	Example
p	Statement	A number is composite.
q	Statement	A number has nontrivial factors.
$\sim p$	Not p, p is false. It is not the case that p.	It is not the case that a number has nontrivial factors.
$\sim q$	Not q, q is false. It is not the case that q.	It is not the case that a number has nontrivial factors.
$p \wedge q$	p and q	A number is composite and has nontrivial factors.
$p \vee q$	p or q. (Inclusive sense)	A number is composite or has nontrivial factors.
$p \longrightarrow q$	If p then q. q only if p. p is a sufficient condition for q.	If a number is composite then it has nontrivial factors.
$p \longleftrightarrow q$	If p then q and if q then p. q if and only if p. p is a necessary and sufficient condition for q.	A number is composite if and only if it has nontrivial factors.
$\sim(p \wedge \sim q)$	It is not the case that p and not q.	It is not the case that a number is composite and does not have nontrivial factors.

Below on this page are illustrated some formulas for valid arguments, with some examples.

The strength of these formulas becomes apparent if we apply one of them to statements with which we are not acquainted. For example:

Let p = A trili is a poli

Let q = A trili has more than two kali

We can now test the truth or falsity of the following statement by fitting it to one of our formulas:

If a trili is a poli if and only if it has more than two kali and this trili has more than two kali, then this trili is a poli. (Note that it fits our last formula and is therefore true.)

Formulas*	Examples
$[(p \longrightarrow q) \wedge p] \longrightarrow q$	If a number is composite then it has nontrivial factors and 12 is composite ∴ it has nontrivial factors.
$[(p \vee \sim q) \wedge \sim p \longrightarrow \sim q]$	A number is composite or it does not have nontrivial factors and 11 is not composite ∴ it does have nontrivial factors.
$(p \longrightarrow q) \longrightarrow (\sim q \longrightarrow \sim p)$	If a number is composite, then it has nontrivial factors ∴ if a number is not composite then it does not have nontrivial factors.
$p \longrightarrow \sim(\sim p)$	If a number is composite then it is not true that the number is not composite.
$[(p \longleftrightarrow q) \wedge q] \longrightarrow p$	If a number is composite if and only if it has nontrivial factors and it has nontrivial factors then it is composite.

*p and q are defined as in the previous table.

It is not recommended, however, that the teacher encourage blind dependence upon formulas, especially with younger learners. A much more dependable tool might be the use of straight thinking associated with Euler's circles and Venn diagrams.

Our development to this point leads naturally to an interesting and fruitful area known as *truth tables*. These, however, will not be developed in this text, but the reader is referred to the *Twenty-fourth Yearbook of the National Council of Teachers of Mathematics,* pages 158–166.

We pause here to emphasize some of the fallacies and pitfalls against which we must guard if we are to develop the techniques, skills and concepts which will lead us to rigorous and logical proof. The following items of caution should be considered:

1. A false premise may lead to a false conclusion even though the syllogism is valid.
   Example: (a) All men are rich.
   (b) This person is a man.
   ―――――――――――――
   (c) ∴ this person is rich.
2. False conclusions may be reached by assuming the truth of a converse.
   Example: All right angles are equal; therefore all equal angles are right angles.
3. False conclusions may be reached by assuming the truth of an inverse.
   Example: If two angles are right angles, then they are equal; therefore if two angles are not right angles, they are not equal.
4. The danger of hidden or implicit assumptions.
   Example: When we are told that Zingo television sets will not distort the picture, we assume other sets will.
5. Circular definitions and circular reasoning.
   Example: An arc degree is an arc ∴ an arc is an arc degree.
   Using a term to define itself.
   Using a theorem to prove itself.
6. Using invalid formulas such as:

$$[(p \longrightarrow q) \wedge \sim p] \rightarrow \sim q$$

$$[(p \longrightarrow q) \wedge q] \longrightarrow p$$

7. Drawing false conclusion from sound premises or ignoring the facts.
   Example: (a) If a figure is a triangle, it is a polygon.
   (b) This figure is a polygon.
   ―――――――――――――
   (c) ∴ this figure is a triangle.

THE NATURE OF PROOF

Let us now explore the nature of proof and some of the strategies used in its establishment. First we should recognize that mathematics is not absolute nor does it make any claim to "eternal truths." Every mathematical system is built as depicted in the accompanying diagram.

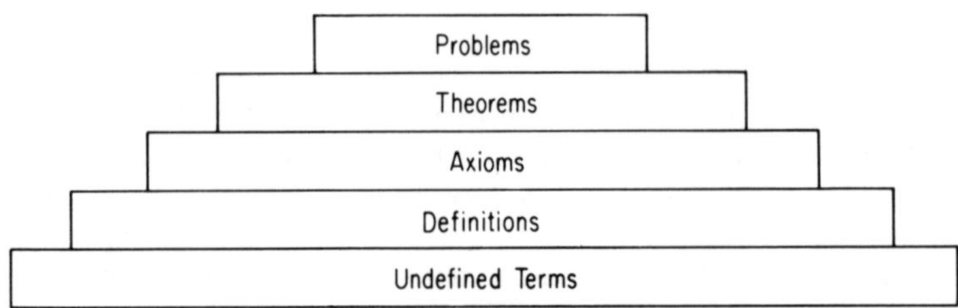

In mathematics, as in any other human endeavor, we must begin somewhere. Once we have agreed upon the undefined terms we can begin to define certain other terms in the light of the undefined terms and our experiences with them. Never should we become too certain of our definitions, since generally they are only a few steps removed from the undefined terms. The strength of our definitions lies not in their evolution, but in their consistency and noncontradiction within the system. Having now accepted the undefined terms and used them in our definitions, we are ready to postulate anything we wish. Axioms and postulates are out-and-out assumptions suggested by experience or based upon the whim of some mathematician. The laying down of axioms or postulates is a free act of human beings. Again as with definitions and undefined terms, their true value lies in their usefulness in strengthening and expanding the mathematical system in consistent and noncontradictory fashion. To the uninitiated this may appear haphazard, but in reality it is not at all so, since the mathematician must choose intelligently or face the discomfort and embarrassment of a poor mathematical system. Having once established a sound underpinning, he can build a system of theorems limited only by his imagination and the power of the system which he has created.

Teachers should assist their students to recognize the structure upon which each branch of mathematics is built and articulate it into a consistent and supporting whole. Modern mathematics is doing much to assist in this endeavor, as evidenced by the use of broad concepts such as sets and ordered pairs which thread themselves vertically through much of mathematics.

As we now look more specifically at how mathematicians prove their theorems, we submit the following description of proof:

Proof, in the broad sense, consists of any means of gaining assurance that a conclusion is valid. In its narrower sense it refers to methods of reasoning such that any doubt as to the validity of a solution must refer to the assumptions upon which it is based, rather than to the logical necessity of the inferences drawn from them.

In order to appreciate the accepted scope for proof, it is desirable to realize that there are some areas in which conviction properly remains undefended, in which there is no place for proof. In those cases where it is appropriate and possible to question bases of belief, there are several familiar and reasonable methods for establishing conviction.

Before we look at various kinds and strategies of proof we should make two facts clear. First, no amount of agreement is conclusive in mathematics. A mathematician may show that a hypothesis holds for a million cases, but unless he can exhaust the cases he has proven nothing. This is not to say that he has not improved the plausibility of his hypothesis. Second, one instance of failure suffices to shatter a hypothesis. Such rigor may seem unfair to many people, but the mathematician would have it no other way. He recognizes that the reasoning of mathematics is virtually devoid of prejudice and emotion and he adheres to the rules, neither giving or asking quarter.

STRATEGIES OF PROOF

We now examine some strategies of proof:

1. Proof by counterexample.
   As pointed out earlier, one counterexample is sufficient to disprove an hypothesis. This rule of the game is often helpful in disproving propositions which may require examination. For example, we may prove that

   $$\frac{x^2 - 49}{x - 7} = x + 7$$

   is not always true by exhibiting the case where $x = 7$.
   Another simpler example is the proof that not all odd whole numbers are prime. We simply exhibit the counterexample nine.
2. Detaching an antecedent.
   When we have an implication such as $p \longrightarrow q$, we call p the antecedent and q the consequent. If our inference is valid and we can prove p, then q follows. For example: If a figure is a quadrilateral, it is a polygon. *ABCD* is a quadrilateral; therefore it is a polygon. In our chart of valid arguments this appeared as $[(p \longrightarrow q) \wedge p] \longrightarrow q$.
3. Developing a chain of propositions.
   This consists of repeated application of 2 above. For example: *ABCD* is a square, and all squares are quadrilaterals, and all quadrilaterals are polygons; therefore *ABCD* is a polygon. Symbolically,

   $$[r \wedge (r \longrightarrow q) \wedge (q \longrightarrow p)] \longrightarrow p$$

   where r = a figure is a square
   q = a figure is a quadrilateral
   p = a figure is a polygon
   If r is true and $r \longrightarrow q$, then q is true; and if q is true and $q \longrightarrow p$, then p is true.

4. Proving a conditional.

   There are three possible attacks here.

   (a) Assume the antecedent and argue the consequent. *Example*: If a triangle is equilateral, it is equiangular. We assume it equilateral and argue it equiangular by any means at our disposal.

   (b) Prove its contrapositive. *Example*: In proving (a) above, we would prove: If a triangle is not equiangular, it is not equilateral. This is justified by the law of contraposition, viz., $[(p \longleftrightarrow q) \longleftrightarrow (\sim q \longrightarrow \sim p)]$. In cases where the consequent is a conjunction, we use repeated applications of a simple conditional. Assume the antecedent and argue each part of the conjunction (conjunct) separately. *Example*: If a line bisects the vertex angle of an isosceles triangle, it bisects the base and is perpendicular to it. We first prove the line bisects the base and then prove it is perpendicular to the base.

   (c) A third way of proving a conditional $p \longrightarrow q$ is to find some statement r so that you can prove $p \longrightarrow r$ and $r \longrightarrow q$ then $p \longrightarrow q$ follows. *Example*: Prove $3/4 = .75$. First prove $3/4 = 3 \cdot 25/4 \cdot 25 = 75/100$. Then prove $.75 = \dfrac{.75 \cdot 100}{100} = 75/100 \quad \therefore 3/4 = .75$

Another strategem of proof draws upon the *law of the excluded middle*. For example, if we wish to prove p is true we can show that $\sim p$ is false, then p must be true. Symbolically $\sim(\sim p) \longrightarrow p$. For example, if we wish to prove that the real number $\sqrt{2}$ is irrational, we may do so by proving that the statement that it is not irrational (it is rational) is false. This kind of proof is actually used to prove the $\sqrt{2}$ is irrational. This method is known as *reductio ad absurdum*, or reduction to an absurdity.

Indirect proofs are another means of establishing proof; that is, we may prove a statement by eliminating all other possibilities. For example, if we wish to prove line $AB \perp CD$, we consider all the possibilities:

1. AB does not intersect CD
2. AB intersects CD at $90°$
3. AB intersects CD at an angle $\neq 90°$

If we now can disprove 1 and 3, we know that $AB \perp CD$.
Symbolically,

$$[(p \vee p \vee r \cdots \vee z) \wedge ((\sim q) \wedge (\sim r) \wedge \cdots (\sim z))] \longrightarrow p$$

Another useful stratagem of proof lies in proving two or more statements are equivalent. For example, we may wish to prove that $[3x - 5 = + 7]$ is equivalent to $x = 6$. Here we must keep in mind that equivalence is a biconditional situation ($\longleftrightarrow$) meaning "if and only if." It thus becomes necessary to prove:

1. If $(3x - 5 = x + 7)$, then $x = 6$

2. If $x = 6$, then $(3x - 5 = x + 7)$

Since both of these cases are conditionals, whatever strategies are allowable with conditionals can be used here.

By applying the proper axioms to $3x - 5 = x + 7$ we can obtain $x = 6$ and by reversing the application of the axioms we can get from $x = 6$ back to $3x - 5 = x + 7$ which proves the equivalency.

$3x - 5 = x + 7$	Problem
$(3x - 5) + (-x) = (x + 7) + (-x)$	If $a = b$, then $a + c = b + c$
$2x - 5 = 7$	$a + b = b + a$; $(a + b) + c = a + (b + c)$ and $a + (-a) = 0$
$[2x + (-5)] + (+5) = 7 + (+5)$	If $a = b$, then $a + c = b + c$
$2x = 12$	$(a + b) + c = a + (b + c)$; $a + (-a) = 0$
$x = 6$	If $a = b$, then $a \cdot c = b \cdot c$

Now reversing the process,

$x = 6$	Problem
$2x = 12$	If $a = b$, then $a \cdot c = b \cdot c$
$2x + (-5) = 12 + (-5)$	If $a = b$, then $a + c = b + c$
$2x - 5 = 7$	Adding,
$(2x - 5) + x = 7 + x$	If $a = b$, then $a + c = b + c$
$3x - 5 = x + 7$	$a + b = b + a$ and adding

Quite a different situation is encountered in the equation

$$\frac{A^2 - 36}{A - 6} = 6.$$

If we apply the proper axioms to this expression we obtain what appears to be two equivalent expressions $A = 0$ and $A = 6$. By reversing the sequence of axioms on $A = 0$ we can get back to the original, but not so with $A = 6$. This situation results from the fact that if $A = 6$ then the original is undefined because of the resulting zero denominator.

The work appears as follows:

1.

$A = 0$	Given
$A^2 = 0$	If $a = b$, then $a \cdot c = b \cdot c$ and $A \cdot 0 = 0$
$A^2 - 36 = -36$	If $a = b$, then $a + c = b + c$; $c = -36$
$\dfrac{A^2 - 36}{A - 6} = \dfrac{-36}{A - 6}$	If $a = b$, then $a \cdot c = b \cdot c$; $c = \dfrac{1}{A - 6}$
$\dfrac{A^2 - 36}{A - 6} = \dfrac{-36}{-6}$	If $a = b + c$ and $c = d$, then $a = b + d$ and $a + 0 = a$
$\dfrac{A^2 - 36}{A - 6} = +6$	Division

2. When we begin with $A = 6$ we encounter difficulty. The reader is challenged to try it.

INDUCTIVE PROOF

Inductive reasoning is the process by which generalizations or conclusions are derived from observation of a series of particular instances or facts. The probable truth of a conclusion reached by induction increases with the number of diverse instances from which the conclusion is verified—assuming that no case of failure has been encountered. Inductive reasoning may be observational, experimental, intuitive, or concrete. The reasoning of the physicist is inductive, for he makes experiments and draws conclusions from the particular results obtained. In social sciences, birth rates, number of unemployed persons, and rates of interest are examples of elements studied to obtain useful results which are in accord with experience. Here again the reasoning is inductive. Inductive proof is proof by sense.

In reality there is no such thing as a rigorous inductive proof for propositions whose cases are inexhaustible. As was implied earlier in this chapter, proof by mathematical induction actually is a misnomer since the reasoning involved is really deductive.

DEDUCTIVE PROOF

To understand the meaning of proof in the rigorous sense, the student must advance beyond the stage of inductive reasoning.

Basic to deductive proof is the principle of *formal implication*, often known as the "if-then" principle, which we discussed earlier. This principle applies to situations in which if certain assumptions (premises, propositions) are granted, then the conclusions (inferences, deductions) that necessarily follow must also be granted.

It is very important that young learners be led to understand the nature of proof as we have described it above. Early experiences in rigorous proof are, therefore, desirable. Some of the earliest rigorous proofs available to students are the following.

Example 8-2

Prove that if □ is a whole number and is not divisible by two, then it is odd.

Reasoning: All whole numbers are either odd or even, if a number is divisible by two it is even, this number is not divisible by two, therefore it is odd.

Note that all proofs are dependent upon some basic facts arising from logic, definitions, axioms, or previously proven theorems. In this case the proof is dependent upon:

1. All whole numbers are either odd or even.
2. If a number is divisible by two it is even.

The *law of the excluded middle* tells us that a whole number is either divisible by two or it is not divisible by two. In this case we are told in the proposition that the number is not divisible by two. If it is not divisible by two, then it is not even (definition given). Now, since there are only two possibilities and we have excluded one of them, the other must be true.

Example 8-3

Prove that two is the only even prime.

Basic information essential for the proof:

1. Definition of divisibility
2. Definition of a prime
3. Definition of an even whole number

From here we accomplish the proof by exhausting the possibilities and applying the indirect method. In other words, all even whole numbers greater than two are divisible by themselves, by one and by two. They therefore have more than two divisors and are not prime. The even whole number 0 is divisible by all whole numbers except itself, and is therefore not prime. We have now considered all even whole numbers other than two and have shown that none of them are prime. The old T format, for arranging a formal proof in mathematics, where we placed the statements on the left and the reason on the right, is no longer popular. This was a holdover from Euclidean geometry and was not essential. It may be used, however, if students prefer it but a good logical and mathematically sound narrative form will do as well.

Proofs of Some Theorems

Let us now prove several other theorems beginning with $a \times 0 = 0$. One might, of course, argue that this theorem should also be accepted as an axiom, but we must begin our proofs at some point and this seems to be as good a beginning as any.

Theorem 8-1. Prove $a \times 0 = 0$

Proof:

1. $0 = 0 + 0$	Axiom: $a + 0 = a$
2. $a \times 0 = a \times (0 + 0)$	Axiom: If $a = b$, then $a \cdot c = b \cdot c$
3. $a \times 0 = (a \times 0) + (a \times 0)$	Axiom: $a\,(b + c) = ab + a \cdot c$
4. $(a \times 0) + 0 = (a \times 0) + (a \times 0)$	Axiom: $a + 0 = a$
5. $0 = (a \times 0)$	Axiom: If $a = b$, then $a + c = b + c$

Theorem 8-2. Prove $a \times (b) = -\,(a \times b)$

Proof:

1. $b + (-b) = 0$	Axiom: $a + (-a) = 0$
2. $a \times [b + (-b)] = a \times 0 = 0$	Axiom: If $a = b$, then $a \cdot c = b \cdot c$
	Axiom: $a + b = b + a$
3. $(a \times b) + [a \times (-b)] = 0$	Axiom: $a\,(b + c) = a \cdot b + a \cdot c$
4. $a \times (-b) = -\,(a \times b)$	Axiom: If $a = b$, then $a + c = b + c$
	Axiom: $a + 0 = a$

Theorem 8-3. Prove $(-a) \times (-b) = (a \times b)$

Proof:

1. $[(-a) + a] \times (-b) = 0$	Axiom: $a \cdot 0 = 0$ and $a + (-a) = 0$

2. $(-a) \times (-b) + a \times (-b) = 0$	Axiom: $a(b + c) = a \cdot b + a \cdot c$
3. $(-a) \times (-b) + [-(a \times b)] = 0$	Theorem 8-2, above
4. $(-a) \times (-b) = -[-(a \times b)]$	Axiom: If $a = b$, then $a + c = b + c$
	Axiom: $a + 0 = a$
5. $(-a) \times (-b) = (a \times b)$	Axiom: $-(-a) = a$; The opposite of $(-a)$ is a.

In closing this section, it is again pointed our that mathematics students should not be led to believe that plane or solid geometry is the only or even the best example of rigorous mathematical proof. Actually any branch of mathematics will serve equally well if the development has been built upon basic laws, principles, axioms, definitions, and undefined terms.

MATHEMATICAL FIELDS

A field is a system having a set of elements with equality and addition and multiplication defined such that:

1. The elements of the system are commutative and associative with respect to multiplication and addition.
2. Multiplication of the elements is distributive over addition.
3. The uniqueness and closure laws for both addition and multiplication hold in the system.
4. The additive law of zero holds in the system: $a + 0 = a$
5. The law of the additive inverse holds in the system: $a + (-a) = 0$
6. The multiplicative law of one holds in the system: $a \cdot 1 = a$
7. The law of the multiplicative inverse holds in the system: $a \cdot 1/a = 1$, $a \neq 0$

There are many different fields of members both finite and infinite. Among the common infinite ones are:

1. The field of all rational numbers
2. The field of all real numbers
3. The field of all complex numbers

Among the common infinite sets of numbers the following are not fields:

1. The positive rationals
2. The integers
3. The primes

Teachers should encourage students to test many systems to determine whether or not they are fields. This is usually done by merely applying the field axioms and searching for counter examples.

MODULAR ARITHMETIC

A good application of testing for a field can be had from the area of modular arithmetic. In elementary mathematics the material here is often referred to under the heading of *clock arithmetic* or *finite arithmetic.* Teachers will recognize that this area is of considerable significance in higher mathematics where it becomes involved with congruences in the number-theory field. In elementary mathematics we use modular arithmetic chiefly as a novelty and motivator for broadening the understanding of the field axioms. It does, however, have other elementary applications such as explaining the casting out of nines in arithmetic. We will proceed to introduce this area by means of the clock.

Let us suppose that we began work at 12 o'clock, and worked 14 hours, at what hour on the clock would we complete our work? Students investigating problems of this nature will quickly see that we can always obtain the hour on the clock by casting out as many groups of twelve as we can.

The answer to the above problem is 2 o'clock, and if we had worked 40 hours the answer would be 4 o'clock. We get these as follows:

$$14 - (1.12) = 2 \text{ and } 40 - (3.12) = 4$$

The students can check these results with the assimilated clock face.

After the experimental groundwork has been established students can move to the six-hour clock, and from here they are ready for the generalizations of modular arithmetic.

If we consider an arithmetic mod 5 based on our clock experience we can now set up an addition chart and a multiplication chart as follows (since our operations are different than usual we will circle our operational signs):

⊕	0	1	2	3	4
0	0	1	2	3	4
1	1	2	3	4	0
2	2	3	4	0	1
3	3	4	0	1	2
4	4	0	1	2	3

⊗	0	1	2	3	4
0	0	0	0	0	0
1	0	1	2	3	4
2	0	2	4	1	3
3	0	3	1	4	2
4	0	4	3	2	1

Let us now check this system for closure, uniqueness, and the field axioms. Note that since this is a finite arithmetic the charts above are not just basic facts—they are all the addition and multiplication facts in the system. We now proceed with the check:

1. $\forall a,b$; $(a + b)$ and $(a \cdot b)$ are elements of the set.
   Examples: $(3 + 4)$ is in the set and is 2
   $(2 \cdot 3)$ is in the set and is 1
2. $\forall a,b$; $(a + b)$ is always the same element of the set.
   $(a \cdot b)$ is always the same element of the set.
   Examples: $(2 + 3)$ is always zero and
   $(3 \cdot 4)$ is always two.
3. $\forall a,b; a + b = b + a$ and $a \cdot b = b \cdot a$
   Examples: $2 + 4 = 4 + 2$ and $3 \cdot 4 = 4 \cdot 3$
4. $\forall a,b,c;\ a + (b + c) = (a + b) + c$, and $a\,(b \cdot c) = (a \cdot b) \cdot c$
   Examples: $3 + (2 + 4) = (3 + 2) + 4$, and $2 \cdot (3 \cdot 4) = (2 \cdot 3) \cdot 4$
   $3 + 1 = 0 + 4$ $\qquad$ $2 \cdot 2 = 1 \cdot 4$
   $4 = 4$ $\qquad$ $4 = 4$
5. $\forall a,b,c;\ a\,(b + c) = a \cdot b + a \cdot c$
   $3\,(4 + 2) = 3 \cdot 4 + 3 \cdot 2$
   $3 \cdot 1 = 2 + 1$
   $3 = 3$
6. $\forall a;\ a + 0 = a$ — *Example*: $4 + 0 = 4$
7. $\forall a;\ a + (-a) = 0$ — *Example*: $2 + 3 = 0$ and for every element there is some number which behaves like $(-a)$ to produce zero.
8. $\forall a;\ a \cdot 1 = a$ — *Example*: $4 \cdot 1 = 4$
9. $\forall a \neq 0;\ a \cdot 1/a = 1$ — *Example*: $3 \cdot 2 = 1$ and in each case there is an element which behaves like $1/a$ to produce one.

Here, then, we seem to have finite system which satisfies the field axiom. At this point the students are encouraged to set up the charts for mod 6. In this particular experience it will be found that there is not an element which behaves like $1/a$, in the axiom $a \cdot 1/a = 1$, for every element of the set. Further experimentation will show that all prime mods produce fields while the composites do not.

Teachers are cautioned to use the more difficult sections of this chapter with care. In some cases only the mathematically gifted will master the intended concepts, but with proper teacher interpretation a great deal of the material is useable over a wide range of elementary school students.

PROBLEMS

1. If a number is greater than seven then what do you know about it in comparison to numbers other than seven?
2. What do you know about a number which is neither $>$ nor $<$ 8?
3. Negate the following:
   (a) John is older than Mary.

(b) Susan is not younger than Joe.
(c) Joe is the same age as Jane.

4. Write 10 mathematical statements which may be classified as simple implication or conditional.

5. Write five mathematical statements which are biconditional.

6. Is a mathematical definition always biconditional?

7. Explain why the law of the excluded middle is so named.

8. State the law of noncontradiction, and explain the appropriateness of the name.

9. Write the following propositions in if-then form:
(a) All right angles are equal
(b) All even whole numbers greater than two are composite
(c) Vertical angles are equal
(d) Prime whole numbers have exactly two integral divisors.

10. Fit an example to the following model of the chain rule of inference:

$$p \longrightarrow q \text{ and } q \longrightarrow r, \quad \text{therefore } p \longrightarrow r$$

11. Write the converse, inverse and contrapositive for the following:
(a) If two angles are vertical, then they are equal.
(b) If a number is rational, then it can be written in the form a/b, where a and b are integers and $b \neq 0$.
(c) If a figure is a rectangle, then it is a quadrilateral.
(d) If two integers are odd, then their sum is even.

12. Give an original example of each of the cases of illogical reasoning illustrated in this chapter.

13. What are the building blocks of mathematical systems?

14. What does a mathematician mean by an indirect proof?

15. Distinguish between inductive and deductive reasoning. Is there such a thing as inductive proof?

16. Prove or disprove the following propositions:
(a) All whole numbers are either odd or even.
(b) If a number is divisible by two it is an even integer.
(c) Two is the only even prime.
(d) The $\sqrt{2}$ is irrational.
(e) All quadrilaterals are rectangles.

17. Prove the theorem $(-a) \times (-b) = a \times b$, using whatever axioms you need and the theorem $a \times (-b) = -(a \times b)$

18. Show that the set of rational numbers constitutes a field by applying the field axioms.

19. Show that the set of positive rationals does not constitute a field by showing that at least one of the field axioms fails.

20. Apply the field axioms to an arithmetic mod 7 and determine whether each has an interpretation in this system.

21. Repeat Prob. 20, using an arithmetic mod 6.

Chapter 9

Space and Relationships Within It

THE NATURE OF SPACE

Space relationships are concerned with location, shape, and size. The child confronts these basic concepts early in life and usually displays a natural interest which deserves careful nurturing as he relates the geometric realities of his concrete experiences to the abstractness of his imagination. The elementary schools have often been content to let the child's understandings of geometry evolve with little concern for either accuracy or continuity. Generally we have done only what the child's interest has demanded, and often we have done this poorly. As evidence of our shortcomings in this area, witness the confusion that exists in the minds of many junior high school students with regard to the difference between a square and a cube, or a circle and a sphere, or by what is meant by an angle, perpendicular lines, etc. The elementary school program has generally leaned heavily upon the upper grades to handle geometric measurement and the formal high school courses in plane and solid geometry to carry the other concepts and relationships of geometry. Actually this procedure cannot be defended in the light of either observation or research. Geometric understandings and skills unfold as naturally with the child's age and experience as do the understanding and skills associated with numbers. Furthermore, the concepts associated with geometry are closely tied to the concepts associated with numbers and the two taught simultaneously tend to support and clarify one another.

Let us then explore a possible sequence of development leading toward an understanding of space and the important relationships associated with it.

Children should be led to understand space as a set of points. Each of these points represent an exact or fixed location and cannot move. (Space thus becomes a set of all possible locations.) The earth and every object on it, in it, or outside it can now be identified by a subset of this total set of points. We think of a point as being so small that it has no size at all. No instrument has a sharp enough point to designate the exact location of a point. For convenience we draw pictures of certain collections or sets of these points by using pencil marks on paper or chalk marks on the chalkboard, but actually even a single dot which we think of as being a picture of a point covers more points than we could ever count. However, the picture does help us to talk about a point; and we say that the dot represents or "stands for" a point. Since points cannot move, if we make a dot on a sheet of paper to represent a point in space and then we move the paper, the dot now represents a different point or location in space.

CURVES AND SURFACES

We have already said that all objects in space may be identified as a set of points; let us now talk about the object which we will call a *curve*. (At this point it should be made clear to the child that an object is not necessarily something that we can recognize by our senses but may be something which we can only imagine in our minds.) We will merely say that a curve is the set of all points which we pass through in going from one point to another. In the accompanying illustration are some picture of curves from point A to point B.

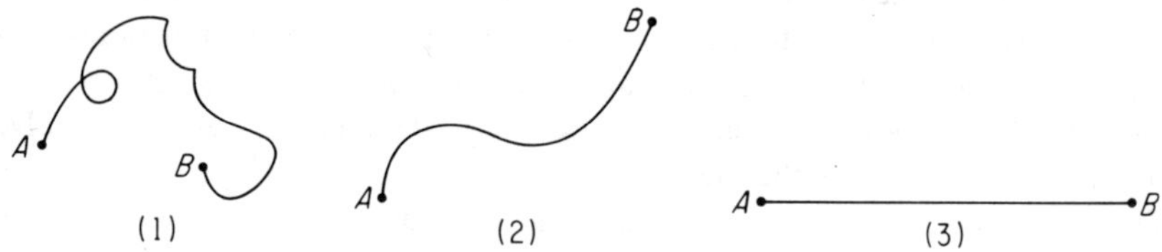

Sketch (3) drawn with aid of a straightedge is the shortest or most direct path from A to B. It is called a line segment[1] and is written $\overline{AB}$. The picture on the paper is merely a picture or model of this line segment and represents all the points passed through in going from A to B. It should be noted here that according to our mathematical description of a curve, the picture in sketch (3) is a curve, even though it may not agree with what we commonly think of as a curve. A line segment may also be thought of as being a set of points in space identified by the edge of a straightedge when the straightedge is held stationary in space. Now if we extend the line segment in each direction without specifying a limit, we have illustrated the concept of a line. This representation is pictured by the use of arrows on the extensions as follows:

The line segment $\overline{AB}$ need not be designated in the picture of a line. We may draw it thus:

Note that in our concept of a line we have purposely avoided saying that the line

[1] Line and line segment as used in this chapter are understood to be straight.

segment may be extended infinitely far in each of two directions, since we do not know what happens to a line in infinite space. Actually, some mathematicians have conjectured that it may not behave in the infinite at all as it does in the finite.

If we hold a smooth surface (such as a piece of paper) stationary in space and then imagine that the paper has no thickness, we may think of the points in space identified by this surface as a curved surface. We picture a curved surface as follows:

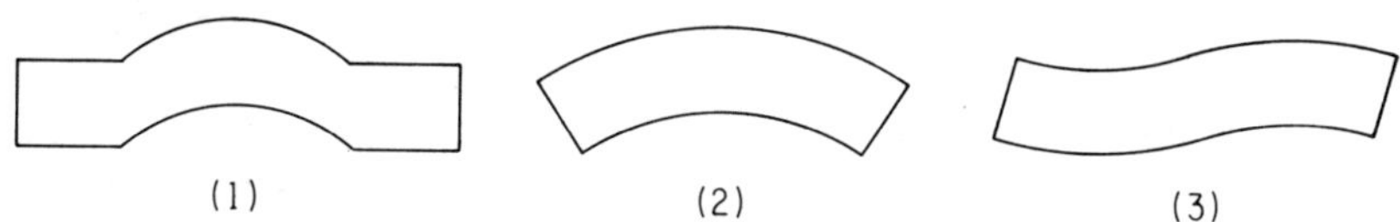

(1) (2) (3)

Now if the surface is smooth and flat, like that of a piece of glass, and if we continue to think of it as having no thickness, and if in this case we do not specify a limit to its width or length, we have now pictured in our minds what is known as a plane. It can be seen that if we read the third dimension into our illustrations, some of the points in each set may not lie in the plane of the paper. For this reason they do not represent a plane. Note that we may also picture a plane as the set of points in space identified by this special kind of surface held stationary in space. For convenience when we speak about any definite part of a plane (that is, limit the width and length) we will call this part of a plane a *plane area or region*. If we wish to speak of a limited surface which is not flat, we will call it a *curved area or region*. Collectively, curved regions and plane regions are known as *surface regions*. Note now that in each concept we are talking about a set of points and in each case this set of points is infinite. Even though a segment is limited as to length and a surface region is limited as to width and length, this in no way limits the number of points in any one of these sets or regions.

GENERALIZATION IN SPACE

We are now ready to begin drawing generalizations from our newly developed concepts:

1. Between any two points of a line there is always a third. This supports our concept of a point having no dimensions. It also indicates that there are just as many points on a short segment as on a long one. This is illustrated as follows:

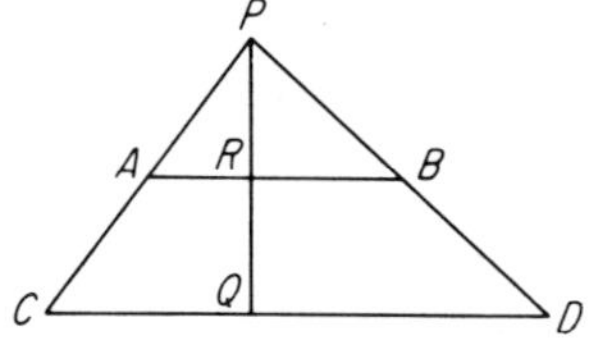

For any point on $\overline{CD}$ there is a corresponding point of $\overline{AB}$ as shown by extending $\overline{CA}$ and $\overline{DB}$ to meet at P. We can now choose any other point on $\overline{DC}$, say Q, and identify its companion point R on $\overline{AB}$. This may be repeated indefinitely. In the language of mathematics, generalization number one above is covered by the statement that the points on a line are dense.

2. If we draw a line through any two points of a plane, every point of the line will lie in the plane. This leads us to conclude that a plane contains an infinite number of lines, since there is an infinite number of points in the plane.
3. The points in a plane are dense. That is, within the triangle formed by any three nonlinear points in a plane a fourth point may be found.
4. The points in space are dense. That is, within any tetrahedron in space there is always a point.
5. Through a line in space an infinite number of planes may be drawn, as shown.

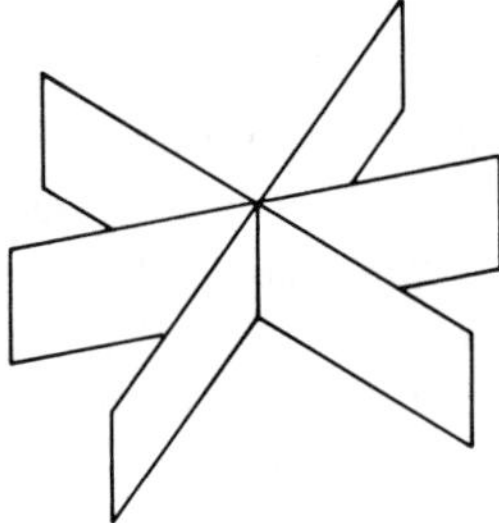

6. Any three noncolinear points of space are contained in only one plane.
7. If two different lines of space intersect their intersection set contains only one point. Illustration:

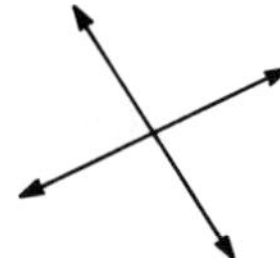

8. If a line and a plane intersect, either their intersection contains only one point (sketch 1) or the set of points comprising the line is a subset of the set of points comprising the plane, i.e., the line lies in the plane (sketch 2).

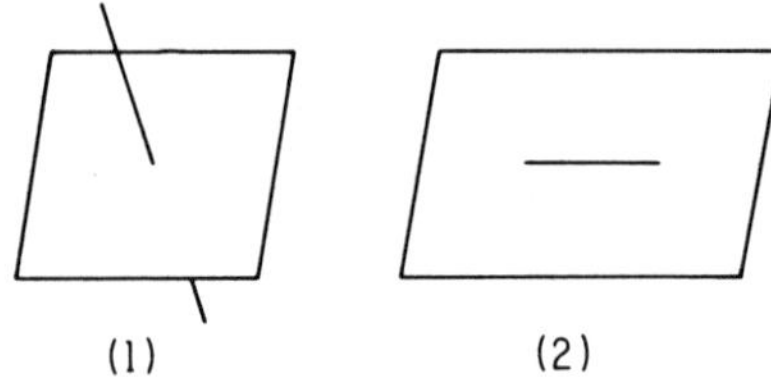

9. If two planes intersect their intersection is a line, as shown.

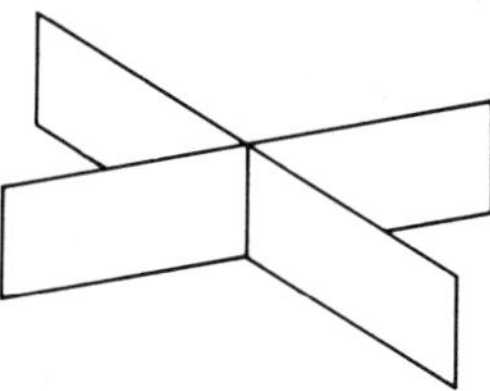

10. Any point on a line divides the line into two half-lines. The dividing point is the boundary between the two half-lines and belongs to neither. The boundary point together with either half-line is known as a *ray*. The ray is $A \cup B$, where set A is the boundary point and set B is either half-line. A ray is represented thus:

11. Any line in a plane divides the plane into two half-planes. The line is the boundary between the half-planes and belongs to neither.
12. Two points are said to be on the same side of a line if they lie in the same half-plane. If they lie in opposite half-planes, they are on opposite sides of the line.
13. A plane angle is the union of the two sets of points identified by two rays having a common end point.

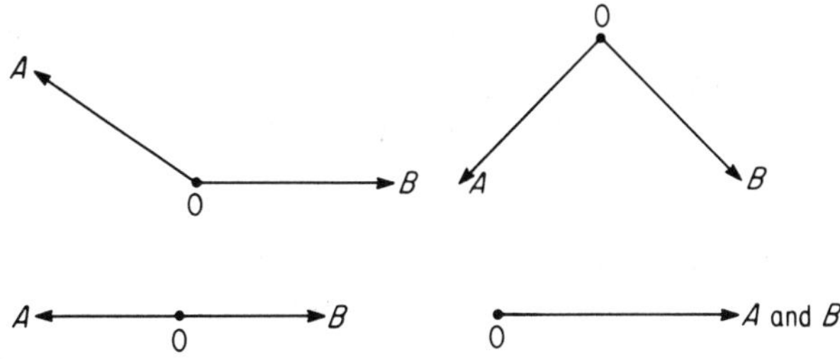

14. The interior of an angle consists of the intersection set of the half-planes identified by each ray and its associated half-line.

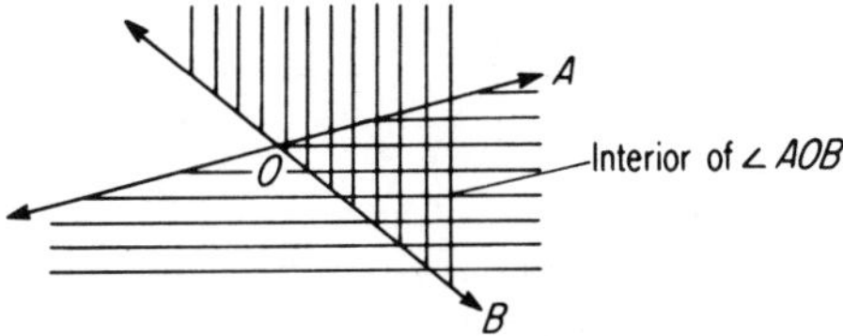

15. An angle degree is an angle of such size that if 360 of them were placed side by side around a common vertex, we would have an angle whose

interior would include all of the points in a plane except those on a single ray.

16. Angles are classified as follows:

0° angle . . . . An ∠ whose interior contains no points.

Perigon . . . . An angle whose interior includes all the points in a plane except those on a single ray. It contains exactly 360 angle degrees.

Acute angle . . . . . An angle whose interior is a nonempty set involving less than the points designated by a quarter-plane. It contains more than 0 and less than 90 angle degrees.

Right angle. . . . . . An angle whose interior is the set of points designated by a quarter plane. It contains exactly 90 angle degrees. The rays of such an angle are said to be perpendicular at the vertex. A line is perpendicular to a plane if it is perpendicular to every line in the plane which passes through the intersection of the line and plane.

Obtuse angle . . . . . An angle whose interior is a set of points designated by more than a quarter-plane but less than a half plane. It contains more than 90 but less than 180 angle degrees.

Reflex angle . . . . . An angle whose interior is a set of points designated by more than a half-plane but less than a perigon. It contains more than 180 but less than 360 angle degrees.

Straight angle . . . . An angle whose interior is a set of points designated by a half-plane. It contains exactly 180 angle degrees.

17. Dihedral angles are comprised of the union set of two intersecting planes. They are measured by the plane angle formed when a plane is passed perpendicular to the line of intersection of the two planes.

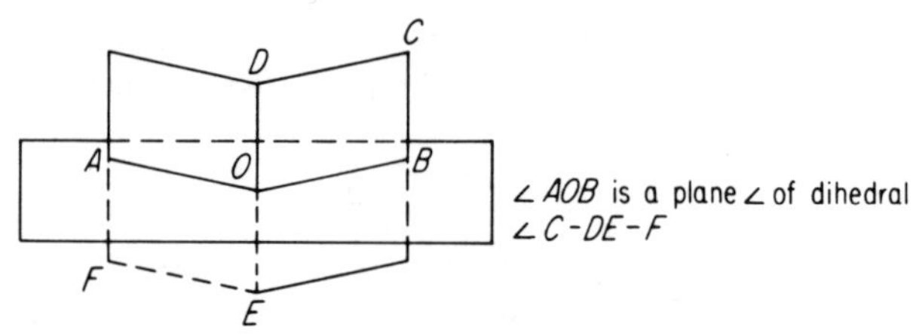

18. When three or more planes intersect at a common point, a polyhedral angle is formed. The planes forming these angles intersect in pairs and form dihedral angles.

19. If a curve has all of its points lying in the same plane and begins and ends at the same point, we call it a *plane closed curve* or a *plane geometric figure*. Actually any set of points in a plane comprise a plane geometric figure whether it is closed curve or not. Samples of plane closed curves are shown in the drawing. These are also plane regions.

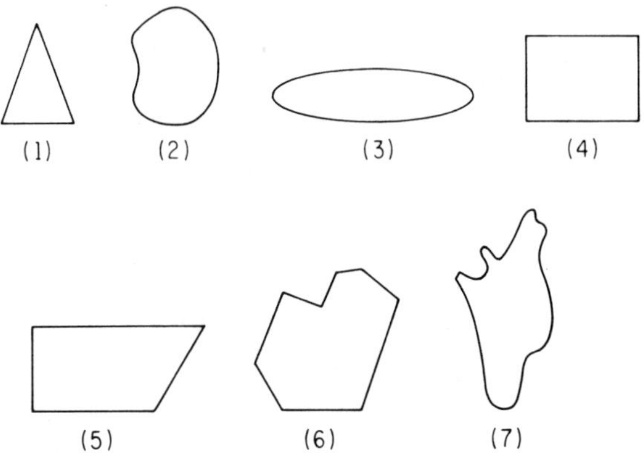

PLANE REGIONS

Some of the simple closed curves of plane geometry have special names, as given in the table.

Polygon	A plane closed curve comprised of the union of sets of points identified by line segments. These segments are called sides of the polygon. Figures (1), (4), (5), and (6) on the adjacent sketch show polygons. Polygons are classified as follows:
Regular polygon	A polygon whose sides are congruent and whose interior angles (angles formed by the sides) are congruent. Any other polygon is *irregular.*
Convex polygon.	A polygon such that a segment joining any two points of the polygon is either in the polygon or its interior (1), (4), (5). Any other polygon is concave (6).
Triangle	A polygon comprised of three segments (1).
Quadrilateral	A polygon comprised of four segments (4), (5).
Parallelogram	A quadrilateral whose opposite line segments are equal (4).
Rhombus	A parallelogram, all of whose line segments are equal.
Square	A rhombus, two of whose line segments meet at right angles.
Rectangle	A parallelogram, two of whose adjacent line segments are perpendicular (4).

Trapezoid . . . . A quadrilateral, two of whose opposite line segments are parallel (5).
Pentagon . . . . A polygon comprised of five line segments.
Hexagon. . . . . A polygon comprised of six line segments.
Heptagon . . . . A polygon comprised of seven line segments.
Octagon . . . . A polygon comprised of eight line segments.
Decagon . . . . A polygon comprised of ten line segments.
Dodecagon . . . . A polygon comprised of twelve line segments.
Circle. . . . . The set of all points in a plane each equidistant from a single point in the plane. The single point is called the center of the circle, the segment from the center to any point on the circle is called the *radius* of the circle. A segment through the center of the circle and ending on the circle is called a *diameter*. A segment joining any two points of a circle is called a *chord*. A line through a point outside a circle and intersecting the circle at two points is called a *secant*. A line touching a circle at only one point is called a *tangent*. A chord, its subtended arc, and the points within these boundaries form a region known as a *segment* of a circle. This region naturally has area. The region identified by two radii, the arc which they intercept and the points within these boundaries is known as a *sector* of a circle. The angle formed by two chords drawn from the same point on a circle is known as an *inscribed angle*. The perimeter of a circle is called the *circumference*. An angle formed by two radii is called a *central angle*.
Ellipse . . . . The set of all points is a plane such that the sum of the distances from two fixed points in the plane to any one of them is constant.

Triangles are classified in terms of their sides and angles as follows:

Right triangle . . . . A triangle having one right angle
Obtuse triangle . . . . A triangle having one obtuse angle
Acute triangle . . . . A triangle all of whose angles are acute
Scalene triangle . . . . A triangle having no two sides equal
Isosceles triangle . . . . A triangle having two equal sides
Equilateral triangle . . . . A triangle having all three sides equal
Right isosceles triangle . . . . A triangle having one right angle and two equal sides

A plane closed curve consists only of the points on the curve. Our definition of a curve (it will be remembered) included straight lines and straight-line segments. The points in the interior of a plane closed curve do not include the points of the curve. When the points of the curve and the interior of the curve are taken together, we call this union of sets a *plane region*. When we find the area of a plane closed curve, we are actually finding the area of the plane region determined by the curve and its interior.

SPACE REGIONS

When four or more plane regions are placed together in such a way as to completely enclose a portion of space, we call this combination of plane regions a *closed surface*.

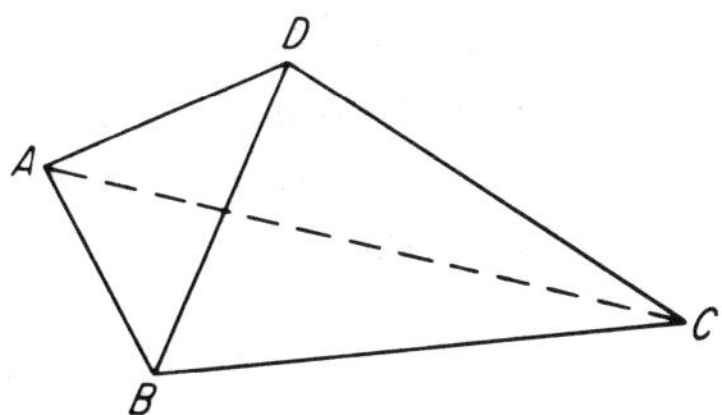

ABD is a triangular region; *ABC* is a triangular region; *ADC* is a triangular region; *BDC* is a triangular region; and together they form a pyramid *ABCD*.

Closed surfaces may be formed, however, by using regions other than plane regions. For example, we might form closed surfaces by using plane regions alone, a curved region alone, more than one curved region, or curved regions and plane regions in combination. A simple example is the closed surface formed by slicing a rubber ball and sealing the open section with a circular plane region. Other examples follow.

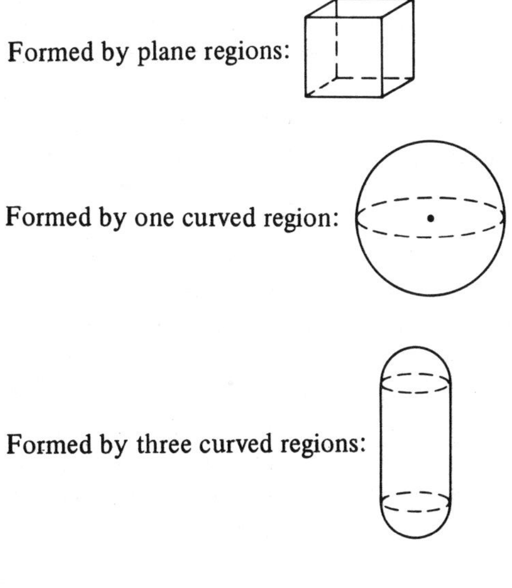

Formed by a curved region and two plane regions:

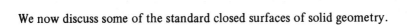

We now discuss some of the standard closed surfaces of solid geometry.

1. Prism

Consider a polygon in a plane and a line 1 intersecting the polygon but not in the plane of the polygon. The set of lines intersecting the polygon and parallel to line 1 comprise a curved surface. This surface extends any distance up and down, but if we now cut it by two parallel planes, the closed surface so formed is called a *prism*. Each of the plane regions forming the prism is called a *face* of the prism. The two parallel faces are called the *bases*, and the remaining faces are known as *lateral faces*. The intersection of any two faces is called an *edge*. The intersection of two lateral faces is called a *lateral edge*.

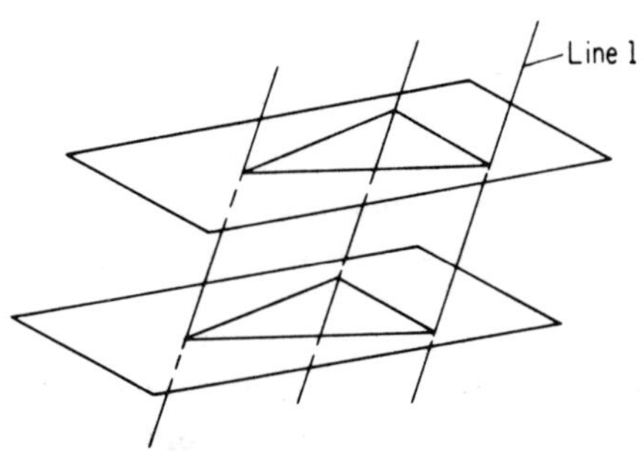

It can readily be seen that the prism is a union of the faces. It is a closed surface and points in the interior of the prism are not points of the prism. When we speak of the volume of a prism we are speaking of the prism and its interior.

Prisms are often identified by the shape of their bases. They are therefore spoken of as triangular prisms, rectangular prisms, pentagonal prisms, etc. When the lateral edges are perpendicular to the bases the prism is known as a *right prism*.

The prism as well as all other closed surfaces are composed only of the plane and/or curved regions. Any closed surface divides space into two sets of points other than the surface itself. The points inside the surface are known as the *interior of the closed surface*, and the points outside are known as the *exterior of the closed surface*. The closed surface is the boundary between the two sets and is not included in either. One must pass through the closed surface to get from an interior point to an exterior point. We call the union of a closed surface and the points in its interior a *space region*. Just as a plane region has area so a space region has volume. The prism and its interior therefore has volume.

2. Pyramid

If we consider the union of all lines which pass through a point *P* not in the plane of the polygon, we get a surface as shown. The surface consists of two identical parts separated by the point *P* called the *vertex*. Each of these parts is known as a *nappe*. If we now intersect one of these nappes with a plane, we obtain a closed surface known as a *pyramid*. A pyramid has edges, a polygonal

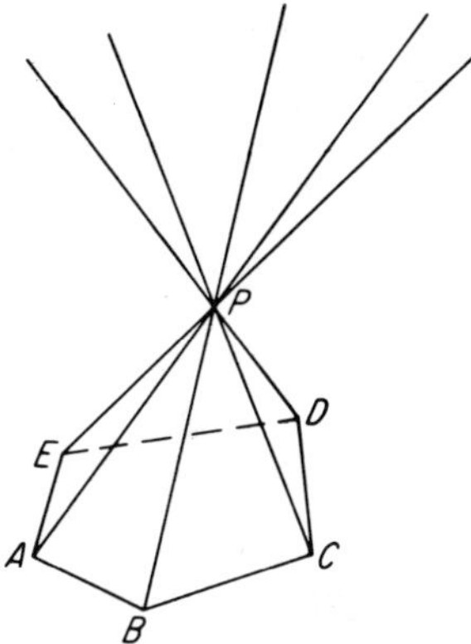

base, triangular faces, and a vertex. They are classified by the shape of their bases, being triangular pyramids, rectangular pyramids, etc. When we speak of the volume of a pyramid, we refer to the space designated by the pyramid and its interior.

A closed surface consisting entirely of polygonal regions is called a *polyhedron*. Prisms and pyramids are polyhedrons. A triangular pyramid is called a *tetrahedron*. A polyhedron is convex if the segment joining any two points of it lies either in the polyhedron or its interior. All other polyhedrons are concave. A convex polyhedron consisting entirely of congruent regular polygons is called a *regular polyhedron*. There are but five (except for size) regular polyhedrons possible.

3. Cylinder

If we modify the manner in which we generate a prism by beginning with *any* plane closed curve and construct a closed surface, we then have a cylinder. In fact, since a polygon is a closed curve, we may think of the prism as a special case of the cylinder. It will be noted that since the bases of a cylinder are not polygons some or all of the vertical faces become curved regions rather than plane regions. The bases, edges, faces, and interior of a cylinder are defined just as for a prism. Circular cylinders (cylinders whose bases are circular regions) are the most common. A circular cylinder whose lateral surface is perpendicular to its bases is called a *right circular cylinder*. Some examples of cylinders are shown in the sketches.

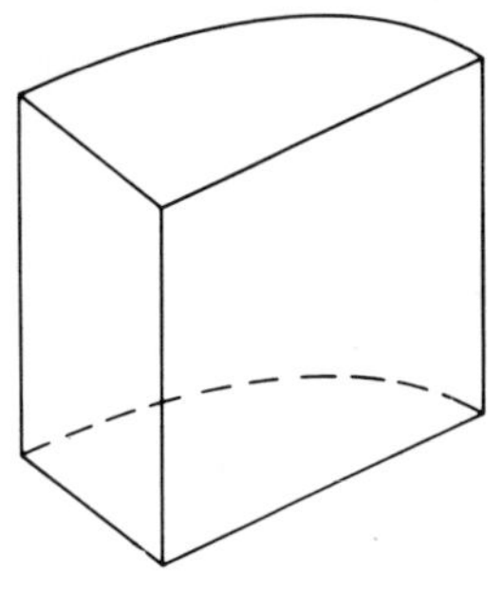

Two plane vertical faces and one curved vertical face

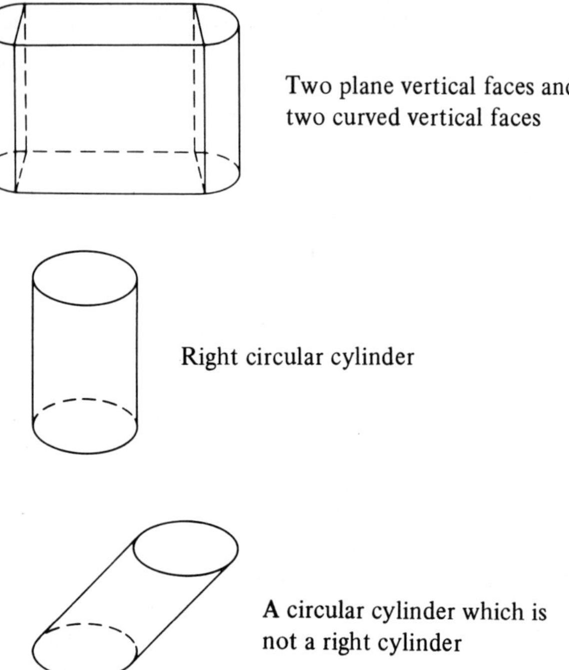

Two plane vertical faces and two curved vertical faces

Right circular cylinder

A circular cylinder which is not a right cylinder

The space region consisting of the cylinder and its interior has volume as does that of a prism.

4. Cone

The generation of a conical surface and of a cone is exactly like that of a pyramid, except that we do not restrict the base to a polygon. Any convex closed curve will serve as a base. Again we have a vertex and two nappes and a plane region intersecting the nappe. The part of the nappe between the vertex and this plane region constitutes a *cone*. It can be seen that a pyramid is just a special type of cone. A circular cone is obtained when the closed curve used in the generation of the surface is a circle. A right circular cone is obtained when all of the segments from the vertex to the circle bounding the base are equal. The space region formed by the cone and its interior is properly considered to have volume.

5. Sphere

A sphere consists of the set of all points in space which are at a distance r from a specified point O. The point O is called the *center* of the sphere and the distance r is called its *radius*. Since a sphere is also a closed surface, the space region formed by the sphere and its interior has *volume*. The intersection set of the points of a plane through the center of the sphere and the set of points of the sphere itself is a *great circle* of the sphere. The intersection set of the set of points of plane intersecting the sphere but not passing through the center of the sphere and the set of points of the sphere identifies a *small circle* of the sphere. A half sphere is known as a *hemisphere*.

Illustrated on the sphere are:

(a) Center: *O*
(b) Radius: *OA*
(c) Diameter: *BE*
(d) Great circle: *BFEG*
(e) Small circle: *CD*
(f) Hemisphere

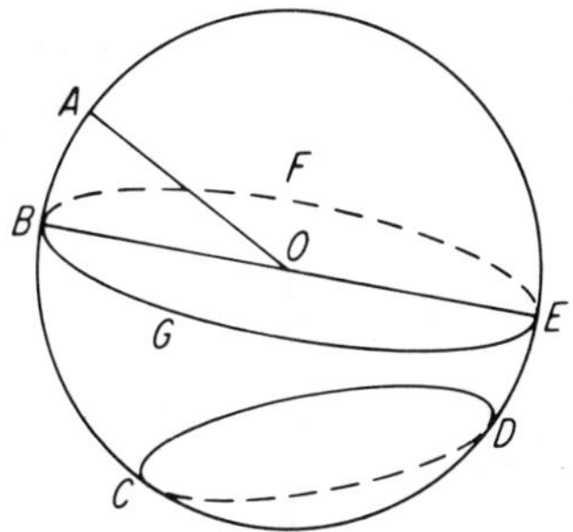

Whenever two arcs of great circles *ACBD* and *AFBE* originate from the same point *A* on a sphere, a spherical angle *CAF* is formed. This spherical angle is measured by the dihedral angle *COF* formed by the planes of their circles.

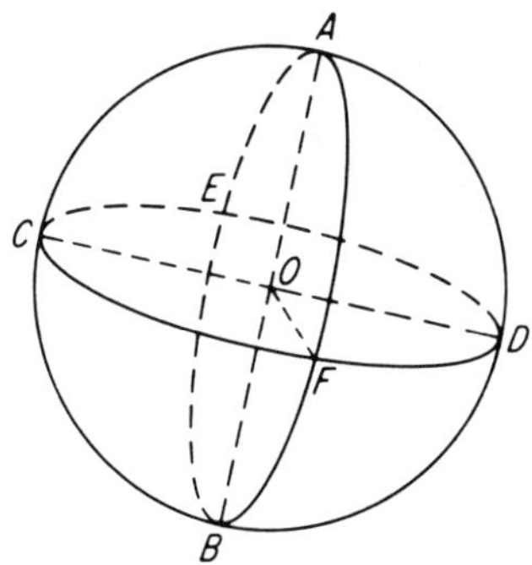

Closed unions of arcs of great circles form spherical polygons on the sphere. The points of the sphere within this closed union of arcs are called the *interior* of the polygon. The polygon and its interior are called a *spherical region*. A *lune* (*ABCD* in the sketch) is a curved region and consists of the union of points of two great semicircles and the points of the sphere enclosed by them. A lune has area.

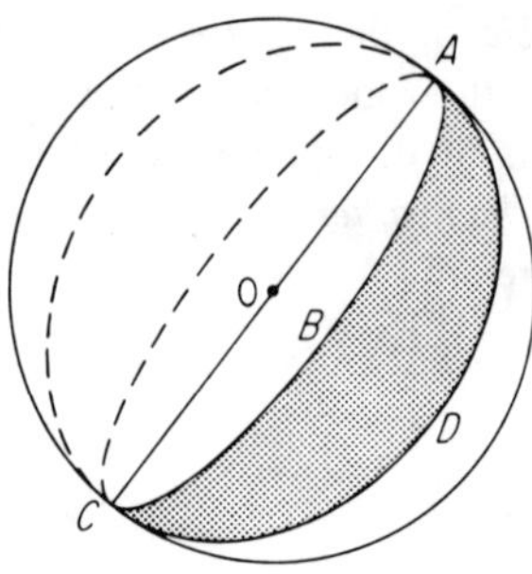

A *zone* is the union of the sets of points of two circles of a sphere whose planes are parallel and the set of points of the sphere located between them. A zone has area. The circles *AB* and *CD* are called the *bases* of the zone, and the distance between the planes of the two circles is called the *altitude* of the zone.

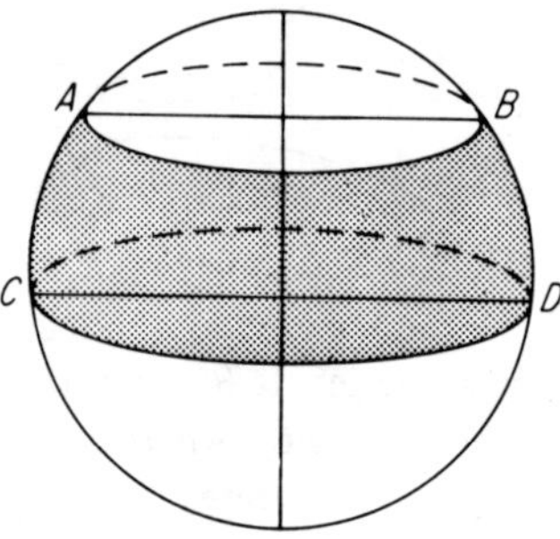

A spherical pyramid is the union of the sets of points identified by a spherical polygon and its interior and the plane regions formed by each side of the spherical polygon and the radii of the sphere drawn from the ends of these sides. The spherical pyramid together with its interior has volume. The base of the spherical pyramid *ABCO* is the spherical polygon, *ABC*. Its altitude is the radius of the sphere. Its vertex is the center of the sphere.

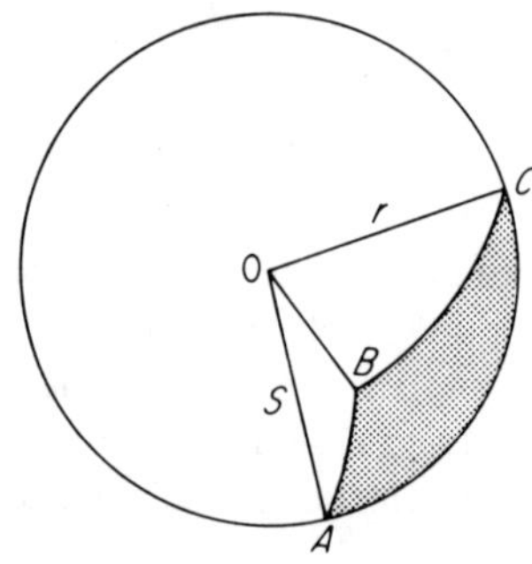

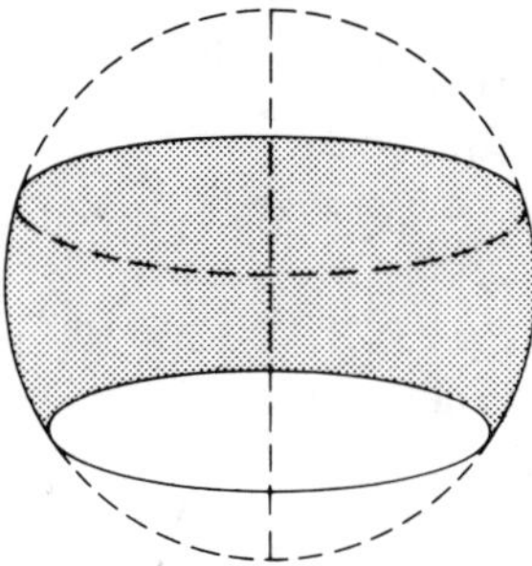

A spherical segment is the union of the sets of points of a zone and the plane regions identified by the bases of the zone. These plane regions are called the *bases of the segment*, and the distance between them is called the *altitude* of the spherical segment. A spherical segment and its interior has volume. A spher-

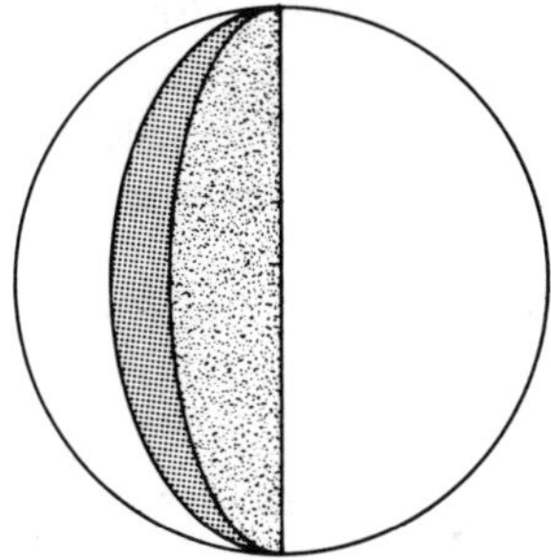

ical wedge is the union of sets of points of a lune and the plane regions identified by the arcs of the lune and the radii of the sphere drawn from the ends of the arcs. A spherical wedge (*ABCDO*) and its interior has volume.

FORMULAS FOR MEASURING REGIONS

To this point in our development we have laid the basic foundations for understanding space relationships. We have identified the basic undefined terms, definitions, and concepts necessary for measurement of geometric figures and have opened the way for deciding upon further axioms, as well as for postulating and proving or disproving geometric propositions.

Since we have already discussed the nature of measurement in Chapter 8, we will at this point list the formulas for perimeter, area, and volume of geometric figures. The development of these formulas follows the listing, however, these formulas should be introduced and used only after the student's maturity and experience will allow for understanding, and even then this understanding may need to be based on experimentation and intuition. The more common of the formulas for linear measure follow:

Perimeter of square = $4s$
Perimeter of rectangle = $2W + 2L$
Perimeter of triangle = $a + b + c$
Perimeter of parallelogram = $2S_1 + 2S_2$ S_1 and S_2 are adjacent sides
Perimeter of rhombus = $4S$
Perimeter of trapezoid = $P_1 + P_2 + N_1 + N_2$ P_1 and P_2 are the parallel sides N_1 and N_2 are the nonparallel sides.
Perimeter of polygon = $S_1 + S_2 + S_3 + \cdots S_n$
Perimeter of regular polygon = NS N = the number of sides
Circumference of circle = $2\pi r$ or πd

Formulas for square measure or area (the students' later experience should include proofs of these formulas):

Area of square = S^2
Area of rectangle = $W \cdot L$
Area of triangle = $1/2 b \cdot h$, where h is altitude
Area of parallelogram = $b \cdot h$, where h is altitude
Area of rhombus = $b \cdot h$, where h is altitude
Area of trapezoid = $1/2 h(b + b')$, where h is altitude, b is the lower base and b' the upper base
Area of regular polygon = $1/2 A \cdot P$, where A is the apothem and P the pe-imeter
Area of circle = πr^2
Lateral area of a prism = $P \cdot e$, where e = lateral edge and P = perimeter of a right section
Lateral area of a regular pyramid = $1/2 S \cdot P$, where S = slant height and P = perimeter of the base
Lateral area of a right circular cylinder = $c \cdot e$, where e = an element and c = the circumference of the base
Lateral area of a cone = $1/2 c \cdot S$, where c = circumference of the base and S = slant height
Surface area of a sphere = $4\pi r^2$

Formulas for cubic measure or volume:

Volume of cube = e^3, where e = an edge
Volume of rectangular parallelepiped = $W \cdot L \cdot h$
Volume of parallelepiped = $B \cdot h$, where B = the area of the base and h = its altitude
Volume of prism = $B \cdot h$, with B and h as in parallelepiped
Volume of pyramid = $1/3 B \cdot h$, where B = area of base and h = altitude
Volume of cylinder = $B \cdot h$, where B = area of base and h = altitude
Volume of cone = $1/3 B \cdot h$, where B = area of the base and h = altitude
Volume of sphere = $4/3 \pi r^3$

DEVELOPING THE FORMULAS

The development of the formulas for measuring the common geometric figures should be carefully developed probably in conjunction with measurement and should evolve in the student's experience over many grade levels, beginning in the primary grades. By the time the student has reached the upper grades he should be able to show how each of the formulas is derived and be able to use each formula with understanding. With the concept of linear measure already established, these formulas are quite obvious, since the student need only think of laying the segments (sides) of these figures out in a straight-line segment and measuring their length. The one exception we have is the circle, and this can be handled in meaningful ways, as described below.

The students will already be familiar with the irrational number pi and will remember that it came from dividing the circumference of any circle by its diameter. Thus $\pi = c/d$. Now applying the axiom, if $a = b$, then $a \cdot c = b \cdot c$, and using d as c we get $\pi d = \frac{c \cdot d}{d}$, and since $d/d = 1$ for all $d \neq 0$ we now have $C = \pi d$ since $d = 2r$, then C also equals $2\pi r$. Using rational approximations of π the students can now check the formula, using many circles.

The foundations for area measurement were established in chapter 7 on measurement, and we there found how to get the number of square units in a rectangle or square. Capitalizing on these concepts we can help the students discover the area formulas for the other geometric figures. A brief summary follows.

Parallelogram

By moving triangle 1 of parallelogram *ABCD* to position 2 we have an equivalent area which is now a rectangle whose base is equal to $\overline{AD}$, and whose width is the height *h* of *ABCD*.

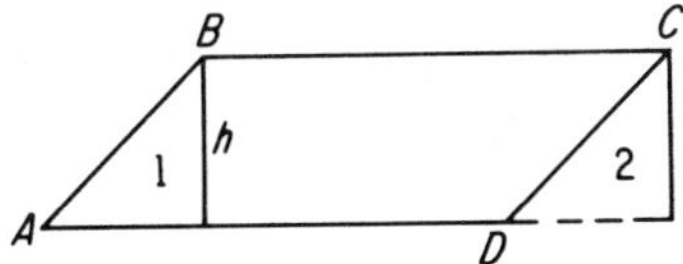

Triangle

By constructing ΔBCD on ΔABC to form parallelogram *ABCD*, it becomes apparent that the area of ΔABC will be one half that of parallelogram *ABCD*.

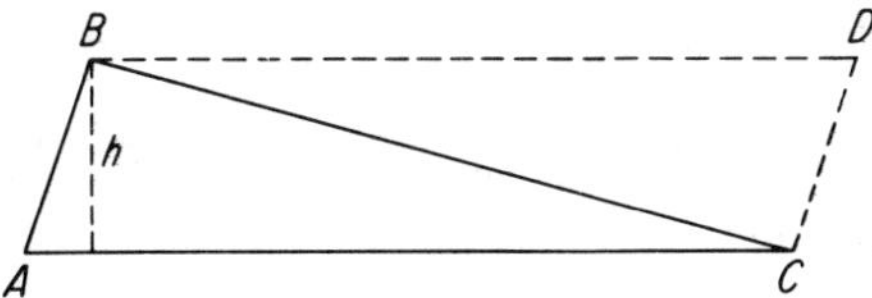

Rhombus

Merely a special case of the parallelogram.

Trapezoid

By drawing a segment between the midpoints of $\overline{AB}$ and $\overline{CD}$ we cut the trapezoid into two parts which can be fit together to form parallelogram $AEGH$ whose base $\overline{AH} = \overline{AD} + \overline{BC}$ and whose altitude is $\frac{1}{2}h$.

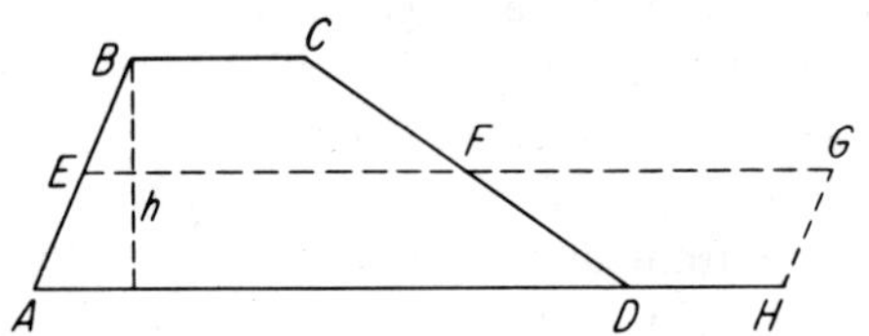

Regular Polygon

The area of $\Delta A0B = {}^1\!/_2 \overline{AB} \cdot a$ and for all the Δ it would be six times as much or, area of polygon $= 6 \cdot {}^1\!/_2 \overline{AB} \cdot a$ but $6 \cdot \overline{AB} = P$ the perimeter of the polygon, then area $= {}^1\!/_2 \cdot a \cdot P$. The development may, of course, be extended to a regular polygon of any number of sides.

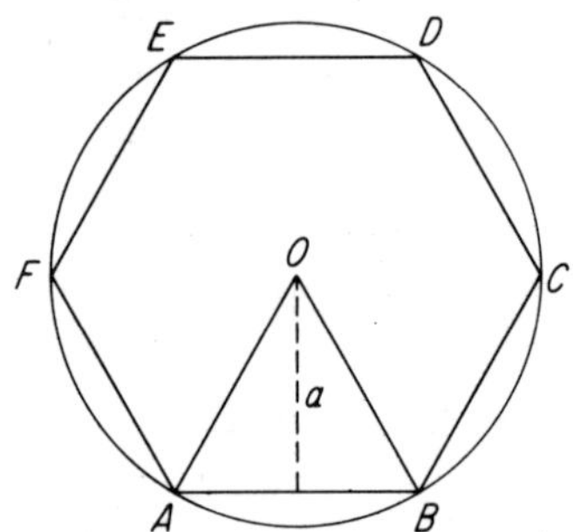

Circle

Using the idea above, it can be seen that if we keep doubling the number of sides of the polygon that the perimeter of the polygon will approach the circumference of the circle and the apothem of the polygon will approach the radius of the circle. We can therefore replace P by C and a by r in the formula $A = {}^1\!/_2\, a \cdot p$ and it becomes $A = {}^1\!/_2 \cdot c \cdot r$, but since $c = 2\pi r$, we now have $A = \pi r^2$.

The lateral areas and total surface areas of closed surfaces can be developed in a like manner for most closed surfaces. The sphere will present some diffi-

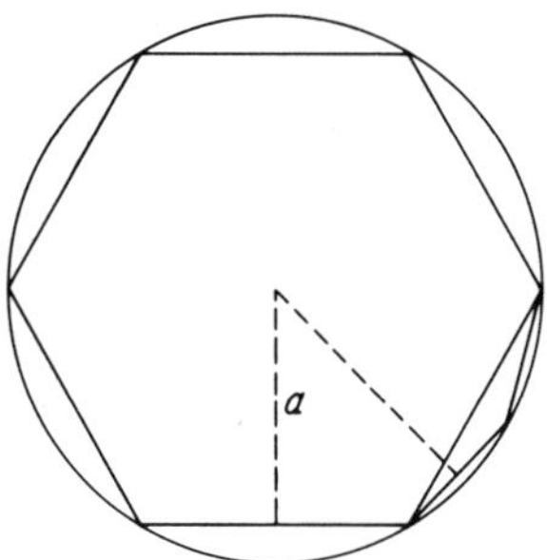

culties with younger students and can probably best be handled by experimentation.

Volume

Again using the ideas from Chapter 7 on measurement, we quickly handle the formulas for the cube and the rectangular prism and parallelepiped. In the elementary school it is perhaps best to develop the formulas for the volume of the pyramid, cone, cylinder, and sphere by experimentation.

It is recommended that a basic volume kit be available. These kits should have a plastic sphere, cylinder, and cone constructed so that the radii of the base of the cone and cylinder are the same as the radius of the sphere. The construction of the plastic figures should be such that the radius of the sphere includes the thickness of the plastic, while the radii of the cone and cylinder do not. This allows the sphere to fit inside the cylinder. Also the height of the cylinder and cone should be twice the radius of their bases. It is also well that the kit include a cubic-inch dipper with which students can check the formulas. Also, all the plastic figures should have small openings so that sand or water can be poured into them. At this point we establish that the volume of the cylinder will be the number of inch cubes that can be placed on the base (since it is a circle we can determine this) multiplied by the height, as this tells the number of layers of cubes which the cylinder will hold.

It is now apparent that the experimentation would include showing that the cone holds one-third as much water as the cylinder, and that when the opening in the sphere is sealed with tape and it is immersed in the cylinder filled with water, two-thirds of the water will be forced out. If we consider that the volume of the cylinder is the area of its base multiplied by its height, or $\pi r^2 \cdot h$, and that $h = 2r$, we now get $2\pi r^3$ and 2/3 of $2\pi r^3 = 4/3\pi r^3$, which is the formula for the volume of the sphere.

The volume of the pyramid may now be compared with the volume of a right prism having the same base and height as the pyramid. Here we will discover as with the cone and cylinder that the volume of the pyramid is one-third the volume of the corresponding prism. Verification by means of the cubic-inch dipper is now in order for all of the plastic models.

MEASURING ANGLES AND ARCS

In the chapter on measurement we have already classified angles by size. We used an angle degree as our unit of measure. Let us discuss this measurement further.

1. An angle of one degree or *angle degree* is a small angle such that if 360 of them are arranged in a successive adjacent manner they will make a perigon. Stated in other words, they will comprise the complete angular measure around a point. Now angle degrees are subdivided into minutes and seconds as follows:

   (a) $1° = 60'$, read "one degree equals 60 minutes"

   (b) $1' = 60''$, read "one minute equals 60 seconds"

2. The length of the rays of an angle has nothing to do with its size. For example, angle A and angle B in the sketch are equal:

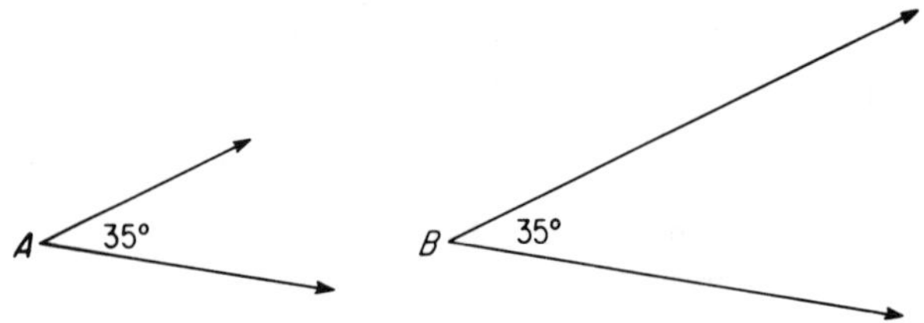

3. Angles are often measured with an instrument called a *protractor*, illustrated in the sketch.

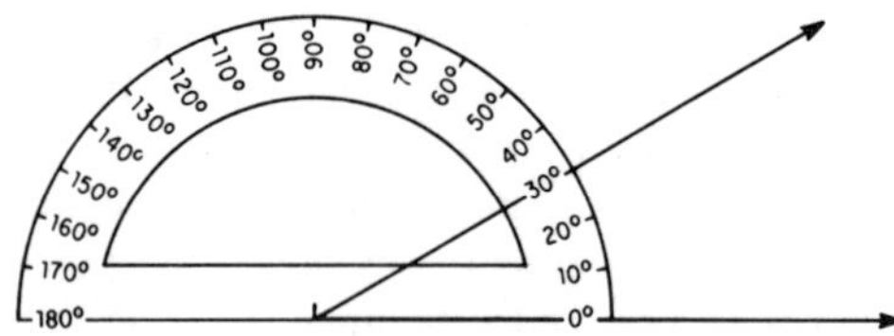

4. Angles can be measured independently of the circles which can be drawn using the vertex of the angle as center. When such circles are drawn the angle is called a *central angle* of the circle or circles.
5. Arcs of circles are measured by using a unit called an *arc degree*. This unit is 1/360 of the circle from which it is taken. Because of this latter fact, arc degrees are always the same size on a particular circle but the

size of an arc degree will vary from circle to circle, depending on the radius.

6. Note that an angle degree is a small angle while an arc degree is an arc.

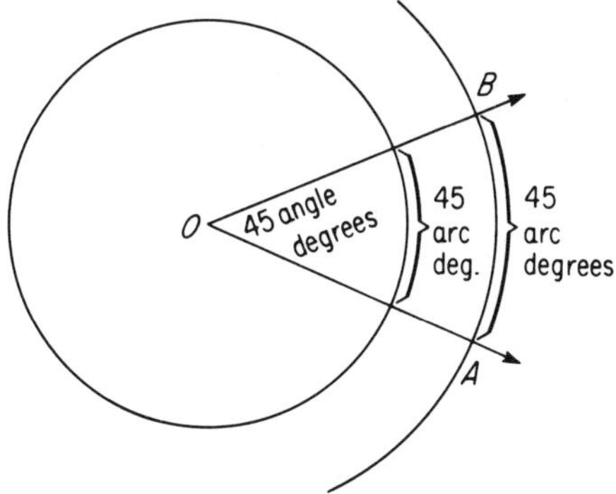

7. There is a relationship between an angle degree and an arc degree whenever a circle is drawn with the vertex of the angle as center. The situation is then as illustrated in the adjacent sketch. Note that if we draw a larger concentric circle the arc cut off by the $\angle AOB$ is still 45 arc degrees, but the arc degree has now become larger.
8. From the above we note that whenever we have a central angle drawn in a circle, one angle degree will cut off one arc degree.

CONGRUENCE

At this point we introduce the concept of congruence, which will be helpful in identifying further axioms and proving certain propositions. We define two or more segments as being congruent if their measurements in a common linear unit are identical. For example, we say the $\overline{AB} \cong \overline{CD}$ providing they have identical measures. Furthermore, a congruence relation is always reflexive, symmetric, and transitive. That is if segments AB, CD, EF are congruent then,

1. $\overline{AB} \cong \overline{AB}$ a segment is congruent to itself.
2. If $\overline{AB} \cong \overline{CD}$, then $\overline{CD} \cong \overline{AB}$.
3. If $\overline{AB} \cong \overline{CD}$ and $\overline{CD} \cong \overline{EF}$, then $\overline{AB} \cong \overline{EF}$.

Segments need not lie in the same plane in order to be congruent. The same definitions hold true for angles, the measures now being expressed in angular degrees. Furthermore, this definition holds for plane angles, dihedral angles, and polyhedral angles–except that we do not mix them. Now we extend our concept of congruence to plane closed curves made up of only plane angles and segments. We define such closed curves as being congruent if and only if the respective angles are congruent, and the respective segments are congruent.

AXIOMS AND POSTULATES IN THE PLANE

We are now prepared to identify some further axioms and postulates. We list these without comment, recognizing that their acceptance and understanding by students will require a great deal of intuitive and experimental geometry.

1. A segment may be constructed ≅ to a given segment.
2. An angle may be constructed ≅ to a given angle.
3. A given segment can be bisected, or construct a ⊥ bisector of a segment.
4. A third ray may be constructed from the vertex of an angle which will produce two ≅ angles, each half the size of the original angle.
5. Two or more triangles having three sides of one respectively congruent to the corresponding sides of the others the ⓢ△ are themselves congruent.
6. Two or more triangles having two sides and the included angle of one respectively congruent to the corresponding sides and angles of the other triangles are themselves congruent.
7. Two or more triangles having two angles and the included side of one respectively congruent to the corresponding angles and sides of the others are themselves ≅.
8. From a point not on a line, a line can be constructed perpendicular to the given line.
9. From a point on a given line, a line can be constructed perpendicular to the given line. (This postulate is actually covered by 3 above.)
10. Angles having the same number of degrees are equal and congruent.
11. If B and A are two angles such that $\angle B < \angle A$, then $\angle A > \angle B$.
12. For any two angles A and B, either $\angle A < \angle B$, $\angle A \cong \angle B$, or $\angle A > \angle B$.
13. If $\angle A = \angle B$, and $\angle B < \angle C$, then $\angle A < \angle C$.
    " " " " " $\angle B = \angle C$, then $\angle A = \angle C$.
    " " " " " $\angle B > \angle C$, then $\angle A > \angle C$.
14. Supplements of congruent angles are themselves congruent.
15. Complements of congruent angles are themselves congruent.
16. If $\angle B > \angle A$ then $\angle A < \angle B$ (also holds for segments).
17. If $\angle A = \angle B$ and $\angle B \cong \angle C$, then $\angle A = \angle C$.
    " " " " and $\angle B < \angle C$, then $\angle A < \angle C$.
    If $\angle A < \angle B$ and $\angle B < \angle C$, then $\angle A < \angle C$.
    " " " " and $\angle B \cong \angle C$, then $\angle A < \angle C$.
    If $\angle A > \angle B$ and $\angle B > \angle C$, then $\angle A > \angle C$.
    " " " " and $\angle B \cong \angle C$, then $\angle A > \angle C$.

CONSTRUCTIONS

Many elementary school students are now having the experience of doing the basic constructions listed previously. These are done by use of the compasses and straightedge only. For primary-grade students compasses without the sharp metal point are now available. These eliminate the dangers of injury and give younger students an opportunity to enjoy the constructions.

1. A segment may be constructed ≅ to a given segment.

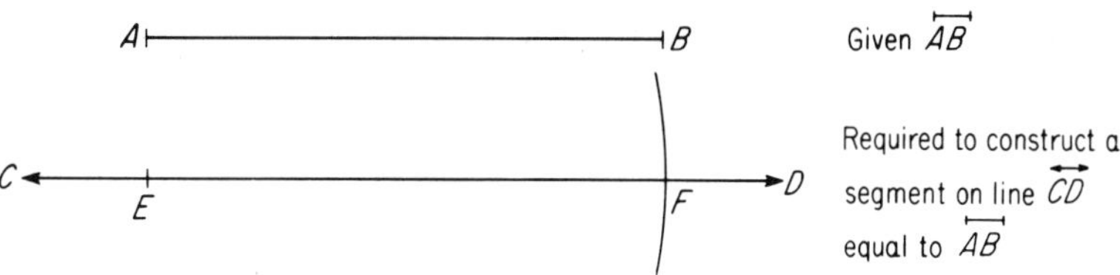
A
B
C
E
F
D
Given $\overline{AB}$
Required to construct a
segment on line $\overleftrightarrow{CD}$
equal to $\overline{AB}$

Construction

(a) Set compasses to radius $\overline{AB}$
(b) Place point of compasses at any point E on $\overleftrightarrow{CD}$
(c) Cut an arc intersecting $\overleftrightarrow{CD}$ at F
(d) $\overline{EF} = \overline{AB}$

2. Construct an angle ≅ a given angle.

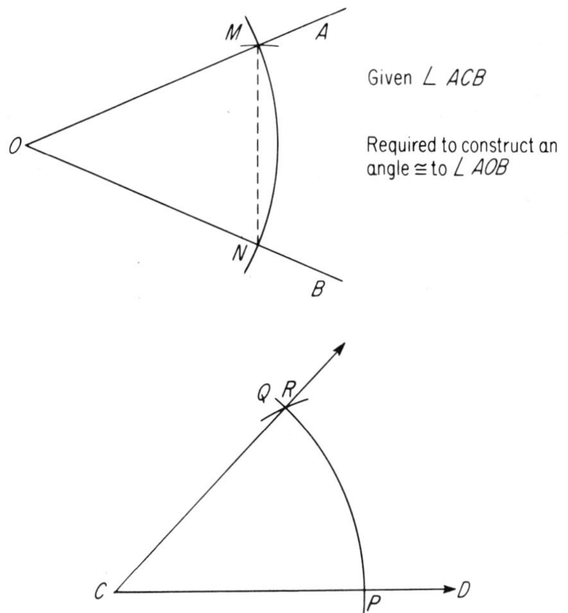
M
A
O
N
B
Given ∠ ACB
Required to construct an
angle ≅ to ∠ AOB
Q
R
C
P
D

Construction

(a) Draw ray $\overrightarrow{CD}$
(b) Using O as center and any convenient radius, draw an arc intersecting $\overrightarrow{OA}$ at M and $\overrightarrow{OB}$ at N.

(c) Using C as center and the same radius, draw an arc intersecting $\overrightarrow{CD}$ at P and extending well above $\overrightarrow{CD}$.
(d) Set compasses to radius $\overline{MN}$.
(e) Using P at center and radius $\overline{MN}$, cut an arc intersecting $\overset{\frown}{PQ}$ at R
(f) Draw $\overrightarrow{CR}$. Now $\angle DCR \cong \angle ADB$.

3. Construct the ⊥ bisector of a segment.

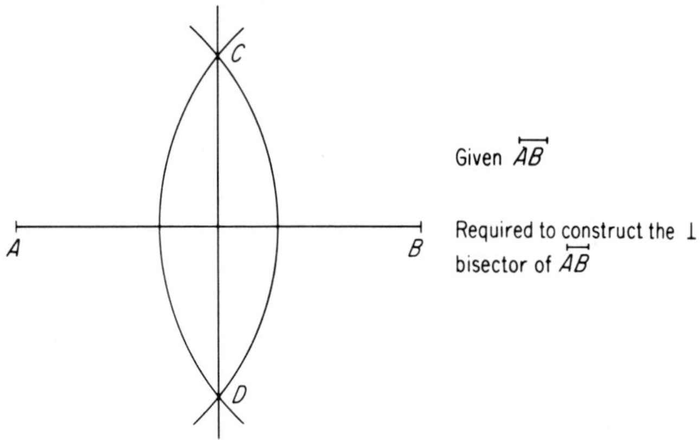
C
A
B
D
Given $\overline{AB}$
Required to construct the ⊥ bisector of $\overline{AB}$

(a) Using A as center and any radius greater than $1/2\ \overline{AB}$, cut an arc.
(b) Using B as center and the same radius, draw another arc intersecting the first at C and D.
(c) Draw $\overleftrightarrow{CD}$.
(d) $\overleftrightarrow{CD}$ is the ⊥ bisector of $\overline{AB}$.

4. A third ray may be constructed from the vertex of an angle which will produce two ≅ angles, each half the size of the original angle.

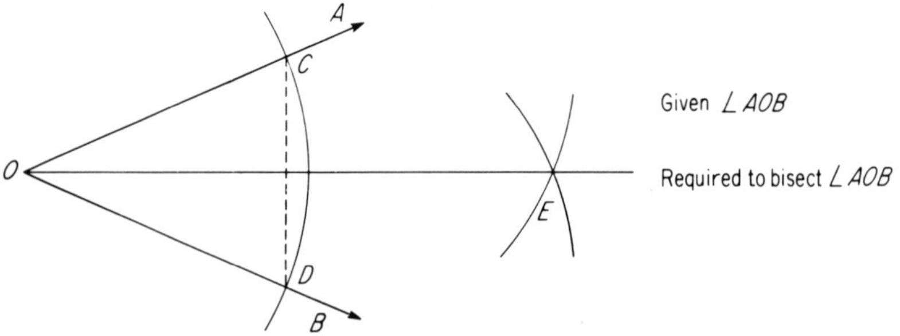
A
C
O
E
D
B
Given ∠ AOB
Required to bisect ∠ AOB

Construction

(a) Using O as center and any convenient radius, cut an arc intersecting $\overrightarrow{OA}$ at C and $\overrightarrow{OB}$ at D.

(b) Using C and D as centers and any radius greater than $\overline{CD}$, cut arcs intersecting at E.
(c) Draw $\overrightarrow{OE}$.
(d) $\angle EOC \cong \angle EOB$.

5. From a point not on a given line, a line can be constructed ⊥ to the given line.

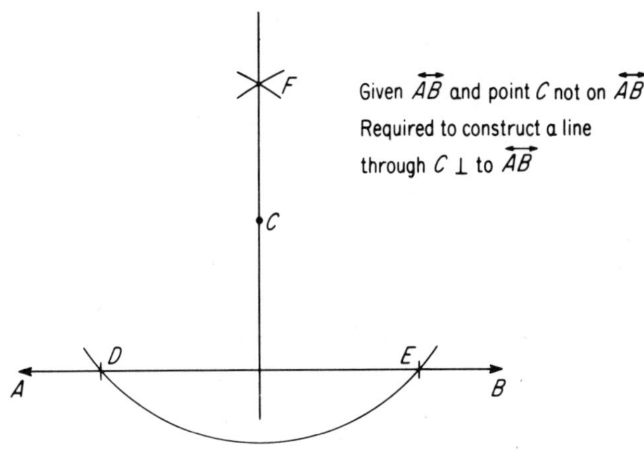

F
Given $\overleftrightarrow{AB}$ and point C not on $\overleftrightarrow{AB}$
Required to construct a line
through $C \perp$ to $\overleftrightarrow{AB}$
C
D
E
A
B

Construction

(a) Using C as center and radius greater than the distance to $\overleftrightarrow{AB}$, cut an arc intersecting $\overleftrightarrow{AB}$ at D and E.
(b) Using D and E as centers and any radius greater than $\overline{DE}$, cut arcs intersecting at F.
(c) Draw $\overleftrightarrow{FC}$.
(d) $\overleftrightarrow{FC} \perp \overleftrightarrow{AB}$.

6. From a point on a given line, a line can be constructed ⊥ to the given line.

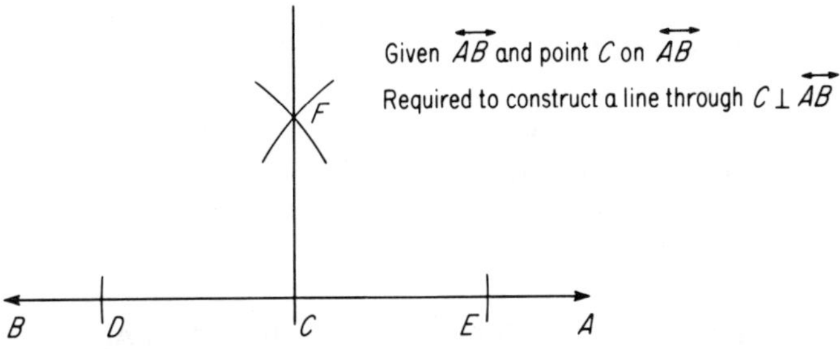

Construction

(a) Using C as center and any convenient radius cut arcs intersecting $\overleftrightarrow{AB}$ at D and E.
(b) Using D and E as centers and any radius greater than $\overline{DC}$ cut arcs intersecting at F.

(c) Draw $\overleftrightarrow{FC}$.
(d) $\overleftrightarrow{FC} \perp$ to $\overleftrightarrow{AB}$ at C

AXIOMS AND POSTULATES IN THREE-DIMENSIONAL SPACE

1. If a line L does not lie in a plane P but has at least one point in L, then L and P have exactly one point in common.
2. If two distinct planes have at least one point in common, they have precisely a line in common.
3. There are at least four points that are not in any one plane.
4. There is exactly one plane containing any three noncollinear points.
5. Each plane in three-dimensional space satisfies all the postulates of plane geometry.
6. The postulates of congruence of segments, angles, and triangles hold whether or not the segments, angles, and triangles are in the same plane.

With the definitions and postulates developed to this point we are now in a position to prove many theorems and problems of both plane and three-dimensional geometry. In practice this should be done extensively and with rigor, drawing upon the nature of proof developed in a previous chapter and allowing students to develop their own theorems and problems as well as the sequence in which they are treated. They should not be protected against trying problems that cannot be solved at this stage or even some that have no solution. A few problems which might be examined at this stage are listed below with no intent to be either exhaustive or sequential.

THEOREMS OF TWO-DIMENSIONAL SPACE

1. The base angles of an issosceles triangle are equal. (Also its converse.)
2. Vertical angles are congruent.
3. An exterior angle of a triangle is greater than either opposite interior angle.
4. In any triangle the side opposite the greater angle is the greater. (Also its converse.)
5. The sum of any two sides of a triangle is greater than the third.
6. If a triangle is equilateral, it is equiangular. (Also its converse.)

This is an excellent place to review converses, inverses, and contrapositives as they relate to geometry.

THEOREMS OF THREE-DIMENSIONAL SPACE

1. If a line is perpendicular to two intersecting lines, it is perpendicular to the plane determined by the intersecting lines.
2. There is exactly one plane perpendicular to a line at a point of the line.
3. There is exactly one plane perpendicular to a line and containing a point not on the line.

4. The sum of two face angles of a trihedral angle is greater than the third face angle.
5. The sum of the face angles of a convex polyhedral angle is less than four right angles.

Since this experience will likely constitute the first formal and rigorous geometric proofs encountered by the student, it is recommended that he hypothesize his own propositions and prove them where possible, realizing that he may not be able to solve all he can hypothesize, either because his hypotheses are false or because he does not yet have sufficient background and skill in geometry and logic. Actually in many cases his lack of background may be due to limitations in postulates.

PARALLEL LINES

The concept of parallel lines in space is an essential and basic idea of geometry. We define parallel lines as being sets of points in a plane, each set being determined by a straight line and whose respective intersection sets are empty.

A straight line and a plane are parallel if their intersection set is empty. Two planes are parallel if their intersection sets are empty. Two or more rays are said to be parallel if the lines containing them are parallel. Rays are said to have the same direction if and only if they are parallel and both on the same side of a line through their vertices.

That parallel lines exist seems to be intuitively acceptable, and actually there are several proofs of the theorem: if L is any line and A any point not on L, then there exists at least one line through A parallel to L. While these proofs seem to be perfectly acceptable, it is of more than passing interest to note that mathematicians have shown that it is impossible to prove from the other postulates of Euclidian geometry that there is no more than one line through a given point parallel to a given line. In fact, Johann Bolyai, after trying in vain to prove the truth of the parallel postulate by using the other postulates, decided to assume that a second parallel could be drawn through the point. Using this postulate he was able to set up what is now known as a non-Euclidian geometry. This, along with other non-Euclidian geometries based on different postulates, has been found to be extremely useful in modern astronomy and physics. It does not make sense to ask which geometry is true, since each is based on a different postulate system, and each serves a unique purpose. Actually, mathematicians design geometries as engineers design bridges, and in either case it is a matter of function rather than truth or falsity.

DIAGRAM OF A GEOMETRIC SYSTEM

This summary of the basic concepts of geometry is not intended to be exhaustive. It merely portrays a sequential development of a branch of mathematics which is, in its overall development, not unlike any other branch of

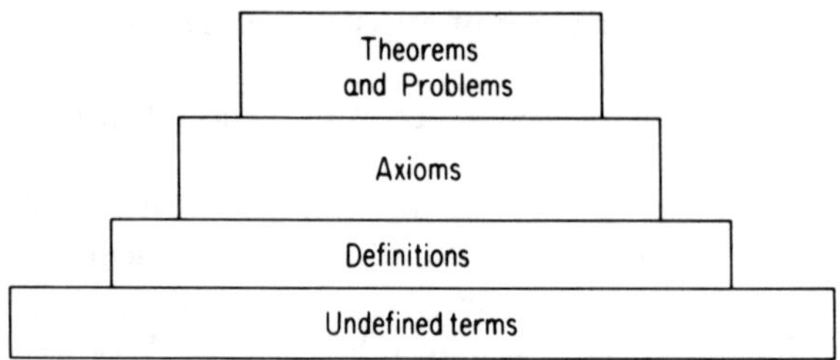

mathematics. The following diagram similar to that used earlier in this text is again appropriate.

Once the three foundation blocks are established, the hypotheses associated with this system can be tested; that is, we can prove, disprove, or be forced to leave undecided the truth of falsity of any proposition falling within the realm of our system. The trick, of course, is to establish the three bottom blocks with maximum power but in a strictly consistent and noncontradictory manner.

PROBLEMS

1. Explain in detail how you would assist a sixth-grade student to understand the following geometric concepts:

   (a) Point
   (b) Space
   (c) Curved line
   (d) Line segment (curved and straight)
   (e) Plane
   (f) Half-line
   (g) Half-plane
   (h) Half-space
   (i) Angle
   (j) Interior of an angle
   (k) Exterior of an angle
   (l) Geometric figure
   (m) Curved surface
   (n) Plane region
   (o) Space region
   (p) Surface region
   (q) Closed curve
   (r) Closed surface

2. Which of the items in Prob. 1 above would you consider to be undefined terms and which defined terms?
3. State the definitions of the defined terms in Prob. 1 above.
4. State how you would explain to an elementary student that
   (a) The points on a line are dense.
   (b) The points in a plane are dense.
   (c) The points in space are dense.
   (d) The number of points on a one-inch segment is as great as the number on a two-inch segment.
5. How would you illustrate concepts 5 through 19, pages 195-199 to a group of sixth-graders?
6. What space regions are elementary students likely to encounter in their experience?
7. Illustrate how you would develop the following formulas with students:
   (a) Perimeter of a rectangle
   (b) Perimeter of a square

(c) Perimeter of a parallelogram
(d) Perimeter of a triangle
(e) Perimeter of a rhombus
(f) Perimeter of a trapezoid
(g) Circumference of a circle

8. Illustrate how you would develop with students the area formulas for the geometric figures mentioned in Prob. 7 above. Include visual aids.

9. Assuming you have a volume kit available, state how you would develop with elementary students the formulas for the volume of the following space regions:

(a) Rectangular prism
(b) Cube
(c) Parallelepiped
(d) Right prism (regular polygon base)
(e) Cylinder (right circular)
(f) Pyramid (regular polygon base)
(g) Cone
(h) Sphere
(i) Hemisphere

Assume your volume kit contains the following:

1. Plastic foot cube
2. 155 plastic inch cubes
3. Plastic cylinder (open top) same height as diameter of base
4. Plastic cone same base and height as cylinder above
5. Plastic pyramid (regular polygon base)
6. Plastic prism with same base and height as pyramid above
7. Plastic sphere with diameter same as the height of cylinder in part 3
8. Plastic dipper (one cubic inch capacity)

10. Describe an angle degree.

11. Describe an arc degree.

12. Is it true that the number of angle degrees in a central angle will be the same as the number of degrees in the arc cut off by its rays? Discuss.

13. Add $45°57'30''$ and $60°57'45''$.

14. Discuss the critical factors in the use of protractor.

15. Explain in detail how you would teach the basic constructions to elementary school children.

16. How do the axioms of arithmetic relate to geometry?

17. Devise means of encouraging students to discover some of the postulates and theorems of geometry.

18. Under what circumstances are a plane and a straight line parallel?

19. How do non-Euclidean geometries differ from Euclidean geometries in terms of their parallel postulates?

Chapter 10

Supplemental and Enrichment Topics

PURPOSE OF THE CHAPTER

This chapter is designed to familiarize and make readily available to pre-service and in-service teachers some supplemental and enrichment topics which will provide for the specific interests of a wide range of students as well as meet the needs of the mathematically apt student who needs challenge beyond the basic concepts generally taught in the elementary school.

Neither the number of topics nor the individual developments are intended to be exhaustive. Some of the topics chosen are currently being considered for inclusion in some basic elementary mathematics textbook series and could well become standard text content within the next few years. Regardless of what happens in this direction, these are defensible mathematics topics which many teachers will use and enjoy with their students.

Many of these developments relate closely to concepts and topics discussed earlier in this text and taught generally in the elementary students' text. They thus become usable extensions appropriate for interspersion at these particular points in the sequence. When used in this manner the topics serve as horizontal acceleration, whereas their use after completion of a basic text places them in the vertical acceleration category.

GOLDBACH'S CONJECTURES

The use of primes in multiplication and division has been extensive throughout the text. The basic theorem of arithmetic which states that, "any composite can be uniquely factored into primes," has also been emphasized. Furthermore, it has been proven that two is the only even prime and that the number of primes is infinite. In 1742 Goldbach conjectured that:

1. Any even whole number greater than four may be written as the sum of two odd primes.

2. Any odd whole number greater than seven may be written as the sum of three odd primes.

Proofs for these conjectures have not been found to date. No one has, however, discovered a counterexample.

Students will enjoy applying these conjectures to the appropriate whole numbers and running them as far up the whole number scale as they can. Illustrations follow:

Conjecture 1	*Conjecture 2*
6 = 3 + 3	9 = 3 + 3 + 3
8 = 5 + 3	11 = 5 + 3 + 3
10 = 5 + 5 or 7 + 3	13 = 7 + 3 + 3 or 5 + 5 + 3
12 = 7 + 5	15 = 5 + 5 + 5 or 7 + 5 + 3
14 = 7 + 7 or 11 + 3	17 = 11 + 3 + 3 or 5 + 5 + 7
16 = 11 + 5 or 13 + 3	19 = 13 + 3 + 3 or 11 + 5 + 3
18 = 13 + 5 or 11 + 7	

Note that in the solutions there is often more than one way to illustrate the conjecture. In other words, the breakdown is not necessarily unique.

If this supplemental topic is used with elementary students, caution must be taken to avoid confusion with the more basic facts concerning primes. Actually these conjectures are of little use mathematically except as they may serve as a review of primes and the operations of addition and subtraction. They do assist students to distinguish the subsets of the whole numbers known as the odd and even whole numbers. It should also be observed that these conjectures lead to an excellent open-ended assignment for students in which they may pursue the whole numbers as far up the scale as they wish.

PYTHAGOREAN NUMBERS

The famous theorem discovered and proven by Pythagoras is one of the most practical and often-used theorems in mathematics. The theorem itself may be stated in two forms one of which is arithmetic, the other geometric. These two statements follow:

1. The square of the length of the hypotenuse of a right triangle is equal to the sum of the squares of the lengths of the other two sides.
2. The area of the square constructed upon the hypotenuse of a right triangle is equal to the sum of the areas of the squares constructed upon the other two sides.

Over two hundred proofs have been devised for this theorem, and many noted mathematicians as well as laymen have been engaged in exploring it. It is perhaps noteworthy that James A. Garfield, the twentieth president of the United States, devised a proof for this theorem which still bears his name.

Associated with the theorem are triples of numbers which obey the Pythagorean relationship. These are called Pythagorean numbers, and various formulas have been devised for their determination. Elementary students will do well to discover some Pythagorean triples by observation and trial and error. The classical primitive triple (3,4,5) is an excellent beginning point. Students will quickly discover that multiples of this classical triple also produce Pythagorean triples, and that the multiplier need not be integral, indeed not even rational or positive. Some students may discover that all numbers a, b, and c such that

$$a = m^2 - 1$$
$$b = 2m$$
$$c = m^2 + 1$$

where m is any integer, will produce triples with the Pythagorean property. As soon as they discover a triple which does not result from these formulas such as (5,12,13) the search is on again and eventually the students will want to examine the numbers generated by

$$a = m^2 - n^2$$
$$b = 2mn$$
$$c = m^2 + m^2$$

These formulas will produce all the nonnegative integral Pythagorean triples when m and n are relatively prime and $m > n$.

If these restrictions are removed and m and n are allowed to range over the reals the resulting a, b, and c still obey the Pythagorean relation. This is brought about by the fact that the relation $[(m^2 + m^2)]^2 = (2mn)^2 + [(m^2 - n^2)]^2$ is an identity. Additional mathematics of Pythagorean triples is concerned with forms of primes which can be expressed as the sum of two squares. These observations, along with the trigonometric implications of these numbers, are beyond the scope of this treatment.

PROBLEM

Generate five sets of primitive Pythagorean triples by using the formulas above. Verify your triples by applying the theorem to them.

HISTORICAL ALGORISMS AND PROCESSES

Many algorisms and processes have come to us from other people and cultures. Some are simplified versions of difficult operations and many are adaptations to primitive cultures. These processes have interest for us today chiefly in terms of why they work. It is with this purpose in mind that elementary students are encouraged to examine them in depth. The explanations that follow are not proofs but logical interpretations which many elementary school children can with teacher encouragement discover and understand.

THE SAND-BOARD OR SCRATCH METHOD OF ADDING

Suppose that we wish to add 786 and 467. The usual algorism produces the sum 1253. Note, however, that this sum can be obtained as follows:

	2	5	
1	~~1~~		
	~~1~~	~~4~~	
		~~1~~	3
	~~7~~	~~8~~	~~6~~
	~~4~~	~~6~~	~~7~~
1	2	5	3

We first add seven and six to get 13 which we place above, with the three over the six. Whenever we involve a number in addition we cross it out. We then add eight and six and place the 14 above, with the four over the one. We next add seven and four and place it above, with the one over the one. We now add four and one to obtain the five at the top, and one and one to obtain the two at the top. We now pick up the digits not crossed out and place them in their proper order in the sum.

By placing the original addends in their proper place-value columns and including whatever additional columns we will need for the sum, it can be readily seen why the method works. Notice that we do not need to carry from one column to the next, since we keep adding until we have only a single digit for each column. The process including the place-value columns is shown below.

1000	100	10	1
	2	5	
1	~~1~~		
	~~1~~	~~4~~	
		~~1~~	3
	~~7~~	~~8~~	~~6~~
	~~4~~	~~6~~	~~7~~
1	2	5	3

Use the scratch method to add the following:

1. 964 + 87
2. 9230 + 596
3. 82.46 + 938.7

PEASANT MULTIPLICATION

Assume we wish to multiply 63 $\times$ 27; we proceed as follows:

63	27
126	13
~~252~~	~~6~~
504	3
1008	1
1701	

We place the multiplicand in one column and the multiplier in another. We then consecutively double each number in one column while taking half of each number in the other column, and continue this until the column in which we have been taking half results in one. Note that in taking one-half we ignore remainders. We now cross out any numbers in the left-hand column which are opposite an even number in the right-hand column. The product is now obtained by adding the remaining numbers in the left-hand column.

We can understand this process if we write 27 into base two which gives 11011_2 which in turn means $2^4 + 2^3 + 0 + 2^1 + 1$. If we now set up the problem as

$$63\,(2^4 + 2^3 + 0 + 2^1 + 1)$$

we get

$$\begin{aligned} 63 \cdot 2^4 &= 63 \cdot 16 = 1008 \\ 63 \cdot 2^3 &= 63 \cdot 8 = 504 \\ 63 \cdot 0 &= 0 = 0 \\ 63 \cdot 2^1 &= 63 \cdot 2 = 126 \\ 63 \cdot 1 &= 63 = 63 \\ & \overline{1701} \end{aligned}$$

These products are those we added in the left-hand column.

Even numbers in the right-hand column are crossed out because in converting the multiplier to base two we will either have a one or a zero in the respective place-value column, and if in the process of successively dividing the multiplier by two we get an even quotient, this indicates that the multiplier was divisible by a higher power of two and will be taken care of in the next higher place-value column. A zero thus appears in the column under consideration and the corresponding number in the left-hand column will not be involved, since the zero factor forces the product to zero. The arrangement which follows may help to explain this.

63	.....	1	.....	2^0
126	.....	2	.....	2^1
~~252~~	.....	~~4~~	.....	2^2
504	.....	8	.....	2^3
1008	.....	16	...	2^4
1701	.....	27_{10}	=	11011_2

Use peasant multiplication to find:

1. 92×65
2. 108×86
3. 946×34.3
4. 8.9×28.4

FINGER MULTIPLICATION, OR SLUGGARDS RULE

If we wish to multiply two integral factors both of which are > 4 and < 10 we may do so by using our fingers in the following manner.

Raise as many fingers on one hand as the number by which the first factor exceeds five. (We call this the *excess* of the number over five). Now do the same for the second factor, using the other hand. Now add the raised fingers on the two hands and place the sum in the tens place. Multiply the number of fingers which are down on the two hands and place the result in the units place, if it is a one-digit number, and the resulting number will be the product of the original factors. If the product of the fingers down produces a two-digit number, place the units digit in its proper place and add the tens digit to the tens digit previously obtained.

Examples

1. $7 \times 8 = 56$

Excess of 7 over 5 = 2 therefore raise two fingers on one hand.
Excess of 8 over 5 = 3, therefore raise three fingers on the other hand.
Adding fingers up we get 2 + 3 = 5 and put in tens place.
Multiply fingers down $3 \times 2 = 6$ for units digit. Product is now 56

2. $6 \times 5 = 30$

Excess on one hand = 1
Excess on other hand = 0
Adding fingers up we get 1 + 0 = 1 for tens place multiplying fingers down we get $4 \times 5 = 20$. Placing zero in units place and adding two to one for the tens place we get 30.

This is explained on a specific example $7 \times 8 = 56$ as follows:

Excess of 7 = 2; Excess of 8 = 3; 2 + 3 = sum of excesses
(5 − 2) = fingers down on one hand
(5 − 3) = fingers down on other hand

Applying the rule,

$$10\,(2 + 3) + (5 - 2)\,(5 - 3) = 50 + 6 = 56$$

$$(5 + 2)\,(5 + 3) = 25 + (2 \cdot 5) + (3 \cdot 5) + 6 = 25 + 10 + 15 + 6$$
$$= 25 + 25 + 6 = 50 + 6 = 56$$

In general,

Let a = excess of first factor or fingers up on one hand

Let b = excess of second factor or fingers up on other hand

First factor is then $(5 + a)$ and second factor is $(5 + b)$

$$(5 - a) = \text{fingers down on first hand}$$
$$(5 - b) = \text{fingers down on second hand}$$

Applying the rule,

$$10(a + b) + (5 - a)(5 - b) = 10a + 10b + 25 - 5a - 5b + ab = 25 + 5a + 5b + ab$$

But product of original factors

$$(5 + a)(5 + b) = 25 + 5a + 5b + ab$$

which is the same as the product obtained from the rule.

Use finger multiplication to do the following:

1. 6 X 5 =
2. 9 X 7 =
3. 8 X 8 =
4. 7 X 7 =
5. 6 X 9 =
6. 8 X 5 =

CASTING OUT NINES

The process of casting out nines is often used in checking addition. The check is done as follows.

825	adding the digits and subtracting as many nines as possible gives 15 - 9 = 6
647	same process, 17 - 9 = 8
1472	same process, 14 - 9 = 5

Now if we add 6 + 8 = 14 and cast out nine, we get 5, thus checking with our sum. Notice that if we were to take out as many as possible of any number say 7 merely by division the check would work. For example,

$$825 \div 7 = 117 + \text{remainder of } 6$$
$$647 \div \quad = \ 92 + \text{remainder of } 3$$

and adding 6 + 3 = 9 and dividing by seven we get a remainder of 2. Also, 1472 ÷ 7 = 210 + remainder of 2.

It appears then that the explanation will be concerned with why we can add the digits and then cast out nine and still get the same remainder as that obtained by division. Let us examine one of the numbers used in the example by first writing it in expanded notation.

$$825 = 8 \cdot (100) + 2 \cdot (10) + 5$$

The right-hand member of this could also be written

$$\begin{aligned} 8\,(99 + 1) + 2\,(9 + 1) + 5 &= (8 \cdot 99) + (8 \cdot 1) + (2 \cdot 9) + (2 \cdot 1) + 5 \\ &= (8 \cdot 99) + (2 \cdot 9) + (8 + 2 + 5) \end{aligned}$$

Now note that the first two terms of this expression $(8 \cdot 99)$ and $(2 \cdot 9)$ are certainly divisible by 9, because of the 99 and 9 factors, so we need only examine the remaining part of the expression $(8 + 2 + 5)$ for divisibility by nine in order to get the remainder. It will be noted then that $8 + 2 + 5$ is the sum of the digits of 825. Note also that the treatment used on this three-digit number will apply equally well applied to integers having greater place value, since $1000 = 999 + 1$, $10000 = 9999 + 1$ etc.

In the checking of multiplication we proceed much as we did in addition. For example,

74	casting out nines we get 2
48	casting out nines we get 3
592	
296	
3552	casting out nines we get 6

Again we could show that dividing by any number and considering the remainder will serve as a check and our previous explanation of how adding the digits and then casting out nine produces the remainder is still valid.

Note that when we add the digits of a number and get a number having two or more digits that we can repeat the process for casting out the nines of this sum. This is justified by the same explanation used on the original number. This check does not catch reversal of digits, since the sum of the digits is not altered.

Add the following and check your results by casting out nines.

1. 294 + 68
2. 7869 + 2968
3. 87640 + 839
4. 5.648 + 956.7

Multiply the following and check your results by casting out nines:

1. 29 × 846
2. 871 × 2064
3. 8572 × 9684
4. 35.4 × 839.27

Use the casting out of nines to check both the addition and multiplication in the following problem.

$$297 \cdot (846 + 9385) =$$

THE SQUARE-ROOT ALGORISM

In Chapter 4 we discussed several methods of extracting square root, one of which was the algorism. While many elementary students wish to use this algorism it is generally very difficult for them to understand its inner workings. In fact, the explanation of the general case is beyond the understanding of most elementary students. We will here, however, examine a specific case carefully in an effort to give some understanding of why the algorism works, and then present the general case for use with gifted elementary school children.

Let us review an application of the algorism to the problem.

Find: $\sqrt{1\ 8\ 4\ 9}$

$$
\begin{array}{r|l}
 & \ \ 4\ \ \ 3 \\
\hline
 & \overline{1\ 8}\ \overline{4\ 9} \\
 & 1\ 6 \\
\hline
8\ 0 & 2\ 4\ 9 \\
8\ 3 & \underline{2\ 4\ 9} \\
\hline
\end{array}
$$

Now let us analyze this application of the algorism

$$(43)^2 = (40 + 3)^2 = (40)^2 + 6 \cdot 40 + 9$$

which can be written

$$(40)^2 + 3\ [(2 \cdot 40) + 3]$$

Now let us arrange our work more nearly like the algorism above:

$$
\begin{array}{r|l}
 & 40 \quad + 3 \\
\hline
 & (40)^2 + 3\,(2 \cdot 40 + 3) \\
 & (40)^2 \\
\hline
(2 \cdot 40) + 0 & 3\,(2 \cdot 40 + 3) \\
(2 \cdot 40) + 3 & \underline{3\,(2 \cdot 40 + 3)} \\
\hline
\end{array}
\qquad \text{OR} \qquad
\begin{array}{r|l}
 & 4\ 0\ +\ 3 \\
\hline
 & 1\ 8\ 0\ 0\ +\ 4\ 9 \\
 & 1\ 6\ 0\ 0 \\
\hline
8\ 0\ +\ 0 & 2\ 0\ 0\ +\ 4\ 9 \\
 & \qquad \text{OR} \\
8\ 0\ +\ 3 & 2\ 4\ 0\ +\ 9 \\
 & \underline{2\ 4\ 0\ +\ 9} \\
\hline
\end{array}
$$

Note that $3\,[(2 \cdot 40) + 3] = 249$, which is identical to the original algorism.

General Development of the Algorism

The square of any integer may be written in expanded notation and thus take a polynomial form. For example,

$$(43.2)^2 = (40 + 3 + .2)^2 \text{ which is of the form}$$

$$(X + Y + Z)^2$$

$$(X + Y + Z)^2 = X^2 + 2XY + Y^2 + 2XZ + 2YZ + Z^2$$

$$= X^2 + Y\,(2X + Y) + Z\,(2X + 2Y + Z)$$

Let us now place this expression into the usual square root bracket and apply the algorism.

$$
\begin{array}{r|l|l}
 & \multicolumn{2}{l}{X + Y + Z} \\
\cline{2-3}
 & \multicolumn{2}{l}{X^2 + Y(2X + Y) + Z(2X + 2Y + Z} \\
 & \multicolumn{2}{l}{X^2} \\
\cline{2-3}
2X + 0 & \quad Y(2X + Y) & \\
2X + Y & \quad \underline{Y(2X + Y)} & \\
\cline{1-1}
 2X + 2Y + 0 & Z(2X + 2Y + Z) & \\
 \underline{2X + 2Y + Z} & \underline{\underline{Z(2X + 2Y + Z)}} &
\end{array}
$$

Specifically,

$$(43.2)^2 = (40 + 3 + .2)^2 = (40)^2 + 3\ (80 + 3) + .2\ (80 + 6 + .2)$$

$$
\begin{array}{r|l}
 & 40 \quad + \quad 3 \quad + .2 \\
\cline{2-2}
 & (40)^2 + 3\ (80 + 3) + .2\ (80 + 6 + .2) \\
 & (40)^2 \\
\cline{2-2}
(2 \cdot 40) + 0 & 3\ (80 + 3) \\
(2 \cdot 40) + 3 & \underline{3\ (80 + 3)} \\
\cline{1-1}
(2 \cdot 40) + (2 \cdot 3) + 0 & .2\ (80 + 6 + .2) \\
\underline{(2 \cdot 40) + (2 \cdot 3) + .2} & \underline{\underline{.2\ (80 + 6 + .2)}}
\end{array}
$$

$$(43.2)^2 = 1866.24$$

$$\sqrt{1866.24} = 43.2$$

By carefully following this development the shortcut steps in the algorism become meaningful. Use the detailed breakdown shown above to extract the square root of 3226.24.

THE METRIC SYSTEM

The advantages of the metric system over our awkward English system of measurement hardly needs restatement at this point. Just how early we can effectively introduce the metric system into the elementary school remains unanswered. Our cultural dependence on the English system continues to harass us, and primary-grade children bring little if any of the metric system to the classroom. To date our major obligation seems to be the imparting of a functional understanding of the English system as a means of meeting the cultural needs.

All wishful thinking aside, it appears that we will be burdened with a dual system of measurement for some time to come. However, once we have achieved a degree of competency in the English system adequate for our basic needs we surely should begin to develop proficiency in the metric system which is also part of culture, having been recognized by the U.S. Congress as early as 1866.

Let us look then at this most logical system which is calibrated in the decimal scale and which possesses a most beautiful relationship among the measures of length, weight, and capacity. The metric system is built upon three basic units –the liter, the gram, and the meter. All other units of measure are power-of-ten multiples of these basic units. The units smaller than the basic units of course requiring a power of 10 smaller than one.

Having learned the basic terms for capacity, weight, and length the student will move to the prefixes which distinguish the units within a category. These are defined below:

milli	.001
centi	.01
deci	.1
Basic unit–meter, gram or liter:	
deka	10
hecto	100
kilo	1000

The relationships existing among the basic units are as follows:

1. The weight of one cubic centimeter of pure water at 4°C is one gram.
2. One thousand cubic centimeters equals one liter.
3. One liter of pure water at 4°C equals a kilogram.

Conversion of units within the system is obviously very simple because of the power-of-ten relationship. Conversion from the English to the metric and vice versa may be made by means of the following conversion factors:

1 meter $\approx$ 39.37 in.
1 gram $\approx$ .035 oz
1 liter $\approx$ 1.057 qt

Teachers working with elementary school students will do well to provide themselves with the following visual aids:

1. A wall chart of the metric system
2. A liter and quart container
3. A meter stick and yardstick
4. A gram and an ounce weight

Convert each of the following to the system and units indicated:

1. Convert 78.74 in. to meters.
2. Convert 2.5 meters to feet.
3. Convert 12 oz to grams.
4. Convert 1,000 grams to pounds.
5. Convert 250 miles to kilometers.

GEOMETRY OF THE EARTH

Elementary students need to have a basic and functional understanding of the geometry of the earth. Two basic ideas concerning the earth are here in order:

1. The earth will be considered as a sphere in locating places on its surface.
2. The earth will be considered as a plane in measuring its surface.

In locating points on the earth a system similar to rectangular coordinates will be employed. The equator will serve as the prime latitude or x-dimension and the meridian through Greenwich England as the y-dimension. The lines of latitude other than the equator itself are really small circles of the earth and their planes are parallel to that of the equator. These parallels are measured in arc degrees, minutes, and seconds ranging from 0° to 90° north and south latitudes. The meridians are all great circles of the earth through the poles. They also are are measured in degrees, minutes and seconds east and west of the prime meridian. When the globe is shown with the North Pole at the top of the page and Greenwich in the foreground, the meridians to the right of Greenwich are east longitude until reaching the Greenwich great circle on the opposite side of the globe. Going to the left from the prime meridian is considered west longitude with similar limitation. The diagram illustrates how a point P is located on the globe by means of this arrangement.

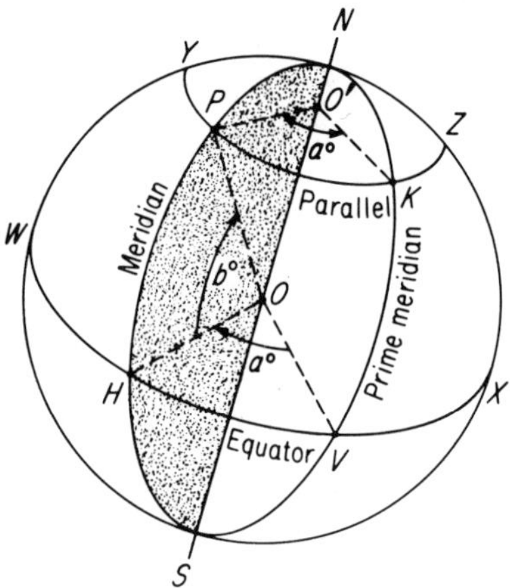

To find the longitude and latitude of point P in the preceding figure proceed as follows:

Go from V along the equator to H, a distance of $a°$ of arc as shown by the central angle VOH. Then go along the meridian from H to P, or $b°$ of arc as shown by the central angle HOP. P is then located at $a°$ west longitude (west because P is west of the prime meridian) and $b°$ north latitude. The longitude may be measured along the small circle through P as well as along the equator, because angle $KO'P$ equals angle VOH.

The following types of problems are now in order:

1. Find to the nearest five degrees the latitude and longitude of the following:
   (a) Moscow, Russia
   (b) Makasar, Indonesia
   (c) Durban, Union of South Africa
   (d) Seward, Alaska

2. What large city is nearest the following locations:
   (a) 35°N latitude 140°E longitude
   (b) 35°S latitude 150°E longitude
   (c) 10°S latitude 72°W longitude
   (d) 65°N latitude 150°W longitude
3. What latitude is the tropic of cancer? The tropic of Capricorn?
4. Name several islands near the 180° meridian.
5. Is the 180° meridian known as east or west longitude?
6. What island is nearest the origin of the global grid?

Land Measure on the Surface of the Earth

The U.S. Coast and Geodedic survey is based upon the following factors:

1. In the original survey 35 principal points were established astronomically across the United States.

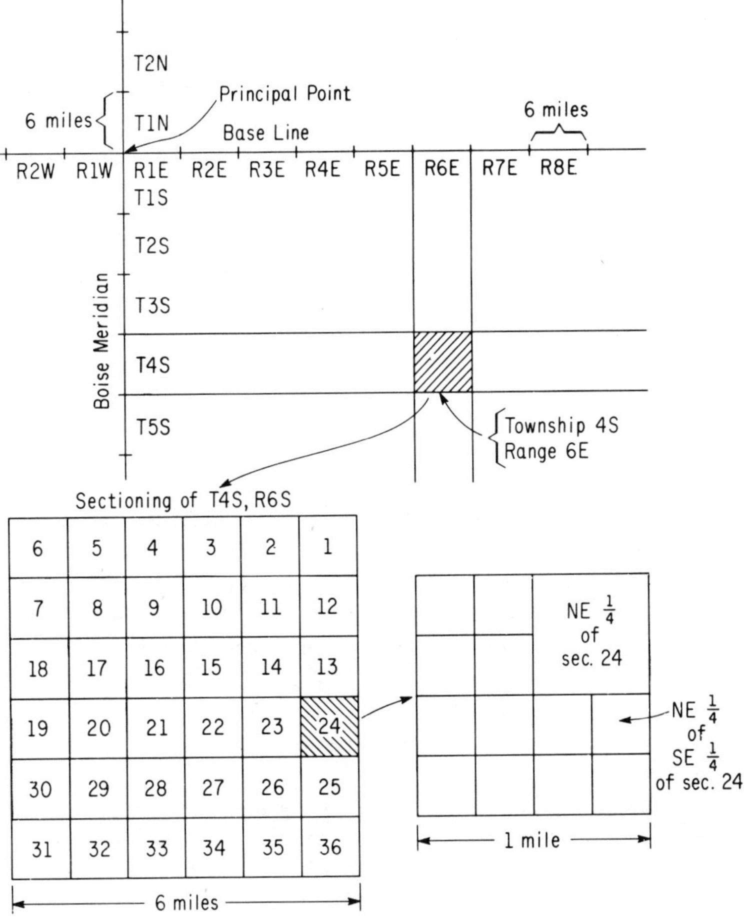

2. At each principal point a principal meridian was established.
3. Ranges were laid out in six-mile-wide strips, beginning at the principal meridian. The ranges are thus located between successive meridians six miles apart. Each range is numbered east and west of the principal meridian.
4. Every 24 miles east and west of each principle meridian a guide meridian is established.
5. The ranges are cut into six-mile squares called *townships*. These are numbered north and south of the principal point.
6. A particular township is located by giving the number of the township north and south of the principal point and east and west of the principal meridian through this principal point.
7. Each township is divided into sections one mile square, resulting in 36 sections per township.
8. Losses in area due to the curvature of the earth are deducted from the section located in the N.W. corner of each township.
9. The sections of a township are numbered 1–36 beginning in the N.E. corner and numbering successively to the west to section 5, then moving south to the next section which is 7, then to the east successively to section 12, then south to 13 and then west, etc., until section 36 is finally located in the S.E. corner.
10. Each section is approximately one mile square and contains 640 acres. The location of a particular parcel of land may be described as follows: N.E. quarter of section 24 township 4 S range 6 E Boise Meridian. (The prime meridians are often identified by the name of the region rather than by number.)

SYSTEMS OF OPEN SENTENCES

Our discussion of open sentences in this text has been pretty well limited to one sentence and one variable per problem. Many situations in mathematics lead us into more than one sentence and more than one variable. This is especially true in the modern day, when industrial and research organizations may be confronted with situations requiring hundreds of variables and hundreds of open sentences for their solution. Such problems become very practical through computer-assisted solutions.

At this level we shall, however, restrict ourselves to two variables and two open sentences, recognizing that the picture will be extended at the higher instructional levels.

As we worked with one variable and one open sentence we interpreted our solution on a number-line graph. We shall now consider two variables in two open sentences and will interpret our solutions on a two-dimensional graph which we call a *rectangular coordinate system*. As explained elsewhere in this text, this type of graph can be conjectured from imposing a second number line at right angles to our usual number line at point zero and with the positive numbers above the zero point.

Let us now seek the simultaneous solution of the following two open sentences:

1. $X + Y = 10$
2. $2X - Y = 5$

First we observe that sentence 1 has an infinite number of solutions among which are $X = 8$ and $Y = 2$, also $X = 6$ and $Y = 4$. We write these solutions as ordered pairs and the solution set becomes {(8,2), (6,4), etc.} Now if we plot this equation on the graph by the conventional procedure we obtain a straight line passing through the two points shown in the solution set. Further, if we read the coordinates of any other point on this line we find they too make the sentence true. It appears then that all the ordered pairs contained in the "etc." of our solution set lie on this line.

Similarly, if we find two ordered pairs which make sentence 2 true i.e., {(3,1), (6,7) etc.}, and plot these on the graph, we have a straight line which represents the graph of all the ordered pairs that make this sentence true. If we consider now the coordinates of the intersection of the two lines, we find this ordered pair makes both sentences true which of course it should since it lies on both lines. (See graph.)

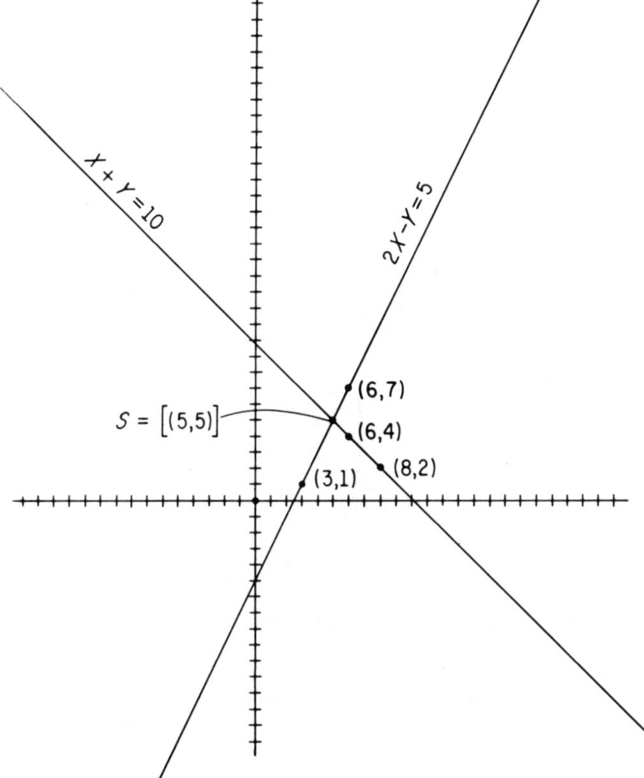

Note that (5,5) makes both sentences true, i.e.,

$$x + y = 10; \quad 5 + 5 = 10$$
$$2x - y = \ 5; \quad (2 \cdot 5) - 5 = 10 - 5 = 5$$

Let us look now at a pair of open sentences, one of which is an equation and the other an inequality:

1. $2X + Y = 12$
2. $X - Y > 4$

We first plot the equation $X - Y = 4$, using the same procedure previously taught. We call this line *CD*. We note now that the coordinates of any point to the right of this line makes the open sentence $X - Y > 4$,true. For example, suppose we consider the point (6,1) we see that $6 - 1 > 4$. Points on the line or to the left of the line do not make the open sentence true, i.e., (6,2) gives us $6 - 2 > 4$ which is false, and (3,1) gives us $3 - 1 > 4$, which is also false. We conclude then that solution set for $X - Y > 4$ consists of the shaded area of the graph.

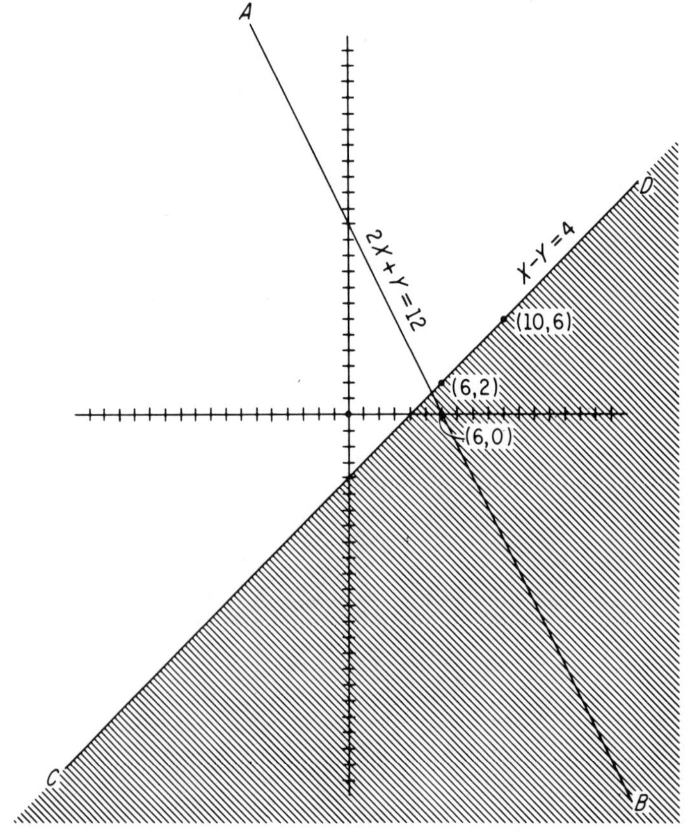

We now plot the graph of $2X + Y = 12$ and find it to be the line AB. Now the coordinates of any point of AB and to the right of CD will make both open sentences true. For example: The point (6,0) substituted in the open sentence $2Y + Y = 12$ gives us $(2 \times 6) + 0 = 12$ which is true, and (6,0) substituted in $X - Y > 4$ gives us $6 - 0 > 4$, which is also true. It appears then that we have found the solution set for the simultaneous pair of open sentences with which we began our problem.

We conclude this topic with some problems and the suggestion that the student explore nongraphical means of solving simultaneous open sentences. Use the graphical method to find the solution set and complement set for the following systems of open sentences:

1. $X + 2Y = 12$
   $X - Y = 6$
2. $3X + Y = 10$
   $2X + Y = 5$
3. $X - Y = 6$
   $X + 2Y > 4$
4. $2X + Y > 4$
   $3X + 2Y > 10$

BASE TWELVE NUMERATION

In Chapter 3 we discussed bases less than ten and discovered certain characteristics which exist in all bases which are constructed similar to our base ten. This experience provides use with adequate foundation material for bases greater than ten and leads us to rewarding supplementary or enrichment topics for those students who quickly master the treatment of bases developed in Chapter 3.

As we develop the base twelve system, we quickly discover that we need two additional basic number symbols to accommodate the duodecade which now corresponds to the decade used in base ten. Let us introduce these symbols to be len (l) and pen (p). As we now set up a one to one correspondence with base ten counting numbers, the numbers in the two bases pair up as follows:

$1_{10}, 2_{10}, 3_{10}, 4_{10}, 5_{10}, 6_{10}, 7_{10}, 8_{10}, 9_{10}, 10_{10}, 11_{10}, 12_{10}, 13_{10}, 14_{10}, 15_{10}, 16_{10}$
$1_{12}, 2_{12}, 3_{12}, 4_{12}, 5_{12}, 6_{12}, 7_{12}, 8_{12}, 9_{12}, l_{12}, p_{12}, 10_{12}, 11_{12}, 13_{12}, 14_{12}$

Note now that in the counting process we can apply some meaningful new names to our numbers by capitalizing upon the term *duodecimal* commonly given to this system, which means "two and ten" and is therefore equivalent to twelve. As we count then, we can perhaps without confusion, use the following terminology, beginning with the integer that follows nine: len, pen, duo-ten, duo-eleven, duo-twelve, and so on up to duo-nineteen, duo-lenteen, duo-penteen, duo-twenty. This process continues through the duo-decades up to duo-ninety-nine, duo-ninety-len, duo-ninety-pen, and then to a new duo-decade. This proceeds as follows: lenty, lenty-one, lenty-two, . . . up to lenty-nine, lenty-len, lenty-pen, then to the last duo-decade penty, penty-one, up to penty-nine, penty-len, penty-pen, and on to duo-one-hundred.

We now construct a place-value chart for base twelve and write into it some of the numbers referred to above.

Base Twelve Place-Value Chart

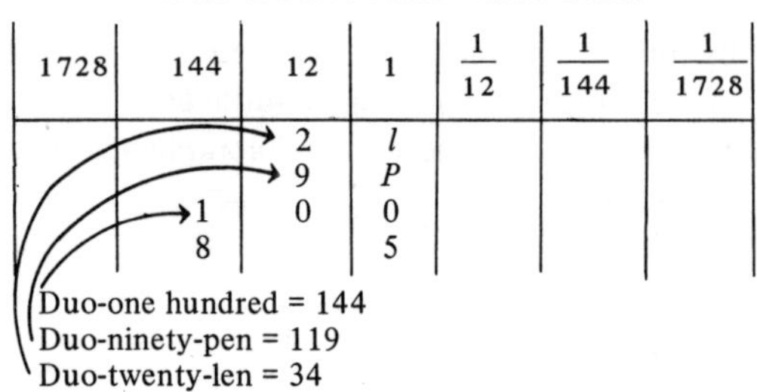

Let us follow up now with some translations to and from base twelve. The symbol $8p5$, which appears in the chart, translates to $8 \times 144 = 1152$, $p \times 12 = 132$, $5 \times 1 = 5$, which summed becomes $1152 + 132 + 5 = 1289$. Translating from base ten to twelve is done logically as follows:

$$2723 = (1 \times 1728) + (6 \times 144) + (1 \times 12) + (p \times 1) = 161p$$

At this point students should be ready to perform the basic operations in base twelve. These operations may be performed either by translation or by the use of charts as was done in the bases used in Chapter 3.

The following are suggested as problems to be used with elementary students who have studied this supplemental topic.

1. Make a basic addition and subtraction chart for base twelve.
2. Make a basic multiplication and division chart for base twelve.
3. Add the following base twelve numbers and check your answer by translating to base ten. Do the problems both by translation and by using the addition chart.
   (a) $3497_{12} + 6258_{12} =$
   (b) $614_{12} + 293_{12} =$
   (c) $5p86_{12} + 197p_{12} =$
4. Subtract the following using both the translation and chart method. Check your answers by translating to base ten.
   (a) $6258_{12} - 3497_{12} =$
   (b) $614_{12} - 293_{12} =$
   (c) $197p_{12} - 5p86_{12} =$
5. Multiply the following using both the translation method and the chart. Check your answers by translating to base ten.
   (a) $274_{12} \times 63_{12} =$
   (b) $8l6_{12} \times 493_{12} =$
   (c) $14p_{12} \times 86p_{12} =$

6. Divide the following using both methods and the check as above.
   (a) $14310_{12} \div 63_{12} =$
   (b) $376116_{12} \div 493_{12} =$
   (c) $753401_{12} \div 86p_{12} =$

CHICKEN ARITHMETIC[1]

Chapter 8 dealt briefly with mathematical fields and modular arithmetic. An interesting takeoff on these two topics centers around a situation described by Dr. James Wolfe as "chicken arithmetic." In this particular situation a hen hatched 13 chicks. In an effort to test her knowledge of arithmetic, Dr. Wolfe removed all of the chicks from her sight, which resulted in a very unhappy, scratching clucking hen. He then returned one chick, which quieted her some. The return of a second chick reduced her anxiety further, until by the time the fifth chick was returned she seemed to be completely content. Dr. Wolfe therefore concluded that the hen could add up to a sum of five but did not discern sharply between five chicks and any number of chicks greater than five. The hen's addition chart could, then, be illustrated as follows:

⊕	0	1	2	3	4	M
0	0	1	2	3	4	M
1	1	2	3	4	M	M
2	2	3	4	M	M	M
3	3	4	M	M	M	M
4	4	M	M	M	M	M
M	M	M	M	M	M	M

where M = many and is specifically 5 or more.

It can be conjectured further that perhaps the hen's basic multiplication chart would be as follows:

⊗	0	1	2	3	4	M
0	0	0	0	0	0	0
1	0	1	2	3	4	M
2	0	2	4	M	M	M
3	0	3	M	M	M	M
4	0	4	M	M	M	M
M	0	M	M	M	M	M

[1]Used with permission of James H. Wolfe, Professor of Mathematics University of Utah, Salt Lake City, Utah.

It is interesting to apply the appropriate test to this situation to determine whether or not the hen's mathematical system constitutes a mathematical field.

At this point the teacher will do well to refer her elementary school students to the definition of a mathematical field found on page 188 of this text and suggest that they test it thoroughly in terms of the existence principle, the uniqueness principle, and the other field axioms.

Note that as in our application of the field axioms to modular systems in Chapter 6 we can give meaning to the additive and multiplicative inverse axioms by merely seeking elements in the system which behave like negatives and fractions, even though the system does not actually contain these. Now try the following questions:

1. In what ways does this system differ from modular arithmetic?
2. Do the existence and uniqueness principles hold in this system?
3. Which of the field axioms hold and which do not in this system?
4. Is the system a field?
5. If the hen could distinguish say up to seven chicks, would this strengthen the system in terms of its becoming a field?
6. Would the system more nearly approach a field if M for the hen had been four or more instead of five or more?

DIVISIBILITY RULES AND WHY THEY WORK

In certain areas of arithmetic it is often convenient to know whether large integers are exactly divisible by the small integers; say 2 through 12. There are many tests for divisibility, all of which have a logical mathematical basis for their truthfulness. While blind application of the rules may appeal to some students, the spirit of contemporary mathematics would also emphasize the reasons why the rules work. Much sound mathematics is involved in these reasons, and they should therefore be thought of as worthwhile mathematical experiences for elementary school students.

Let us examine divisibility, beginning with the number 2. Any integer is divisible by two if the units digit is divisible by 2. The reason for this rule becomes apparent if we examine the expanded notation of a given integer, say 289. $289 = 200 + 80 + 9 = (2 \cdot 100) + (8 \cdot 10) + (9 \cdot 1) = 2(10)^2 + 8(10)^1 + 9(10)^0$, and since this notation indicates that the digit in any place value beyond the units place, is to be multiplied by an integral power of 10 where the exponent is equal to or greater than one, and since such powers of ten are all divisible by 2, the final digit becomes the determining one. We depend here upon the fact that if an integer can be expressed as the sum of addends, each of which is divisible by 2, then the integer is divisible by two. We shall use this without proof at this point.

Any integer is divisible by 3 if the sum of its digits is divisible by 3. The truthfulness of this is enhanced by the following illustration.

$$
\begin{aligned}
924 &= (9 \cdot 100) + (2 \cdot 10) + (4 \cdot 1) \\
&= 9 \cdot (99 + 1) + 2\,(9 + 1) + (4 \cdot 1) \\
&= (9 \cdot 99) + (9 \cdot 1) + (2 \cdot 9) + (2 \cdot 1) + (4 \cdot 1) \\
&= (9 \cdot 99) + (2 \cdot 9) + (9 \cdot 1) + (2 \cdot 1) + (4 \cdot 1) \\
&= 9 \cdot 99 + 2 \cdot 9 + (9 + 2 + 4)
\end{aligned}
$$

Since the first two terms are divisible by 3 because of the 9 factor, the final divisibility of 924 depends upon the sum $(9 + 2 + 4)$, which are the digits of 924.

Any integer is divisible by 4 if the integer formed by the first two digits taken alone is divisible by 4. For example, 8760 is divisible by 4, since 60 is divisible by 4. This rule results from the fact that any integer with three or more digits may be written as $n(100)$ + the number formed by the last two digits, (where n = an integer), and since $n(100)$ is always divisible by four because the factor 100 is divisible by 4. The divisibility of the original integer thus depends upon the divisibility of the number formed by the last two digits.

A second method of testing for divisibility by 4 consists of applying the test for 2. If the number is not divisible by 2, it is not divisible by 4. If it is divisible by 2, take 2 out as a factor and test the remaining factor for 2. If this factor is divisible by 2, then the original number was divisible by 4.

An integer is divisible by five if the last digit is zero or five. Again as with our test for 2, since all multiples of integral powers of 10 beyond 10^0 are divisible by five, the divisibility depends upon the units digit. Example: $8435 = (8 \cdot 1000) + (4 \cdot 100) + (3 \cdot 10) + (5 \cdot 1)$, and the first 3 addends must be divisible by 5, since they have integral powers of 10 beyond 10^0 as factors. The divisibility is then decided by the units digit.

Divisibility by 6 is probably most easily determined by testing for 2 and 3. If the integer satisfies the divisibility rules for both 2 and 3, then it is divisible by $2 \cdot 3 = 6$. Furthermore, if an integer fails either the test for 2 or 3, then it is not divisible by 6.

Since a divisibility rule is designed to shorten the determination of divisibility beyond the actual division, no rule for division by seven is presented here.

Any integer may be tested for divisibility by 8 by three successive applications of the rule for divisibility by 2. This is done by testing the original number and removing 2 as a factor where possible, then doing the same two more times if possible. This test results from the fact that $2 \cdot 2 \cdot 2 = 8$. If the divisibility test for 2 fails at any of the three stages, then the number is not divisible by 8.

An integer is divisible by 9 if the sum of its digits is divisible by 9. This stems from the following demonstration:

$$
\begin{aligned}
6813 &= (6 \cdot 1000) + (8 \cdot 100) + (1 \cdot 10) + (3 \cdot 1) \\
&= 6(999 + 1) + 8(99 + 1) + 1 \cdot (9 + 1) + (3 \cdot 1) \\
&= (6 \cdot 999) + (6 \cdot 1) + (8 \cdot 99) + (8 \cdot 1) + (1 \cdot 9) + (1 \cdot 1) + (3 \cdot 1) \\
&= (6 \cdot 999) + (8 \cdot 99) + (1 \cdot 9) + (6 + 8 + 1 + 3)
\end{aligned}
$$

Since the first three addends are divisible by 9 because of the nature of the factors, then the divisibility depends upon (6 + 8+ 1 + 3), which is the sum of the digits.

Any integer is divisible by 10 if the units digit of the integer is zero. This follows from the fact that integral powers of 10, where the exponent is greater than zero, are divisible by 10, and no digit other than zero is divisible by 10.

Any integer is divisible by 11 if the difference of sum of the digits in the odd-numbered positions and the sum of the digits in the even-numbered positions is divisible by 11. Positions are determined from right to left. If the subtrahend turns out to be larger than the minuend, add a multiple of 11 to the minuend. Exploration of why the rule works is given for a specific case.

$$\begin{aligned}
94{,}864 &= 9\,(10000) + 4\,(1000) + (8 \cdot 100) + (6 \cdot 10) + (4 \cdot 1)\\
&= 9\,(9999 + 1) + 4\,(1001 - 1) + 8\,(99 + 1) + 6\,(11 - 1) + (4 \cdot 1)\\
&= (9 \cdot 9999) + (9 \cdot 1) + 4\,(1001) - (4 \cdot 1) + (8 \cdot 99) + (8 \cdot 1) + (6 \cdot 11)\\
&\quad - (6 \cdot 1) + (4 \cdot 1)\\
&= (9 \cdot 9999) + 4\,(1001) + (8 \cdot 99) + (6 \cdot 11) + (9 \cdot 1) - (4 \cdot 1) + (8 \cdot 1)\\
&\quad - (6 \cdot 1) + (4 \cdot 1)\\
&= (9 \cdot 9999) + 4\,(1001) + (8 \cdot 99) + (6 \cdot 11) + [9 - 4 + 8 - 6 + 4]
\end{aligned}$$

Now one factor in each of the first four addends is divisible by 11, i.e., (9999), 1001, 99, and 11 are all divisible by 11. Therefore divisibility by 11 for the original number depends upon 9 - 4 + 8 - 6 + 4, which is the sum dictated by the rule.

Any integer is divisible by 12 if it is divisible by 3 and also by 4. If both tests hold the original integer is divisible by 12. If either fails the integer is not divisible by 12.

Divisibility rules for integers beyond 12 are not generally economical except where the rules for all the members of the same set of factors of the integer has already been established. We may then utilize the same approach as used for divisibility by 12.

For example, an integer is divisible by 18 if it is divisible by two and 9. If divisibility by either fails, the integer is not divisible by 18. Another exception to the economy of divisibility rules for integers larger than 12 is illustrated by integral powers of 10 beyond one as an exponent.

Determine whether the following are exactly divisible by the numbers indicated:

1. Is 2472 divisible by 2? by 4? by 6?
2. Is 86295 divisible by 3? by 5? by 10?
3. Is 5496 divisible by 8? by 9? by 12?
4. Is 3228800 divisible by 2? by 3? by 4? by 5? by 6? by 7? by 8? by 9? by 10? by 11? by 12?

SCIENTIFIC NOTATION

Scientists have devised a standard form for writing numbers which is especially useful in the macro and micro world where very large and very small numbers are often encountered. In mathematics this form or method is called *scientific notation* or *standard notation*.

In Chapter 4, we discussed exponents and powers, including negative exponents. We can now very easily draw upon this information to help us with this new notation. Further, our previous treatment of factors and significant digits will help us.

By the method of scientific notation, a number may be expressed as the product of two factors, one factor indicating the significant digits of the given number with the decimal point placed immediately following the digit of the number located at the extreme left, the other factor showing the integral power of 10 necessary to give correct place value to the significant digits. When the zero digits in a given number are known to be significant, they must be given consideration when expressing the number in scientific form. We now illustrate:

1. If a number such as 186,000 is known to be accurate to only three significant digits it is written 1.86×10^5.
2. The number 0.000560 in scientific notation becomes 5.60×10^{-4} since by our rules for significant digits the zero after the 6 is significant or it would not have been shown originally.
3. If the last two digits of 75600 are known to be exactly zeros, that is they are known to be significant, then we write 7.5600×10^4.
4. If the last two digits of 75600 are not known to be exactly zeros, then we write 7.56×10^4.
5. The number 0.00750 in scientific notation becomes 7.50×10^{-3}.
6. The number .0075 becomes 7.5×10^{-3}.

A group of numbers which are successive powers of ten are shown below. They will review for us material which was discussed in the body of this text.

$$10^6 = 1000000$$
$$10^5 = 100000$$
$$10^4 = 10000$$
$$10^3 = 1000$$
$$10^2 = 100$$
$$10^1 = 10$$
$$10^0 = 1$$

$$(10)^{-1} = \frac{1}{(10)^1} = \frac{1}{10} = 0.1$$

$$(10)^{-2} = \frac{1}{(10)^2} = \frac{1}{100} = .01$$

$$(10)^{-3} = \frac{1}{(10)^3} = \frac{1}{1000} = .001$$

$$(10)^{-4} = \frac{1}{(10)^4} = \frac{1}{10000} = .0001$$

$$(10)^{-5} = \frac{1}{(10)^5} = \frac{1}{100000} = .00001$$

Since it will eventually be essential that students be able to translate rapidly to and from scientific notation, they should at the higher-grade levels be encouraged to generalize the procedures, but for the younger students, reasoning and checking are important experience, and such students should not be given the short cut rules by the teacher, but be encouraged to find and use them on their own. Their discoveries may take the following forms:

(a) To write a number in standard form, place a decimal point after the first significant digit on the extreme left, then count the number of digits between the new and the original location of the decimal point, and use this number as the exponent of 10.

(b) In the above process if the new decimal point is to the left of the original location, the sign of the exponent will be positive. If the new location is to the right of the original decimal point, the sign of the exponent will be negative.

More examples follow:

1. $563900 = 8.634 \times 10^5$
2. $263.2 = 2.632 \times 10^2$
3. $0.000543 = 5.43 \times 10^{-4}$
4. $0.00000700 = 7.0 \times 10^{-6}$

In the calculations of science, standard notation leads to valuable shortcuts which all science students will want to know. Compare the procedure necessary in the first problem with that shown in the second. As you will note, they are equivalent problems.

(a) $$\frac{764300000 \times 0.00009876}{42600 \times 0.007321} =$$

(b) $$\frac{7.643 \times 10^8 \times 9.876 \times 10^{-5}}{4.26 \times 10^4 \times 7.321 \times 10^{-3}} =$$

$$\frac{7.643 \times 9.876}{4.26 \times 7.321} \times \frac{10^8 \times 10^{-5}}{10^4 \cdot \times 10^{-3}} =$$

$$\frac{7.643 \times 9.876}{4.26 \times 7.321} \times \frac{10^3}{10^1} = \frac{7.643 \times 9.876}{4.26 \times 7.321} \times 10^2$$

The study of scientific notation is also a preparation for the study of logarithms. Students using the slide rule will surely want to know the mathematical theory which causes it to work so effectively. It is only a short step from scientific notation to the theory back of logarithms base 10.

The following problems are suggested as a continuation of your experience with scientific notation.

1. Change to scientific notation:
   (a) 974000000
   (b) 0.0000634
   (c) 568004
   (d) 0.000702
   (e) 9900000
   (f) 704000
   (g) 0.0000000317
   (h) 7639
   (i) 654.000083
   (j) 20007
   (k) 7.40000000
   (l) 9.000400000
2. Change from scientific notation to regular form:
   (a) 6.34×10^{-6}
   (b) 9.9×10^{6}
   (c) 3.17×10^{-8}
   (d) 7.04×10^{5}
   (e) 7.02×10^{-4}
   (f) 9.0004×10^{6}
   (g) 5.68004×10^{6}
   (h) 7.4×10^{-8}
   (i) 7.639×10^{3}
   (j) 2.0007×10^{4}
3. Place in true standard form:
   (a) 0.742×10^{7}
   (b) 93.70×10^{-3}
   (c) $.04 \times 10^{2}$
   (d) 297.6×10^{5}
   (e) $.42 \times 10^{-5}$
   (f) $.007 \times 10^{10}$
4. Place in standard form then compute:
   (a) $\dfrac{16000000 \times 0.000025}{500000 \times .00008} =$
   (b) $\dfrac{.000004 \times .0000065}{3250000 \times 2000000} =$
   (c) $\dfrac{185000 \times 96000000}{.0000032} =$
5. Set up open sentences and then compute using scientific notation:
   (a) The star closest to the earth is 24,500,000,000,000 miles away when the distance is calculated to three-digit accuracy. How many days will it take light from the star to reach the earth?
   (b) One inch = 0.03937 millimeters. Approximately how many millimeters are there in 10,000 miles?
   (c) If light travels at the rate of approximately 1.86×10^{5} miles per hour, how far does it travel in 1,000 hours?

ABSOLUTE VALUE[2]

In Chapter 4 we defined the absolute value of a number as follows:

1. The absolute value of a positive number is the number itself.
2. The absolute value of a negative number is its additive inverse.
3. The absolute value of zero is zero.

At that time we used absolute value to assist us in stating rules for operating with

[2]M. P. Bridgess (ed.), *Absolute Value*, Supplementary and Enrichment Series (Stanford, Calif: Stanford University, 1966). S.M.S.G.

signed numbers. Absolute value has many other uses and can be explained meaningfully on the number line.

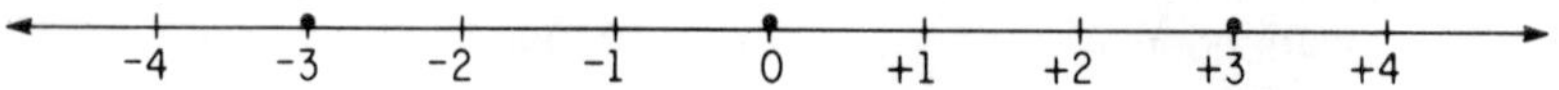

By definition the distance between any two points on the number line is a nonnegative real number. On the number line shown, the distance between the point labeled (+3) and the point O is three units, and the distance between the point labeled (−3) and the point O is also three units. The distance between the point N and the point O, where (N) represents any number, is what we have called the *absolute value* of N. We could then restate the definition of absolute value of a number as the distance between the point representing the number and the point representing zero on the number line.

We use two vertical parallel segments, one on each side of the number, to indicate the operation of taking the absolute value of a number.

Examples of the notation and the results of the operation are:

(a) $|-7| = 7$

(b) $|+6| = 6$

(c) $|0| = 0$

(d) $|-\sqrt{2}| = \sqrt{2}$

(e) $|-\frac{2}{3}| = \frac{2}{3}$

(f) $|.333\ldots| = .333\ldots$

(g) $|-.272727\ldots| = .272727\ldots$

(h) $|-(-3)| = 3$

(i) $|-(-(-5))| = 5$

Which of the following are true and which are false? Defend your answer.

(a) $\frac{2}{3}$ is a nonnegative number

(b) $|\frac{2}{3}|$ is a negative number.

(c) 0 is a nonnegative number.

(d) $-\frac{3}{4}$ is a negative number.

(e) $|-\frac{3}{4}|$ is a negative number.

(f) If $\square$ is a negative number then $|\square|$ is a nonnegative number.

(g) If $\square$ is a real number, then $|\square|$ is a nonnegative number.

(h) $|\square|$ is greater than $\square$ if $\square$ is a negative number.

(i) $-17 < |-3|$

(j) $3 \nless |-3|$

(k) $|-2| < |-3|$

(l) $|-6| > |4|$

(m) $|\sqrt{9}| < |-4|$

(n) $|-3|^2 = 9$

(o) $|+3|^2 < -9$

(p) $3^2 = |-9|$

(q) $4 < |-8|$

Now do the following:

1. Write a subset of set A consisting of the absolute values of the elements in set A.

$$A = \{-3, -2, -1, 0, +1, +2, +3\}$$

2. Consider the operation of taking absolute values. Are all nonempty subsets of real numbers closed under this operation? Defend your answer.

3. If every element of a subset of the real numbers is accompanied in the subset by its opposite will the set be closed under the operation of taking absolute value. Illustrate your answer with some examples.

4. Is the set of integers closed under the operation of taking absolute value? Defend your answer.

5. Is it true that $|-6| = -(-6) = 6$?

6. Does Prob. 5 tell us that the absolute value of a negative number is its opposite? Write each of the following as a single-digit numeral:

(a) $-[|-3| + |-4|]$
(b) $9 - |-5|$
(c) $|-3| \times |+2|$
(d) $5 - |6 - 7|$
(e) $|-12| \div 3$
(f) $-(|-4| - 2)$
(g) $-(-5 + |-3|)$
(h) $|-3| \times [|-4| - |2|]$
(i) $[|-2| + |+5|] \div |-7|$
(j) $|[|-2| - |-3|]|$

The absolute value of a placeholder can occur in an open sentence and the solution set can often be determined by observation. When the solution set has been determined it can be graphed on the number line unless it is empty. Let us find and graph the solution set for $|\square| < 2$. **U** = the real numbers. The solution set contains such elements as $-\frac{3}{4}$, $-\frac{3}{2}$, $0, \frac{2}{3}, \frac{5}{3}$, -1, $+1$ all of which make the sentence true. Elements such as $-7, \frac{5}{2}$, -2.3, $2.272727\ldots$, 2, $-1.999\ldots$ are in the complement set and make the sentence false. The solution set consists of all the real numbers between -2 and 2, as shown in the graph. Note that -2 and 2 are not included.

Write the solution set for each of the following open sentences, then graph each solution set on a number line.

(a) $|\square| = 5$
(b) $6 - 2|\square| = -2$
(c) $|\square| > 3$
(d) $-|\square| \leqslant \square$
(e) $\square \leqslant |\square|$
(f) $|\square| > -1$
(g) $|\square| \geqslant 0$
(h) $|\square| < 0$

Write an open sentence for each of the following graphs using at least one absolute-value symbol.

(a) 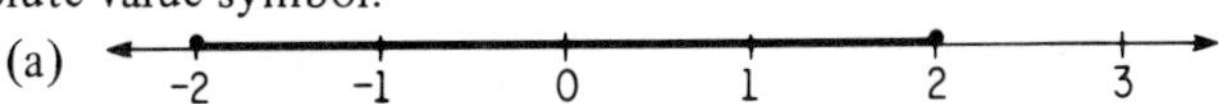

(b) 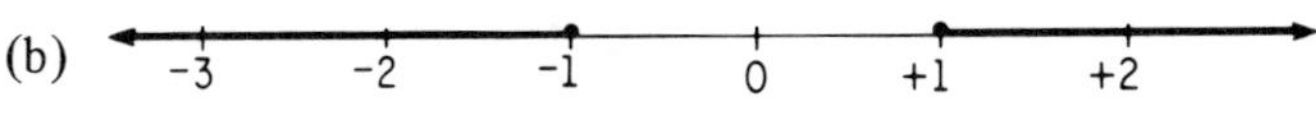

(c) 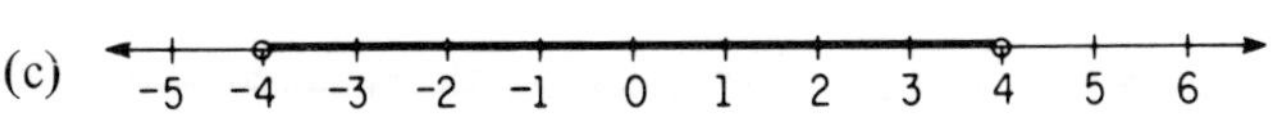

How would the graph of the compound sentence $\square > -|-4|$ and $\square < 4$ compare with (c) above?

Note that we can write the compound sentence above as $-4 < \square < 4$ and this sentence and your answer to (c) above are equivalent open sentences.

At this point we would do well to review our rules for operating with positive numbers, negative numbers, and zero. Notice from our recent developments and our rule for adding two negative elements that we could write $(-3) + (-2) = -[|-3| + |-2|]$ and when we write the right-hand member of this equation as a single number we get (-5) which substantiates our rule.

In like manner, we can write $(-4) \cdot (-5) = +[|-4| \cdot |-5|]$ and solving our right-hand member illustrates the rule for multiplying two negative elements, and also produces the correct product.

We have explored only two of the rules here but our work could be extended to include them all. These experiences lead us to many worthwhile extensions of the field axioms to include the negative elements and other uses of absolute value in roots, two-dimensional graphing, quadratic open sentences, complex numbers and vectors. These, however, are beyond the scope of this treatment.

SLIDE, TURN, AND FLIP (TRANSFORMATIONS)

In our study of geometry you will recall that any set of points in a plane constitutes a plane geometric figure. If we have a plane geometric figure consisting of just three points say, A, B, and C, mark them clearly and place a marble on each of them, we could then shake the plane so that some or all of the marbles would come to rest on a new point of the plane. Let us assume that the marble which was on point A now comes to rest on a new point which we will call A'. The marble which was on point B comes to rest on point A formerly occupied by the marble which moved to A'. The marble which was on point C comes to rest on a new point C'. All three marbles have moved, and in so doing make a path. The path could have taken any particular marble back to its original position, to a position originally occupied by one of the other marbles or to an entirely new position. In our case, the diagram shows what happened.

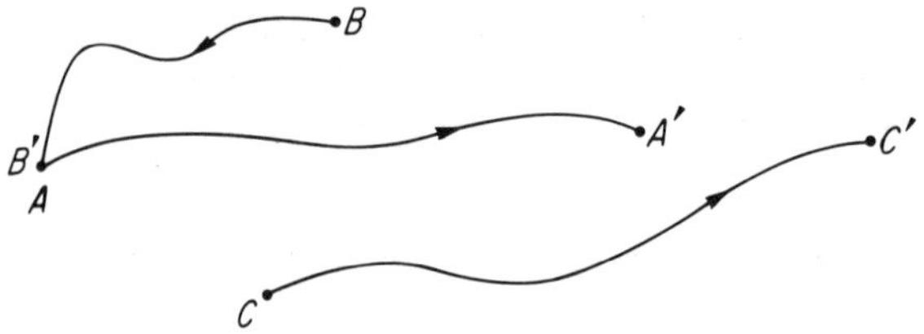

During this maneuver, each of the original points is paired with one and only one of the final points. Such pairing of points is called a *transformation*, and is denoted by writing $A \longrightarrow A'$, $B \longrightarrow A$, and $C \longrightarrow C'$. In the pairing A' is called the *image of A*, B' is called the *image of B*, and C' is called the *image of C*. Also, A is called the *preimage of A'*, B is called the *preimage of B'*, and C is called the *preimage of* C'. If a marble goes back to its original point and it was originally on, say point D, then we write $D \longrightarrow D$, and D is called a *fixed point* of the transformation. If each point has one and only one image point and each image point has one and only one preimage point, then the transformation is called a one-to-one mapping.

Now let us limit our transformations a bit by making every marble move in the same direction and the same distance. In the example we begin with three marbles located at points x, y, and z and move each marble exactly two inches along the parallel dotted paths, bringing them to rest on the new points x', y', z'.

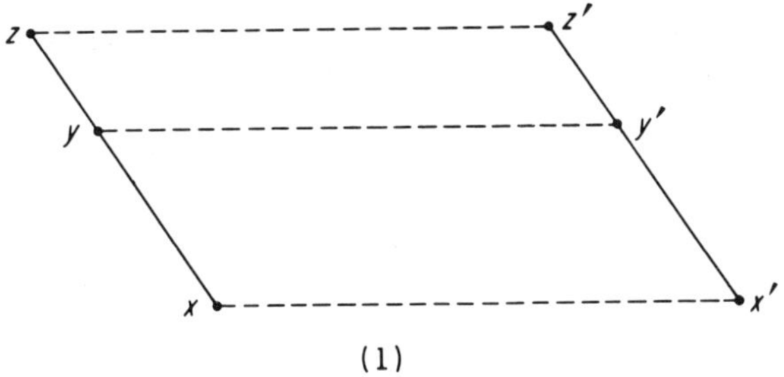

(1)

We now have $x \longrightarrow x'$, $y \longrightarrow y'$, and $z \longrightarrow z'$, and we have a one-to-one mapping. Now if we consider all the points on the segment going from point x to point z (written $\overline{xz}$), we have mapped all of the points of $\overline{xz}$ on to $\overline{x'z'}$, furthermore, if we had had marbles on every point of $\overline{xz}$, each would have moved two inches along a path parallel to $\overline{xx'}$. Such a transformation is called a *parallel translation*, or for convenience young students may call it *sliding*.

From our previous experience we note that sliding causes all the image points on $\overline{x'z'}$ to be in the same relative position as their corresponding preimage points in $\overline{xz}$. For example, if point y is between point x and z on $\overline{xz}$, then point y', is between point x' and point z' on $\overline{x'z'}$. Furthermore, the measure of $y'z'$ is the same as the measure of $\overline{yz}$. We conclude then, that not only did the parallel translation or sliding map all the points of one segment into the points of another segment, but the distances between points on the image segment were preserved (left unchanged).

We can now apply this same transformation (sliding) to all the points of a triangle with similar results and if necessary, there may be repeated applications of this transformation.

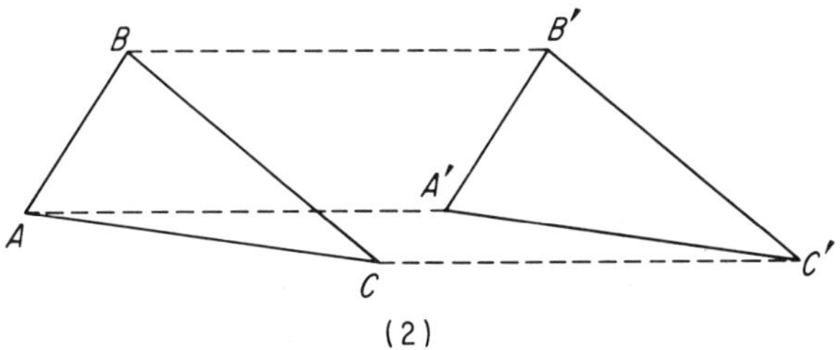

(2)

Because the distance between any two points of triangle lettered $A'B'C'$ (written $\Delta A'B'C'$) is left unchanged from what they were in the preimage, we can conclude that the measures of such things as the angles, the altitudes, the perimeters, and the areas are left unchanged. The size and shape of the triangles are therefore, unchanged and we say that ΔABC is $\cong$ (congruent) to $\Delta A'B'C'$. We see then, that two congruent geometric figures, say P and Q, must display a one-to-one correspondence between the points of P and the points of Q which leaves distances unchanged (invariant). This concept of congruence is very valuable in the study of geometry.

Let us now explore another kind of transformation. Consider a phonograph record on a turntable. Mark the center of the record with an O. Mark another point A on the record with a piece of chalk. Now turn the switch on and off quickly. Point A will move along the dotted path to a new location in the plane, say A'.

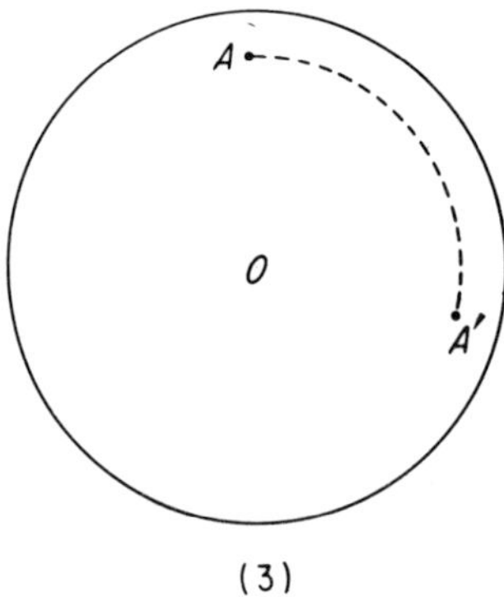

(3)

Now let us redo the figure and add some more lines so that we can investigate what happens under this kind of transformation called *rotation*, (turning).

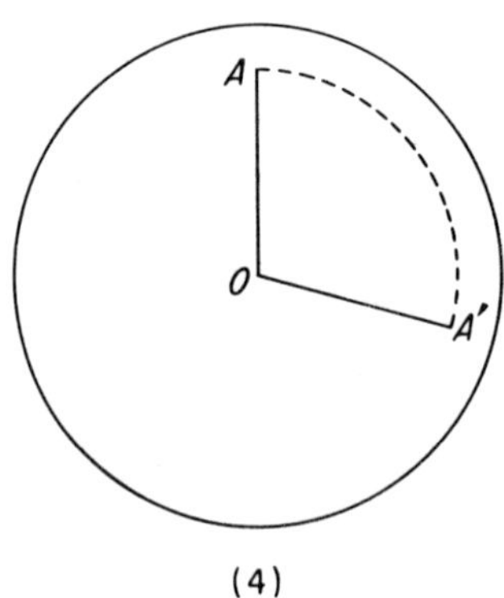

(4)

Note now that the measure of $\overline{OA}$ did not change under the turning. Also all of the points of $\overline{OA}$ have an image in $\overline{OA'}$, every point on $\overline{OA}$ having moved along arcs concentric to $\widehat{AA'}$ (the dotted arc), except point O, which is a fixed point.

Let us now extend this figure to include some more points and lines.

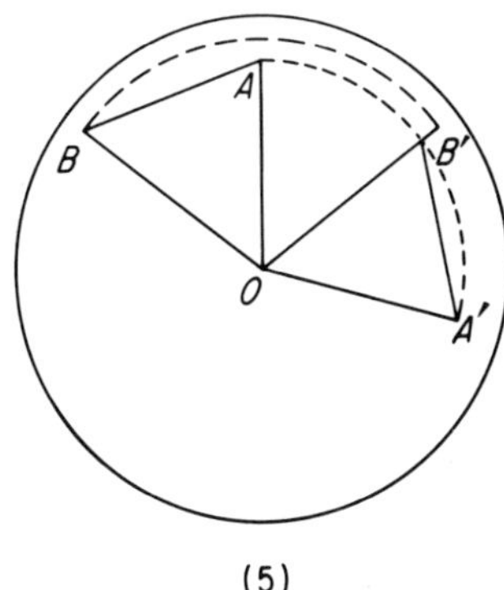

(5)

Note that we have added point B before turning the disk and that after turning, B' becomes the image of B. $\overline{OA'}$ is the image of $\overline{OA}$, and $\overline{OB'}$ is the image of $\overline{OB}$. This makes the measure of $\overline{OR'}$ equal to the measure of $\overline{OA}$ and the measure of $\overline{OB'}$ equal the measure of $\overline{OB}$. It appears then, that a turning (rotation) transformation leaves the distances unchanged.

Remembering our definitions of rays and angles from Chapter 7, we observe that we have rays and points which form angles in sketch (5), and that the measure of $\angle AOB$ equals the measure of Angle $A'O\,B'$, (written $m \angle AOB = m \angle A'O\,B'$). Also $m \angle BAO = m \angle B'A'O$ and $m \angle ABO = m \angle A'B'O$. Thus the measures of these angles were left unchanged under this transformation. Notice, too, that we could not get the image $\overline{A'B'}$ of $\overline{AB}$ by using a parallel translation. Our turning transformation was, therefore, essential in this situation.

Turning transformations also allow for repeated applications using the same or different fixed points as centers of rotation.

Let us now examine some situations in which it becomes apparent that a third kind of transformation is essential if we are to get a one-to-one mapping. Note that in sketches (6) and (7) our slide or turn transformations even with repeated application or in combination will not explain how the figures on the right can be images of those on the left.

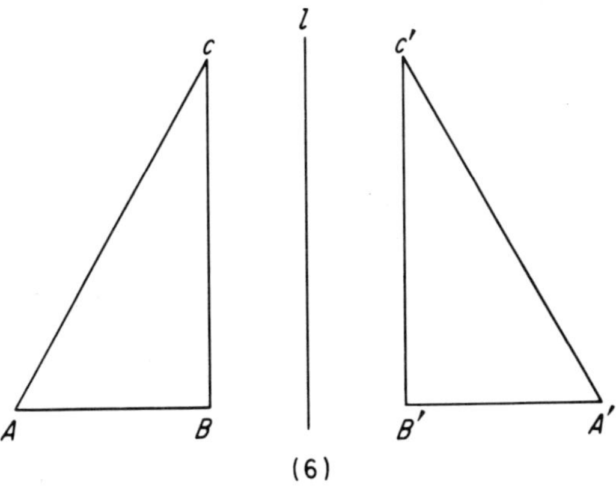

(6)

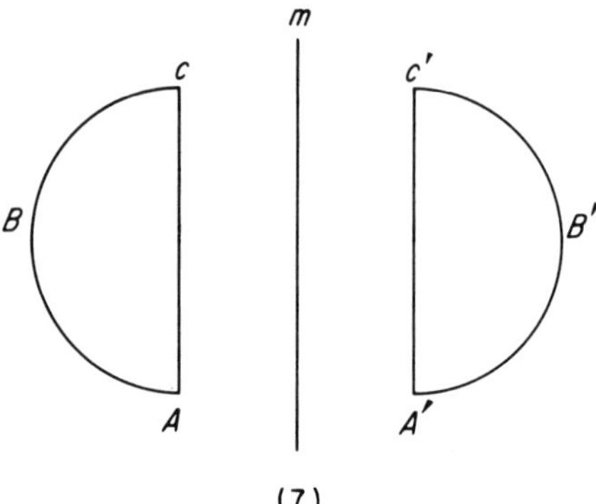

(7)

But let us investigate other possibilities. Suppose we should fold the paper along the lines l and m in (6) and (7), this then would map the points of the figure on the left on to the points of the figure on the right in both cases. If we should flip over the figure on the left and then apply a slide transformation, this would also map the points properly. This is called a *reflection transformation*, but we will call it a *fold transformation* if we use the first method and a *flip-slide transformation* if we use the second. It can be seen that this type of transformation preserves distances, angles, and areas, but it does not preserve the clockwise or counterclockwise order of the points as they occur on a closed figure or plane region. Note in (6) that the preimage labels A, B, and C go counterclockwise while the image labeling goes clockwise.

PROBLEMS

1. Does a slide transformation preserve the order of labeling?
2. Draw a triangle and its image triangle which can be achieved by a sliding transformation alone.
3. Draw a triangle and its image triangle which requires both turn and slide transformations.
4. Draw a triangle and its image triangle which can be achieved by a fold transformation.
5. Can your triangle in Prob. 4 above be achieved by flip and slide transformations?
6. Draw a triangle and its image which can be achieved by flip and turn transformations.
7. In Prob. 6, which point in your turn transformation was fixed and used as a center of rotation?
8. Under a slide translation of a segment are the image and preimage always parallel?
9. In the figure below explain what transformations were applied to get the image $\triangle A''B''O'$ from the pre-image $\triangle ABO$. The two dotted lines with arrows were drawn to help you get started.

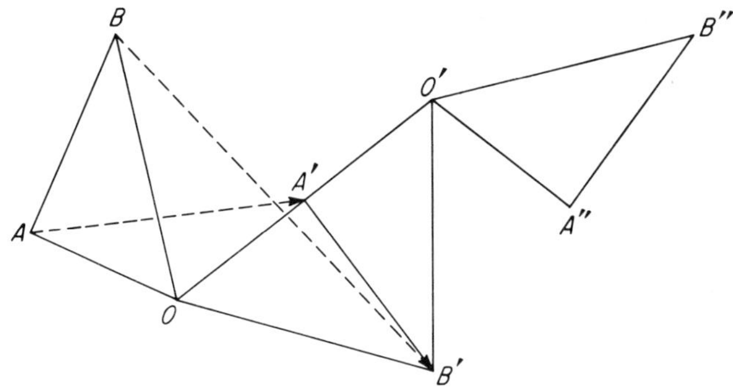

10. Is $\triangle ABO \cong \triangle A''B''O'$?

11. Was the order of labeling retained?

12. Under what circumstances do a flip and a fold turn out to be the same transformation?

TOPOLOGY FOR ELEMENTARY STUDENTS

Topology is an unusual and exciting kind of mathematics which deals with sets of points in space. It is more than ordinary geometry and deals with properties of position which disregard changes in size and shape. If you draw a simple closed curve on a rubber sheet and identify a point on the rubber and inside the curve, no matter how you stretch the sheet, the point will always be inside the curve. Note that the shape of the curve changes, also its length. If we mark a path on the sheet from point A to B, both of which are on the sheet, we cannot destroy this path by stretching or bending the sheet. Furthermore, the path will not cross itself nor will it have any breaks in it. That is, it will not stop and then start again except at its ends.

In Chapter 9 we spoke of plane regions and observed that each plane region divided the points of the plane into three subsets, namely, the points inside the region, the points outside the region, and the boundary points. In topology we have a similar situation, except that the points of our flexible surface (rubber sheet), need not remain in a plane. Note, however, that any point on the sheet is either inside our boundary or outside the boundary (8).

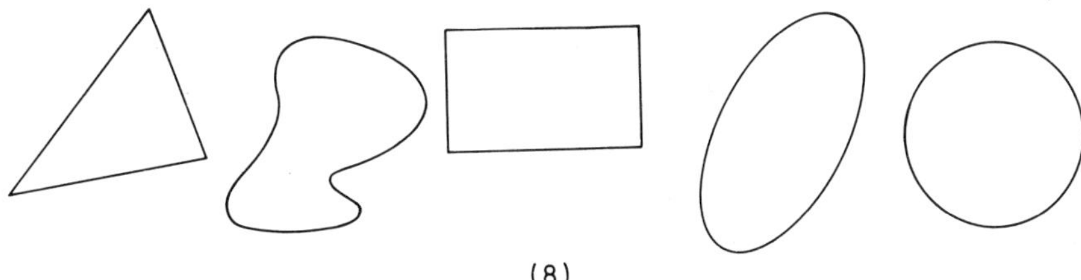

(8)

By stretching and bending the rubber sheet, a simple closed curve drawn on the sheet can take on many shapes and need not retain a constant length, interior area, or be confined to a plane. The closed curve incloses a surface region and separates this region from the outside region. To get from the inside to the outside region, the path will cross the closed curve.

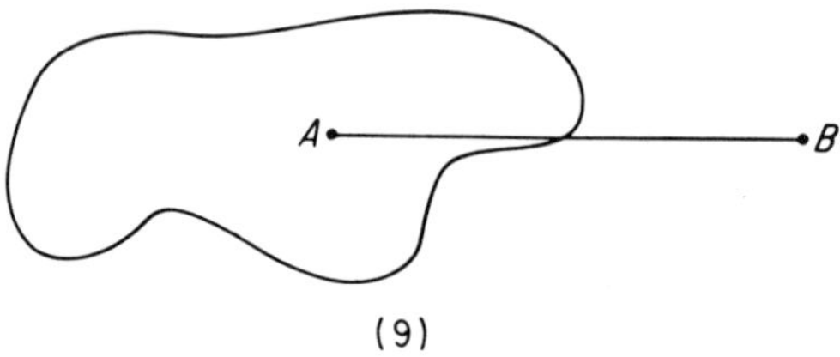

(9)

A straight line, segment AB, sketch 9, on the rubber sheet may become a continuous path of any shape and the points A and B need not remain fixed. In topology such a path is called an arc. Note again that the points of the path are not confined to a plane, A and B are not stationary, nor does the distance between the points A and B remain constant.

Topology concerns itself not only with simple closed curves, but often the closed curves have several inside regions. Again the shape of the regions (both interior and exterior), may change, the length of the boundaries vary, the areas of the enclosed surfaces are not fixed and the surface is not restricted to a plane. See sketch 10.

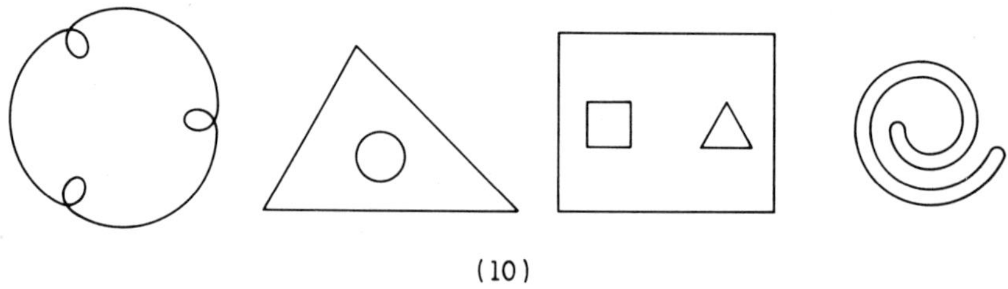

(10)

Topology deals with closed surfaces as well as closed curves. As we learned in Chapter 9, a simple closed surface divides space into two space regions, that inside the closed surface and that outside the closed surface. To get from one space region to the other, the path must cut the closed surface. The closed surfaces of topology consist of spheres, cubes, prisms, and all other closed surfaces in all their distortions. Again, areas, volumes, distances, and position of points are not retained in these topological figures. Topology also deals with closed surfaces which are not simple, i.e., those that consist of more than one space region. See sketch 11.

To this point in our development it appears that some of the properties of figures which were important in geometry have lost their importance while new

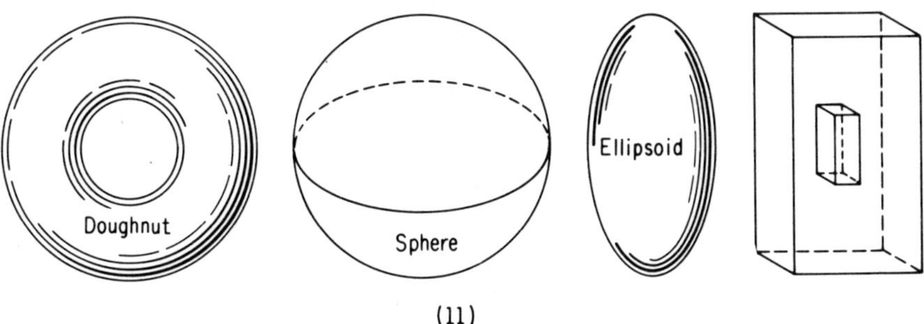

(11)

properties of importance have emerged. Let us tabulate this observation in a table:

Properties of Figures Which Are Important in Geometry	Properties of Figures Which Are Important in Topology
1. Size (length, area, volume)	1. Inside and outside of both surface and space regions.
2. Shape	2. No breaks in curves or holes in surfaces.
3. Sharp distinction between plane regions and surface regions.	3. Regions (both surface and space) are retained during distortion.
4. Sharp distinction between straight lines and curved lines.	4. Topological figures may have many inside surface or space regions.
5. Most elementary closed curves are simple ones. (have one inside and one outside)	5. Distortions are not necessarily confined to a plane.
6. Figures remain rigid during a particular consideration.	6. Faces, edges, and corners give way to regions, areas, and vertices or points.
7. Points remain fixed.	

The Swiss mathematician, Leonhard Euler, is credited with having introduced topology through his analysis of networks. A network is composed of arcs, and vertices. The language and rules of the network game are as follows:

1. If the number of paths or arcs to a particular vertex is even, the vertex is said to be even.
2. If the number of paths or arcs to a particular vertex is odd, the vertex is said to be odd.
3. A network is traveled by passing over all the arcs exactly once without lifting your pencil from the paper.
4. A vertex may be passed through any number of times.
5. A network is closed if there is at least one path leading from any vertex to every other vertex.

Euler's laws for tracing networks are given below. See if you can verify them on the famous Koinigsberg bridge network sketched in (12) and by drawing other networks which illustrate his conclusions.

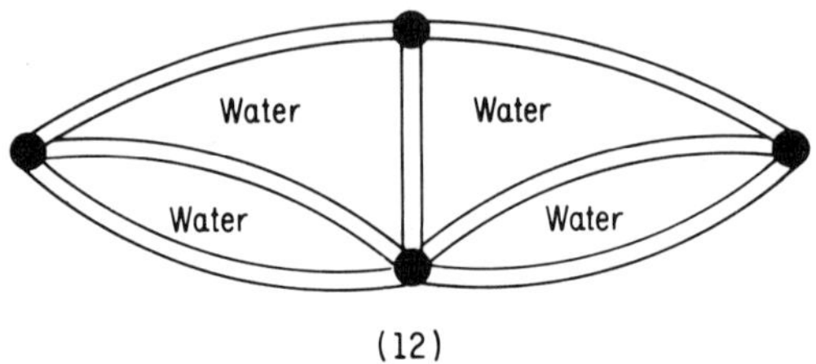

(12)

Euler's Laws:

1. A closed network always has an even number of odd vertices.
2. A closed network of all even vertices can always be traced without traveling any arc twice.
3. If a closed network contains two and only two odd vertices, it can be traced without traveling any arc twice by starting at an odd vertex.
4. If a closed network contains more than two odd vertices, it cannot be traveled in one journey without retracing an arc.
5. In a closed network, $V + R = A + 2$, where A = number of arcs, V = number of vertices, and R = number of regions into which the network divides the surface.

One of the unsolved network problems relates to map coloring. If we have a map which constitutes a closed network, an interesting problem arises in determining the number of different colors that will be necessary so that countries or states with common borders will not have the same color. To date no one has found a need for more than four colors, but this result has never been proven to be adequate for all possible situations. Try your hand at refuting the conjecture that four different colors are adequate.

The Moebius strip is a famous topological surface. Most of the surfaces with which we are acquainted have two sides, but the Moebius strip has only one side.

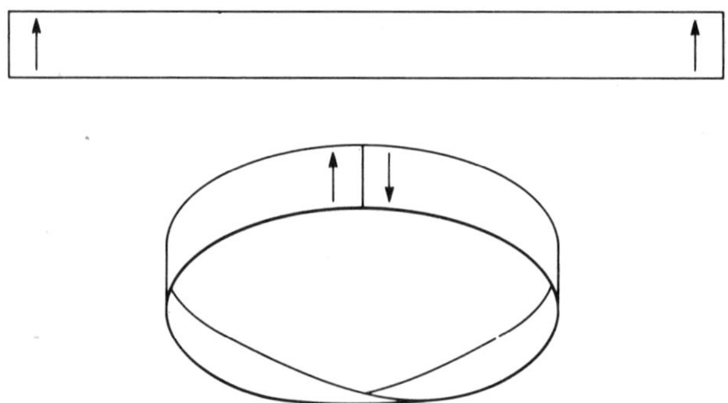

A Moebius strip can be made by cutting a strip of paper approximately 3 inches wide and 3 feet long and giving the strip a half-twist before gluing the ends together. What happens if you now draw a line in the middle of the strip and continue it the full length of the strip? Now paint only one side of the strip. Was this possible? What happened? Cut the strip lengthwise along a line in the middle of its width. What happened? (See accompanying illustration for making strip.)

Now cut another Moebius strip along a line located one-third its width from one edge. What happened?

Excellent sample lessons on topology for elementary school children can be found in *Twenty-Seventh Yearbook of the National Council of Teachers of Mathematics*, pp. 153–164.

Symbols

$=$	is equal to
$\neq$	is not equal to
$\approx$	is approximately equal to
$>$	is greater than
$\not>$	is not greater than
$<$	is less than
$\not<$	is not less than
$\geqslant$	is greater than or equal to
$\not\geqslant$	is not greater than or equal to
$\leqslant$	is less than or equal to
$\not\leqslant$	is not less than or equal to
$\subseteq$	is a subset of
$\subset$	is a proper subset of
$\supset$	is a superset of
$\cong$	is congruent to
$\in$	is an element of
$\notin$	is not an element of
U	universal set
S	solution set
$\overline{S}$	complement set
$\sim P$	negation of statement P
$P \rightarrow Q$	statement P implies statement Q
$P \leftrightarrow Q$	statement P is true if and only if statement Q is true
$P \vee Q$	statement P or statement Q
$P \wedge Q$	statement P and statement Q
$\forall n$	for all elements of the universal represented by n
$\cup$	union of two sets
$\cap$	intersection of two sets
a^{-n}	is interpreted as $\frac{1}{a^n}$ where $a \neq 0$
$\parallel$	is parallel to
$\perp$	is perpendicular to

$\lvert X \rvert$	absolute value of X
$\sqrt{\ }$	positive square root of
$\sqrt[n]{a}$	nth root of a
$\overleftrightarrow{AB}$	straight line containing points A and B
$\overline{AB}$	straight line segment with end points A and B
$\overrightarrow{AB}$	ray from point A through point B
(a,b)	ordered pair a and b
$\{a\}$	set containing element a
$\square, \triangle, \cdot$	frames, place holders or nonspecified elements
$\{\ \}$	the empty or null set
XRY	x is in the relationship R to Y
ΔL	change in L
$\Delta^2 L$	change in ΔL
M	master set, often used as a selection set not having all the elements in the universe.
$\triangle ABC$	triangle with vertices A, B, and C. Applies to any polygon
$\angle ABC$	angle with point B as vertex
$\{\square \mid \square > 5\}$	the set of all $\square$ in the universal set such that $\square$ is greater than 5
$F = \{(x,y) \mid x \in d, y \in r, \text{and } R(x,y)\}$	definition of a relation having two variables
A_n	where A and n are whole numbers greater than zero, used to designate distinct elements of a set such as $\{2_1, 2_2, 3_1\}$.
$a:b$	ratio of a to b
$\exists_x$	for some element x of the universal set
$.232132113 \longrightarrow$	indicates that the pattern continues infinitely and this never becomes periodic
$.272727...$	indicates that pattern repeats infinitely and is periodic. Also written $.\overline{27}$

Glossary

abacus: a counting device which can be adjusted to do arithmetic in any base.

absolute value (of a number): The absolute value of a non-negative number is that number, and the absolute value of a negative number is the opposite of that number.

abundant number: a whole number the sum of whose proper divisors is greater than the number. For example 12, the sum of its proper divisors is $1 + 2 + 3 + 4 + 6 = 16$.

acute angle: an angle having a measure between 0° and 90°.

addend: one of the numbers added to find a sum. The addends in $4 + 7 + 9$ are 4, 7, and 9.

addition: a binary operation with a pair of numbers called addends which results in a third number called the sum.

additive identity: a number n for which it is true that $x + n = x$. For real numbers, 0 is the additive identity, since $x + 0 = x$.

additive inverse (of a number): the number which, when added to the original number, makes the sum zero. If x is the additive inverse of y, then $x + y = 0$.

adjacent sides (of a polygon): two sides which share a common vertex.

algorism (algorithm): a plan or procedure followed in carrying out a numerical operation.

altitude (of a parallelogram): a segment connecting two opposite sides or extensions and perpendicular to each.

altitude (of a triangle): a segment from a vertex of a triangle perpendicular to the opposite side or its extension.

amicable numbers: a pair of numbers such that the sum of all proper divisors of each number is equal to the other number.

angle: the union of two rays which have the same beginning point.

area: a measure of a surface region involving area and square units.

array: an orderly arrangement of set elements in rows with the same number of elements in each row.

associative property of addition: when three numbers are added, the order of adding the numbers does not affect the sum. In general, $a + (b + c) = (a + b) + c$.

Associative property of multiplication: when the product of three numbers is found, the product is not affected by the order of multiplying. In general $(a \times b) \times c = a \times (b \times c)$.

axiom: a basic assumption for which no counter-example has been found within the designated master set.

base (of a numeration system): the number used as the basic set, the number of the first collection used. For example, 10 is the base of the decimal system, and 2 is the base of the binary system.

biconditional: a theorem whose converse is also true.

binary numeration system: numeration system in base two. For example, $11010_{two} = 26_{ten}$.

binary (operation): an operation involving only two numbers. All of the basic operations are binary. When more than two numbers are to be added or multiplied, they must be grouped by pairs.

braces: symbols or signs used to designate a set. Braces are also used as symbols of grouping, for example, $5 - \{2[4 - (3 - 1)]\}$.

cardinal number: number used to tell the number of elements in a set.

Cartesian coordinate system: a reference frame consisting of two perpendicular number lines in a plane. Also called "rectangular coordinate system."

chicken arithmetic: a take-off from modular arithmetic.

circumference: the measure of the length of a circle.

clock arithmetic: Similar to a modular arithmetic.

closure: A set is closed under a given operation if the result of operating on an element or elements of a set also belongs to the set. For example, the set of whole numbers is closed under addition because the sum of any pair of whole numbers is a whole number.

collinear points: points which belong to one line.

commutative property: An operation is commutative if the result is independent of the order of the pair of elements used. Addition is commutative because $4 + 2 = 2 + 4$, and likewise, multiplication is commutative because $3 \times 4 = 4 \times 3$.

complement (of a set): Set A is a complement of set B if and only if A consists of all elements of the universal sets which are not in B. The symbol for the complement of B is $\overline{B}$.

composite number: a whole number different from one, and zero which is not a prime number.

concave polygon: a polygon which is not convex.

congruence: the relationship between two geometric figures which have exactly the same size and shape.

convex polygon: a polygon such that a segment connecting any two points in the interior is a subset of the interior.

coordinates (of a point): an ordered number pair which designates the x-value and y-value of a point on a rectangular graphing system.

coplanar: belonging to the same plane.

counting numbers: the set $\{0,1,2,3,...\}$. In many texts it is the set $\{1,2,3,...\}$.

cube root: one of three equal factors which produce a number. For example, $\sqrt[3]{8} = 2$ because $2 \times 2 \times 2 = 8$.

curve: the set of points lying along any non-straight line in space.

decade: a set of ten consecutive whole numbers beginning with a multiple of 10.

deficient number: a whole number the sum of whose proper divisors is less than the number.

degree (angle): one three hundred sixtieth of the angle measure around a point in a plane. It is a small angle and of constant size.
degree (arc): one three hundred sixtieth of the circle from which the arc is taken. It is an arc as contrasted with an angle degree which is an angle.
denominator: the number named by the lower numeral in a fractional numeral. For example, the denominator of $\frac{2}{3}$ is 3.
density: the property of a set of numbers in which there is always a third number between any two given numbers. The set of rational numbers is dense.
diagonal: a segment connecting two nonadjacent vertices of a polygon.
diameter (of a circle): a segment connecting two points of a circle and passing through the center.
difference: the result of subtracting one number from another number or from itself. For example, in $12 - 5 = 7$, 7 is the difference, and in $12 - 12 = 0$, 0 is the difference:
digit: a basic numeral. In base ten there are ten digits: 0, 1, 2, 3, 4, 5, 6, 7, 8, 9.
directed real number: a positive or a negative real number.
disjoint sets: sets which have no common elements.
distributive property: a property of multiplication which states that the multiplication operation is distributive with respect to addition. The following is an illustration: $6 \times (3 + 4) = (6 \times 3) + (6 \times 4)$. In general, $a \times (b + c) = (a \times b) + (a \times c)$.
divisor (of a whole number): three is a divisor of fifteen because $15 \div 3 = 5$; that is, the quotient is a whole number and the remainder is 0.
divisor of a whole number (trivial): one and the whole number itself.
dodecagon: a 12-sided polygon.
duodecimal numeration system: numeration system in base twelve. For example, $111_{\text{twelve}} = 157_{\text{ten}}$.
element (of a set): a member of a set.
empty set { }: a set which has no members.
endpoint (of a segment): the endpoints of $\overline{AB}$ are A and B.
equal sets: sets having exactly the same members.
equiangular triangle: a triangle with each angle measure equal to 60°.
equilateral triangle: a triangle in which each side has the same measure.
equivalent sets: Two sets are equivalent if their elements can be brought into one-to-one correspondence.
Erathosthenes' sieve: a method for identifying primes.
Euler's circles: circles used in diagramming relations and operations with sets.
existence principle: there exists at least one result within the master set for every operation.
exponent: In 2^3, 3 is the exponent. It tells how many times 2 is used as a factor in a product $(2 \times 2 \times 2)$. This definition holds only for positive integral exponents.
exterior of an angle: the set of all points which are not in the interior of an angle and not on the angle.
factor (of a number): a divisor of the number; one of the numbers used in a product. For example, 5 and 7 are factors of 35 because $5 \times 7 = 35$.

field: a structure that is closely associated with the study of arithmetic and algebra. The axioms of a field include closure, associativity, commutativity, distributivity, identity, and inverse.

finite set: a set which has a finite number of members.

fraction: a non-directed number which has a name of the form $\frac{a}{b}$ where a and b are integers and b does not equal zero.

fundamental theorem of arithmetic: every composite number can be expressed uniquely as a product of primes.

geometric figure: a set of points.

greatest common divisor *GCD* **(of two or more numbers)**: the greatest integer by which each of a given set of integers is divisible.

half-line: one of the two subsets into which a point separates a line.

half-plane: one of the two subsets into which a line separates a plane.

half-space: one of the two subsets into which a plane separates space.

heptagon: a seven-sided polygon.

hexagon: a six-sided polygon.

Hindu-Arabic numeration system: the system of base ten numeration now used in many countries.

hypotenuse: the side in a right triangle which is opposite the right angle.

identity element for addition: the identity element for addition is zero. Zero added to any number is that number.

inproper fraction: a fraction greater than one.

inequality: a number sentence showing that two expressions are names for different numbers, for example, $3 \neq 5$ or $n - 5 < 2$.

infinite set: a set which has an infinite number of members.

integer: a directed whole number or 0.

interior of an angle: the set of all points "inside" the angle.

interior of a triangle: the set of all points "inside" the triangle.

intersection (of two sets): the set which consists of only those elements which belong to both of the two sets.

inverse: see additive and multiplicative.

inverse operation: addition and subtraction are inverse operations, as are multiplication and division. An inverse or opposite operation undoes or neutralizes the operation of which it is the opposite.

irrational number: a real number which has no name of the form $\frac{a}{b}$ $(b \neq 0)$, with a and b integers. Example: $\sqrt{5}$.

is greater than ($>$): Example: $5 > 3$.

is greater than or equal to ($\geqslant$): Examples: $5 \geqslant 3$; $5 \geqslant 5$.

is less than ($<$): Example: $3 < 5$.

is less than or equal to ($\leqslant$): Examples: $3 \leqslant 5$; $3 \leqslant 3$.

is not equal to ($\neq$): Examples: $5 \neq 3$.

isosceles triangle: a triangle in which two sides have the same measure.

lattice of points: an array of points arranged in a rectangle or square or an infinite number of points so arranged.

least common multiple, *LCM* (of two or more numbers): the least number of which each of the two or more given numbers is a factor. For example, *LCM* of 6 and 14 is 42 because 42 is the least number divisible by both 6 and 14.

leg (of a right triangle): a side in a right triangle which is adjacent to the right angle.

matching sets: two sets between which there exists a one-to-one correspondence.

mathematical sentence: a sentence expressing a mathematical fact. $6 \times 3 = 18$, $4 + 2 > 5$, $6 + 2 = m$, and $6 - 4 \neq 7$ are examples of mathematical sentences.

member (of a set): a number or any other thing which belongs to the set.

midpoint (of a segment): a point which divides a segment into two segments each of the same measure.

multiplication: an operation on two or more numbers called factors to obtain a third number called the product.

multiple of a whole number: a product of that number and any whole number.

multiplicative law of one: the product of any number N and one is N. Symbolically $N \times 1 = N$.

multiplicative law of zero: the product of any number N and zero is zero. Symbolically $N \times 0 = 0$.

multiplicative inverse: the product of any non-zero number and its inverse is one. Symbolically $N \times \frac{1}{N} = 1; N \neq 0$.

multiplicand: the second of two factors used to form a product.

multiplier: the first of two factors used to form a product.

natural numbers: the set $\{1,2,3,4,5,6,...\}$.

negative real number: an opposite of a positive real number. Each negative real number is less than 0.

noncollinear points: points which are not on the same line.

non-repeating non-terminating decimal: Example: .5151151115⟶.

non-specified element of a set: a place holder for a number in an open sentence.

null set: empty set, that is, a set with no members. The symbol for it is $\emptyset$ or $\{\ \}$.

number field: a set of numbers and two operations obeying the field axioms.

number line: a series of points on a straight line representing various subsets of the real numbers.

number sentence: a sentence involving numbers (see mathematical sentence).

number system: a set of numbers having one or more operations defined in the set.

numeral: a name of a number.

numeration system: a system of writing names of numbers.

numerator: the number named by the upper numeral in a fractional number. For example, the numerator of $\frac{2}{3}$ is 2.

obtuse angle: an angle having more than 90° and less than 180°.

obtuse triangle: a triangle having one obtuse angle.

octagon: an 8-sided polygon.

one-to-one correspondence: a matching between two sets so that to each element of one set there is assigned exactly one element of the second set and vice versa.

open sentence: a number sentence that contains one or more place holders. Such a sentence is neither true nor false until each place holder is replaced by a numeral.

opposite (of a number): the negative number with the same absolute value. The opposite of a negative number is the positive number with the same absolute value. The opposite of 0 is 0.

ordered pair of numbers: an ordered pair (a,b) has two properties: (1) $(a,b) \neq (b,a)$ if $a \neq b$; (2) $(a,b) = (c,d)$, if and only if $a = c$ and $b = d$.

ordinal number: a number used to identify the position of one of the things in an ordered set of things.

origin: the point in the coordinate plane assigned to the pair (0,0).

parallelogram: a quadrilateral in which pairs of opposite sides are parallel.

pentagon: a polygon with five sides.

percent, %: $1\% = .01 = \frac{1}{100}$.

perfect number: a number which is equal to the sum of all its proper divisors. For example, 6 is a perfect number because $6 = 1 + 2 + 3$ and 1, 2, and 3 are all proper divisors of 6.

perimeter (of a polygon): the sum of the measures of all sides of a polygon.

perpendicular (lines): two lines intersecting each other so that right angles are formed.

place value: place value of 3 in 3247 is three thousand.

plane: any set of points which can be thought of as a flat surface.

plane region: a definite portion of a plane.

point: a location in space.

polygon: a plane geometric figure having three or more segments as sides and enclosing a plane region.

positive real number: a real number which is greater than 0.

power: a number shown by means of a base and an exponent. For example, 4 is the second powet of 2, because $4 = 2^2$.

prime factor (of a number): a factor which is a prime number.

prime number: a whole number which has exactly two divisors, 1 and the number itself. In the set of integers primes have exactly four divisors.

prism: a space figure formed by two congruent parallel polygons and the parallelograms which connect their corresponding segments.

product: the result of multiplying a pair of numbers. For example: in $3 \times 4 = 12$, 12 is the product.

proper divisor of a whole number: any integral divisor of the number, excluding the number itself. For example, the proper divisors of 10 are 1, 2, and 5.

proper subset: a proper subset of set S is any subset not equal to S.

propórtion: a statement of equality between ratios.

pyramid: a geometric figure having a polygon as a base, triangular faces and enclosing a space region.

pythagorean relation: In a right triangle, if a and b are measures of the two legs and c is the measure of the hypotenuse, then $a^2 + b^2 = c^2$, and conversely.

quadrant: one-fourth of the plane outlined by the coordinate system, not including the points on the axes.

quadrilateral: a polygon with four sides.

quotient: the result of dividing one number by another number or by itself. For example, in $12 \div 6 = 2$, 2 is the quotient; in $18 \div 18 = 1$, 1 is the quotent.

radius: a segment connecting any point of a circle with its center.

ratio: the quotient of a pair of numbers. Example: $\frac{3}{7}$ or 3 : 7.

rational number: a real number which has a name of the form $\frac{a}{b}$ $(b \neq 0)$, a and b integers. Example: $\frac{5}{7}$.

rational number of arithmetic: the same as fraction.

ray: a half line and its boundary point.

real numbers: the union of the set of rational numbers and the set of irrational numbers.

reciprocal: multiplicative inverse. The quotient of 1 divided by a number is the reciprocal of that number. There is no reciprocal for 0. The product of any number and its reciprocal is 1.

rectangle: a 4-sided polygon with opposite sides parallel and 1 right angle.

rectangular coordinate system: See **Cartesian coordinate system.**

rectangular prism: a prism in which each face is a rectangle.

region (plane): a specific portion of the plane.

region (space): a specific portion of space.

regrouping: a term used to replace the old terms of "carrying" and "borrowing."

regular polygon: a polygon with all sides of the same measure and all angles of the same measure.

relative error (of a measurement): the quotient obtained when the greatest possible error is divided by the measurement.

relatively prime (numbers): two whole numbers with 1 as their only common factor.

repeating decimal: a decimal numeral in which a block of one or more digits repeats indefinitely. For example, .253253253 . . ., also written as $.\overline{253}$.

rhombus: a parallelogram having two adjacent sides equal.

right triangle: a triangle which has one right angle.

right angle: an angle whose measure is 90°.

scalene triangle: a triangle in which no two sides have the same measure.

scientific notation: a number expressed as the product of a number between 1 and 10 and the correct power of ten. For example, 237 in scientific notation is 2.37×10^2.

scratch method (of addition): a method of performing addition, as used in Europe, in which digits are erased or crossed out successively as their sum is recorded above them.

segment: a set of points containing two endpoints and all points of the straight line between the two endpoints.

set: a collection of things or elements.

set builder notation: notation of the form $A = \{x/x = 6\}$, read "A is the set of all elements of the universal set represented by x such that x equals six."

sieve of Erathosthenes: a means of screening the prime numbers from the positive set of integers.

signed number: a number designated as either positive or negative. For example, -5 is a signed number sometimes written as $^-5$.
simple closed curve: a closed curve which does not intersect itself.
solution set: a number belongs to the solution set of an open sentence if the number makes the sentence true and is a member of the universal set.
space: the set of all points.
special numbers: the whole numbers zero and one.
sphere: the set of all points in space which are a given distance from a point inside the sphere called the center of the sphere.
square root: that number which when taken 2 times as a factor gives the number for a product. For example, $\sqrt{36} = 6$ because $6 \times 6 = 36$.
square root algorism: a method of finding a square root of a number.
subset (proper): Set A is a proper subset of set B if every member of A is a member of B and set A contains at least one less element than set B.
subtraction: an operation with two numbers called the sum and the given addend which results in the identification of the other addend. In general, $a - b = n$ if $n + b = a$.
successor (of a number): the whole number immediately following the given whole number. For example, 5 is a successor of 4.
sum: the result of adding a pair of numbers. For example, in $2 + 7 = 9$, 9 is the sum.
terminating decimal: a decimal with a finite number of digits. For example, .3702 is a numeral for a terminating decimal.
tetrahedron: a solid with four triangular faces.
theorem: a statement which has been proven to be true.
trapezoid: a trapezoid is a quadrilateral with one pair of parallel sides.
triangle: a union of three segments, in which each pair of segments has one common point.
twin primes: a pair of primes which differ by 2. For example, 11 and 13 is a pair of twin primes, because each number is a prime and $13 - 11 = 2$.
union (of two sets): the set consisting of the members which belong to one or the other of the two given sets (includes members belonging to both sets).
uniqueness principle: the principle which states that every operation in arithmetic has only one result.
unit fraction: a fraction with a numerator 1, such as $\frac{1}{2}, \frac{1}{3}, \frac{1}{12}$.
universal quantifier: $\forall_x$, read, for every number x in the universal set.
universal set: the set of all things which are chosen for a particular study.
Venn diagram: a pictorial method of showing relations and operations with sets.
vertex (of an angle): the point of intersection of the two rays of an angle.
vertex (of a polygon): the point of intersection of two adjacent sides.
whole numbers: the set of whole numbers is 0, 1, 2, 3, 4, 5, 6, . . .
***x*-axis**: the horizontal line in the rectangular coordinate system.
***y*-axis**: the vertical line in the rectangular coordinate system.
zero: see page 112 for the many roles of *zero* in the various subsets of the real numbers.
zone (of a sphere): the portion of a spherical surface included between two parallel planes.

Square and Cube Table

N	N^2	$\sqrt{N}$	N^3	$\sqrt[3]{N}$	N	N^2	$\sqrt{N}$	N^3	$\sqrt[3]{N}$
1	1	1.000	1	1.000	26	676	5.099	17576	2.962
2	4	1.414	8	1.260	27	729	5.196	19683	3.000
3	9	1.732	27	1.442	28	784	5.291	21952	3.037
4	16	2.000	64	1.587	29	841	5.385	24389	3.072
5	25	2.236	125	1.710	30	900	5.477	27000	3.107
6	36	2.449	216	1.817	31	961	5.568	29791	3.141
7	49	2.646	343	1.913	32	1024	5.657	32768	3.175
8	64	2.828	512	2.000	33	1089	5.745	35937	3.208
9	81	3.000	729	2.080	34	1156	5.831	39304	3.240
10	100	3.162	1000	2.154	35	1225	5.916	42875	3.271
11	121	3.317	1331	2.224	36	1296	6.000	46656	3.302
12	144	3.464	1728	2.289	37	1369	6.083	50653	3.332
13	169	3.606	2197	2.351	38	1444	6.164	54872	3.362
14	196	3.742	2744	2.410	39	1521	6.245	59319	3.391
15	225	3.873	3375	2.466	40	1600	6.325	64000	3.420
16	256	4.000	4096	2.520	41	1681	6.403	68921	3.448
17	289	4.123	4913	2.571	42	1764	6.481	74088	3.476
18	324	4.243	5832	2.621	43	1849	6.557	59507	3.503
19	261	4.359	6859	2.668	44	1936	6.633	85184	3.530
20	400	4.472	8000	2.714	45	2025	6.708	91125	3.557
21	441	4.583	9261	2.759	46	2116	6.782	97336	3.583
22	484	4.690	10648	2.802	47	2209	6.856	103823	3.609
23	529	4.796	12167	2.844	48	2304	6.928	110592	3.634
24	576	4.899	13824	2.884	49	2401	7.000	117649	3.659
25	625	5.000	15625	2.924	50	2500	7.071	125000	3.684

Measurement Tables

LINEAR MEASURE

12	inches (in.)	= 1 foot (ft)
3	ft	= 1 yard (yd)
16½	ft	= 1 rod (rd)
5½	yd	= 1 rd
320	rd	= 1 mile (statute)
1760	yd	= 1 mile (statute)
5280	ft	= 1 mile (statute)
1	nautical mi	= 1.15 statue mi

SURFACE MEASURE

144	sq in.	= 1 sq ft
9	sq ft	= 1 sq yd
30½	sq yd	= 1 sq rd
160	sq rd	= 1 acre
640	acres	= 1 sq mi
43,560	sq ft	= 1 acre

VOLUME MEASURE

1728	cu in.	= 1 cu ft
27	cu ft	= 1 cu yd
9.69	cu rds	= 1 acre ft
231	cu in.	= 1 gal
1	cu ft	= 7.48 gal

DRY MEASURE

2	cups	= 1 pt
2	pt	= 1 qt
4	qt	= 1 gal
8	qt	= 1 peck (pk)
4	pk	= 1 bushel (bu)

LIQUID MEASURE

4	gills	= 1 pint (pt)
2	pt	= 1 quart (qt)
4	qt	= 1 gallon (gal)
42	gal	= 1 bbl of oil
8⅓	lb	= 1 gal water

AVOIRDUPOIS WEIGHT

16	ounces (oz)	= 1 pound (lb)
100	lb	= 1 hundredweight (cwt)
20	cwt	= 1 ton = 2000 lb
62.428	lb	= 1 cu ft of water
2240	lb	= 1 long ton

ARC AND ANGLE MEASURE

60	arc sec (″)	= 1 arc min (′)
60	arc min	= 1 arc degree (°)
360	arc degrees	= 1 circle
60	angle sec (″)	= 1 angle minute (′)
60	angle minutes	= 1 angle degree (°)
360	angle degrees	= 1 perigon
1	radian	$= \frac{180}{\pi}$ degrees (angle or arc)

1′ of arc on a great circle of the earth = 1 nautical mile

MISCELLANEOUS

12	doz	= 1 gross
144	units	= 1 gross
500	sheets	= 1 ream
π		= 3.14159

Index